Readings in Existential Psychology and Psychiatry

STUDIES IN EXISTENTIAL PSYCHOLOGY AND PSYCHIATRY

SERIES EDITOR: KEITH HOELLER

Published

Dream and Existence

Heidegger and Psychology

Merleau-Ponty and Psychology

Readings in Existential Psychology and Psychiatry

Sartre and Psychology

Readings in Existential Psychology and Psychiatry

Edited by

Keith Hoeller

Humanities Press
New Jersey

Originally published as Volume XX, nos. 1, 2, and 3 of
Review of Existential Psychology & Psychiatry

First published in this format 1994 by Humanities Press International, Inc.,
Atlantic Highlands, New Jersey 07716

Library of Congress Cataloging-in-Publication Data

Readings in existential pyschology and pyschiatry / edited
by Keith Hoeller.
p. cm. — (Studies in existential pyschology and pyschiatry)
"Originally published as volume XX, nos. 1, 2, and 3 of Review of
existential psychology and pyschiatry"—T.p. verso.
Includes bibliographical references.
ISBN 0-391-03840-0 (pbk.)
1. Existential psychology. 2. Existential psychotherapy.
I. Hoeller, Keith. II. Series.
BF204.5.R43 1993
150.19′2—dc20 93-24311
CIP

A catalog record for this book is available from the British Library.

Printed in the United States of America

Contents

CONTENTS

Preface

KEITH HOELLER

This special issue of the *Review of Existential Psychology & Psychiatry* has been put together to honor the publication of the *Review*'s twentieth anniversary volume. It is the fifth volume to appear in the *Review*'s companion book series, *Studies in Existential Psychology & Psychiatry.* For over two decades, the *Review* has dedicated its pages to the study of human experience from the existential and phenomenological perspectives. Briefly, this has meant a thoroughly interdisciplinary approach to the questions of human existence which we all face in our day-to-day lives. For centuries, these questions have been asked and answered by the philosophers, and it is thus appropriate that existential psychology has turned to the existential philosophers for both questions of principle and method. However, in our time these are questions that invariably are asked and answered by psychologists, psychiatrists, and their clients, often during the process of psychotherapy. Thus, over the years a great many of the articles in the *Review* have been written by some of the leading psychotherapists of our time.

The volume begins with basic theoretical considerations concerning existential psychology and psychiatry, and proceeds immediately to the practice of psychotherapy. The following chapters deal with major issues raised by existential psychology and are arranged in alphabetical order from Anxiety to Will. The book closes with a selected bibliography in the field. With three exceptions, all of the articles originally appeared in the *Review of Existential Psychology & Psychiatry.* The exceptions are the "Introduction" and "Selected Bibliography," which I have written and compiled especially for this volume, and Medard Boss's article, "The Unconscious—What is It?" which has been especially translated for this collection and appears here in English for the first time.

In spite of the wealth of publications in the field, this is the first such collection of essays published since Rollo May edited *Existential Psychology* (Random House) in 1961. It is meant to serve both as an introduction to the field for the beginner and as a refresher for the expert. Many of the essays included here are classics in existential psychology and psychiatry, and are well worth reading again and again.

From its humble beginnings in 1959 as a mimeographed pamphlet entitled *Existential Inquiries,* the *Review* has sought to publish articles which offer an alternative to the reductionistic theories of psychoanalysis and behaviorism. Far from seeing the individual as at the mercy of either unconscious or environmental determinants, existentialism sees the person as an acting agent within a particular world. If I had to choose the most fundamental principle of existential psychology, it would be this commitment to the freedom of the individual, and thus to the possibility of choice and change. It is this view of the individual that has been responsible for the major contributions of existential psychology, whether it be R. D. Laing's discovery of meaning in schizophrenia, or Binswanger's ability to find choice in the suicide of a woman from a previous era.

I would like to take this opportunity to thank the people who have contributed essays to this volume. I would also like to express my gratitude to our current Editorial Board, as well as to all our predecessors on the *Review* who have worked so hard over the decades to make this journal a distinctive voice in psychology and psychiatry.

Readings in Existential Psychology and Psychiatry

I. Existential Psychology and Psychiatry

An Introduction to Existential Psychology and Psychiatry

KEITH HOELLER

It has been thirty years since the publication of *Existence: A New Dimension in Psychiatry and Psychology,* edited by Rollo May, Ernest Angel, and Henri F. Ellenberger.[1] In his historical introduction to the field of existential and phenomenological psychology, Herbert Spiegelberg calls this book "the most important event in the development of American phenomenological existentialism."[2] For the first time, English-speaking readers gained an introduction to the field which had been growing rapidly in Europe. In addition to first translations of classic articles by Ludwig Binswanger, Erwin Straus, Eugene Minkowski, Viktor Von Gebsattel, and Roland Kuhn, this volume contained lengthy introductions to existential psychology and psychiatry.

The decade (1959-68) following the publication of *Existence* saw a proliferation of books and journals in the field. In 1959 *Man's Search for Meaning,*[3] by the Austrian psychiatrist Viktor Frankl, appeared in English. Rollo May was asked to contribute an essay on "The Existential Approach" to Silvano Arieti's *American Handbook of Psychiatry.*[4] Rollo May also began a mimeographed journal entitled *Existential Inquiries,* which in 1961 became the *Review of Existential Psychology & Psychiatry* (1961-Present), with Adrian Van Kaam as its first editor.[5] In 1960 the *Journal of Existential Psychiatry* (1960-70), edited by Jordan Scher, was also founded.[6] The *Journal of Humanistic Psychology* began the same year (1960-Present).[7] In 1960, R. D. Laing's first book, *The Divided Self,*[8] appeared, followed the next year by *Self and Others.*[9] In 1961, the book *Existential Psychology,* edited by Rollo May, was published; it contained important articles by May, Abraham Maslow, Herman Feifel, Carl Rogers, and Gordon Allport and a selected bibliography by Joseph Lyons.[10] This same year, the psychiatrist Thomas Szasz published his highly influential work, *The Myth of Mental Illness.*[11]

In 1962 Heidegger's *Being and Time,*[12] Merleau-Ponty's *Phenomenology of Perception,*[13] and Medard Boss's *Psychoanalysis and Daseinsanalysis*[14] all appeared in English translations for the first time. Eugene Gendlin's *Experiencing and the Creation of Meaning*[15] and Thomas Kuhn's controversial book, *The Structure of Scientific Revolutions*[16] were published the same year. In 1963 Jacob Needleman published a lengthy introduction to the work of Ludwig Binswanger, along with several first translations of his work, under the title, *Being-in-the-World.*[17] In 1964 the extremely important series, *Studies in Phenomenology and Existential Philosophy,*[18] originally edited by John Wild and later by James Edie, began publishing a monumental collection of first translations and original works in the field.

In 1965 an English edition of Michel Foucault's ground-breaking work, *Madness and Civilization,*[19] was published in Pantheon's series, *World of Man: A Library of Theory and Research in the Human Sciences,* edited by R. D. Laing. The same year James F. T. Bugental published his important book *The Search for Authenticity: An Existential-Analytic Approach to Psychotherapy.*[20] In 1966 two books were published by frequent contributors to the *Review of Existential Psychology & Psychiatry:* Adrian Van Kaam's *Existential Foundations of Psychology*[21] and Leslie Farber's *The Ways of the Will.*[22] *Phenomenological Psychology,*[23] a collection of papers by Erwin Straus, was also published in 1966. In 1967 Joseph Kockelmans' important collection of essays was published in a widely distributed paperback, *Phenomenology: The Philosophy of Edmund Husserl and Its Interpretation,*[24] as well as his important critical introduction, *Edmund Husserl's Phenomenological Psychology.*[25] Perhaps still the best collection of introductory articles published on the subject, *Existential Philosophers: Kierkegaard to Merleau-Ponty,*[26] edited by George Schrader, also appeared this year. 1968 saw the appearance of *Disclosing Man to Himself,*[27] by the existential-humanistic psychologist Sidney Jourard.

This is merely the barest of overviews, meant to convey the explosion of significant publications which appeared in the decade following *Existence.* It does not even begin to cover the many translations of Heidegger, Sartre, Merleau-Ponty, and Nietzsche that regularly appeared, or the hundreds of articles being published in the various philosophical and psychological journals. (A "Selected Bibliography of Existential Psychology & Psychiatry,"[28] prepared by the author, may be found at the back of this volume.)

In a selected bibliography of the field prepared only a decade after *Existence,* it was estimated that the number of items it would take to make a comprehensive bibliography would number over a thousand. It is safe to say that a similar comprehensive bibliography today would number several thousand entries in the English language alone. In the last decade there have been several signs of the continuing growth and acceptance of the field of existential psychology and psychiatry. The classic textbook *Theories of Personality,* by Calvin Hall and Gardner Lindzey, was first published in 1957, a year before *Existence.* By 1970, when they published their second edition, "existential psychology" was deemed to merit its own chapter alongside the contributions of Freud, Jung, Rogers, and Skinner. Writing in the third edition (1978), the authors summarize the positive contribution of existential psychology as follows:

> It had an almost immediate impact on the thinking and practices of a number of psychologists and has been one of the chief influences in bringing about the emergence of new viewpoints and techniques, especially in the areas of counseling and psychotherapy . . . Whatever the future of existential psychology may be—and at the present time it appears to have sufficient vigor and vitality to last

a long time—it has already served at least one important function. That function is to rescue psychology from being drowned in a sea of theories that have lost contact with the everyday world and with the "givens" of experience.[29]

Much has happened since this assessment to justify its optimism. In 1980 the Stanford psychiatrist Irvin Yalom, best known for his book *The Theory and Practice of Group Psychotherapy*[30] published *Existential Psychotherapy,*[31] the first comprehensive textbook in the field. In 1983 *The Clinical Psychology Handbook,*[32] edited by Michel Hersen, Alan Kazdin, and Alan Bellack, contained chapters by Hugh Urban on "Phenomenological-Humanistic Approaches"[33] to personality theory, and by Constance T. Fischer and William F. Fischer on "Phenomenological-Existential Psychotherapy."[34] In 1984 in his textbook *Current Psychotherapies,* Raymond Corsini added a chapter on "Existential Psychotherapy," written by Rollo May and Irvin Yalom.[35] According to Corsini, this chapter was added in large part due to the request of the teachers using his textbook.[36]

And of course throughout the past decade the *Review of Existential Psychology & Psychiatry* has published a series of important collections on major existential thinkers and their impact on psychology and psychiatry: *Heidegger & Psychology,*[37] *Sartre & Psychology,*[38] *Merleau-Ponty & Psychology,*[39] *Dream & Existence* (by Michel Foucault and Ludwig Binswanger),[40] and now this volume, *Readings in Existential Psychology & Psychiatry.*[41] Edited by Keith Hoeller, all are now available to the book trade in the Review's companion book series, *Studies in Existential Psychology & Psychiatry.*[42]

EXISTENTIALISM AND PHENOMENOLOGY

All of these books have a heritage in the 19th and 20th Century philosophical movements called existentialism and phenomenology. While these two movements have often had similar adherents and have often overlapped in their viewpoints, the words existentialism and phenomenology do have two different meanings, which I would like to elucidate in the following brief sketch by concentrating on the meaning of the word "existence," primarily as it appears in Kierkegaard and Heidegger.

The Existential Tradition in Philosophy

Although Albert Camus declined to be associated with the word "existentialism," as Jean-Paul Sartre had used it, he is nevertheless rightly considered to be a major existential thinker. Camus opens his book *The Myth of Sisyphus* with what he considers to be the most fundamental question in philosophy:

> There is but one truly philosophical problem, and that is suicide. Judging whether life is or is not worth living amounts to answering the fundamental question of philosophy. All the rest comes later . . . whether or not the world has

> three dimensions, whether the mind has nine or twelve categories—comes afterwards. These are games; one must first answer . . . These are facts the heart can feel . . . .[43]

That philosophy should be concerned with matters of life and death, with the ultimate questions of the meaning of life, with how to live "the good life," is a belief shared in common by the existentialists. And if we take this as a basic belief, then it is certainly appropriate to see the question of human existence running through philosophy back to the early Greeks.

Indeed, the very first fragment of western philosophical writing by Anaximander reads: "And the source of coming-to-be for existing things is that into which destruction, too, happens, 'according to necessity; for they pay penalty and retribution to each other for their injustice according to the assessment of Time.'"[44] Birth and death happen, then, according to a larger order, and this order is an ethical one, in which justice is arbitrated by time. As Heidegger will remark 2500 years later, there is an intimate and necessary connection between being and time.

Certainly Socrates and Plato are concerned with life's ultimate questions. The picture Plato gives us of Socrates in dialogue with his students, encouraging them to think for themselves, represents a precursor to modern-day psychotherapy. In his book *Mind and Madness in Ancient Greece: The Classical Roots of Modern Psychiatry,* Bennett Simon goes so far as to entitle one chapter on Plato, "The Philosopher as Therapist."[45]

At the time Socrates was in a battle with the Sophists over the souls of the youth of Athens. The Sophists claimed that they could take your son and make him better, help him to live "the good life." They claimed to have both the knowledge and the skills to impart their wisdom—for a fee. In his Introduction to *The Last Days of Socrates,* the translator Hugh Tredennick writes of the Sophists: " . . . they aimed at producing cleverness and efficiency rather than wisdom and goodness; and they charged fees for their services—which shocked the philosophers, but was good psychology as well as good business, since people take seriously what they have to pay for."[46] In short, they were concerned with technique above all else, especially as regards rhetoric and persuasion. And their idea of the good life was not much different than it is today in the popular culture: success in one's career and financial matters, a good reputation, and having enough personal power to be able to aid your friends and relatives, and to harm your enemies.

Socrates, on the other hand, was concerned with a different kind of good life: doing the right thing, based on a rational principle, regardless of the consequences to one's fame, family, or fortune. He claimed not to have any knowledge to impart, and while he did accept charity from his friends, he did not exact a fee for his talk. He believed that each person, through dialogue with a philosopher who acted as a kind of midwife to the soul, could find for himself the eternal truths necessary to live justly in this world and to pass on to the next.

However, it was not always easy to distinguish between the Sophists and the true philosophers, as Plato himself makes clear in his dialogue, *The Sophist*. The Sophists themselves were also controversial and under suspicion. It is clear that at his trial Socrates was in part accused of Sophistic practices. Actually, had he deliberately employed their techniques for the purpose of swaying his jurors, he might have been acquitted. But Socrates instead chose to remain true to his beliefs, and he did not, as was customary, beg for his life, or play on the sympathy of the large jury. Socrates, practicing what he preached at his trial, paid for his beliefs with his death, and became the West's most famous suicide.

While there are certainly other instances of philosophy addressing life's fundamental questions after Plato (e.g., St. Augustine's *Confessions*, Pascal's *Pensées*, etc.), there is enough of a philosophical turn away from existential themes in the history of philosophy that Heidegger makes the claim that, after the (early) Greeks, Being (*Sein*) itself (or perhaps better: what it means to be) is forgotten.

This forgetting tends to enshrine reason at its helm and to move further away from Camus's facts of the heart. At the beginning of the modern era, Descartes defines man as the thing who thinks (*res cogitans*). This is what most determines us as human beings. And we are thinking things over against a world of objects (*res extensae*). After Descartes splits the world into subject and object, Kant will try, but fail, to get back to "the thing in itself." And the early nineteenth century German philosopher Hegel will try to lay a rational system over human being, going so far as to say: "the real is the rational and the rational is the real."

Søren Kierkegaard's Existentialism

Søren Kierkegaard, the acknowledged father of existentialism, will try to change all of this. Writing in reaction to Hegel, Kierkegaard will once more try to resurrect philosophy's concern with life's ultimate meaning. In an early journal entry (August 1, 1835) in which Kierkegaard is concerned to find his purpose in life, he argues that it is not his goal to find objective truth, to develop a new system of philosophy. He says philosophy would not be important, "if it had no deeper meaning *for me and my life*."[47] In what may be one of the earliest uses of the word "existence" in its modern meaning, he goes on to say:

> This was what I needed to lead a *completely human life* and not merely one of *knowledge*, so that I could base the development of my thought not on—yes, not on something called objective—something which in any case is not my own, but upon something that is bound up with the deepest roots of my existence [*Existents*], through which I am, so to speak, grafted into the divine, to which I cling fast even though the whole world may collapse. *This is what I need, this is what I strive for.*[48]

Thus from the very beginning of Kierkegaard's thought it was his goal to write something which would deal not merely with arm-chair philosophizing, but with "the deepest roots of my existence." Subtitling several of his works with the adjective "psychological," Kierkegaard will try to encourage his readers as well to address their lives in this manner by showing them mirror portraits of fictitious, though plausible, lives. Kierkegaard describes what he calls "spheres of existence" or "stages on life's way."

In 1844, Kierkegaard outlines these stages in his first book, *Either/Or* (2 Vols.).[49] The first volume vividly describes the life of the Aesthete, who though fascinated with death is afraid to choose life. The paradigm of the Aesthete is Don Juan. He seeks pleasure and to live for the moment. His relations to others are characterized by his perpetual romantic conquests, which leave him empty. He is not really engaged in the world; afraid, he holds himself back in all matters. He merely plays a comfortable role, whereby he attempts to write all the scripts. Oddly (at least to himself), his pursuit of excitement leaves him in a state of perpetual boredom ("the root of all evil," he says), and thinking of suicide (melancholy is his "most faithful mistress").

In Volume II, Kierkegaard holds out an opposing world-view: the Ethicist. The paradigm is that of a calm, sedate judge, who has made his commitments. He has chosen to marry and to love one woman for the rest of his life. As a judge, he is involved in his community and he rules his life by reason and a firm set of ethical principles. His life, so he claims, is in perfect order.

Kierkegaard ends his first book with only a hint that the Ethicist, who indeed appears quite boring to the Aesthete, may not entirely have his life together. While the Aesthete avoids life by refusing to immerse his true self in it and by avoiding concrete choices, the Ethicist has so thoroughly given himself over to the world and his various projects that he has held too little of himself back. He runs the risk thereby of losing himself if his projects should fail. One is left with the feeling that if the Judge's wife were to die, or if here were to lose his job, he and his world would die too.

In later works, like *The Sickness Unto Death,*[50] Kierkegaard outlines a third stage which he calls the Religious, although it may include someone who at first is devoutly defiant of God. He enters his famous "knight of faith," who on the outside may appear to be little different than the tax collector. This person may be passionately involved with his projects, but does not identify with them. He retains his very self, even if these projects should collapse, and thus retains the heart of a self to help him through a time of crisis.

How does one get from one stage, from one sphere of existence, to another? By means of facing up to the Ultimate Either/Or: either choosing to change or to die. To do this, one must choose despair. This flies in the face of all treatment of depression today, but it is one of the major tenets of existential psychology that despair and crisis are not necessarily bad things to be tranquilized and cured as quickly as possible. There are times when one must look at one's life closely, including the tragic parts, in order to learn from them. In Leslie Farber's words, there is "the therapeutic despair,"[51] which holds tremendous possibility for self-acceptance, growth and positive change.

For Kierkegaard, as with all existentialists, anxiety may be exactly the right catalyst for serious reflection and change in one's life. This reflection is often occasioned by a change from outside our control, which produces profound anxiety and a summons for awareness. In *The Myth of Sisyphus,* Camus puts it this way: "It happens that the stage sets collapse . . . one day the "why" arises and everything begins in that weariness tinged with amazement."[52] In the same journal entry cited above, Kierkegaard writes:

> When he struggles along the right path, rejoicing in having overcome temptation's power, there may come at almost the same time, right on the heels of perfect victory, an apparently insignificant external circumstance that pushes him down, like Sisyphus, from the height of the crag. Often when a person has concentrated on something, a minor external circumstance arises that destroys everything.[53]

In *The Concept of Anxiety,* Kierkegaard brings together many of the themes of existentialism:

> Hence anxiety is the dizziness of freedom, which emerges when the spirit wants to posit the synthesis and freedom looks down into its own possibility, laying hold of finiteness to support itself. Freedom succumbs in this dizziness. Further than this, psychology cannot and will not go. In that very moment everything is changed, and freedom, when it again rises, sees that it is guilty. Between these two moments lies the leap, which no science has explained and which no science can explain . . . I will say that this is an adventure that every human being must go through—to learn to be anxious in order that he may not perish either by never having been in anxiety or by succumbing in anxiety. Whoever has learned to be anxious in the right way has learned the ultimate . . . Anxiety is the possibility of freedom . . . .[54]

Edmund Husserl's Phenomenological Philosophy

The year 1900 saw not only the publication of Freud's *Interpretation of Dreams,* but also Husserl's *Logical Investigations.* Husserl would attempt to found "philosophy as a rigorous science," using the method of phenomenology. Briefly, bracketing out all presuppositions, the philosopher would describe the phenomena in order to get at their essence, "to the things themselves." In one of the versions of the method, the eidetic variation, Husserl would ask the researcher to begin a regress starting by eliminating the characteristics of an object until only the most essential remained: that without which the thing would not be this or that. This method of description could also be used in human experience as well, selecting out various aspects of the *Lebenswelt,* the life-world, in order to illuminate a particular human phenomena. Thus began the phenomenological movement.

Husserl's return to experience and his phenomenological method of description have been quite useful for existential psychology. However, it should be clear even from my brief description that Husserl's method contains some strains of philosophy which run counter to existentialist thought. These are primarily his Cartesian elements, with the emphasis on an ego-subject set over against the world-object, and the Platonic notion of eternal forms or essences. Starting as Husserl does, for example, in his *Cartesian Meditations,* with "the transcendental ego," it then becomes a problem to get back to the world of other people, to intersubjectivity, a problem which plagued Descartes' original enterprise. In addition, Husserl's essences sound familiar to readers of Plato, and recall to mind the idea of Plato's eternal forms. Existentialism's whole goal has been to overcome the idea of fixed essences, in order to flesh out all the contours of finite, lived existence.

Martin Heidegger's Existential Turn

With the statement that "higher than actuality stands *possibility,*" Husserl's student, Martin Heidegger, takes the phenomenological method and gives it "an existential turn" in his book *Being and Time* (1927).[55] Acknowledging the human element in any human investigation, Heidegger believes that rather than being presuppositionless, the investigator must lay out his or her presuppositions for us to see and examine. And since philosophical investigations cannot have the character of objectivity à la the natural sciences, his phenomenology is a hermeneutic one, i.e., it is always interpretive.

Heidegger's claim is that philosophy has forgotten the meaning of Being, or what it means to be, and it is his task to ask the "question of Being" once again. This task is the prerogative of "fundamental ontology," which was the discipline of the ancient Greeks devoted to asking the most fundamental questions of Being. But before he begins, there are a couple of circles his questioning raises. The first, commonly known as "the hermeneutic circle," is that as soon as he raises the question of the meaning of Being, the first question to arise is that it is a particular being, the human being, who is asking the question. There is an intimate relation between the questioner and the question:

> Thus to work out the question of Being adequately, we must make an entity—the inquirer—transparent in his own Being . . . . This entity which each of us is himself and which includes inquiring as one of the possibilities of its Being, we shall denote by the term "Dasein."[56]

Thus, it is first necessary to investigate human being, Dasein, itself, and Heidegger undertakes in Division One of *Being and Time* a "preparatory fundamental analysis of Dasein." (In German, Dasein means "existence," or more literally, "being-there.") But where to begin? "The essence of Dasein lies in its existence."[57] Heidegger thus outlines his *Daseinsanalysis,* detailing the ontological characteristics of what it means to be a human being.

Being-in-the-World

First and foremost is the idea of world. We are not isolated, encapsulated egos. We are always a being-in-the-world, i.e., a being in relation. We are immersed in the natural world around us (*Umwelt*) and in the world with other humans as well (*Mitwelt*).

And how are we primarily in the world? For the most part, Heidegger says, the "who" who occupies the world is *das Man,* the impersonal one, the they, the Joneses. We primarily live in the world without thinking, that is to say, inauthentically. (In German, *uneigentlich* literally means "not one's own"). We just go along accepting the values that have been handed down to us. Before we ever start thinking, we are already living, and we are fundamentally living inauthentically.

Nevertheless, at the heart of human being, there is care, as the unifier of human existence. Briefly, although for the most part we are only concerned with the most superficial aspects of what it means to be a human being, care remains at the center of our existence. And while *das Man* gives us only a partial glimpse at what it means to be, there is a way to have access to the full potentiality of Dasein.

Anxiety, Guilt, and Death

Division Two of *Being and Time* is called "Dasein and Temporality." We all know that we will die. But we do not think about it, we try not to dwell on it. In fact, we get rather nervous about people who do think about it. Yet death holds the clue to grasping the meaning of Being as a whole. And while we are not likely to face up to death of our own accord, it is possible that anxiety may propel us to do so. For Heidegger, moods are, quite simply, a way of knowing. And anxiety may compel us to face the fact that we will die, and that this fact distinguishes us as humans. Knowing we will die, we can grasp our life as a whole and see that we are fundamentally guilty. By guilt Heidegger means that we are responsible not only for our choices, but even for those things which, by our choices, we have not chosen. We could have chosen otherwise. We could also live otherwise, certainly otherwise than *das Man* has dictated. And this means heeding the call of conscience, which urges us to live up to our potential, and in a state of resoluteness, knowing we will die, choosing who our selves will be.

In a short essay written only two years after *Being and Time,* Heidegger echoes Kierkegaard's *The Concept of Anxiety.* For Heidegger, the most fundamental metaphysical question is Leibniz's "Why is there something rather than nothing at all?" The answer to this question is to be found in a mood, the mood of anxiety. Heidegger himself describes the importance of anxiety for making the "qualitative leap," which Heidegger refers to in "What is Metaphysics?" (1929) as "transcendence":

> Does such an attunement, in which man is brought before the nothing itself, occur in human existence? This can and does occur, although rarely enough and only for a moment, in the fundamental mood of anxiety . . . If in the ground of its essence Dasein were not transcending, which now means, if it were not in advance holding itself out into the nothing, then it could never be related to beings nor even to itself. Without the original revelation of the nothing, no selfhood and no freedom . . . Being held out into the nothing—as Dasein is—on the ground of concealed anxiety is its surpassing of beings as a whole. It is transcendence.[58]

EXISTENTIAL PSYCHOLOGY AND PSYCHIATRY

It has been commonly assumed that Freud had two contradictory strains running through his thought: on the one hand, there is the natural scientist trying to map out the psyche on a landscape similar to medical science (most epitomized by the 1895 "Project for a Scientific Psychology"[59]), and on the other hand, there is the Freud of the technique of psychoanalysis whose goal is to liberate the individual patient from his or her sufferings. Boss's account of Heidegger's reaction perhaps best sums up the existential view of Freud:

> During [Heidegger's] perusal of the theoretical, "metapsychological" works, Heidegger never ceased shaking his head. He simply did not want to have to accept that such a highly intelligent and gifted man as Freud could produce such artificial, inhuman, indeed absurd and purely fictitious constructions about homo sapiens. The reading made him literally feel ill. Freud's "Papers on Technique," in which he gives advice on the practical conduct of the therapeutic analysis of the neurotic patient, made Heidegger more conciliatory.[60]

After the publication of Heidegger's *Being and Time* in 1927, a number of psychiatrists and psychologists began to devote their work to the twofold task of a critique of Freud's natural science approach, and a development of a positive theory and therapy emphasizing the liberating aspects of Freud's practice. In 1930 the Swiss psychiatrist Ludwig Binswanger published the first article to be influenced by Heidegger, "Dream and Existence,"[61] in the *Neue Schweizer Rundschau*. The same year *Der Nervenartzt,* a new journal, was founded in Zurich, which would regularly publish articles by Binswanger, Erwin Straus, and others.[62]

Although Binswanger had originally come to phenomenology through Husserl, he called his version of existential psychiatry *Daseinsanalyse,* after Heidegger's analysis of Dasein. Unfortunately, Binswanger's appropriation of Heidegger's ontology did not meet with the approval of Heidegger, who felt that Binswanger had misunderstood and misapplied it.

It would remain for Medard Boss to develop a truly Heideggerian psychiatry. Establishing a life-long personal relationship in 1946, Heidegger eventually agreed even to travel to Zurich to teach Boss' medical students. For seventeen years, beginning in 1958, Heidegger met with between 50-70 such students at Boss' house in Zurich.[63] In addition, Heidegger even gave Boss suggestions for his major work, *Existential Foundations of Medicine and Psychology.*[64]

Existence introduced the English-speaking reader to the European psychiatrists who had been pioneering detailed phenomenological descriptions of their patient's world and interpreting them in the light of an existential view of what it means to be a human being. As a result, numerous concepts in existential and phenomenological philosophy came to be applied concretely in psychiatry and psychology.

After Szasz's major work, *The Myth of Mental Illness* (1961),[65] it became increasingly harder to see psychological conflict as restricted to the isolated person. Szasz had exposed the Wizard of Oz pulling the strings of the purely medical concept of "mental illness." Once the theory was exposed, it became easier to see the obvious political, social, and ethical implications of the medical model of mental illness. To put it bluntly, after Szasz, *all psychology is by definition social psychology.*

Applying Heidegger's insights, the existential psychiatrists put this same concept into a similar formula: being-in-the-world. In other words, psychological conflict is not merely intrapsychic, but interpersonal. Developing a theme originated by Gregory Bateson in his classic double-bind theory of schizophrenia,[66] R. D. Laing and his colleagues applied the concept of being-in-the-world directly to the study of schizophrenia. Traditionally, schizophrenia had been seen (and in many cases, continues to be seen) as caused by a disturbance inside the individual, which, like a disease, may erupt out of nowhere for no particular reason. Indeed, schizophrenia is by definition not understandable in experiential terms.

In *Sanity, Madness, and the Family (1963),*[67] however, Laing and Esterson put schizophrenic patients back within their world again. As a result, their behavior was seen as quite intelligible indeed. The technique was very simple. They simply interviewed (and tape-recorded) the patients interacting with their families. In the context of the family, their mysterious illness made sense. These patients had made choices, or in some cases, failed to make choices, in reaction to the mystifications presented to them in their family relationships. Laing validated his patients perceptions, and earned their gratitude, while at the same time earning the wrath of traditional psychiatry as well.

The Existential Approach to Psychotherapy

Naturally, given the concerns of existential psychology and psychiatry, it has had its greatest impact on psychotherapy. This has been in spite of the fact that there have been virtually no schools or training institutes, let alone a set of techniques developed to expound a particular brand of "existential psychotherapy."

Psychotherapy is one way for an individual to face the ultimate problems of existence. In a recent article, May and Yalom write that "the spirit of existential psychotherapy . . . deals with the *presuppositions underlying therapy of any kind*."[68] In his book, *Existential Psychotherapy,* Yalom identifies four ultimate concerns: death, freedom, isolation, and meaninglessness. Using these concerns as a guide, I would like to give my own brief summary of the presuppositions underlying the existential approach to therapy.

We have seen how much emphasis the existentialists place on death. It would not even be going too far to say that death makes the other three ultimate concerns possible. For the existentialists, we are already living a certain life (in Kierkegaard's words, a "stage on life's way") when we start thinking about our life. This reflection is usually occasioned by the advent of anxiety, which propels us into a search for answers, or a new way to live. This anxiety may provoke the question "Why live at all?" But more importantly, it may also reveal that there are other ways to be. Death reveals freedom through possibility. At the same time, however, death also reveals our isolation, our individuality, since, as Heidegger has put it, it individualizes us since no one else can die our death for us. No one else can choose our life for us. But what should we choose, why choose at all? For Camus, the question of death leads to what he calls the absurd, which is defined as our demand for meaning, and the indifferent world's refusal to hand us one on a platter. If there is to be meaning in the universe, we must, like artists, create it.

These are the fundamental assumptions of an existential approach to psychotherapy. What do they mean in practice? How do existential psychotherapists differ from other therapists? What techniques do they use and how do we tell an existential therapist from other kinds of therapists?

With Socrates we saw the distinction between two types of teachers: the philosopher and the Sophist. Socrates was concerned with the individual's quest for the reality of true self-knowledge and power over oneself, while the Sophists were concerned with the appearance of wisdom and the achievement of political power over others. Both used techniques (Socrates had his dialectic, the Sophists had their rhetoric), and it was often hard to distinguish them from each other. Indeed, one of the indictments against Socrates was the accusation of his making the weaker argument appear to be the stronger one, a common Sophistic technique of oratory.

We also saw that Kierkegaard's knight of faith was impossible to tell by outward appearance as well. He could resemble the tax collector. Heidegger also gave us no guidelines to distinguish on an everyday level between someone who was living life authentically and someone who was not.

But why should this distinction be so difficult in the realm of existential psychotherapy? After all, there is no such difficulty in distinguishing between the other major types of therapies, whether they be Freudian, cognitive-behavioral, or even, for that matter, Rogerian, in their orientation. All of the above have a relatively set theoretical outlook and a corresponding set of techniques.

Part of the difficulty in distinguishing between existential therapy and other types of therapies lies in the fact that existential therapy has been consistently resistant to systematization and the development of one particular set of techniques and applications. I would now like to suggest why this has been so, and why it is likely to remain so.

It has now become common in psychology to speak of the various models or, in Thomas Kuhn's words, paradigms, of psychology. Following Kuhn's *Structure of Scientific Revolutions,* it is acknowledged that psychology is a young science with various competing paradigms. The major paradigms are the medical model, the psychodynamic model, the cognitive-behavioral model, and the existential-humanistic model. If one accepts this structure, and if one accepts that psychology should be a science like other sciences, then it could appear that the existential-humanistic model is one competing paradigm among others, and that, if it wins out in this competition, it might ultimately enthrone itself as the paradigm for a normal science, with a well-defined approach, a particular method (in this case, the phenomenological one), and of course the subject matter of human being.

In earlier papers entitled "Phenomenology, Psychology, and Science, I & II,"[69] I raised the question of whether or not existential psychology was this kind of paradigm, which could ultimately be used as a basis for a new, normal science, or whether or not it was essentially a new kind of paradigm, perhaps the paradigm of paradigms, which would remain a fundamentally critical approach to psychology and psychiatry, resisting its being used as the basis for a new system or another "normal science," in Kuhn's terms.

My reason for raising this issue is that Kuhn makes it clear that in order to be a science, it is necessary that a *single* paradigm be adopted, and that *the critical, philosophical stage of development, which he calls "revolutionary science," must ultimately cease,* so that the basic research of normal science can be undertaken. All new entrants in the field would thus be required to adopt this paradigm, as well as its research method. Paraphrasing the conclusions of an early article Kuhn wrote in 1958, four years before publication of *The Structure of Scientific Revolutions,* I wrote that for Kuhn:

Normal science is dogmatic, exclusive, close-minded, authoritarian, and intolerant. It is committed to only one way, secure in its drastically restricted vision, and as narrow and rigid as systematic theology.[70]

Given that existential psychology is committed to freedom, especially the freedom of the individual, and to expanding the possibilities from which an individual might choose, these words should give rise to a pause and a reminder of Kierkegaard's words, cited earlier, from *The Concept of Anxiety:*

Further than this, psychology cannot and will not go. In that very moment, everything is changed, and freedom, when it again rises, sees that it is guilty. Between these two moments lies the leap, which no science has explained and which no science can explain.[71]

As early as 1961, writing in the anthology *Existential Psychology,* Rollo May wrote:

In psychology and psychiatry, the term [existential] demarcates an *attitude,* an approach to human beings, rather than a special school. It is doubtful whether it makes sense to speak of "an existential psychologist or psychotherapist" in contradistinction to other schools. Existentialism is not a system of therapy, but an attitude toward therapy. Though it has led to many advances of technique, it is not a set of new techniques but a concern with the understanding of the structure of human being and his experience that must underlie all techniques. This is why it makes sense . . . to say that every psychotherapist is existential to the extent that he is a good therapist.[72]

In this case, then, the purpose of existential therapy remains much like the role of Socrates' midwife: to help the individual understand himself and his world and to help give birth to a new self. Thus, while the therapist may be quite active and involved in helping the client to explore new possibilities, the responsibility for choice and change still rests with the individual client.

The lack of specific techniques is often frustrating to those who wish to learn existential therapy, and want to know how to actually apply it. It is often not comforting to hear how much a role a philosophical view must play in therapy for those trained in the presumedly scientific techniques of traditional therapies. But as may be gleaned from the above exposition of existentialism and phenomenology, sometimes it is appropriate to resist the urge to do something, anything, for our clients, in order to allow them the responsibility and possibility of being themselves. Perhaps the best articulation for not reducing psychotherapy to one system or one set of techniques, can be found in Szasz's recent Preface (1988) to his book, *The Ethics of Psychoanalysis.*

I envision the therapeutic contract—the understanding between patient and therapist of the nature and purpose of their coming together and their mutual respect for its terms—as providing the practical conditions which make the therapeutic encounter possible. Only that much, and no more, can be articulated or specified. Within that space, the relationship between the participants must be

> as natural, spontaneous, and unrehearsed as is the relationship between other persons who respect (and perhaps are fond of) each other. Accordingly, from such a perspective, there is—there can be—no such thing as a *psychoanalytic technique or psychotherapeutic method*. If a therapist is to help a patient in the ways I describe, then his relationship with his client cannot be, and cannot be reduced to, a technique—just as a person's relationship with members of his family or friends cannot be, and cannot be reduced to, a technique.[73]

If it is correct that the subject matter of psychology or psychotherapy, i. e., human being, does not intrinsically admit of being reduced to a system or a set of techniques, it may very well turn out in the long run that what has often been viewed as existential psychology's greatest weakness—its reluctance to systematize itself— may well turn out to be its greatest strength, and ultimately its greatest usefulness for psychology and psychotherapy as a whole.

NOTES

1 May, Rollo, Angel, Ernest, and Ellenberger, Henri F., *Existence: A New Dimension in Psychology & Psychiatry* (New York: Basic Books, 1958).

2 Spiegelberg, Herbert, *Phenomenology in Psychology & Psychiatry* (Evanston: Northwestern University Press, 1972), p. 163.

3 Frankl, Viktor E., *Man's Search for Meaning: An Introduction to Logotherapy* (New York: Simon & Schuster, 1959).

4 May, "The Existential Approach," in *American Handbook of Psychiatry,* Vol. II, ed. Silvano Arieti (New York: Basic Books, 1959), pp. 1348-61.

5 *Review of Existential Psychology & Psychiatry* (1961-Present), ed. Keith Hoeller (Seattle, WA).

6 *Journal of Existential Psychiatry* (1960-70), ed. Jordan Scher (Chicago, IL).

7 *Journal of Humanistic Psychology* (1960-Present), ed. Thomas C. Greening (San Francisco, CA).

8 Laing, R. D., *The Divided Self: An Existential Study in Sanity and Madness* (New York: Pantheon, 1960).

9 Laing, *Self and Others* (New York: Pantheon, 1961).

10 May (ed.), *Existential Psychology* (New York: Random House, 1961).

11 Szasz, Thomas S., *The Myth of Mental Illness: Foundations of a Theory of Personal Conduct* (New York: Harper & Row, 1961).

12 Heidegger, Martin, *Being and Time,* trans. John Macquarrie and Edward Robinson (New York: Harper & Row, 1962).

13 Merleau-Ponty, Maurice, *Phenomenology of Perception,* trans. Colin Smith (New York: Humanities Press, 1962).

14 Boss, Medard, *Psychoanalysis and Daseinsanalysis,* trans. Ludwig Lefebre (New York: Basic Books, 1962).

15 Gendlin, Eugene, *Experiencing and the Creation of Meaning* (Glencoe: The Free Press, 1962).

16 Kuhn, Thomas, *The Structure of Scientific Revolutions* (Chicago: University of Chicago Press, 1962).

17 Binswanger, Ludwig, *Being-in-the-World: Selected Papers of Ludwig Binswanger,* ed. Jacob Needleman (New York: Basic Books, 1963).

18 *Studies in Phenomenology and Existential Philosophy,* ed. James M. Edie (Evanston: Northwestern University Press).

19 Foucault, Michel, *Madness and Civilization,* trans. Richard Howard (New York: Pantheon, 1965).

20 Bugental, James F. T., *The Search for Authenticity: An Existential-Analytic Approach to Psychotherapy* (New York: Holt, Rinehart, & Winston, 1965).

21 Van Kaam, Adrian, *Existential Foundations of Psychology* (Pittsburgh: Image Books, 1966).

22 Farber, Leslie, *The Ways of the Will: Essays Toward a Psychology and Psychopathology of the Will* (New York: Basic Books, 1966).

23 Straus, Erwin W., *Phenomenological Psychology: Selected Papers of Erwin Straus,* trans. Erling Eng (New York: Basic Books, 1966).

24 Kockelmans, Joseph J. (ed.), *Phenomenology: The Philosophy of Edmund Husserl and Its Interpretation* (New York: Doubleday/Anchor, 1967).

25 Kockelmans, *Edmund Husserl's Phenomenological Psychology: A Historico-Critical Study* (Pittsburgh: Duquesne University Press, 1967).

26 Schrader, George Alfred (ed.), *Existential Philosophers: Kierkegaard to Merleau-Ponty* (New York: McGraw-Hill, 1967).

27 Jourard, Sidney M., *Disclosing Man to Himself* (New York: Van Nostrand Reinhold, 1968).

28 Hoeller, Keith, "Selected Bibliography of Existential Psychology & Psychiatry," in *Readings in Existential Psychology & Psychiatry,* ed. Keith Hoeller (Seattle: Review of Existential Psychology & Psychiatry, 1990), pp. 297–309.

29 Hall, Calvin S., and Lindzey, Gardner, *Theories of Personality* (New York: John Wiley & Sons, 1978, 3rd ed.), pp. 340 & 343.

30 Yalom, Irvin D., *The Theory and Practice of Group Psychotherapy* (New York: Basic Books, 1975).

31 Yalom, Irvin D. *Existential Psychotherapy* (New York: Basic Books, 1980).

32 Hersen, Michel, Kazdin, Alan E., and Bellack, Alan S., *The Clinical Psychology Handbook* (New York: Pergamon Press, 1983).

33 Urban, Hugh, "Phenomenological-Humanistic Approaches," in Hersen et al., pp. 155-75.

34 Fischer, Constance T. and William F., "Phenomenological-Existential Psychotherapy," in Hersen et al., pp. 489-505.

35 May and Yalom, "Existential Psychotherapy," in *Current Psychotherapies,* ed. Raymond Corsini and Danny Wedding (Itasca: Peacock Publishers, 1989, 4th ed.), pp. 363-402.

36 *Ibid.,* p. ix.

37 Hoeller (ed.), *Heidegger & Psychology* (Seattle: Review of Existential Psychology & Psychiatry, 1988).

38 Hoeller (ed.), *Sartre & Psychology* (Seattle: Review of Existential Psychology & Psychiatry, 1983).

39 Hoeller (ed.), *Merleau-Ponty & Psychology* (Seattle: Review of Existential Psychology & Psychiatry, 1985).

40 Foucault, Michel and Binswanger, Ludwig, *Dream & Existence,* trans. Forrest Williams (Seattle: Review of Existential Psychology & Psychiatry, 1986).

41 Hoeller (ed.), *Readings in Existential Psychology & Psychiatry* (Seattle: Review of Existential Psychology & Psychiatry, 1990).

42 Hoeller (ed.), *Studies in Existential Psychology & Psychiatry* (Seattle: Review of Existential Psychology & Psychiatry, 1986-Present).

43 Camus, Albert, *The Myth of Sisyphus,* trans. Justin O'Brien (New York: Random House, 1956), p. 3.

44 Kirk, G. S. and Raven, J. E., *The Presocratic Philosophers* (Cambridge: Cambridge University Press, 1963), pp. 106-07.

45 Simon, Bennett, *Mind and Madness in Ancient Greece: The Classical Roots of Modern Psychiatry* (Ithaca: Cornell University Press, 1978).

46 Plato, *The Last Days of Socrates,* trans. Hugh Tredennick (New York: Penguin, 1969), p. 7.

47 Kierkegaard, Søren, *Either/Or,* Vol. II, trans. Howard V. and Edna H. Hong (Princeton: Princeton University Press, 1987), p. 362.

48 *Ibid.,* pp. 362-63.

49 *Ibid.*

50 Kierkegaard, Søren, *The Sickness unto Death,* trans. Howard V. and Edna H. Hong (Princeton: Princeton University Press, 1980).

51 Farber, Leslie, "The Therapeutic Despair," in his *The Ways of the Will,* (New York: Basic Books, 1966), pp. 155-83.

52 Camus, Albert, *The Myth of Sisyphus,* trans. Justin O'Brien (New York: Random House, 1956), p. 10.

53 Kierkegaard, *Either/Or,* Vol. I, p. 365.

54 Kierkegaard, *The Concept of Anxiety,* trans. Reidar Thomte (Princeton: Princeton University Press, 1980), p. 61 & 155.

55 Heidegger, *Being and Time,* p. 63.

56 *Ibid.,* p. 27.

57 *Ibid.,* p. 67.

58 Heidegger, "What is Metaphysics?" in *Basic Writings,* ed. David Farrell Krell (New York: Harper & Row, 1977), pp. 102, 105-06, 108.

59 Freud, Sigmund, "Project for a Scientific Psychology," *The Freud Reader,* ed. Peter Gay (New York: Norton, 1989), pp. 86-89.

60 Boss, Medard, "Martin Heidegger's Zollikon Seminars," *Heidegger & Psychology,* ed. Keith Hoeller (Seattle: Review of Existential Psychology & Psychiatry, 1988), p. 9.

61 Foucault, Michel and Binswanger, Ludwig, *Dream & Existence* (Seattle: Review of Existential Psychology & Psychiatry, 1986).

62 Spiegelberg, Herbert, *Phenomenology in Psychology and Psychiatry,* p. 102.

63 Boss, "Martin Heidegger's Zollikon Seminars," p. 9.

64 Boss, Medard, *Existential Foundations of Medicine and Psychology* (New York: Jason Aronson, 1979.

65 Szasz, *The Myth of Mental Illness,* 1961.

66 Bateson, Gregory, *Steps to an Ecology of Mind.*

67 Laing and Esterson, *Sanity, Madness, and the Family,* 1963.

68 May and Yalom, "Existential Psychotherapy," in Corsini and Wedding, p. 374.

69 Hoeller, Keith, "Phenomenology, Psychology, and Science I," *Heidegger & Psychology,* pp. 147-75; "Phenomenology, Psychology, and Science II, *Merleau-Ponty & Psychology,* pp. 143-54.

70 *Ibid., Heidegger & Psychology,* p. 166.

71 Kierkegaard, *The Concept of Anxiety,* p. 61.

72 May, Rollo, "The Emergence of Existential Psychology," in *Existential Psychology,* ed. May, p. 15 (2nd ed).

73 Szasz, Thomas S. *The Ethics of Psychoanalysis,* 1988 (originally published in 1963), pp. xii-xiii.

Existential Psychology as a Comprehensive Theory of Personality

ADRIAN VAN KAAM

The relation of existential psychology to other psychologies may be unclear to many. A great number of writings on existential psychology are more confusing than enlightening. There are those who say that existential psychology is Adlerian, others that it is all in Heidegger, Merleau-Ponty and Jean-Paul Sartre, others again that is encompassed in Freud or Jung, still others that it is identical with Tolman's behaviorism, and so on.

No trend of psychology has been claimed to be identical with so many others. This makes us think that something in existential psychology itself must give rise to all these identifications. We believe that it is the comprehensive scope of existential psychology which leads to this confusion. This confusion will not cease until psychologists become clearly aware of the specific nature of comprehensive psychology, which is totally different from the nature of the differential psychologies which necessarily preceded and made possible the emergence of a comprehensive scientific theory. For existential psychology is fundamentally a comprehensive scientific theory which attempts to integrate the contributions of the various areas of the behavioral sciences. It needs for this integration basic comprehensive notions concerning man's very nature. Existential psychology finds some of these broad concepts by means of the existential attitude towards man. The further development of existential psychology is based on the constant dialogue between these comprehensive hypothetical notions—obtained by the existential-phenomenological attitude—and the contributions of the different schools of psychology and psychiatry. The *Review of Existential Psychology and Psychiatry* expresses this state of affairs in the definition of its purpose when it announces that it "seeks to advance the understanding of human existence by encouraging the dialogue between the behavioral sciences and the phenomenology of man, and to point towards the integration of the theories and data of psychology and psychiatry into a science of man based on increasing knowledge of his essential nature."

This dialectical relationship explains why representatives of different schools of psychological or philosophical thought recognize their own insights in this growing scientific theory. However, as a result of this, to identify existential psychology with any particular existential philosophy or with any particular school of psychology leads to confusion. Existential psychology partakes of all and identifies with none. On the other hand, all of them can partake of existential psychology without identifying with it as such and without losing their own irreplaceable function in the growth of the science of behavior. One could compare this with comprehensive theoretical physics as illustrated in the theory of relativity. The findings of many outstanding physicists were integrated within this comprehensive theory; and vice versa, many areas of physics profited from the new comprehensive formulations. But this comprehensive theory did by no means do away with the necessity of continued research in the various domains of physics; it only stressed the advantages of a continuous dialogue between newly emerging theoretical physics on the one hand and the specialized fields of physics on the other.

THE DIALECTICAL RELATIONSHIP OF EXISTENTIAL PSYCHOLOGY TO DIFFERENTIAL PSYCHOLOGIES

Psychology, psychiatry and psychotherapy uncovered many phenomena of behavior and a wealth of relationships between them. Distinguished psychologists and psychiatrists throughout the years developed theories of personality to account for those phenomena and their interaction. The ultimate aim of every science is systematic explanation and orderly understanding. Therefore, the science of psychology now moves towards the construction of comprehensive theories which may be capable of integrating the phenomena and the theoretical constructs uncovered or created by the various schools of psychology, psychiatry and psychotherapy.The phenomena which have been reported and interpreted by the different schools of psychotherapy are related to one another because they are expressions of the nature of man. Therefore, each one of these phenomena can be better understood when seen in its reference to other phenomena which are described and explained by other schools of psychology. However, the mutual reference of these phenomena uncovered by various schools remains unclear and only implicit as long as they are not integrated. For they are expressed in the different languages which are created by the different approaches in psychology. Their interrelationship can be made explicit only when they are expressed in the same language or—what is analogous—integrated in a common frame of reference. Such a common frame of reference can be based only on a phenomenological description of the fundamental structures of the original experiences which are interpreted differently by the various approaches in psychology. For this structure of an experience underlies as a common ground the different interpretations given to it by the representatives of the various schools of psychology. A comprehensive theory of psychology, however, presupposes the integration not only of these experiences but also of their interrelationships with one another and with human nature as such. Such an overall integration is feasible only on the basis of a synthesizing idea or theoretical construct concerning man's nature which is comprehensive enough to connect all these findings without distortion of their original contribution. Phenomenological descriptions were necessary in order to uncover the original phenomena on which the interpretations of the various schools were based. In order to find what binds those phenomena with one another and with the nature of man we need the method of existential phenomenology. Existential phenomenology tries to describe man's very nature. Doing so, it presents us with constructs which seem really comprehensive and thereby capable of integrating the phenomena which we have found by means of phenomenology. The notion of existence is one of these comprehensive concepts. The term existence refers to the fact that it is man's essence to find himself bodily together with others in the world. He exists, literally, he stands out bodily with others in the world. In other words, this notion unites the subjective, physiological, objective and social aspects of the behavior of man. The student of behavior has to split up this reality into many aspects in order to study them in isolation. As a result we have a variety of psychologies such as social, behavioral, physiological, introspectional, psychoanalytical and other psychologies. We should like to reintegrate the phenomena which are discovered when behavior has been studied from these various isolated viewpoints. But this reintegration presupposes a return to our original experience of behavior in its unity before it was split up methodically into a variety of profiles. It is for this reason that the notion of man's existence seems useful for reintegration. This notion is used in existential psychology as an integrational construct as follows: a concept that refers to observed phenomena and that can be used for the integration of the greatest number and variety of phenomena and relationships observed by the different schools of psychology and psychiatry.

Existence or existential is the fundamental construct used in this comprehensive theory of psychology. Many more constructs are needed to develop a full theory. We call them subordinated constructs, such as mode of existence, existential world, existential transference, the centered self, ontological security and insecurity. They have the function of connecting the phenomena uncovered by the various schools of psychology with the fundamental construct of existence.

It may be clear by now that a central task of a comprehensive existential psychology is the discovery of existential constructs which can integrate the contributions of the various differential psychologies. All differential psychologies can be subsumed under three main categories. They all study behavior, but they concentrate predominantly on one or the other main aspects of behavior. Behavior is always the bodily interaction of a subject with a situation. Some psychologies are mainly interested in the dynamic psychology of the subject, others in measurable bodily characteristics of behavior, others again in the cultural-social or, briefly, situational determinants of behavior. We call these series of psychologies differential psychologies and their constructs differential constructs. Existential psychology and existential constructs must transcend differential psychologies and differential constructs in order to integrate them within a common open frame of reference.

We have mentioned some of the theoretical constructs used in existential psychology. We shall now list and discuss the necessary characteristics or constituents of existential constructs. This discussion will deepen our insight into existential psychology and into the necessary prerequisites for its sound scientific development as a comprehensive theory of psychology.

Existential constructs should transcend the predominantly subjective, objective, or situational connotations of differential constructs; they should represent fundamental human characteristics; they should be rooted in experience; they should not be function-oriented but person-oriented.

The rest of this paper will be given to a discussion of these four constituents of existential constructs.

THE FIRST CONSTITUENT OF EXISTENTIAL CONSTRUCTS: THE TRANSCENDENCE OF THE PREDOMINANTLY SUBJECTIVE, OBJECTIVE OR SITUATIONAL CONNOTATIONS OF DIFFERENTIAL CONSTRUCTS

Differential psychologies specialize in the study of one of the three main dimensions of behavior. They are forced to do so because of scientific-methodological reasons. The development of Western thought, however, tended to transmute these methodological distinctions into absolute ones. This absolutism leads to subjectivism, objectivism, and situationalism. This unfortunate state of affairs makes it necessary for us first to remove from existential constructs all subjectivistic, objectivistic, and situational connotations; secondly, to consider the development in our culture of an absolute dualism; and, finally, to assess the impact of this dualism on academic and psychoanalytic psychologies.

Subjectivism, which dominated the most recent periods of Western culture, tended to reduce the full meaning of man's psychology to only the subjective dimension of man's being. Man is explained in such an impoverished notion as a subject who is initially separated from the reality in which he lives. Such a view is not rooted in our spontaneous full experience of a man as a meaningful intentional whole who is self-evidently present to reality. It posits *a priori* that man is first of all an isolated entity which implies that there must be in principle an absolute split between man and reality.

Such a fundamental subjectivism leads necessarily to considering man as fundamental objectivism which holds that man can only represent in his consciousness isolated objects from which he is absolutely separated. But man is from the beginning—by his very being—open for the fullness of reality which, therefore, will appear in the light of his understanding to the degree that he is faithful to his fundamental openness. Being man, therefore, does not mean that there is first of all an isolated self or subjectivity, which then later transcends its isolation in order to represent to itself objectified isolated pieces of a completely foreign reality "out there" as does a camera or a tape recorder.

Psychology studies intentional behavior. Intentional behavior of man in its concrete givenness is always a particular realization of his original openness for reality. Therefore, psychology always studies in the last analysis some behavioral relationship of man to himself, to the others and to the things. For man can develop only what he fundamentally is, and he is basically always already a behavioral relationship with reality. This behavioral relationship which man is modifies itself according to the inexhaustible variety of situations in which reality may manifest itself and according to the stand which man may take towards reality. Existential psychology, therefore, is a comprehensive theoretical psychology of human behavior that is conceived as a Gestalt of observable differentiations of an original intentional-behavioral relationship of man to the world. Behavior is thus the observable differentiation of man's intentional relationships. We can emphasize in this behavioral relationship for methodical reasons, first, the intending subject pole, man; secondly, the embodiment of this intentionality in measurable behavior; and finally, the "situated" object-pole of this intentional behavior.

Every differential psychology should concentrate on one of these main profiles of man's existence. This concentration presupposes a temporary abstraction of the aspect concerned from the whole of man's behavior. This methodical restriction will give rise to methodically restricted constructs. It is, however, an essential task of existential psychology to steadily unmask any restricted constructs which are paraded as absolute symbols of the *whole* reality of human behavior.

We shall now briefly review the history of modern psychology in order to see where and how the philosophical tendency to transmute certain methodological restricted constructs into absolute ones arose.

DESCARTES AND THE DUALISM IN ACADEMIC PSYCHOLOGY

The French philosopher René Descartes conceived of mind and body as two really distinct substances. Both mind and matter in his thinking are complete and self-sustaining, and each one has one principle attribute, respectively, thought and extension. Mind is a thinking thing and the body is an extensive thing.

This view gave rise to two mutually exclusive starting points, namely, mind and body, or man and world. Each philosophical system which arose after Descartes adopted one of these starting points and denied or neglected the other. Either consciousness or body and world were emphasized by the post-Cartesian philosophers. Idealistic philosophies stressed consciousness, while empiricistic philosophies paid attention only to body and world which were considered to be of the same order.

Almost every scientific psychology was rooted in idealism or empiricism. For scientific psychology emerged in a cultural atmosphere which was satiated with Cartesian dualism and its implicit presence in idealism and empiricism. Every attempt to found a scientific psychology, therefore, started from an idealistic or an empiricistic view of human nature. Idealism led in psychology to introspectionism, which considered the contents of consciousness the legitimate and exclusive object of the new science. Empiricism, on the other hand, gave rise to behaviorism,which saw quantifiable bodily behavior isolated from the consciousness as the exclusive subject matter of a scientific psychology.

The introspectionists chose to study in isolation one of the partners separated by Descartes, namely, the *res cogitans*, the thinking consciousness. The behaviorists, meanwhile, concentrated their efforts on the other isolated partner, namely, the mechanistic stimulus-response body machine, the *res extensa*. Both neglected the inherent "worldly" aspect of man's behavior. This aspect too became split off from the original whole as an isolated entity and gave rise to environmental and cultural social psychologies, which originally tended to treat the environment as a factor in itself insulated from intentional behavior. A truly comprehensive psychology of existence as a whole should use fundamental constructs which are neither introspectionistic nor behavioristic, but which transcend the methodical limitations of both in order to integrate the findings of both, without distortion, into a higher unity.

DESCARTES AND THE DUALISM IN ANALYTIC PSYCHOLOGY

Descartes' dualism gave rise to idealism and empiricism which in turn led to a dualism in academic psychology. Is psychoanalytic theory also influenced by Cartesian dualism?

An appraisal of Freud's contribution from the viewpoint of comprehensive psychology leads to the conclusion that he too worked within the contemporary framework of Cartesian dualism. His view is evidently not based on the assumption of an original existential unity between man and world. Man in Freudian theory is biologically fixed as a pattern of innate instinctive drives prior to his having any dealings with a world which is in principle alien to his being. The world is not constitutive of his existence but purely a collection of foreign objects to be reacted to by his fundamentally fixed biological structure.

The isolated world out there, as Freud sees it, is only "reacted to" with a pre-structured instinctive impulse which is ready and eager to grasp and seize it in a pre-determined way. This subjectivistic view of man led Freud to the notion that civilization was a menace to the wholesome development of the autonomous subject, and that neurosis was fundamentally a conflict between the isolated instinctual subjectivity and any form of culture. While Freud elucidated important characteristics of the subject pole of existence, he ignored the possibility that man's neuroses may be due to a psychological factor which affects his existence as a whole, which means the subject-pole as well as the "situated" object pole. Is destructive aggression, for instance, a primary instinct to hurt or destroy which is already pregiven as such in the isolated subject? Or should it be considered in the light of the world of the subject as a response evoked by an existential situation which is experienced as obstructive, thwarting, and interfering? The overwhelming sexual and aggressive impulses which we find in certain neurotic patients seem to be not merely innate forces in isolated subjects but are just as much responses to a frustrating life situation embedded in the structure of existence during the history of its development. Freud, however, did not envision the development of the personality in terms of a differentiating encounter of subject and world in which both the subject and the world encountered are constitutive of man's actual being. He thought of men much more as victims of the constant search for the release of subjective tension in a strange and hostile world which had to be used for the highest possible fulfillment of the needs of the subject.

Freud created an inner mental world in the individual separate from and divorced from the "real-world-out-there." Soon he needed the constructs of projection and introversion to handle the contacts between this so-called inner world and the outer world. Impulses and emotions, however, are not isolated objects which exist in themselves within an isolated "psyche" but dynamic aspects of man's modes of existence in the world. Conflict is not an endopsychic affair, but the outcome of two or more incompatible modes of existence.

Freud's theory—especially his later ego theory—was further developed by Anna Freud, Wilhelm Reich, Melanie Klein, Hartmann, Kris, Alexander, Loewenstein, Winnicott and others. This later development shows a considerable growth towards a less dualistic view of man and his world but seems still unable to transcend completely the original split between man and world on which psychoanalytic theory is based. Nevertheless the contribution of psychoanalytic theory to our understanding of man is tremendous and should be carefully integrated within an existential synthesis.

Carl Jung, also, is subjectivistic in his approach. He fills the subject box with objects different from Freud's choices—objects such as archetypes and a racial unconsciousness. Human development becomes for him a wholly internal, somewhat mystical process within the isolated subjectivity. He points to significant experiences the formulation of which, however, can be purified from the dualistic theoretical influence.

A British group of psychoanalysts, notably Melanie Klein, Fairbairn, Winnicott and Guntrip recognized the impact of the culture, but fell back at the same time on the isolated subject-box-theory by their sophisticated theory of psychic internalization of the environment as an inner world. The Cartesian split is revived in their theory to such a degree that man is conceived as living in two worlds at the same time, inner and outer, psychic and material. The "internal objects" psychology of this group can also be seen as a result of the fact that they selected the imaginary aspect of human behavior as their perspective. This imagination is not considered as in principle world-oriented and world-revealing but as part of a relatively insulated and autonomous subjective structure. There is a tendency to stress the endopsychic situation and internally generated troubles at the expense of the impact of the outer world here and now. Fairbairn even concludes that the original distinction of Freud between the conscious and the Unconscious now becomes less important than the distinction between the *two worlds of outer reality and inner reality.*

The quality and quantity of clinical material presented by this British group compels respect; so does the quality of their theorizing. They represent an original and unusual contribution to psychoanalytic theory which goes far in bridging the gap between psychoanalytic and other theories. Their refreshing insights and discoveries lend themselves to integration within a comprehensive psychology of human behavior. Their constructs, nevertheless, while worthwhile and necessary from their differential viewpoint, are not comprehensive enough to present a truly comprehensive basis for an integrative theory of personality.

"SITUATIONAL" ANALYTIC PSYCHOLOGY

The Cartesian split led to introspectionism and behaviorism in academic psychology. An analogous development took place during the evolution of psychoanalytical theory. The cultural interpersonal school of psychoanalytic thought represented by Adler, Harry Stack Sullivan, Karen Horney and Erich Fromm gave rise to a series of differential theories which are bound together by the viewpoint of the culture, the civilization, the "others," the world. They rejected the idea that man's impulsive and emotional behavior emerged from innate instinctive drives within the organismic box. They substituted the perspective of environmental conditions, social pressures, cultural patterns, for the perspective of autonomous instinctual subjectivity. This series of differential psychoanalytic theories stress that culture molds character and that neurosis arises out of disturbances in human relationships. They tend, however, towards an exclusively cultural explanation which implies an underestimation of the relatively free subject pole which interacts with his culture. This state of affairs mirrors the situation in academic psychology where introspectionism was onesidedly concerned only with inner processes "within" the subject, while original behaviorism was geared to the perspective of the outside stimuli. They try to explain neurosis solely in terms of culture-pattern and external social pressures.

The series of differential psychologies which are initiated by the perspective of the "situated" object-pole of existence illustrates strikingly the importance of differential psychologies. They elucidate one aspect of human existence in a most remarkable fashion. They are able to see the whole of human reality in the light of this one perspective. For this "situational" aspect is everywhere present in man even in the most inner reaches of his being. Their onesidedness is laudable and fruitful as a methodological principle and should be maintained and fostered as a source of insight into one aspect of human existence. By the same token, however, it will be impossible to use these differential constructs for a comprehensive scientific theory which is the very transcendence of these aspects in order to assign to them respectfully their appropriate location in a conceptual comprehensive structure which points to human behavior as a whole.

We conclude that the first necessary and sufficient constituent of a comprehensive existential theory and of comprehensive existential constructs is the transcendence of exclusively subjectivistic, objectivistic, and situational connotations which are methodologically justifiable in differential theories.

THE SECOND CONSTITUENT OF EXISTENTIAL CONSTRUCTS: THE REPRESENTATION OF THE FUNDAMENTALLY HUMAN CHARACTERISTICS OF MAN

Introduction

Differential psychologies deal with the various isolated profiles of human behavior. Many of these profiles when taken in isolation from man as a whole are characterized by features, processes and laws which seem similar to certain features, processes and laws that can be observed in animals, plants and inanimate objects. These similar aspects, however, which we can observe in the behavior of man are abstracted from the whole of man's behavior and objectivated for methodological reasons of research. The *full* meaning of these isolated features of behavior can be grasped only when they are reintegrated in the whole by comprehensive existential psychology. Their full sense becomes clear when perceived again in the light of those properly human qualities of man as a whole which characterize all profiles of his behavior and their mutual interdependency. Those comprehensive, all-pervading, specifically human qualities cannot be squeezed into the mechanical models of certain differential psychologies such as stimulus-response, punishment-reward, tension-reduction, or homeostatic models. Such frames of reference are equally applicable to non-human beings. Consequently, those "sets" of mechanistic constructs "catch" precisely that in man which is *not* specifically and exclusively true of human behavior as such. The foundational constructs of anthropological psychology, therefore, should point to precisely those unique qualities that make man distinct and set him apart from every other type of being. Such uniquely human qualities which pervade all profiles, features, and processes of human behavior will present us with the synthesizing ideas which can connect the data and theories of differential psychologies. Only such constructs will facilitate a systematic integration, explanation, and orderly understanding of human behavior.

Philosophical Anthropology

Comprehensive psychology has thus to create constructs which represent the specific human characteristics of behavior. The discipline which is traditionally concerned with the fundamental characteristics of man is philosophical anthropology. Philosophical anthropology studies the being of man, his nature or his essence. The existential psychologist who has to deal with contemporary man in clinic, laboratory, hospital and consulting room, and who has to integrate not only the past but also the most recent discoveries of contemporary differential psychologies, is necessarily interested in concepts and formulations of contemporary philosophers who verbalize the contemporary predicament and self-awareness of man. However, he does not assume philosophical concepts blindly but evaluates them in the light of the contemporary and historical contributions of differential psychologies in order to estimate their applicability to those contributions and therewith their usefulness for comprehensive theory construction. One reason for the usefulness of many ontological concepts for comprehensive integration is their universality, their applicability to all behavior of all men. When constructs about behavior are obtained not by an ontological but by a merely empirical study of a certain group of men, then they will be capable of integrating only the data which pertain to a certain group of men in a specific culture. Only constructs which are obtained from an explicitation of man's very being are in principle broad enough to integrate all psychological data from all periods of human history, from all classes of men, and obtained by all differential psychologies.

Certain differential psychologies, on the other hand, may have their own implicit philosophical anthropology which fits only the specific aspect of behavior which they study. The integration of the contributions of these differential psychologies presupposes, therefore, that the integrational theorists make explicit their specific ontological assumptions. Only then is a dialogue possible between the fundamental anthropological philosophy represented in the foundational constructs of comprehensive theory and those anthropological philosophies which underlie the differential psychologies. This dialogue will clarify whether or not the anthropological philosophy which underlies the differential psychology is sufficiently comprehensive to encompass the discoveries of other differential psychologies. If not, it will be necessary for the integrational theorist to purify the factual differential contributions and statements of all unwarranted extrapolations due to the implicit underlying philosophy. Only such a purification can clarify that which is really and exactly established in scientific observation by the differential psychologist. Such an operation on the basis of comprehensive anthropological constructs is performed by means of the foundational dialectical method in comprehensive theory. This method is based on the principle that scientifically established data of differential theories can never exclude one another and are always open to integration, while implicit philosophical anthropologies underlying these differential psychologies may prove to be incompatible with one another. In this case, the theoretical interpretations may also be incompatible in so far as they are influenced by these incompatible underlying philosophical anthropologies.

The criterion which thus determines the selection of existential constructs is the *principle of applicability*. The principle of applicability states that the *comprehensive scientific theorist of human behavior should borrow no philosophical assumption or construct unless it can be used most adequately for the integration and explanation of the greatest number and variety of the findings of the various differential psychologies because of its applicability to these findings*. This judgment regarding the adequacy of an assumption or statement is thus a *selective* judgment, a psychological and not a philosophical judgment.

THE THIRD CONSTITUENT OF EXISTENTIAL CONSTRUCTS: THE ROOTEDNESS IN EXPERIENCE

A comprehensive existential construct points to a fundamental human characteristic as it is found in real life. It is, consequently, crucial for such a construct to be based on our experience of man himself and not on wishful thinking, subjective imagination, or theoretical prejudice *about* man. In other words, comprehensive existential constructs have to be purified from all distorting wishes and prejudices which are not in harmony with our fundamental experience of the human reality. Therefore, the first task of the foundational theorist is to study in the light of experience constructs offered to him by various philosophies and differential psychologies. He will ask himself what is really experience in these constructs or judgments and what is only a hypothetical explanatory conceptualization contained in these judgments. An existential construct should be based on a real experience of human behavior. This experience may prove to be mistaken or to be contaminated by prejudice; then the construct should be corrected or rejected. It is for this reason that a comprehensive construct is only an approximation of fundamental human qualities. Nevertheless, experience can be the only root of the comprehensive construct and can never be replaced by theories, hypotheses, models, unverified philosophies, social or political views. The comprehensive theorist will build his theory on comprehensive constructs, but the construct itself should never be rooted in a theory but in the firm ground of reality experience. For the same reason the comprehensive existential theorist will borrow from philosophy only those concepts which are rooted in experience and verifiable in experience. The further development of those existential constructs should be an explicitation of what is implicit in the experience which is expressed by the constructs. As we have seen earlier, the integration of the contributions of the differential psychologies presupposes also a study of what in the formulations of the differential psychologies is based on real experience in order to distinguish it from unverified models, hypotheses, and implicit philosophies. Only then is a dialogue possible between the experience of human behavior as a whole expressed in existential constructs and the experience of isolated profiles of human behavior as found by a purification of the formulations of differential psychologies.

The methods necessary for the rooting of comprehensive differential constructs in experience are the methods of natural observation and the phenomenological method. Natural observation places us as it were in the field of phenomena to be studied and enables us to describe these phenomena in their first appearance. The phenomenological method leads us to the inner structure of these phenomena and liberates our perception of this structure from personal and cultural prejudice which is still unchecked in natural observation and description.

The requirement that the comprehensive constructs of personality theory should be rooted in our experience of characteristically human qualities implies that one kind of philosophy seems preferable to other kinds when there is a question of borrowing constructs. Most useful seems to be the kind of philosophy that attempts to root itself in a critical phenomenology of human experience. For only such philosophies attempt to develop on the basis of experience concepts which relate in principle to all that is necessarily true of all human qualities.

THE FOURTH CONSTITUENT OF EXISTENTIAL CONSTRUCTS: PERSON-ORIENTED AND NOT FUNCTION-ORIENTED

Existential constructs differ distinctly from the constructs of differential psychologies in terms of personal versus functional orientation. Various differential psychologies which study certain aspects of behavior in isolation from man's behavior as-a-whole are able to cast their theories in the form of impersonal functions or equations. Such differential psychological operations can be performed only with abstracted isolated variables which are objectivated after having been obtained by means of a dissecting analysis of the reality under study.

Existential psychology, however, has to start from human existence in its wholeness if it ever hopes to reintegrate these unrelated abstracted profiles into a meaningful self-consistent synthesis. This specific task of comprehensive psychology requires a terminology appropriate to itself for it cannot operate on the same lines as the differential psychologies. The system of constructs of an existential psychology has to refer to existence as a "living" personal intentional whole as it appears in real life situations. It is only on this basis that comprehensive psychology will be able to create a synoptic view of human behavior arising out of a synthesis of the knowledge available in the differential psychologies. The human or personal qualities and dynamics which are characteristic of man in his natural union with the world cannot be adequately represented by a terminology which is peculiar to physiology, physics, or mathematics. In that case we would make anthropological data fit an impersonal infra-anthropological theory instead of developing a theory suitable to the data. Existential psychology transcends differential psychologies precisely at the level where the human person emerges as the unique all-encompassing intentional Gestalt. On this ultimate level of integration the mathematical, statistical, physical, physiological, neurological, biological, or biochemical constructs are of no avail, no matter how well they served in differential psychologies on lower levels of integration.

On this highest level of integration of intentional behavior the use of, for instance, mathematics would alter the identity of the subject matter. The expression of intentional behavior in mathematical symbols would necessarily alter the conception of the personal nature of the subject one is dealing with. Human intentional behavior as personal, existential, or qualitative, and not as quanti-mechanical but only by an anthropological or personal model. The existential constructs which compose this personal model form a new terminology capable of representing phenomena of human behavior as personal, existential or qualitative, and not as quantitative, functional, and mechanical. These existential constructs are qualitative in nature and refer to the intentional presence of man in a world which has personally significant meanings to him.

Certain differential psychologies are forced to depersonalize their abstracted profiles of behavior in order to detect how far those profiles are still under the impact of certain biochemical or physical laws. Such a depersonalization, however, would be impossible for a comprehensive science which studies man precisely in his very distinctness from the objects of physics, chemistry, biology, and neurology. Existential psychology studies the intentional-functional behavior of persons who exist together with other people in a meaningful world. This intentional-functional behavior shows also certain process-like mechanical features which can be abstracted from this behavior for close observation and study by differential psychologists. But these features are peripheral and not the unique core of intentional behavior. Nevertheless, they should be taken into account and be reintegrated by the existential psychologist in his comprehensive synthesis. Therefore, existential constructs are indisputably more personal when compared with the functional thought-forms in which most differential psychologies cast their theoretical formulations and factual findings. It would be unscientific to represent human-behavior-as-such with constructs of differential psychologies which point to only certain mathematical, physiological, biological, functional, or physical attributes which human behavior has in common with other species but which precisely for that reason are as such not specifically human. In that case we would transfer a construct from an object in differential psychology to which it properly belongs to the object of a comprehensive psychology of personality to which it would apply only in an improper way. Such an animal-morphism, biomorphism, or machine-morphism would be highly metaphorical and imply an artificial impersonification of the personal. While such a metaphorical use of language is interesting from a literary point of view, it is misleading in science where we prefer an objective statement of fact. The literary statement that man is *like* an animal, or *like* a subtle machine, or *like* a plant which responds to the stimulus of light is metaphorically true and based on resemblances which are really present and found by comparison. The differential psychologies make some of these resemblances the total isolated object of their investigations. In that case these constructs are *literally* valid for those differential psychologists within their isolated domain of investigation. But the statements made by such a differential psychology about isolated impersonal aspects of behavior become metaphorical when applied to human existence in its personal wholeness. The structural differentiations of behavioral existence which were studied in isolation by differential psychology are perceived in existential psychology as *personal* differentiations. This means that these differentiations are necessarily permeated by those unique human characteristics which are represented in the fundamental existential constructs. Each differential aspect of human behavior is perceived in existential psychology as still a person who is existing intentionally in some way and not as an impersonal function going on in isolation. The impersonal aspects of such differential aspects of the human person discovered by differential psychologies are not denied, however, but respectfully integrated within this view of the whole. All impersonal human states are in a sense pseudo-impersonal in so far as we can always find some meaningful personal presence behind them which uses, abuses, submits to, is indifferent to, rebels against, neglects, affirms, denies, or represses those functions and features which are available to him in his organism and environment and which follow within themselves certain biochemical, neurological, physical laws to which the intentional agent has to adapt himself.

The total human self and its existential differentiations can thus be cast in existential and in differential constructs. The existential constructs also represent the human reality as a whole in so far as this unique humanity is present in its existential differentiations. The differential constructs represent the reality of the many resemblances between the human reality and other physical and biological realities in the universe. Therefore, two different languages are necessary in psychology: the existential language to describe man as an existing Gestalt or person and the functional or process language to account for the functional resemblances between man and other objects. Psychologists should be careful not to mix the two series of constructs and to talk metaphorically about man as a living person by using terms that belong to the differential study of some of his isolated aspects. The same would be true if the differential psychologist would apply existential terminology to the abstracted and objectivated profile of behavior which he studies. In such a case, the existential terminology would become as metaphorical as the differential terminology when applied to man as a total living existence. It is as metaphorical to describe a neuron as a person as to describe a person as a neuron.[1]

We may now summarize the differences between differential psychologies and comprehensive existential psychology in respect to the collection of data and the formation of theory.

I. Differential psychologies.
   1. Empirical collection of data.
      Observation of isolated processes, functions, and features of behavior. Ideally in controlled experimental laboratory situations.
   2. Theory formation.
      Explanatory theories about isolated behavioral processes, functions, and features expressed in functional, mechanical, or mathematical constructs.

II. Existential psychology.
   1. Empirical collection of phenomena.
      a. Observation and experience of human behavior as a whole pervaded and characterized by uniquely human characteristics. Ideally in a situation of personal relationships.
      b. Use and integration of the observations of differential psychologies and of other disciplines in so far as they are relevant to the full understanding of human behavior as a whole and in all its aspects.
   2. Theory formation.
      a. Explanatory theory about human behavior in its "lived" intentional entirety in terms of personal, i.e., meaningfully motivated activities expressed in existential terms—that is to say, in terms appropriate to the personal existential nature of the object of study.
      b. Integration of the theoretical explanations of differential psychologies and other disciplines in so far as they are relevant to the full explanation of human behavior as a whole and in all its aspects.

NOTE

1 I am indebted to Harry Guntriss' book, *Personality Structure and Human Interaction*. For some of my formulations in the last section of this article where I discuss person-oriented constructs. In spite of my genuine admiration for this work, I find myself in fundamental disagreement with its main line of thought which is onesidedly geared towards psychoanalytic theory, does not do justice to other differential psychologies, and is still influenced by remnants of Cartesian dualism.

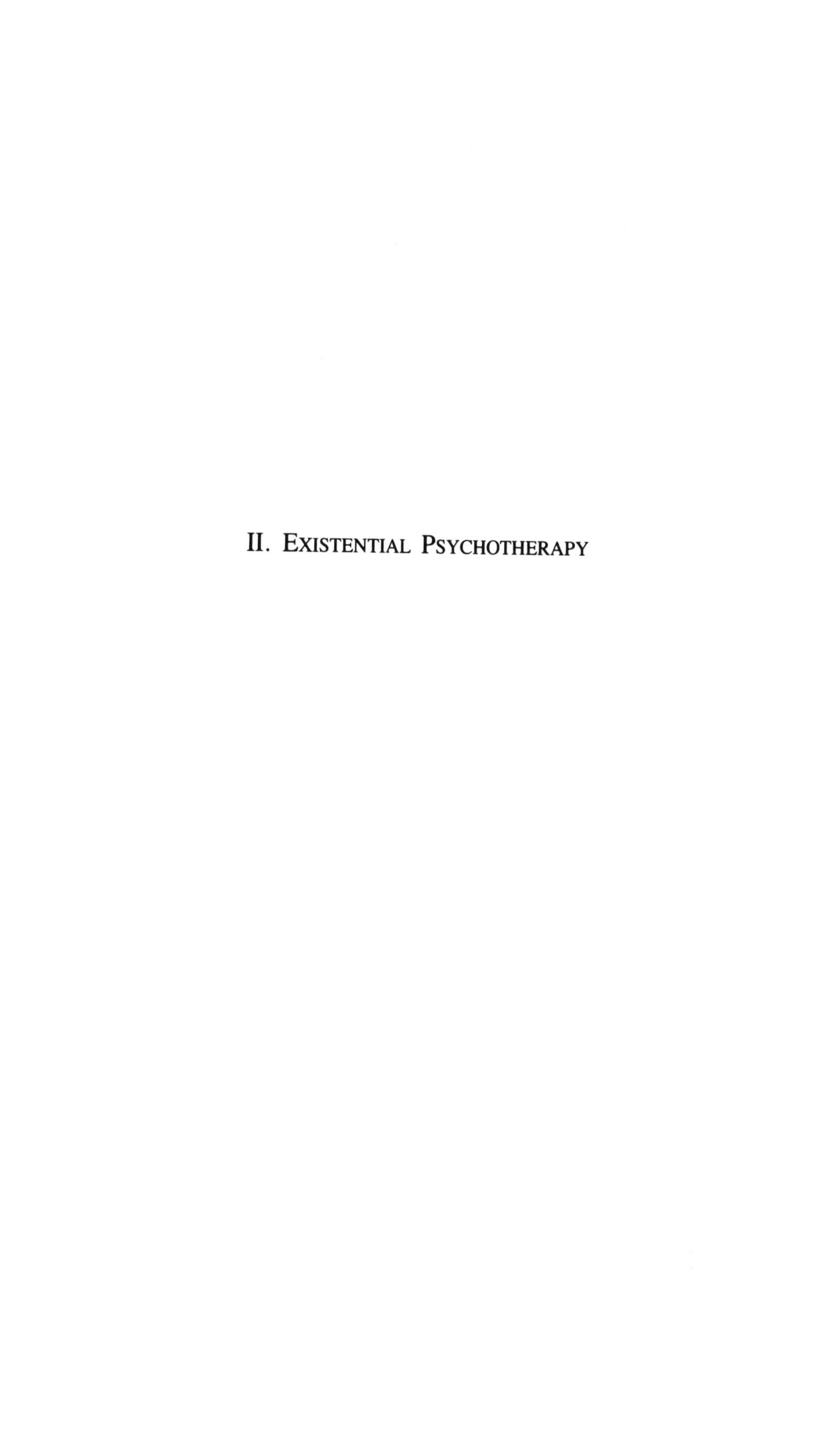

II. Existential Psychotherapy

Existentialism and Psychotherapy

PAUL TILLICH

1. EXISTENTIALISM AND ESSENTIALISM

The task given to me is a formidable one, provoking justifiable anxiety. In all schools of psychotherapy there are many concepts which have proved more or less useful for directing research as well as practical work, but which are devoid of a philosophical foundation and, consequently, without critical and uniting principles. As a non-expert in this vast realm of theory and practice, I can only pose the question of a possible philosophical foundation for psychotherapy on the basis of my own thought, in which the existentialist element has a definite place, although I would not call myself an existentialist.

It is an indication that one has misunderstood existentialism if one uses it without reference to its opposite. Philosophical ideas necessarily appear in pairs of contrasting concepts, like subject and object, ideal and real, rational and irrational. In the same way, existentialism refers to its opposite, essentialism, and I would be at a loss to say anything about the one without saying something about the other. The easiness with which the term existentialism and its derivatives have lately become the talk of the intellectual market is because from the very beginning in America, after the Second World War, the term existentialism was used without reference to its opposite. Indicative for the general situation is the fact that the term essentialism did not even exist in the early discussions of existentialist philosophy. But it seems to me that in a group which seeks for an existentialist psychotherapy, the implicit reference to essentialism should be brought into the open.[1]

Instead of giving an abstract definition of essentialism and existentialism, I will point to an example par excellence, the nature of man. One can describe man's essential nature and one can describe man's existential predicament. Both tasks have always been performed but often the one has tried to eliminate the other. In religious thought, for instance, the view of man's predicament has frequently overshadowed the view of his essential nature. One can say this of ancient Gnosticism as well as of some forms of radical Protestantism. If man's estranged predicament is so much emphasized that his creative goodness appears completely destroyed, an impressive but untenable theological existentialism arises. Some theologians of the Reformation period, like the great church historian, Flacius, as well as some recent theologians like the early Karl Barth, have taken this position. None of them would have denied or even minimized the doctrine of creation and with it man's essential goodness, but they did not draw from it the consequences for the doctrine of man. The divine was cut off from the human without "point of contact." Man was seen as a mere object of divine action and man's productive activities in culture and history were devaluated. This is the theological existentialism without the essentialist frame in which classical theology had stated it.

But the main stream of existentialist thought was running through philosophy, the arts and literature. In contrast to the situation in the last three years after the Second World War, when most people identified existentialism with Sartre, it is now common knowledge in this country that existentialism in the western intellectual history starts with Pascal in the 17th century, has an underground history in the 18th century, a revolutionary history in the 19th century and an astonishing victory in the 20th century. Existentialism has become the style of our period in all realms of life. Even the analytic philosophers pay tribute to it by withdrawing into formal problems and leaving the field of material problems to the existentialists in art and literature.

There are, however, only rare moments in this monumental development in which an almost pure existentialism has been reached. An example is Sartre's doctrine of man. I refer to a sentence in which the whole problem of essentialism and existentialism comes into the open, his famous statement that man's essence is his existence. The meaning of this sentence is that man is a being of whom no essence can be affirmed, for such an essence would introduce a permanent element, contradictory to man's power of transforming himself indefinitely. According to Sartre, man is what he acts to be.

But if we ask whether his statement has not, against its intention, given an assertion about man's essential nature, we must say, certainly, it has. Man's particular nature is his power to create himself. And if the further question is raised of how such a power is possible and how it must be structured, we need a fully developed essentialist doctrine in order to answer; we must know about his body and his mind and, in short, about those questions which for millenia have been discussed in essentialist terms.

Only on the basis of an essentialist doctrine of freedom does Sartre's statement have any meaning. Neither in theology nor in philosophy can existentialism live by itself. It can only exist as a contrasting element within an essentialist framework. There is existentialist philosophizing but there is not, and cannot be, an existentialist system of philosophy. The answers given by existentialists to the questions they raise in their analyses are derived from essentialist traditions. Existentialism is an element within a larger frame of essentialism and it exists only as such an element, even in its most radical anti-essentialist statements. In order to describe the negative in being and life, one must see its impact on the positive. For only through this impact does the negative have reality. There is no existentialist description of the negativities of the human predicament without an underlying image of what man essentially is and therefore ought to be. The cutting power of existentialist novels, paintings, even philosophical analyses of man's predicament, is rooted in the implicit contrast between the negativities they show and the positives they silently presuppose.

But now we must ask the converse question: Is pure essentialism possible? It is possible only if man's searching mind is subjected to a strict censorship, prohibiting all those questions in which man asks about his existence within his world. Plato did not accept such censorship. He was aware of the conflict between the essential and the existential element in reality. And if he talked about the "destiny of the soul," namely, of man's predicament in space and time, he did not use dialectics, but myth. He is the greatest example of a union of essentialism with existentialist elements. In the Middle Ages, existentialist descriptions of the human predicament were present in monastic self-scrutiny and in the penitential manuals for priest-confessors. These manuals contain materials which in many respects are an anticipation of the insights elaborated in the psychotherapeutic schools of the 20th century. In Protestantism, this concrete material disappeared, but certainly not the question of man's predicament. In philosophy the problem came to a dramatic height in the conflict between Descartes and Pascal in the 17th century. Both men stood in the Platonic-Augustinian tradition, both were creative mathematicians, and mathematics was always the pattern for essentialist thinking. But while Descartes reduced the elements to a minimum, Pascal put them against his own and Descartes' essentialist emphasis.

Ever since, this tension has remained alive, although in the modern period it has been under a definite predominance of the essentialist element. A change took place with the existentialist revolt against Hegel's essentialism in the middle of the last century and with the major victory of the existentialist attitude in the 20th century. But this victory does not mean that the tension has ceased between the two approaches to reality. And a slight recovery of essentialism seems to be noticeable, especially in the arts within the last decade.

2. THE PHILOSOPHICAL MATRIX OF PSYCHOANALYSIS

Seen in the background of this development, the question of the relation of existentialism and psychoanalysis can be asked in more definite terms. The term "psychoanalysis" has shared the fate of a large group of important concepts that have grown beyond the limits of their original meaning and in this way have received an increased significance and a growing indefiniteness. This makes it necessary to determine the sense in which psychoanalysis shall be used in its confrontation with existentialism.

Originally it meant a therapeutic technique, a refinement and transformation of earlier techniques. But this was possible only on the basis of a new understanding of the psychological processes which produce both the necessity and the possibility of psychotherapy. "Psychological processes" is a name for processes in the living *Gestalt* which we call "man." No understanding or even description of them is possible without an image of this *Gestalt*, without a doctrine of man in the several dimensions of his being. No therapeutic theory can be developed without an implicit or explicit image of man. But we must go beyond this step. No doctrine of man is possible without a general understanding of the general processes of life, their trends and their ambiguities. And finally, no understanding of life processes is possible without a doctrine of being and of the structure of being universally.

This consideration shows the basis of the question, how is psychoanalysis related to existentialism? The question is two-sided. The psychoanalytic practice is not only dependent on the doctrines of man and life and of being, but these doctrines are also dependent on the practice of psychoanalysis. Every practical dealing with reality provides experiences which have theoretical impact. This insight is as old as the gospel of John when it speaks of doing the truth and it is as new as Marx in his earlier writings when he fought against the separation of theory and practice. And it is as old and as new as the main emphasis of Nietzsche and the American pragmatists when they tried to reunite action and knowledge. Therefore, it is not astonishing that Freud's analytic practice became the source of ideas which changed the whole intellectual climate of the 20th century.

Unfortunately, the philosophical matrix in which the psychoanalytic techniques were conceived was rather inadequate to the implications and consequences of their conception. The naturalistic (and in some respect, idealistic) presuppositions of Freud do not fit the immense contribution he has made indirectly to the existentialist analysis of the human predicament. Therefore, it is a justifiable attempt by the different Neo-Freudian groups to overcome this inadequacy and, by doing so, to correct some shortcomings of the therapeutic method which follows from the inadequacy of Freud's philosophical presuppositions. This is what existentialist psychotherapy also tries to do. I believe that such a task is necessary, not only for psychotherapeutic practice but also for the contemporary intellectual situation.

If my philosophical assumptions are correct, an important consequence follows: It cannot only be existentialist, it must also be essentialist thought which provides the philosophical matrix for the psychoanalytic practice. Existential psychotherapy is almost a truism; for disease is one of the central existential concepts. Therefore, let us not talk of existentialist psychoanalysis as such but of a possible philosophical matrix of psychoanalysis, being aware of the fact that every constructive philosophy and theology unites essentialist and existentialist elements. In order to understand sin, the theologian must understand creative goodness. In order to understand estrangement, the philosopher must understand that from which we are estranged, namely, our own essential nature. This means psychotherapy must remain aware of its dependence on the doctrine of man, on the doctrine of life, on the doctrine of being. As psychotherapy, it cannot create such a philosophy, though it can influence it.

This is a difficult relationship. The problem is the same as it is in all creative functions of the human spirit. Always and inescapably they have a philosophy in their background. We must bring this into the open and subject it to criticism and transformation. On the other hand, all creative functions of man's spirit must contribute to a philosophy which deals with all of them. This mutual dependence of philosophy and the other functions of the spirit produces a perpetual problem. For more than fifty years, I have been laboring under this problem in relation to the philosophy of religion; and I am consoled that now other groups are in the same predicament and will have to labor probably more than fifty years under the same problem. As a group of healers you cannot identify yourselves with a particular philosophy; but you cannot do without a philosophy. Instead of attempting a general answer, I want to give a description of some exemplary situations, thus leading to the next consideration: philosophical problems of psychoanalytic procedures.

3. PHILOSOPHICAL PROBLEMS OF PSYCHOANALYTIC PROCEDURES

Naturalism, the philosophy from which Freud came, is together with idealism the main expression of an essentialist philosophy. Freud's determinism was his naturalistic heritage, his moralism was his idealistic heritage. And in both he represented the basic attitude of the victorious and "Victorian" industrial society of the 19th century. But with the empirical rediscovery of the old philosophical concept of the unconscious, he broke through his own moralism, and with the concept of sublimation, he broke through his determinism. The first, the rediscovery of the unconscious, was the confirmation of the inability of autonomous morals to lead man to his fulfillment. It was the destruction of the philosophy of the "men of good will," which is so rampant in American Protestantism. Freud showed the ambiguity of goodness as well as of evil, and in doing so, he helped to undercut Protestant moralism. This perhaps was the most important existentialist contribution of psychoanalysis to the doctrine of man. Man is not what he believes himself to be in his conscious decisions.

This is the point where Freud is a true existentialist in the sense of all existentialist descriptions of man's predicament. He is certainly not the moralistic idealist he sometimes gives the impression of being, especially in relation to sex. And he is not a determinist either, towards which his naturalistic heritage seemed to push him. I don't look for indeterministic utterances of Freud. They probably could not be found. And they should not, because the traditional fight between determinism and indeterminism is a dead issue. But I look at his concept of sublimation, which philosophically is completely unelaborated.

Sublimation is the act which transforms something not sublime into something sublime. And the sublime is a concept which deserves highest standing in formulating a philosophy of life. The structure of life shows that the sublime is the greatest potentiality of life. It is not a mere transformation of the not sublime; then it would be only another form of it. But the sublime is something qualitatively new, it demands a creative act—and this means freedom, in a meaningful sense of the word. It belongs to the theories wherein Freud was "behind" himself—in that he tried to derive sublime things, like works of art, from non-sublime things like early psychological disturbances of the artists. But the very concept of the sublime requires that such disturbances be looked at as occasions and not causes of the creation of the sublime. This is not an existentialist but an essentialist question. It refers to man's essential nature and to the central concept in which converge all elements in man's essential nature, the concept of freedom. I do not mean the so-called "freedom of the will" (an obsolete concept), but the power of man to react centrally to a stimulus, by deliberation and decision.

This explains the fact to which Rollo May drew my attention, that in so many of his patients' dreams there appears the necessity of deciding. His patients have not yet lost the awareness that sublimation goes through decision, and that the power of deciding makes men human. This consideration is an essentialist one—although it shows the pre-condition for the possibility of man's existential self-loss. This should lead to the acknowledgement that biological and sociological methods of interpretation are by no means sufficient in order to explain the drive towards the sublime. The centered act of the centered self is the source of sublimation. This is a basic statement of an essentialist doctrine of man and is as necessary for psychoanalysis as the existentialist insight in the determining function of the unconscious is for morality and religion.

After these examples of existentialist as well as of essentialist elements in which psychoanalysis must find a solid philosophical ground, let me speak of a phenomenon in which elements of both sides are effective. I point to the difference and confusion of existential and neurotic anxiety, of existential and neurotic guilt, of existential and neurotic emptiness. I believe that Freud is partly responsible for the confusion because of his inadequate philosophical foundations which did not admit the distinction between essential goodness and existential distortion. The decisive question here is whether one believes that it is possible to remove by successful analysis not only neurotic forms of anxiety but also its genuine forms—the anxieties of finitude, of guilt, of emptiness. Of course, no one would deny that a completely successful analysis is highly improbable, but many analysts assert that in principle both forms of anxiety can be removed, because there is no qualitative difference between them. They all can be treated as neurosis, capable of being healed. This would include the anxiety of having to die, the anxiety of having become guilty, the anxiety of lacking a meaning of life. This however would imply, at least in principle, that the analyst is able to remove from human beings the awareness of their finitude, and consequently their basic anxiety; that he would be able to convince men who have become guilty that they are not really guilty; that he would be able to answer the question of the meaning of life to his patients. But all this is not realistic.

Actually the situation is quite different. Neurotic anxiety is misplaced compulsory anxiety, and not the basic anxiety about everything being finite. Basic anxiety is anxiety about being bound to the law of coming from nothing and going to nothing. Neurotic guilt is misplaced compulsory guilt feeling and not the existential experience of being guilty of a definite concrete act which expresses the general estrangement of our existence, an act for which responsibility cannot be denied, in spite of the element of destiny in it. Neurotic emptiness is a compulsory flight from meaning, even from that remnant of meaning which makes the experience of meaninglessness possible. It is the expression of an unreflective and unsophisticated understanding of men and life if these neurotic phenomena are confused with the universal structures of existence which make neurotic phenomena possible. No great physician has ever claimed that he can change the biological structures of life; and no psychotherapist from whatever school he comes should claim that he can change the structures of life in the dimension of self-awareness usually called the psychological dimension. But he can assert that he may heal disorders which follow from the relation of man's existential to his essential nature. Here are very obvious reasons why psychoanalysis needs a philosophical matrix.

There are other reasons, some existentialist, some essentialist. I can only point to them. What do norms of thought and action mean in relation to the therapeutic process? For Freud, the "superego" is the name for the consciousness of norms. But the material of the superego is taken from the "id." It has no standing in itself, no objective validity. It has only the power of psychological oppressiveness. The reason for this construction is that Freud did not distinguish the essential structure of man's being, from which forms and principles are derived, and their existential distortion in the images of the superego. Certainly, there are images of destructive power in most human beings; but they are not identical with man's essential nature.

Essential norms, if obeyed, fulfill and give the joy of fulfillment because they represent our own essential being against our existential distortion. Religious commandments, for instance, express a concrete understanding of man's essential nature. The superego gives arbitrary commands and produces unhappiness and revolt. Dr. Hanna Colm writes about the revolt of children, not only against oppressive education, but also against the lack of any direction. This is an interesting confirmation of the assertion that norms and principles are an expression of our essential being. In view of these facts, the distinction between essential and existential elements in human nature becomes empirically verifiable. In spite of this, the general acceptance of the id-ego-superego scheme has blinded many scholars against the distinction of the essential and the existential in human nature.

A further problem is that of the relation between the analyst and the patient in the therapeutic process. A person becomes a person in the encounter with other persons, and in no other way. All functions of our spirit are based on what I call the moral self-realization of the centered self. This is what morality is—not the subjection to laws. The only way in which this can happen is the limiting encounter with another ego. Nature is open to man's controlling and transforming activity indefinitely, but man resists such control. The other person cannot be controlled like a natural object. Every human being is an absolute limit, an unpierceable wall of resistance against any attempt to make him into an object. He who breaks this resistance by external force destroys his own humanity; he never can become a mature person.

This interdependence of man and man in the process of becoming human is a judgment against a psychotherapeutic method in which the patient is a mere object for the analyst as subject. The inevitable reaction then is that the patient tries in return to make the analyst into an object for himself as subject. This kind of acting and reacting has a depersonalizing effect on both the analyst and the patient. The transference phenomenon should be reconsidered in the light of a "philosophy of encounter," in which existentialist and essentialist elements are united.

My last example is the phrase "being-in-the-world" (Heidegger), which plays a great role in existentialist literature. It points to the fact of "being-with" in spite of our aloneness in the world. But more important for the understanding of man is that he has the potentiality of having a world in contrast to other beings which have only environment. Man breaks through his environment in all directions, his language is his liberation from bondage to a limited situation. But this freedom is not easy to accept and many people turn back from the openness of their world to the prison of their environment. This is another description of the neurotic withdrawal from reality, and one which shows the neurotic character of many forms of seemingly normal behavior, as in conformism and submission to absolute authorities. Without sharp essentialist distinction between world and environment, such approaches to the phenomenon of neurosis have no foundation.

Existentialism has discovered many characteristics of man's predicament which are able to provide a philosophical matrix for psychotherapy. But this does not mean that there should be a definite marriage between existentialism and psychotherapy. It is an alliance which should not be exclusive. Without a powerful essentialist frame the alliance would not hold. It would fall into vagueness and irrelevance, both on the philosophical and the psychotherapeutic side. But it is the task of a philosophical matrix in all realms of man's intellectual life to help these realms towards definiteness, clarity, fundamental principles and universal validity.

NOTE

1 Here the distinction between existential and existentialist should be brought out: "Existential" points to the universally human involvement in matters of genuine concern; "existentialist" points to a philosophical movement which fights the predominance of essentialism in modern thought, be it idealistic or naturalistic essentialism.

On the Phenomenological Bases of Therapy

ROLLO MAY

PRESENT RELATIONSHIP BETWEEN PHENOMENOLOGY AND PSYCHOTHERAPY

I must begin this evening with a disclaimer more modest than some other papers today. I speak as a practicing psychoanalyst, and what you hear from me may seem to you not only second hand phenomenology but may appear to have only a third hand relationship to phenomenology as it has been discussed here today. I do not apologize for this, nor must you construe my modesty as an apology, because the work that we do in psychotherapy in dealing with living human beings in trouble and suffering justifies not only our doing our best to help them clinically but also our doing our best to try to understand what goes on. And we must do this whether it fits philosophical definitions or not. To paraphrase Dr. Spiegelberg this afternoon, we must rush in even where angels and purists dare not tread.

I speak of psychotherapy rather than existential psychotherapy. I do not believe there is a special school of therapy to be put in a category of "existential." I think existential, rather, refers to an attitude toward human beings and a set of presuppositions about these human beings. I shall be talking about intensive psychotherapy, whether it be of the Freudian, Jungian, Sullivanian or any other school.

When Dr. Straus assigned me this topic, "The Phenomenological Bases of Psychotherapy"—which I accepted and so must bear full guilt—I discovered very quickly that it was too ambitious. I do not believe we are ready yet to build a bridge between phenomenology and psychotherapy. There exist beginnings of this bridge: as we have known, and heard again today, there is the exceedingly important work of Straus and other phenomenological psychiatrists like Minkowski and Binswanger, whose work I believe will be increasingly more important for psychotherapy in the future, and psychologists like Buytendijk and Merleau-Ponty. But as Binswanger himself has been the first to say, the connection between phenomenology and psychotherapy is at present only indirect. There are required several steps between pure phenomenology on one hand and psychology and psychiatry on the other hand; this is given by our existential problem rather than by our lack of ability to formulate. I certainly do not deny the many interrelationships between phenomenology and different kinds of therapy. But I believe our present over-all task is one of building. When they build a bridge in New York over the East River, part of the bridge reaches out from Brooklyn and part from Manhattan; we are in process of such a construction, with phenomenology on one side and psychology on the other reaching out toward a meeting. What I want to do tonight is to make you aware of some of the problems in this construction, which means problems in the relationship between psychotherapy and phenomenology; and if I succeed in describing these problems I shall be content.

Jean Paul Sartre writes that we are not yet ready to formulate an existential psychoanalysis, arriving at this conclusion, somewhat ironically, in the chapter entitled, "Existential Psychoanalysis," in his book, *Being and Nothingness.* I think he is correct, both with respect to an existential psychoanalysis and even a phenomenological one. It is significant, incidentally, that Sartre in his book takes seriously Freud and psychoanalysis and the problems that lie therein—an attitude that one commends to other philosophers. Sartre then sets out to demolish the deterministic aspect of the theory of Freud. This deterministic emphasis, Sartre believes—and I think rightly—destroys the reality and significance of man. That is, if we use such determinism as our method, we shall end up with everything except our living patient. Sartre then goes on to point out that only the adumbrations of an existential psychoanalysis are now present, for example in some biographies, and makes his most important point, that the psychoanalysis we seek must be grounded in ontology. I quote from his book: "The final discoveries [of ontology] are the first principles of psychoanalysis."

THE DIRECT CONFRONTATION OF FREUD

Let me begin by saying that the initial consideration in understanding the relationship between phenomenology and psychotherapy is that we confront directly the work of Sigmund Freud. If we try to bypass Freud we shall be guilty of a kind of suppression. For what Freud thought, wrote and performed in therapy, whether we agree with it or not, permeates our whole culture, in literature and art and in almost every other aspect of western man's self-interpretation. Freud obviously had more influence on psychology and psychiatry than any other man in the twentieth century. Unless we confront him directly, consciously and unflinchingly, our discussions of therapy will always hang in a vacuum.

We cannot, furthermore, dismiss Freud simply by stating our disagreements with him. One summer twenty-five years ago I was on an island in Maine finishing a thesis on psychotherapy. A friend that I made there, a young Catholic priest with whom I used to go swimming and fishing, happened one day to be up in my room and saw on my shelves a number of books by Freud. He immediately explained to me in twelve succinct sentences why Freud was wrong. Since this was before psychotherapy was read either in Protestant or Catholic theological seminaries, I wondered if he knew anything about the master from Vienna. I asked him if he had read any books by Freud. He answered, "Oh, yes, everybody in our seminary is required to read one book." I thought this was very enlightened, so I inquired the name of the book. The title, he said, was *Freud Refuted*. This incident always comes back to my mind when I read the writings, especially of the deviant schools: I read a great deal about Freud refuted, but what I fail to find is that Freud himself is directly and seriously confronted.

I believe the issue with Freud must be joined on two fronts. We need first to appreciate and ask the meaning of the vast changes amounting in many ways to sheer revolution that Freud's impact has had upon Western man's image of himself. And secondly, we need to face the fact that the image of man he consciously sought and worked toward—an image amazingly contradictory at many points to his mythology—is inadequate, and must be superceded by an understanding of the nature of man that is adequate to man as the *human* being.[1] I propose that a task that needs to be done is a phenomenological analysis of Freud and the meaning of his impact upon Western culture. Not being competent to perform that task, at least not in this situation, I shall offer some remarks on how I see the underlying meaning of this impact on our image of man.

First, *Freud tremendously enlarged the realm of human consciousness*. The meaning of his elaboration and elucidation of what he called "the unconscious" (or what I prefer to call "unconscious potentialities of experience") was a radical breaking of Victorian rationalism and voluntarism. I shall deal later this evening with the problem of the "unconscious"; but here I want only to emphasize that he uncovered the vast areas in which human behavior and motives are influenced, molded, pushed, and in neurotic cases determined, by forces which are much vaster and more meaningful than those encompassed in Victorian rationalism. His contribution was to enlarge the sphere of human personality to include the depths, i.e., the irrational, the so-called repressed, unacceptable urges, the instinctual forces, bodily drives, anxiety, fears, forgotten aspects of experience *ad infinitum*.

His elucidation of "wish" and "drive" and his unmasking of the self-deceit of Victorian will power, also destroyed moralism in the over-simplified sense in which most of us were taught as children. As I was writing this paper, I thought about what I was taught as a child in the Middle West, namely, that I could completely decide my destiny by any resolution I might make on New Year's Day or in church on any Sunday when the whim might strike me. This amazing piece of arrogance really amounted to my playing God. I've learned since that God moves in much more mysterious ways, and that the destiny of myself and other human beings springs from deeper levels in the human heart and soul than we were led to believe in our liberalized and enlightened West. This Victorian belief in will power was really the dedication to the manipulation of nature, to the rule of nature with an iron hand (as in industrialism and capitalism) and then to the rule of one's own body with the same iron hand, to the manipulation of one's self in this same way (which is evident not only in the ethics of Protestanism but also in other religious systems of our day, and is particularly present in the non-religious ethics on Madison Avenue which are not softened by a sense of sin or a principle of mercy). Now this manipulation of one's self on the basis of the concept of will power needed to be undermined; and I think it was one of Freud's great contributions that by elucidating the infinite number of wishes, drives and other motivations of which we, at any given moment, may not be conscious, he made the above kind of will power and moralism impossible. Since Freud's time, the moral problem has not been lost but placed on a deeper level; and the problems of guilt and responsibility have to be confronted on this profound level. Rightly understood, these earthquakes that Freud produced in western culture, earthquakes that shook the self-picture of modern western man to its base, imply a humility that can be very liberating.

I shall later indicate how I believe the inadequacies of Freud played into an undermining of modern man's sense of individual responsibility. But here let me say that there are curious implications in Freud's psychological determinism that we generally overlook, implications which point in the direction of psychological freedom. I notice with my patients the strange fact that their reaction to an interpretation by me often does not depend so much on whether the interpretation is true or not, but rather centers on the liberating implications in *my act* of making an interpretation. The patient seems to be hearing, in my interpretation, the words, "Your problem has deeper inner roots than you realized; you can stand outside the problem and deal with it." This reminds me of Spinoza's statement, "Freedom is the recognition of determinism."

From these brief indications of how I believe a phenomenological approach to Freud could and should be undertaken, I now pass on to the central part of my paper, a discussion of the relationship, as I see it, between phenemonology and psychotherapy.

PROBLEMS FOR PHENOMENOLOGY AND PSYCHOTHERAPY

We psychotherapists look to phenomenology to give us a way to an understanding of the fundamental nature of man. What we need are norms concerning man which have some degree of universality. Whenever we confront a patient, we presuppose some answer to the question, "What constitutes this being as a *human* being?" We cannot get this understanding of the nature of man from our study of illness, for the various categories of illness themselves can be understood only as distortions in the patient's realization of his nature, as blockages in his endeavors to actualize aspects of his nature.

I have said "understanding" of man. I could say "knowledge of the nature of man," or "concept," or "image of man." But "knowledge" sounds too static, "concept" too intellectual, and "image" too aesthetic. No term is entirely adequate. I choose the term *understanding,* in its etymological sense of "standing under," that is, a basic context in which we can encounter and work with our patients.

I shall take up three central problems in psychotherapy which illustrate and exemplify this need for an understanding of the fundamental nature of man. With each problem I hope to show first, the difficulties we have gotten into because we have lacked this understanding. Second, how phenomenology, as I understand it, can give us the norms we need. Third, how neurosis is a distortion of these norms. And fourth, some implications which follow therefrom for our psychotherapy.

First, I take up *the problem of defining health, illness and neurosis*. In our fields we have been in the strange position of deducing our image of the normal, healthy man from sickness and neurosis. The people who don't break down don't come for help; and the kind of problem which does not fit our techniques we tend not to perceive. Since we know neurosis (and many forms of psychosis) only by virtue of the fact that the sufferers therefrom cannot fit into our society, and since we understand illness by virtue of our techniques, we are bound to end up with a view of man which is a mirror of our culture and our techniques. This inevitably results in a *progressively empty* view of man. Health becomes the vacuum which is left when the so-called neurosis is cured; or on the psychosis level, if a man can stay out of jail and support himself, we call that vacuum health. This empty view of health (filled only by some vague biological assumptions about "growth," "satisfactions of libido," and so forth) has had much to do with the general tendencies in our day toward ennui, passionlessness, emotional and spiritual emptiness. The empty view of health often puts psychiatry and psychology, as well as other forms of science, on the side of making life increasingly more possible and longer at the price of making existence more boring. From this point of view we can understand why our patients often show a strange lack of zest for getting better, for they may not be so irrational in suspecting that neurosis is more interesting than health, and that health may be the corridor to apathy.

This negative, progressively empty view of health—which I believe is implied in classical psychoanalysis as well as other disciplines—led inevitably to a swing to a frankly *social-conformist* definition of health. In this the norms of health are drawn from the requirements of the culture. This is the distortion, and the sometimes real error, of schools like Horney's and my interpersonal school: they hover dangerously on the edge of conformism, the next step in which is "the organization man." I do not mean that this is what Freud or Horney or Sullivan at all intended. I mean the lack of an adequate concept of the nature of man has made the definition of health inevitably empty, and into that vacuum rush such imposters as "adjustment," "fitting in," "according one's self with the realities of the society" and so on.

Thus we must take seriously William H. Whyte's caution in *The Organization Man,* that modern man's enemies may turn out to be a "mild-looking group of therapists, who . . . would be doing what they did to help you." He refers to the inevitable tendency to use therapy in the service of the social ethos of the period; and thus the process of helping people may actually tend to make them conformist and destroy individuality. This tendency, I believe, increases radically with the recent emergence of "operant conditioning" forms of psychotherapy, which are based on an outspoken denial of any need for a theory of man at all beyond the therapist's assumption that whatever goals he himself and his group have chosen are obviously the best for all possible men.

How can phenomenology help us with respect to our concept of health? When a patient comes in and sits down in the chair opposite me in my consulting room, what can I assume about him? I shall offer some principles which have been helpful to me.[2] *I assume that this person, like all beings, is centered in himself, and an attack on this centeredness is an attack on his existence*. He is here in my office because this centeredness has broken down or is precariously threatened. Neurosis, then, is seen not as a deviation from my particular theories of what a person ought to be, but precisely as the method the individual uses to preserve his own centeredness, his own existence. His symptoms are his way of shrinking the range of his world in order that his centeredness may be protected from threat; a way of blocking off aspects of his environment that he may be adequate to the remainder. We now see why the definition of neurosis as a "failure of adjustment" is inadequate. An adjustment is exactly what a neurosis is; and that is just its trouble. It is a necessary adjustment by which centeredness can be preserved; a way of accepting non-being in order that some little being may be preserved. *Neurosis, or illness of various sorts, is the distortion of this need for centeredness*.

I was fortunate recently to be able to discuss these problems with Professor Dorion Cairns of the New School for Social Research, translator of Husserl's *Cartesian Meditations*. Professor Cairns pointed out that my principle of centeredness has its parallel in Husserl's emphasis on *integration*. Husserl believed that inherent in man, and in mind as such, is the "drive" toward consistency, the need for the increasing of experience and the integration of this experience. Thus life is not simply a random, haphazard series of events and observations but has form and potential meaning. Mental activity is *protentive*.

The second problem I wish to cite on which psychotherapy needs the aid of phenomenology is the relationship between the two people, patient and therapist, in the consulting room. This refers to what is called transference in classical analysis. The concept and description of transference was one of Freud's great contributions, both in his own judgment and in that of many of the rest of us. There are vast implications for therapy in the phenomenon that the patient brings into the consulting room his previous or present relationships with father, mother, lover, child, and proceeds to perceive us as those creatures and build his world with us in the same way. Transference, like other concepts of Freud, vastly enlarges the sphere and influence of personality; we live in others and they in us. Note Freud's idea that in every act of sexual intercourse four persons are present—one's self and one's lover, plus one's two parents. I have always personally taken an ambivalent attitude toward this idea, believing as I do that the act of love at least deserves some privacy. But the deep implications are the fateful interweaving of the human web; one's ancestors, like Hamlet's father, are always coming on to the edge of the stage with various ghostly challenges and imprecations. This emphasis of Freud's on how deeply we are bound each to each again cuts through many of modern man's illusions about love and interpersonal relations.

But the concept of transference presents us with unending difficulties if we take it by itself, i.e., without a norm of relationship which is grounded in the nature of man as such. In the first place, transference can be a handy and ever-useful defense for the therapist, as Thomas Szasz puts it; the therapist can hide behind it to protect himself from the anxiety of direct encounter. Secondly, the concept of transference can undermine the whole experience and sense of reality in therapy; the two persons in the consulting room become "shadows," and everyone else in the world does too. It can erode the patient's sense of responsibility, and can rob the therapy of much of the dynamic for the patient's change.

What has been lacking is a concept of *encounter,* within which, and only within which, transference has genuine meaning. *Transference is to be understood as the distortion of encounter*. Since there was no norm of human encounter in psychoanalysis and no adequate place for the I-Thou relationship, there was bound to be an oversimplifying and watering down of love relationships. Freud greatly deepened our understanding of the multifarious, powerful and ubiquitous forms in which erotic drives express themselves. But eros (instead of coming back into its own, as Freud fondly hoped) now oscillates between being an absurd chemistry that demands outlet and a relatively unimportant pastime for male and female when they get bored watching TV of an evening.

Also we had no norm of *agapé* in its own right. *Agapé* cannot be understood as derivative, or what is left over when you analyze out exploitative, cannibalistic tendencies. *Agapé* is not a sublimination of eros but a transcending of it in enduring tenderness, lasting concern for others; and it is precisely this transcendence which gives eros itself fuller and more enduring meaning.

The phenomenological approach helps us in asking the question: How is it possible that one being relate to another? What is the nature of human beings that *Mitsein* is possible, that two men can communicate, can grasp each other as beings, have genuine concern with the welfare and fulfillment of the other, and experience some genuine trust? The answer to these questions will tell us *of what* transference is a distortion.

As I sit now in relationship with my patient, the principle I am assuming is as follows; *this being, like all existing beings, has the need and possibility of going out from his centeredness to participate in other beings*. Before this man ever made the tentative and oft-postponed steps to phone me for an appointment, he was already participating in imagination in some relationship with me. He sat nervously smoking in my waiting room; he now looks at me with mingled suspicion and hope, an effort toward openness fighting in him against the life-old tendency to withdraw behind a stockade and hold me out. This struggle is understandable, for *participating always involves risk:* if he, or any organism, goes out too far, he will lose his own centeredness, his identity. But if he is so afraid of losing his own conflicted center—which at least has made possible some partial integration and meaning in his experience—that he refuses to go out at all but holds back in rigidity and lives in narrowed and shrunken world space, his growth and development are blocked. This was the common neurotic pattern in Freud's day, and is what he meant when he spoke of repression and inhibition. Inhibition is the relation to the world of the being who has the possibility to go out but is too threatened to do so; and his fear that he will lose too much of course may be literally the case.[3]

But in our day of conformism and the outer-directed man, the most prevalent neurotic pattern takes the opposite form, namely, going out too far—dispersing one's self in participation and identification with others until one's own being is emptied. This is no longer the issue of transference, but is the psycho-cultural phenomenon of the organization man. It is one reason too, it seems to me, that castration is no longer the dominant fear of men or women in our day, but ostracism. Patient after patient I've seen (especially those from Madison Avenue) chooses to be castrated, that is, to give up his power, in order not to be ostracized. The real threat is not to be accepted, to be thrown out of the group, to be left solitary and alone. In this overparticipation, one's own consistency becomes inconsistent because it fits someone else. One's own meaning becomes meaningless because it is borrowed from somebody else's meaning.

Speaking now more concretely of the concept of encounter, I mean it to refer to the fact that in the therapeutic hour a total relationship is going on between two people which includes a number of different levels. One level is that of real persons: I am glad to see my patient (varying on different days depending chiefly on the amount of sleep I have had the night before). Our seeing each other allays the physical loneliness to which all human beings are heir. Another level is that of *friends:* we trust—for we have seen each other a lot—that the other has some genuine concern for listening and understanding. Another level is that of *esteem,* or *agape,* the capacity which I think inheres in *Mitwelt* of self-transcending concern for another's welfare. Another level will be frankly *erotic*. When I was doing supervision with her some years ago, Clara Thompson once said to me something I've often pondered, that if one person in the therapeutic relationship feels active erotic attraction, the other will too. Erotic feelings of his own need to be frankly faced by the therapist; otherwise he will, at least in fantasy, act out his own needs with the patient. But more importantly, unless he accepts the erotic as one of the ways of communication, he will not listen for what he should hear from the patient and he will lose one of the most dynamic resources for change in therapy.

Now this total encounter, which I have said can be our most useful medium of understanding the patient, as well as our most efficacious instrument for helping him open himself to the possibility of change, often seems to me to have the resonant character of two musical instruments. If you pluck a violin string, the corresponding strings in another violin in the room will resonate with corresponding movement of their own. This is an analogy, of course: what goes on in human beings includes that, but is much more complex. Encounter in human beings is always to a greater or lesser extent *anxiety-creating* as well as *joy-creating*. I think these effects arise out of the fact that genuine encounter with another person always shakes our self-world relationship: our comfortable temporary security of the moment before is thrown into question, we are opened, made tentative for an instant—shall we risk ourselves, take the chance to be enriched by this new relationship (and even if it is a friend or loved one of long standing, this particular moment of relationship is still new) or shall we brace ourselves, throw up a stockade, hold out the other person and miss the nuances of his perceptions, feelings, intentions? Encounter is always a potentially creative experience; it normally should ensue in the expanding of consciousness, the enrichment of the self. (I do not speak here of *quantity*—obviously a brief meeting may affect us only slightly; indeed, I do not refer to quantities at all, but a *quality* of experience.) In genuine encounter both persons are changed, however minutely. C. G. Jung has pointed out rightly that in effective therapy a change occurs in *both* the therapist and the patient; unless the therapist is open to change the patient will not be either.

The phenomenon of encounter very much needs to be studied, for it seems clear that much more is going on than almost any of us has realized. I propose the hypothesis that in therapy, granted adequate clarification of the therapist, *it is not possible for one person to have a feeling without the other having it to some degree also*. I know you will see many exceptions to this, but I want to offer the hypothesis to ponder and work on. One corollary of my hypothesis is that in *Mitwelt* there is necessarily some resonance, and that the reason we don't feel it, when we don't, is some blocking on our part. Frieda Fromm-Reichman often said that her best instrument for telling what the patient feels—e.g., anxiety or fear or love or anger that he, the patient, dare not express—is what she feels within herself. This use of one's self as the instrument of course requires a tremendous self-discipline on the part of the therapist. I don't mean at all here to open the door simply to telling the patient what you feel; your feelings may be neurotic in all sorts of ways, and the patient has enough problems without being further burdened with yours. I mean rather that the self-discipline, the self-purification if you will, the bracketing of one's own distortions and neurotic tendencies to the extent a therapist is able, seems to me to result in his being in greater or lesser degree able to experience encounter as a way of participating in the feelings and the world of the patient. All this needs to be studied and I believe can be studied in many more ways than we have realized. As I have said, I think there is something going on in one human being relating to another, something inhering in *Mitwelt,* that is infinitely more complex, subtle, rich and powerful than we have generally realized.

The chief reason this hasn't been studied, it seems to me, is that we have had no concept of encounter. Since Freud we have had a clear concept of transference. As one consequence, we have had all kinds of studies of transference—which tell us everything except what really goes on between two human beings. To those of you who feel this evening that your pure phenomenology is being polluted by the psychotherapists, may I say that what we are trying to do as psychotherapists is to get some understanding of man that will enable us at least to see what is going on, and then to study it. We are justified in looking to phenomenology for help in arriving at such a concept which will enable us to perceive encounter itself when so far we have only perceived its distortion, transference. It is especially important, let me add, that we not yield to the tendency in our professions to avoid and dilute encounter by making it a derivative of transference or countertransference.

The third problem is that of "the unconscious." This is a particularly knotty problem in relation to phenomenology. We all know the difficulties inherent in the "cellar" theory of the unconscious—the concept that it is a level below ground where all sorts of entities are stored. And we know how this concept of the unconscious can be used as a blank check on which every kind of cause-and-effect determinism can be written. The negative use of the unconscious is summed up beautifully in a sentence by our friend Erwin Straus: "The unconscious thoughts of the patient are generally the conscious theories of the therapist." Obviously the "cellar" view of the unconscious must be rejected.

But the arguments of Sartre and the other phenomenologists rejecting the unconscious in any form, logical as such arguments are, have always struck me as legalistic and verbalistic. One of Sartre's arguments is that Freud's censor, which is supposed to stand at the gate of the unconscious and decide which thoughts can get through to consciousness, must "know" a great deal; it must "know" what the id knows as well as what can be permitted to come into consciousness. This I accept. But Sartre is only describing here another aspect of the fact that the ways of the mind are complex and subtle indeed. I would agree that any experience of which we are unconscious is to some extent present in awareness, or at least potentially so. The real problem is why the person cannot let himself "know that he knows this." There is no doubt whatever, in my judgment, of the existence and importance of the phenomena Freud was trying to describe when he talked about the unconscious. If we throw this hypothesis overboard, we will the more impoverish ourselves by losing a great deal of the richness and significance of human experience.

How then are we to meet the issue? I find two principles helpful to me here, one having to do with awareness and the other with consciousness. The distinction between these two is critical for our problem. I will state them, beginning with awareness, in reference to my original concept of centeredness, namely, *the subjective side of centeredness is awareness*. Awareness is a capacity we share with animals and much of nature. Indeed, Whitehead and Tillich in their respective ontologies hold that awareness is characteristic of all things in nature, down to the attraction and repulsion between the molecular particles.

Awareness comes from the Anglo-Saxon word "gewaer," meaning alertness to outside dangers. The cognates of the term are "wary" and "beware." Awareness is often correlated in our patients with acting out and paranoid behavior. *It is possible,* that is, *to be aware without being conscious*. We all know the intelligent, often compulsive, patient who can talk for hours with great awareness about what is going on in his life relationships but with no experience whatever that he himself is in on the relationships. I was listening the other day in a supervision group to a tape of a well-educated man who had been in analysis for nine years, who talked at length and very astutely about the mechanisms his wife was using in their relationships, and about the mechanisms between the two; but what struck me was his complete lack of awareness that he was the other half of the relationship—I felt as though I were in a ghostly room hearing a voice but with no person there. Awareness without consciousness is highly depersonalizing.

Thus another principle is not only relevant but necessary. I state it as follows: *Consciousness is the distinctly human form of awareness*. Consciousness is derived from "con" plus "scire," meaning to know with, and it refers to the particularly human capacity not only to know something but to know that I know it. That is, to experience myself as subject in relation to an object, or as I in relation to Thou. I find Erwin Straus' work, such as the perdurable paper which I think will live on for many decades, "The Upright Posture," pertinent and basic to this point. The animal who walks on all fours, like the Chow dog in our family, has infinitely greater awareness in many ways than I have. Our dog's alertness at a great distance by senses of smell and hearing is a source of endless amazement, and makes me feel we human beings are indeed pretty poor specimens from an evolutionary point of view. On our farm this dog can detect other animals or persons coming in the gate way down the road, and, being a Chow, he assumes that those not of our family are of course to be eaten up without further ado. But when man rises on two legs, stands upright and sees, he does not sense at a distance but is aware *of* a distance between himself and the world. This distance I believe is correlated with consciousness. Dr. Plessner's excellent address this morning has, it seemed to me, much to say of significance on this point. The same implications are in Dr.

Straus' paper, "Man, the Questioning Being." We could not question without being aware of the distance between us and the world. Questioning implies that I stand in some significant relationship to the world, and thus is a distinguishing expression of consciousness.

Now I come back to the problem of the unconscious. How shall we interpret unconscious phenomena which are so richly evident in dreams, so significantly present in the whole spectrum of feelings and actions of our patients and ourselves? We must redefine the concept at the outset. One cannot say *the* unconscious, for it is never a place. Nor are things in the sense of entities unconscious; things are not repressed, rather mental processes and potentialities are. I propose as a definition the following: *Unconscious experience is the potentialities for action and awareness which the person cannot or will not actualize*. These potentialities may be nevertheless actualized bodily; denied sexual desires and potentialities are expressed in somatic symptoms, as Freud so well described. But the important point is that the individual will not or cannot let himself be conscious of the desire.

It is critically important, as I have already indicated, to keep the distinction between awareness and consciousness. The patient may well have been "aware" on some level of the experience which is denied and therefore of which he is unconsious. This is why when the patient in psychotherapy has an insight which brings into consciousness some previously unconscious memory or experience, he may say, "I knew it all the time." His point is correct, but his term is partly wrong: he may well have been *aware* of the repressed experience, but he could not let himself *know that he knew it*.

I think when Sartre argues that the censor knew it all the time, he is talking about awareness and not consciousness. The concept "unconscious" is to be understood on the basis of and derived from "conscious," and not the other way around, as the evolutionary thinkers are prone to do. If one wishes to talk in evolutionary terms, one should say that consciousness is a level emerging from awareness; and unconsciousness is a description of the infinite and protean forms of consciousness.

Professor Cairns stated his opinion in discussion with me, that it is "as if" Husserl left a place for unconsciousness by confining himself solely to the description of consciousness. It was also Professor Cairns' opinion that my redefinitions of unconsciousness are, at least to some extent, compatible with Husserl's phenomenology as he understands it.

The implications for therapy of this analysis of unconscious experience are significant. It was said by Freud that the task of the analyst is to make the unconscious conscious. I would put it, rather, that the task of the therapist is to help the patient transmute awareness into consciousness. This process involves all the potentialities which I have described as unconscious, but they are to some extent present in awareness, or at least potentially so. Consciousness consists of the experience, "I am the one who has this world, and am doing something in it." This implies responsibility, *"responding to"* the world.

Thus in transmuting awareness into consciousness, we have a dynamic for change, that is increasing the patient's sphere of consciousness and experience, which inheres directly in the patient's own being. The urge and movement for change and fulfillment does not have to be brought in from the outside, by Victorian voluntarism or by operant conditioning or by modern conformist moralizing. It comes directly out of the patient's own being, and his need to fulfill that being.

NOTES

1 It was Freud's ever present mythology, and his ever ready ability and courage to *think* mythologically, which saved him from the full mechanistic implications of his determinism. The image of man he sought—i.e., one fitting the deterministic categories of natural science of the 19th century—he never succeeded in achieving because his mythology always broke in to bring new dimensions to the image. (A similar thing happens in a different context when Plato tries to think logically about man; at the end of logical categories, Plato's thinking goes into orbit on the wings of a myth.) But when Freudianism crosses the Atlantic ocean, the mythology is the first thing thrown overboard. Thus the mechanism and determinism of Freudianism becomes a more difficult and stultifying problem in this country than in Europe; it makes bedfellows of behaviorism on one side and logical positivism on the other.

2 I call these principles ontological, following Paul Tillich, to whom I am indebted for their philosophical formulation. This paragraph is a re-statement of a section from a previous paper in which I have tried to work out these principles in greater detail, "Existential Bases of Psychotherapy," in *Existential Psychology,* ed. Rollo May, Random House, 1961.

3 Patients will say, "If I love somebody, it's as though all of me flows out like water out of a river, and there'll be nothing left." I think this is a very accurate statement of *transference*. That is, if one's love is something that does not belong there of its own right, then obviously it will be emptied; the whole matter is one of economic balance, as Freud put it.

Logotherapy and the Challenge of Suffering

VIKTOR E. FRANKL

There has been considerable progress in the development of psychotherapy during the last years, inasmuch as a turning is noticeable from the older psychodynamic concept of man as a being mainly concerned with need satisfaction, to the new anthropological view of man whose aim in life was now conceived of as self-actualization and the realization of his own potentialities. We could also say that the category of necessities (in the sense of man's being fully determined by instinctual drives and conditioned by social circumstances) has been replaced more and more by another category, i.e., potentialities to be fulfilled. In other words, we could speak of a re-interpretation of the human being. The whole phenomenon of human existence, however, is ineffable and cannot be circumscribed except by a sentence, the sentence, "I am." This "I am" had first been interpreted in terms of "I must" (i.e., I am forced by certain conditions and determinants, drives and instincts, hereditary and environmental factors and impacts), whereas in the following period the "I am" was understood in terms of an "I can" (i.e., I am able to actualize this or that aspect of myself).

There is still lacking, however, a third concept; for if we want to obtain an appropriate view of the human reality in its full dimensionality we would have to go beyond both necessities and possibilities insofar as we have to bring in—in addition to the "I must" and "I can" aspects of the total "I am" phenomenon—that dimension which would have to be referred to as the "I ought." What I ought to do, however, is in each instance to fulfill the concrete meaning which challenges me in each situation of my life. In other words, at the moment when we brought in the "I ought," we complemented the subjective aspect of human existence, i.e., being, by its objective counterpart, which is meaning.

Only after we have done so, does the present trend of emphasizing self-actualization become justified! Whereas, when self-actualization is made an end in itself and aimed at as the objective of a primary intention, it could not be attained at all. For man would founder in such an attempt to seek directly that which is brought about only as a side-effect. *For only to the extent that man has fulfilled the concrete meaning of his personal existence will he also have fulfilled himself!*

This is in no way contradictory to the theory of self-actualization as presented by Abraham Maslow. For he too seems to me to have taken this fully into account. For instance, when he says "it is possible to call my subjects more objective in all senses of the word than average people. They are more problem-centered than ego-centered . . . strongly focused on problems outside themselves. It may be a task that they feel is their responsibility, duty, or obligation. These tasks are non-personal or unselfish." So, Maslow would certainly agree if

I venture the statement that self-actualization is neither the primary intention nor (to envisage the same thing from a more objective angle and not from the subject's view-point) the ultimate destination of man, but rather an outcome or by-product.

Thus, we can see that when speaking of man's *being* in the world we should not deny that there is also a *meaning in the world*. Only when we have taken into full account this meaning have we supplemented the subjective aspect of human existence by its objective correlate. Not before then have we become aware of existence as being expanded in a polar field of tension between the self and the world.

However, no concept of the world would be adequate then as long as it would be understood in terms of mere projection or self-expression. If, above all, the meaning in the world to be fulfilled by man and the values therein to be realized by him would actually be no more than his "secondary rationalization, sublimations, and reaction formations," nobody would be justified in expecting man to live up to his obligations. As a matter of fact, such pseudo-values totally lack any obligative character when they are understood merely as a mirroring of processes which go on in the individual in an impersonal way or merely as projections and expressions of the inner structure of the respective subject. The world must be seen as essentially more than that. We have to take into account the objectivity of the world which alone presents a real challenge to the subject. However, it would not be enough if we simply refrain from regarding the world and its objects, including values and meanings and their challenge to us as mere self-expression; but we also should beware of regarding the world as a mere instrument serving purposes of our own, an instrument for the satisfaction of instinctual drives, for re-establishing an inner equilibrium, for restoring homeostasis, or a means to the end of self-actualization. This would mean degrading the world and again destroying intrinsically the objective relation of man to the world he "is in." I dare say, man never, or at least not normally and primarily, *sees in the partners whom he encounters and in the causes to which he commits himself merely a means to an end;* for then he actually would have destroyed any authentic relationship to them. Then, they would have become mere tools, being of use for him, but, by the same token, would have ceased to have any value, that is to say, value in itself.

Whenever speaking of meaning, however, we should not disregard the fact that man does not fullfill the meaning of his existence merely by his creative endeavors and experiential encounters, or by working and loving. We must not overlook the fact that there are also tragic experiences inherent in human life, above all that "Tragic Triad"—if I may use this term—which is represented by the primordial facts of man's existence: suffering, guilt, and transitoriness.

Of course, we can close our eyes to these "existentials." Also the therapist can escape from them and retreat into mere somato-or psycho-therapy. Here, "psycho-therapy" is meant in the narrower sense of the term, as against that wider concept of psychotherapy which brings in also the essentially human dimension of the "noetic" in contrast to the psychic. This psychotherapeutic approach is called Logotherapy, and in its frame we have elaborated what is termed "dimensional ontology." Therein, we don't speak any longer of layers or levels of being, for this would imply a disruption of man; to maintain his wholeness and unity we speak of dimensions and differentiate a biological, a psychological, and the essentially human dimension which is called in German *geistig* as against *leiblich* and *seelisch*. Since there is a distinction between *geistig* and *geistlich* (the latter referring to the suprahuman dimension) we are not at a loss. In English, however, spiritual has a religious connotation, but whenever speaking of it Logotherapy has not yet entered the religious dimension. Therefore we prefer to speak, in addition to the biological and psychological dimensions, of a "noological" one. The noological dimension is *ex definitione* what makes man a human being. This would be the case, for instance, when the therapist tries to tranquilize away the patient's fear of death, or to analyze away his feelings of guilt. With special regard to suffering, however, I would say that our patients never really despair because of any suffering in itself! Instead, their despair stems in each instance from a doubt as to whether suffering is meaningful. Man is ready and willing to shoulder any suffering as soon and as long as he can see a meaning in it.

Ultimately, however, this meaning cannot be grasped by merely intellectual means, for it supersedes essentially—or to speak more specifically—dimensionally, man's capacity as a finite being. I try to indicate this fact by the term super-meaning. This meaning necessarily transcends man and his world and, therefore, cannot be approached by merely rational processes. It is rather accessible to an act of commitment which emerges out of the depth and center of man's personality and is thus rooted in his total existence. In one word, what we have to deal with is no intellectual or rational process, but a wholly existential act which perhaps could be described by what I call "Urvertrauen zum Dasein" which, in turn, could be translated by "the basic trust in Being."

Aware now that the meaning of being, or the logos of existence, essentially transcends man's mere intellectuality, we will understand that "logo-" therapy is as far removed from being a process of "logical" reasoning as from being merely moral exhortation. Above all, a psychotherapist—and the logotherapist included—is neither a teacher nor a preacher, nor should he be compared with, let me say, a painter. By this I wish to say that it is never up to a therapist to convey to the patient a picture of the world as the therapist sees it, but rather to enable the patient to see the world as it is. Therefore, he resembles an ophthalmologist more than a painter . . . Also, in special reference to meanings and values, what matters is not the meaning of man's life in general. To look for the general meaning of man's life would be comparable to the question put to a chess player: "What is the best move?" There is no move at all, irrespective of the concrete situation of a special game. The same holds for human existence, inasmuch as one can search only for the concrete meaning of personal existence, a meaning which changes from man to man, from day to day, from hour to hour. Also the awareness of this concrete meaning of one's existence is not at all an abstract one, but it is, rather, an implicit and immediate dedication and devotion which neither cares for verbalization nor even needs it in each instance. In psychotherapy it can be evoked by the posing of provocative questions in the frame of a maieutic dialogue in the Socratic sense. I should like to draw your attention to an experience of such a dialogue during the group psychotherapeutic and psychodramatic activities of my clinic as they are conducted by my assistant, Dr. Kurt Kocourek.

It happened that I stepped in the room of the clinic where he was at the moment performing group therapy; he had to deal with the case of a woman who had lost her son rather suddenly. She was left alone with another son, who was crippled and paralyzed, suffering from Little's disease. She rebelled against her fate, of course, but she did so ultimately because she could not see any meaning in it. When joining the group and sharing the discussion, I improvised by inviting another woman to imagine that she was eighty years of age, lying on her deathbed and looking back to a life full of social success; then I asked her to express what she would feel in this situation. Now, let us hear the direct expression of the experience evoked in her—I quote from a tape: "I married a millionaire. I had an easy life full of wealth. I lived it up. I flirted with men. But now I am eighty. I have no children. Actually, my life has been a failure." And now I invited the mother of the handicapped son to do the same. Her response was the following—again I am quoting the tape: "I would look back peacefully, for I could say to myself, I wished to have children and my wish was granted. I have done my best, I have done the best for my son. Be he crippled, be he helpless, he is my boy. I know that my life was not a failure. I have reared my son and cared for him—otherwise he would have to go into an institution. I have made a fuller life possible for this my son." Thereupon I posed a question to the whole group: "Could an ape which is being used to gain serum for poliomyelitis ever grasp what his suffering should be for?" The group replied unanimously, "Of course it cannot." And now I proceeded to put another question: "And what about man? Man's world essentially transcends an ape's "Umwelt." That is why the ape cannot become cognizant of the meaning of its suffering. For its meaning cannot be found in the "Umwelt" of the animal, but only in the world of man. "Well," I asked them, "are you sure that this human world is something like a terminal in the development of the cosmos? Shouldn't we rather admit that there is possibly a world beyond, above man's world, a world, let me say, in which the question of the ultimate meaning of our sufferings could be answered, and man's quest for this super-meaning could be fulfilled?"

I had but to pose this question, which was answered subsequently by the members of the group in various ways, in personal ways, in no way, however, in a negative sense.

What comes to light here is that the ultimate questions of human existence are on the lips of each "man on the street" and are continually confronting the therapist. It is not necessary, however, to enter into sophisticated debates with the patients.

—"Logos" is deeper than logic . . . .

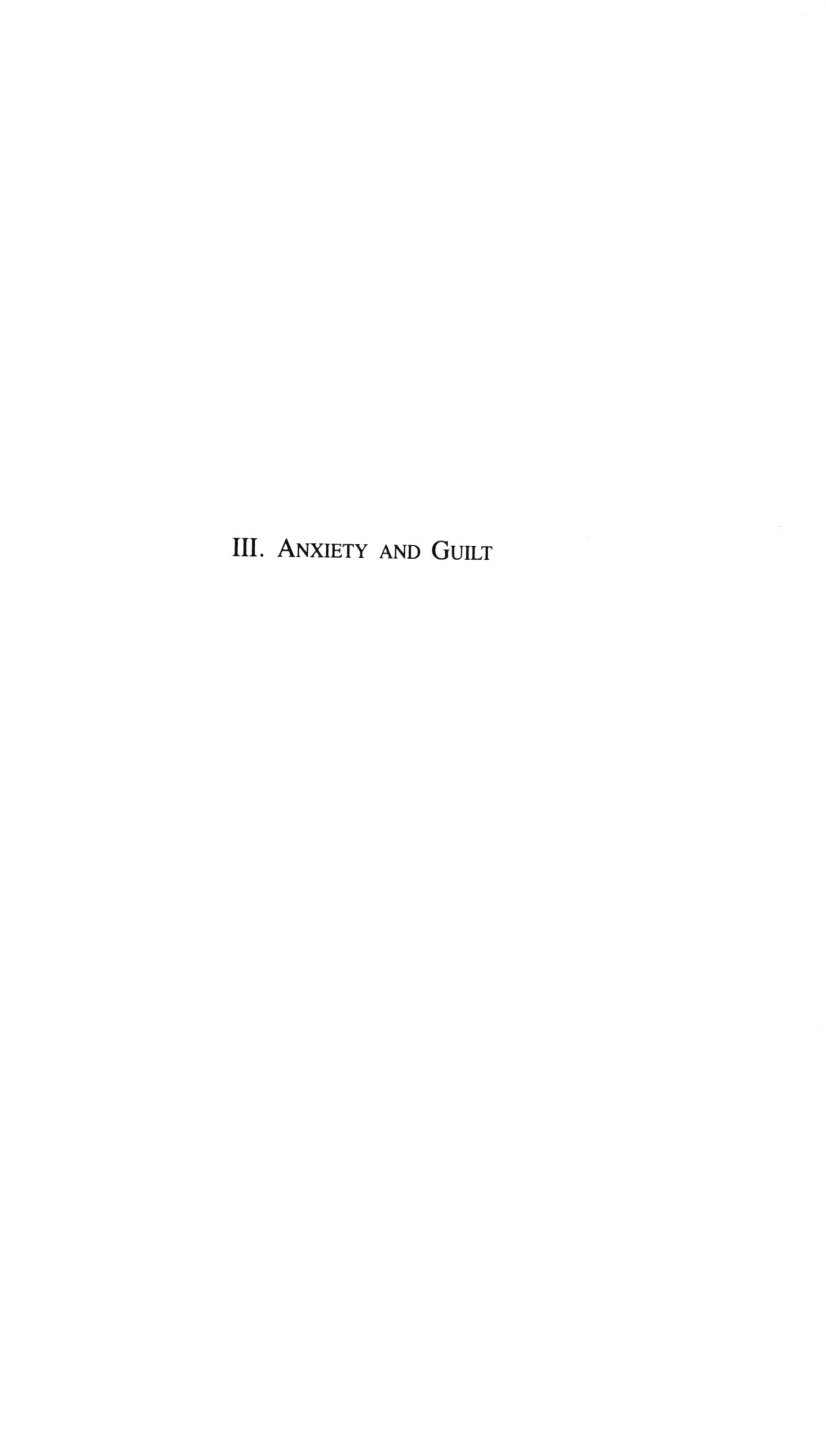

III. Anxiety and Guilt

Anxiety, Guilt and Psychotherapeutic Liberation

MEDARD BOSS

ANXIETY AND GUILT AS BASIC POWERS IN HUMAN LIFE

Anxiety and guilt are basic powers in human life. Many regard them as more powerful and more underlying even than hunger and love. Not the latter but anxiety and guilt are considered in many quarters to be what, in the words of the poet, bind the world inwardly together. If, it is said, anxiety had not driven the very earliest forms of life to preserve themselves by fearful reactions of flight, and if guilt-like inhibitions had not bridled the aggressiveness of animals towards other members of the same species, life on this planet would have annihilated itself long before it had succeeded in producing man, the crown of its evolution.

This view is, to be sure, contested by others who maintain that already in the case of many of the higher mammals anxiety and feelings of guilt are preceded by the protective love and security in the maternal nest and the uninhibited guilt-free high spirits evinced by the young at play. However, we had better leave the history of the evolution of life alone. We were simply not present during the early stages, and for this reason we shall never get beyond the realm of rapidly alternating evolutionary hypotheses. There is, however, one realm where the dominance of anxiety and guilt can be experienced immediately and palpably, confronting us everywhere, and that is the sphere of mental illness in human beings. The psychotherapist meets scarcely a single patient the very substance of whose life is not being eaten away openly or secretly by anxiety and guilt. Only, over the last few decades there has occurred a peculiar and at the same time highly significant transformation in the ways in which our patients' anxiety and guilt come to the surface. At the end of the last century the psychotherapist encountered the phenomena of anxiety mainly in the clamorous symptoms of so-called hysteria. There could be observed in those days in women the obtrusive hysterical defensive gestures of numerous paralyses, convulsions and fits. Anxiety in men still appeared in the First World War in the form of the massive hysterical behavior of so-called victims of shell shock, suffering from a crude shaking of their arms and legs. They were so numerous that entire battalions could be formed from them.

The guilt feelings again struck physicians most conspicuously in compulsive neuroses and above all in the tirelessly proclaimed self-accusations of those suffering from depressions and melancholia. A compulsive neurotic can, let us say, fear that he will become guilty of causing the destruction of the world if he does not without delay recite 99 × 99 times the invocation "Jesus be praised." Although he is himself fully aware intellectually of the absurdity of his penitential act, he is powerless to resist the dictates of his feeling of guilt. A victim of melancholia spends his days and nights, for months and years on end, doing nothing but expressing the desperate complaint that he is guilty of the imminent physical or psychic destruction of his entire family, because once twenty years ago he furtively kissed his parents' housemaid. Nonsense, you will say, sheer lunacy which belongs in a madhouse but which we who are sane need not further concern ourselves with. At the most the people affected by such pathological anxieties and guilt feelings would deserve our pity. Do they really deserve only that? Do they not perhaps deserve very much more in the way of attentive consideration? Could it not be that it is precisely the excesses and discrepancies of their symptoms that would yield especially important insights into the nature and meaning of human anxiety and guilt in general, if only we were prepared to hearken to them in the right way?

Let us, then, not delay our efforts to hear what they have to say, for the voices of our unfortunate criers in the wilderness are becoming fainter and ever more incomprehensible. The hyperdistinct gesticulations of the major kinds of hysteria have all but disappeared in our part of the world. Even the Second World War produced hardly any more cases of hysterical shell shock. For some time now an increasing number of anxieties and guilt feelings of our patients have been creeping into the obscurity of the internal bodily organs. Henceforth they will speak only the alien language of the so-called functional disturbances affecting the heart, stomach and intestines, or of other organ neuroses. At the present time anxiety and guilt are even threatening to sink still more out of sight beneath a cold, glazed façade of a vacuous ennui and behind an icy wall made up of inconsolable feelings of the utter meaninglessness of life. At any rate, the ever growing number of patients whose only complaint is of the void, boring meaninglessness of their existence can leave no psychiatrist in doubt any longer that the illness which could be called boredom neurosis, or the neurosis of the void, is the neurosis of the immediate future. Within every boredom, however, there is hidden an intense ennui. This is clearly revealed already by the German version of its own name. Boredom is "Langeweile," i.e., "lange Zeit," a long while. To have "lange Zeit" uniquivocally means to long for something or somebody very much. In the vast yawning boredom of the modern vacuity neurosis there is concealed a longing which, if it were not warded off with the utmost force, would cause the eruption of an insight into the homelessness and loss of all sheltered security whatsoever. Panic anxiety and abysmal consciousness of guilt would necessarily be the consequence of recognizing that one has lost oneself utterly upon falling into such a bottomless chasm. For this reason the ennui which rules the existence of modern neurotics so often has resort to the deafening 24-hour uproar of our hectic modern life or to the stupor induced by all kinds of medicaments and tranquilizers in order to mask its true meaning.

What, however, is the cause of this ever hardening façade which so utterly conceals the anxiety and guilt of the mental patients of our times behind its frozen emotional immobility? We shall hardly go far wrong if we look for a connection between this phenomenon and the predominance of the Machine in modern life. It is, in fact, the today all-powerful technical spirit that makes us think of ourselves also as but cogs in the mechanism of a gigantic social organization and makes us treat ourselves accordingly. Cogwheels in machinery, however, no longer gesticulate either in a normal or in a hysterical manner; much less then could they engage in free discourse with one another. Also when wheels are pieced together and assembled to form the collectivity of a functional entity of a machine, they then act on one another only in a purely mechanical fashion, bare of all understanding of themselves and of the other wheels, without ceasing to rotate on their own fixed axes.

THE PSYCHOLOGICAL EXPLANATIONS AS INTELLECTUAL SHORT-CIRCUITS

Is it not true, then, that we psychotherapists are utterly helpless in the face of the overpowering modern machine spirit, even when it has cast its spell over our patients? Perhaps we are *quite* helpless only so long as we go on allowing this same spirit to hold in thrall our own professional thinking and acting.

To what an extent, however, it does in fact do just this can only too drastically be demonstrated by the standard theories of today's representative psychologies themselves. On closer examination they all still prove to be governed by the old fundamental working principle which Freud had applied when constructing his psychoanalytic theory. This origin of theirs is clearly betrayed by the most important watchword common to them all: "psychodynamics." However manifold the connotations may have become which are attributed to this term by the different psychologies, its very root remains the "dynamis," the meaning of which has long since been reduced in modern times to forces and energies. It was Freud, though, who has summarized the main intention of his whole psychology with unsurpassed succinctness in the following crucial sentences as early as 1916: "We do not seek merely to describe and classify phenomena but to comprehend them as indications of a play of forces in the psyche, as expressions of goal-directed tendencies which work in unison or against one another. We are striving for a *dynamic conception* of psychic phenomena. *Perceived* phenomena *must* in our conception recede behind the merely *assumed, posited* tendencies."[1] (Author's emphasis in last sentence.)

By this mental procedure of his, Freud had aimed at nothing less than at making the psychic phenomena, too, quantifiable, calculable, predictable, producible—if desired—or repairable—if regarded as pathological symptoms. In the classical method of thinking of all the technical sciences the psychological theories thus hope to discover the "psychodynamic" causal connections obtaining among the different psychic formations, in particular to discover the very first cause in each causal chain. If this, then, could be eliminated, all its following pathological effects and products are thought to have to disappear by themselves.

Caught in this basic concept of our technical sciences, the modern psychologies made use also of that basic mental transformation, naturally, which had proved to be so efficient in one way in the sciences of inanimate nature. The psychological theories, too, turned—without further considerations—a mere sequence of occurrences in time into a causal chain, i.e., into a sequence of phenomena in which always the earlier one was thought to cause, to produce and to bring about the later phenomena.

In accordance with this basic concept many psychologists, for example, began to regard birth anxiety, because it is said to be the very first anxiety in a human life, to be the real cause of all later anxieties, in the first place, to be the prior cause of the infant's "eight months' anxiety" before strangers, then of anxiety before objects with which one has had bad experiences, of anxiety before the scolding parents as well, before teachers, before governmental authorities, before one's fate, and finally to be the cause and model *even* of anxiety before God.

Since, on the other hand, the very first guilt feelings are produced in the child by the commands and prohibitions of the parents, these products of training instilled into the child from the outside were considered to be the cause also of the later stirring of guilt stemming from one's own conscience. Only, in this connection, said the psychologists, the representations of the scolding parents would be projected on the outside world, even farther outward, as it were, but their commands and prohibitions would at the same time be taken into one's inner self, into the conscience or into the so-called super-ego. Therefore, a person is then said to feel guilty before his teacher, the governmental authorities and finally God. Many psychologists extended the theoretical chain of guilt causation still farther back beyond the physical parents to an assumed parricide occurring in the remote past of the human race. As a consequence of such prenatal events, even the new-born infant is said to come into the world already equipped with genetically prepared complexes or archetypal formations in the psyche as the very first causes of anxiety and guilt feelings. However, these extreme, wild hypotheses did not in the slightest alter the character and the object of the psychological theories. Rather it was these hypotheses that really revealed how very important it was for psychology to discover even the very first and thus the presumed *real* cause of human anxiety and guilt, in order to be able psychotherapeutically to reduce their action in the so-called super-ego or conscience of the patient. What would have been more favorable to such a strategy of anxiety and guilt reduction than the contents of precisely these psychological hypotheses? They would after all make it as clear as daylight to suffering patients that their anxiety-inducing representations and their nagging stirring of conscience possessed a purely illusional character, in that they exposed their core and cause as a mere infantile terror no longer having any real basis.

In the reality of psychotherapeutic practice, however, these psychological theories have been far from fulfilling the expectations reposed in them. Their central argument that anxiety and guilt feelings possess a purely illusional character has been so little compelling that nowadays, on the contrary, an increasing number of psychotherapists can be seen abandoning their hypotheses of anxiety and guilt causation as illusions. In point of fact, it has not been possible by psychotherapeutic means to make one single person really free of anxiety and guilt on the basis of these psychological theories, in the way they had promised. The hidden anxiety and guilt feelings in the modern vacuity or boredom neuroses are particularly stubborn in refusing to yield to a psychotherapeutic procedure aiming at dismantling the conscience. How could it be otherwise: The psychotherapists themselves after all know nothing of any meaning and goal because in their own specific world of thought, thinking as they do in scientific-technical terms, in so-called dynamic chains of causation, there are only factual and functional interrelationships that are calculable, predetermined and quite neutral as to meaningful values. How should these psychotherapists be in a position to remedy the boring meaninglessness from which their patients are suffering? They are at the very most able to console themselves for their therapeutic helplessness with new causal hypotheses. They seek such consolation, let us say, in the assumption of a particularly effective death drive or a congenital, primary moral masochism derived from it.

However, the basic principle of the ordinary causal mode of thinking in psychology cannot be justified by anything at all tangible, neither in the original nor in the secondary theorems. It cannot be proved by means of any set of facts, no matter how constituted, that what appears earlier in a life history, simply because it is prior in time, should also be the efficient cause of everything that follows and thus be the given reality itself. Just as little can it be shown why, on the other hand, it would be permissible for the same purely temporal reason to demote all later phenomena to the status of mere secondary products, of reaction or sublimation formations and epiphenomena of what occurs earlier.

What in actual fact is perceivable and ascertainable is solely the regular temporal succession of phenomena. If, however, we think into this temporal sequence of phenomena some kind of causal derivative relationship, we at once brand everything that comes later as something inauthentic, as something merely derived or expressed. In this way we have at the outset abandoned any possibility of grasping the things themselves in their own unmediated reality. Not to mention the fact that such causation theories must also leave the causes assumed to be behind the phenomena wholly indefinite as far as their essential nature is concerned.

Thus it is in the special sphere of human anxiety pure speculation, which can find no support in anything perceivable, not to regard the feats arising very late in a human life, like those of metaphysical nothingness or of the loss of the divine love and eternal life in the hereafter, as authentic and primal human phenomena possessing just as much validity as the early anxieties at the loss of physical integrity, the loss of personal importance and material property or as the still earlier infantile anxieties about the drives or about the loss of maternal security, or even—should anything of the sort exist—the very first anxiety at being born.

Exactly the same objection, however, also has to be raised against a causal derivation of guilt feelings making their appearance *later* from those observed *earlier*. Here again there is not the slightest basis for assigning to the mature guilt feelings of a person over against his fate or God a lesser degree of authenticity or of primacy than to his earlier guilt feelings over against the governmental authorities, teachers, parents. And it is no argument at all in favor of the alleged priority and causal reality of earlier guilt feelings and of the merely unreal, epiphenomenal character of later ones to refer, as is usually done, to the fact that the earlier guilt feelings after all relate to physical, tangible "creditors," to parents and teachers, but that the later ones reveal themselves rather "only" within the so-called mental sphere. Yet such a line of reasoning, if it seeks to have any kind of validity, would at least have to succeed in making it at the very outset understandable how such causation of mental facts by physically tangible phenomena is supposed to come about at all. However, it has already become a truism that not even the classical scientific materialism of the turn of the century has to do with anything primarily material and that its essential concept is an idea, a belief, whose truth content cannot be dealt with scientifically any more than can the articles of Christian faith or Buddhist philosophy.

THE QUEST FOR A FUNDAMENTALLY NEW UNDERSTANDING OF MAN

These considerations may suffice to convince us of the almost total control of the natural-scientific, mechanistic-dynamic way of thinking, moving in chains of cause and effect only, over the realms of present-day psychology and psychotherapy. At the same time they may have made just as stringently evident its inner emptiness and bottomlessness when applied in the field of human existence. If this is the case, however, there can no longer be any doubt as to the consequences of such an insight. We can no longer close our eyes to the fact that by resorting to such an intellectual construction of assumed causes and forces behind the perceived phenomena we forever lose sight of the latter themselves. We thus always fundamentally degrade them at the very outset to something that is merely derived, something that is not sui generis, not authentic in itself.

Consequently, no matter how masterfully we learn in this way to manipulate man's "psyche," the damage inflicted by such a psychological technique easily may in a deeper sense become much greater than what is truly gained by it. Therefore we psychotherapists should realize that it is high time we stopped the practice of always immediately dissecting man with the aid of mechanistic theories erected by our analytical intellect and—by doing so—losing hold of his immediate reality. Not even must we succumb to that usual error of the traditional technical sciences of believing that we can build up the more differentiated structures that are richer in content and more evolved, by proceeding from simpler proto- or partial formations and that we can better understand them as deriving from the latter. Looked at from the standpoint of the thing itself, it is at the outset much more probable that, on the contrary, the more highly evolved given phenomena of our world have more to tell us about their real being, and that in greater detail and more comprehensively, than have the corresponding phenomena while still veiled in the obscurity of the germinal phase of their development, as, for example, in children or in animals. Rather what we must do is to restore an attitude of due reverence before the actual authenticity of all human phenomena alike. We must be capable of allowing what appears before us to remain intact and as what it immediately shows itself to be in the whole frame of references inherent in itself. We have to learn again just to look at the things actually confronting us and to let the phenomena, which we encounter, themselves tell us their meaning and content. Here we have in a nutshell, the fundamental discrepancy between the up-to-now available so-called psychodynamic psychologies and the Daseinsanalysis.

If we accept the challenge of Daseinsanalysis, we shall also have to inquire as to the immediately self-revelatory nature of the unspoiled phenomena of anxiety and guilt. Such a simple questioning permits us to realize, firstly, that anxiety and guilt, both of them, each pose two basic questions of their own. All our understanding of their meaning will depend on the adequacy of the answers to these questions. Every human anxiety has an *Of What,* which it is afraid of, and an *About What,* which it feels alarmed about. Every guilt has a *Something,* which it is owing, and a *Creditor,* to whom something is owing.

a) About the Essence of Human Anxiety

The *Of What* involved in every anxiety is always a crippling attack on the integrity of the human existence. Fundamentally *every* anxiety fears the destruction of the capacity to be, fears the possibility, that is, of not being allowed to exist any longer unimpaired. The *About What* of human anxiety is thus *existence* itself in so far as every anxiety is always concerned and fearful about the existence's continuing integrity.

This applies to the very early so-called drive anxieties that appear in infants. It applies also to all the fears of adults suffering from neurotic anxiety.

In both cases it is always the anxiety about the collapse of their familiar, organized, secured structure of existence and their cosmos into the chaos of the sinister, unknown, overwhelming powers of *sheer* natural vitality. The destruction of the *being-allowed-to-exist* is more obviously feared in the case of the so-called reality fears, at the present time mainly in the fear of nuclear bombs, only that the real atom bomb, the big one, already exploded centuries ago. What we are referring to is that intellectual atom bomb which then began to atomize and to pulverize our world, when the analytical natural sciences took most of the realities of our earth and our heaven and explained them away as a mere assemblage of masses of molecules and wave movements and in so doing destroyed them as the things they had been up to then. Or does a red rose remain, for example, a red rose if it and its redness are in fact regarded henceforth as only an almost empty electric field in which occasional electric charges are rushing around and as a bundle of electromagnetic undulations of measurable frequency and amplitude but its redness as redness is considered to be an illusion of the human brain? It is not surprising that at the very beginning of this scientific and intellectual destruction of the world and of the technological undermining of reality there grew a mounting need for security. Thus it was one of the very first scientific thinkers, the German philosopher *Leibniz* in fact, who conceived also the idea of life insurance companies.

However, could anything display more distinctly and obtrusively than just this greatest and most modern of anxieties about the atom bomb the fact that anxiety actually is at bottom always fear of death, fear *about* existence and fear *of* its annihilation? And again: is it not obvious to man, as nothing else is, that he must one day die? Therefore has not man all his life reason enough to be anxious about his life, to be afraid of his death, his no-longer-being-allowed-to-be? Is anxiety then not necessarily inherent in life as an ever inseparable portion of our existence, not to be eliminated by psychotherapy either?

b) About the Essence of Human Guilt

And now what about human guilt?

In the first place, feelings of guilt *are* by no means easy to distinguish from fears of punishment. We see our children for a long time becoming conscious of guilt only if they have not obeyed a parental command or have violated a parental prohibition and therefore have good reason to expect punishment. Even later, however, guilt and fear of punishment remain very closely linked together. Even behind the obedience men show to their gods or their God there is generally a fear of the punishments of hell. It is not the Christian churches alone that threaten their guilty believers with hell. Long before them the ancient Indian texts depicted in admonishment of the guilty ones among the Hindus scenes of hell which resemble in their very details the organization of the later Inferno of Dante. Not to mention the obligations owing by modern peoples to their governments and state ideologies. How much anxiety at social or even physical damage and annihilation lies at the root of their law-abiding, conscientious activity?

Is not the very clear deduction to be made from all this that there does not exist at all anything resembling an original, authentic, inherent guiltiness in man, that his feelings of guilt are after all merely burned into him from the outside, as the naturalistic psychologies would have it? Many who maintain such an opinion think that they can bolster their theory with two weighty arguments. Firstly, they point out the similarity, in fact the congruence of many people's authority images and mental representations of God with their mental pictures of their physical parents. Does not the language itself speak of a paternalistic State, of the Mother Church, for example? Secondly, they maintain, there are undeniably people who have been able successfully to withstand the relentless barrage of guilt feelings coming from outside, people who egotistically enjoy their lives to the full without any scruples, where both guilt and conscience are totally lacking. Even psychiatry had to give these people a designation and classify them as more or less pronounced cases of "moral idiocy."

In reality, however, these arguments and attempts to derive human guiltiness from something else do not have a leg to stand on. First, all of them have as their basis that scientific assumption—already referred to earlier—which seeks to explain what comes first as the efficient cause of what follows, only because the former appears first. Over and above this, if we look at it carefully, any theory is pure necromancy which believes that it can take an anxiety phenomenon arising out of some kind of external pressure of anxiety and transform it into a guilt feeling. Unless someone really knew how to give a sufficient answer to the question how such a transformation of anxiety into guilt could come about at all. Mounting external pressure from ever more fear-inspiring things will always call forth nothing but anxiety and still more anxiety.

Equally threadbare is the argument which refers to the *congruence* of the guilt feelings of so many allegedly adult citizens over against their political authorities, of so many seemingly grown-up believers over against their priests, with the earlier guilt feelings of children in their relationship to their parents. Is then the fact that many roses do not develop beyond the bud stage and perish as buds an argument that all roses in full bloom are in reality and in truth nothing but deformed rosebuds? On the other hand, is a mature ability-to-feel-oneself-guilty before one's God or one's fate or one's humanity ungenuine and something derivative, projected, only because a state of guilt can also occur in a child before his father? Is the fact that the endlessly vast solar systems with their planets so closely resemble the endlessly small atoms with their nuclei and their electrons a proof that the solar systems are only illusions of the human mind, mental representations of the material atoms of our earth psychologically projected on the heavens?

The second argument indeed, which is supposed to prove the purely secondary character of all human guilt feelings by referring to the occurrence of moral idiocy, resembles the foolish attempt to understand the nature of man from another defective form, from the more familiar intellectual idiocy.

Anxieties may, therefore, appear much earlier in a life history than feelings of guilt, late forms of human guilt phenomena may resemble early ones ever so much, but man's ability-to-feel-oneself-guilty as such is and remains in every guilt phenomenon an autochthonous being-guilty, with its own autonomous origin and essential nature. If the ability-to-be-guilty as such were not an entirely primal feature of man's very nature, no father would ever have been able to instill an awareness of guilt into a defiant son, no priest in a guilty believer, no capitalist boss in a slack employee, no people's commissar in a comrade who has not fulfilled his production quota. Thus not one single psychoanalysis either—against all the expectations bound up with the adoption of the naturalistic theories—has ever succeeded the other way round in making a patient feel really and fundamentally *free* of guilt. At best the various psychotherapies, and we shall come back to this, succeed in modifying the different contents of the guilt feelings of patients, but they never succeed in restoring a person to the guiltless innocence of a new-born child or of a conscience-free savage, the latter being a figment hypothetically posited but not existing at all in reality anyhow.

As to anxiety, therefore, we shall do justice to the human guilt also only if we take whatever concrete guilt phenomena and accept it just as it directly reveals itself to us. However, we then must investigate all the more carefully and in detail its actual nature. In other words: the daseinsanalytic approach must never be misused—as it so often is actually—to serve the purposes of mystically vague and sentimental authors. The genuine daseinsanalytic approach has a thorough and radical strictness of its own which at least equals the exactness of all technical sciences. In our particular case of the daseinsanalytic discussion on human guilt we find a first lead in the language itself. The German word "Schuld" is derived from the Old High German word "Sculd." "Sculd," however, has always signified, and primarily so, merely whatever is lacking and missing and what one owes, be it materially or morally. The same holds true for the English word "debt." Still today the Lord's prayer asks: " . . . and forgive us our debts," certainly not meaning our financial shortcomings only. Less certain is the origin of the word "guilt." Even this expression, though, seems to be derived from the Old English word "guildan," meaning to pay and to pay off, and thus to point to the same double connotation originally as the German "Schuld."

At any rate, it is a fact that a human life always and throughout its course lacks a certain something or other. The life of a child is wanting in respect and obedience over against its father. Then the schoolboy owes his teacher the performance of his school assignments. The adult citizen owes the modern state his cooperation in stepping up the economic production potential. The believer is deficient in the fulfilling of religious precepts, the non-believer owes the fulfillment of his entire life to fate. Most non-believers at least also behave just as if there applied to them as well the old Biblical parable of the buried and the well employed talents.

Man, then, to the end of his days actually seems incapable of coming to terms either with his being-guilty, indebted or with his anxiety. Are anxiety and guilt then both equally heavy and oppressive mortgages on human existence not to be paid off in a lifetime, inalienable from childhood on?

THE WAY INTO THE OPEN

a) The Overcoming of Anxiety

If this were so, clearly all psychotherapeutic endeavors would remain at bottom and forever vain and hopeless undertakings, no matter how many lectures were organized in honor of psychotherapy and existentialism. Or are there, after all, ways leading out into the open? But we said above all anxiety was at bottom: fear of death, of the no-longer-being-able-to-be-there, and death stands always inescapably before us as a consequence of man's inherent finiteness. How is it then that all the same there are in fact people who are without anxiety, and die without anxiety, really without anxiety, who not merely conceal their anxieties behind clamorous displays of aggressive activity? Many children, for example, can be seen breathing their last without anxiety, peacefully and happily smiling. Do they not yet know perhaps what death really means, that in truth what is involved is their actual and complete destruction? However, adults too, lovers, for example, who are well enough aware of the meaning of dying, joyously sacrifice their lives. How many a young vigorous human being has without any anxiety embraced death for his loved one. Heroes, again, we are told, sacrifice their lives without any fear for love of their motherland or a state ideology, or of a better future for mankind. For countless saints dying to the glory of their God was a pure joy. It almost seems as if human life comprised a counterforce to anxiety, showing itself in the phenomena of love, trust, security. Not courage. Courage exists only wherever anxiety is still powerful, against which the courage can fight. Where there is no anxiety to overcome there is no need for courage. But where love, security and trust prevail all anxiety can fade away. Nevertheless, is it not certain that lovers and trusting friends too will one day have to die? Surely enough, and the lover is no less aware of this than the anxious person. Why then is this same prospect of having to die so much dreaded by the ordinary anxiety-ridden person and not at all by lovers? The answer is that one can only be mortally anxious about the continuance of what one is able to regard as being his existence and his possibilities-to-be.

How then if the lover, the trusting friend, the hero and the saint could become aware of more and richer human possibilities-to-be than the ordinary anxious person who nowadays more than ever frets and worries over the possible continuance of what he understands as his ego, his subjectivity, his personality?

Is it not possible perhaps that innumerable people in their mortal anxiety more or less behave as if their being resembled the old skin of a snake in the act of sloughing. From the standpoint of the bursting, perishing old skin which has become too tight, the casting of a skin is, to be sure, a catastrophic event for the old skin which this snakeskin would have every reason to fear as its final destruction if it could conceive of nothing but itself as the totality of the snake's being. And yet for the snake as such and as a totality the sloughing process is the contrary of a dying; it is the creating of more vital space for the animal to go on growing and maturing.

We learn still more about the nature of ordinary human anxiety from many of our dreams. Every analyst, if he only heeds it, can as often as he wishes experience the apparent paradox that his patients dream anxiously of having to die precisely when they stand at the beginning of a new healing phase with fresh developments ahead of them. As an illustration of this let us briefly consider the dreams of a certain twenty-five-year-old woman. When, at the beginning of her psychoanalysis, this patient was still a neurotically stunted person and greatly retarded in her contacts with other human beings, there repeatedly appeared in her dreams one and the same female figure. There always confronted her a woman in a dark grey veil, judging by her outward appearance already a middle-aged woman and in her bearing a person of great vitality and vigorous self-awareness, who mortally frightened the dreamer. Beginning at a definite phase of her treatment, this same Norn, as the patient called her, kept appearing as a judge. She would regularly sentence the patient to death for an unknown but grievous crime. For a long time these dreams ended with the patient awaking with a start immediately before her execution and soaked with perspiration from her fear of death. As the treatment continued, however, this Norn became increasingly friendly, gradually revealed herself and soon appeared as an inviting, mature, vital woman, who wanted to take the anxious dreamer on trips with her. One night even she appeared to the patient as her twin sister—nonexistent in real life—who with her needlework was contributing to her trousseau. From then on and in and through this dream woman, having become now her helpful "alter ego," the patient got the first glimpses of the possibility of her own womanly ripeness and could welcome it. First of all, however, in her dreams she too had only been able to fear the breaking-up of the previous, overly confined, structure of her warped, infantile ways of relating to her world—necessary for the maturing and unfolding of her existence—as anxiety-arousing total annihilation. A great deal of patient psychotherapeutic work had to be done before this woman was in a position to recognize in the necessity of the death of the old, immature modes of behaving her liberation for a more free and wholesome existence.

We have for the time being to leave aside the dream motive of the prosecuted crime of which the dreamer felt herself guilty in the courtroom scenes. We shall only later be sufficiently prepared to understand it.

On the other hand, we shall, beginning now, no longer as a matter of course account for the anxiety-free dying of many children by adducing their all too limited comprehension of the real nature of physical death. We shall, on the contrary, begin to ask whether these children cannot perhaps grasp something more essential about it than the anxiously dying adult imprisoned as he is within his mental conception of being but a subjectivity or a personality, altogether doomed to final annihilation.

It could just as well be that also the fully aware and grown up *lover* can have his eyes opened by his love to a more comprehensive, authentic understanding of the nature of human existence than is possible for the ordinary anxious person fallen prey to his very limited objects and everyday activities. After all, is not the very word "anxiety" itself connected with the Latin "angustia" and the Greek "ancho" (ἄγχω), meaning "narrowness," tying off and strangling? The very word anxiety thus seems to point to the fact that existence, attuned to anxiety, can see itself only as something throttled. In fact, the anxiety of modern man usually restricts self-awareness so much that he can only perceive himself to be, as it were, an isolated trembling waterdrop suspended in the air, but cannot even suspect any more the existence of the ocean from which the drop comes and of which it is essentially a part. On the other hand, within the love relationship towards the world, existence is open to the quite different experience which enables the loving being to recognize that what people ordinarily call dying is the contrary of an inability-to-be-any-longer, is rather an all the more intense surrender to and absorption in the greater entirety of what is loved.

Man's everyday fears then can undoubtedly merge in the love experience which gives him the conviction of belonging directly to a firm and unshakable ground of his existence. It can even give way to a joyous expectation, because in the experience of love the dying of the habitual everyday, mental-physical state is grasped as wholly different from a destruction, is in fact seen to be a transition to a richer and more open kind of existence. The anxious person, however, who would like to brand this love experience as a mere illusion, a metaphysical wish fancy, and so devaluate it, should not forget that he can in no way and by no means prove that his anxiety-cramped range of experience possesses an allegedly greater, more authentic reality. Least of all can he do this by appealing to scientific psychological theories. What is worse, such a fearful person does not even do justice to the full phenomenon of human anxiety itself. He is still far from having heard its actual message, for he would not be anxious in the way he actually is if he had not allowed his own anxiety from the beginning to shrink so that he is only able to see it henceforth from the psychological worm's-eye view of a modern subjectivism centered on the human personality. However, if one keeps oneself really exposed to the full and undissembled essence of anxiety, it is precisely anxiety that opens to man that dimension of freedom into which alone the experiences of love and trust can unfold at all. Anxiety which is freed from subjectivistic pettiness presents the existence of man not only, like love, with the possibility of Something greater and more abundant, but presents it with the direct possibility of that which is completely different from Everything that is and that, after all, as a particular being, cannot be without its limiting limits. In other words, anxiety confronts man with the Great Nothingness, a Nothingness, though, which is the opposite of any nihilistic emptiness, which is rather the cradle of all that is released into being. Anxiety when experienced in its deepest meaning contradicts love as its opposing force so little that it bursts asunder all subjectified, psychologized anxiousness—even continually overcoming itself—and opens up the way of love toward the boundless origin of all things, that no longer merely *is,* that is *beyond* the dichotomy of being and non-being.

b) The Overcoming of Guilt's Burden

There still remains, however, human guilt. Can this too perhaps, just like anxiety, be overcome fundamentally? What is owing then really in all the thousandfold, normal and pathological guilt feelings, in the consciousness of guilt in the child over against his parents and teachers, in that of adults in their relationship to their fellow men, to the State, to God, to fate, to life? And who is the real creditor of all this indebtedness?

Since "guilt," "Schuld" as indebtedness, is what is missing and lacking, the nature of human guilt can be understood only from the standpoint of the fullness and fulfillment of human existence. However, how do things stand with regard to our psychological and medical insights into the entire constitution and nature of man? The situation here has probably never been more lamentable than it is today. Modern philosophers, psychologists and biologists persist in basing their definitions of the nature of man at the very outset on a mass of wholly unclarified concepts and mental constructions. Some start their science of man with the assumption that he is at bottom merely a biological, physical organism with its by-product, mind, attached to it as a more or less meaningless epiphenomenon. Others explain man as a psychosomatic product, as the addition of two organs, the body and the mind. And others again introduce as fundamental concepts into their science of man the notions of an ego, a subject, a person. They all forget, however, to enlighten us as to what these matters which they have made into the fundamental concepts of their science are actually supposed to be essentially. We seek in vain in their writings for adequate elucidation of the basic constitution and nature of these organisms, these organs, these egos, these subjects and persons, which would enable us to grasp why man can with their aid behave at all as he in fact does and for what reasons he is also able to feel himself, among other things, guilty, let us say. If we seek therefore to create really viable preconditions for an understanding of human guilt, we shall have no choice but to start again from the very beginning in our thinking about the nature of man. We have to ask ourselves, for example, what am I like, what kind of beings are we here, to account for the simple fact that I could see you from the very moment I entered this room and could realize that you are my audience of fellow human beings and that you were able to perceive me just as directly as the speaker for this evening? You all know that the most primitive, the purely biological attempt to explain these phenomena proceeds with the assertion that the retina of our eyes is stimulated by rays of light emitted by the external object, whereupon these retinal stimuli are transmitted to the cerebral cortex and there transformed into representations and thoughts. Nevertheless, it is just here that the biologists owe us an answer to the decisive question as to how then such a transformation is supposed to take place, this conversion of chemical-physical excitation processes in the brain cells into intellectually meaningful contents and into an understanding of the apparent events out there for what they are. If some so-called exact scientists really assume, openly or tacitly, the possibility of such an evaporation process, they move in a wholly magical world of their own construction. Where, however, man is posited primarily as a psychophysical organism or as a subject, or a person, the crucial question remains obscure as well, the question, that is, as to how and why these entities of unknown nature succeed from within themselves in somehow getting over to the objects in the outside world, in grasping them and in understanding them?

Fortunately, immediate experience itself shows us that there is not needed at all such an enigmatic transcending on the part of man from out of the interior of a psyche, a subjectivity or a person, because such an Interior simply does not exist. Let us only recollect carefully what actually and really happened when we met here an hour ago! Surely you by no means became aware of yourselves as beings which had been first enclosed inside some kind of bodily organisms that had been sealed in by a skin; nor did you exist primarily inside an ego, in a psyche, in a subject or a person, out of which mental-intellectual containers you would then have had to climb in order to get across to me with your understanding of my personality. Again, I too experienced myself just as little as something to me. Again, I too experienced myself just as little as something existing in my body, something simply pre-existing there within my psyche or my ego. Rather we have all been here together from the very start "out there," present within the total scope of this lecture hall, expanded as it were into all our relationships to what showed itself in this open realm. Above all, however, we have all together at the very outset been at and with the same things concerning us here and now, that is, anxiety, guilt and psychotherapeutic liberation, though each of us in his particular way of relating to them.

Thus, as human beings, we are always and fundamentally existing in this or that relationship to a material or mental thing confronting us, a plant, an animal, a fellow man. We are in all conscience never anything but that comprehending relationship *within* which the phenomena confronting us at any given time can appear originally as what they are, can unfold and reveal themselves in their meaningful and referential connections. Therefore to this day we call everything that is a *phenomenon:* a word derived from the Greek "phainesthai," meaning simply "that which shines forth, which shows itself." However, where something can open up its meaningful content, make its appearance shine forth, show itself and allow itself to be understood, it requires from the very beginning lucidity, brightness, a luminated lucid openness, into which such an appearance can occur, so that a phenomenon can become apparent, present and be-able-to-be. Therefore our most primal and most concrete experience shows us the basic constitution of man as being of the nature of a luminating realm, needed by the phenomena of our world to enable them to become apparent within it and to be. In other words, man's basic nature reveals itself to our immediate perception as that being that our world *needs* as the realm of lucidity necessary for the coming forth, the being-able-to-appear-and-to-be of its phenomena. However, it is just the allowing-oneself thus to-be-claimed and needed, and nothing else, which in his innermost recesses is what man owes to that which is and has to be. Thus all human feelings of guilt in general are rooted in *this* state of owing. *This* state of owing is, if you will, man's existential indebtedness and guiltiness. Consequently, there is not a single phenomenon of the human conscience which would not have to and could not be understood basically as a summons and admonition to discharge the human duty to be a custodian and guardian of everything that has to appear, to be and to unfold in the light of any given human existence.

Thus we also begin to grasp, for instance, what at first was so incomprehensible, that is, the meaning of the grave guilt in the dreams of the anxious patient mentioned earlier who always had to answer to her Norn appearing as a judge. At that time that woman in her neurotic stuntedness and reserve had in fact been extraordinarily remiss in fulfilling the entire range of her existence's possibilities and *by that fact,* by remaining so very much indebted to her destiny as a human being, had really committed the arch-crime against her destiny. Nevertheless, she slowly became healed during the psychotherapeutic treatment and with her waking commissions and omissions to a great extent lived up to her possibilities of meaning-disclosing world-relations in accordance with the demands addressed to her by the phenomena confronting her. Then the grave accusations of her dreams ceased promptly and forever. Clearly, against such a background, the guiltiness and indebtedness of man can no longer be reduced to mere subjective, even to merely externally inculcated psychological guilt *feelings* that could be analyzed away. Man is, by the very terms of his being, guilty and remains in debt to his death. His entire being is not fulfilled until he has accepted and carried out all the possibilities of relationships to the phenomena continually hurled upon him by his future and until he has allowed the emergence of the world which seeks appearance in the light of his existence. Man's future, however, at best has reached him fully and in a genuinely human way in the moment of his dying.

Man, though, is also able to shut his eyes to the demands of what confronts him and makes its demands upon him. It is precisely this possibility either to meet these demands made by that which he encounters or to evade and refuse them, that constitutes the fundamental characteristic of human *freedom*. If he freely assumes his being-guilty, his being indebted, over against his given existential possibilities, if he decides in this sense in favor of having-a-conscience and accordingly *wanting*-to-let-himself-be-used and engaged as the luminating world-openness, then he no longer feels the essential being-indebted and being guilty of human existence as a *burden* of guilt and an *oppression* by indebtedness. The burden and oppression are overcome in the joyous readiness to place himself without reservation at the disposal of all phenomena as the light and clearing into which they can appear and unfold, and as their custodian. At the same time there is opened up to man the inexhaustible meaningfulness of his existence, resulting from his being claimed and needed by everything that seeks to emerge and to be in the light of his existence. This evidently and primarily determines also the "moral" behavior of man by itself. There is no longer any more need of nebulous ethical values, hanging somewhere in the air which subsequently would have to be dragged in to account for his "ethical" actions.

In this way the human being-guilty loses the oppressive character of a load and a burden just as we first saw anxiety overcome itself and give up its constrictive nature. In both cases the only thing to do was to allow our insights to advance just slightly beyond the metaphysical subjectivism of our modern psychology.

THE NEW UNDERSTANDING OF MAN AS BASIS FOR PSYCHOTHERAPEUTIC LIBERATION

These insights into the nature of human anxiety and guilt can now also become the supporting basis of the psychotherapeutic liberation of sick people from the fetters of their psychoneurotic symptoms. We should even go so far as to say that, if entirely devoid of this kind of knowledge, no psychotherapist worthy of the name will get along. Nevertheless, are there not renowned physicians and even philosophers who assert the very contrary, who warn psychotherapists against getting involved in questions concerning their patients' existence? These philosophers maintain that the psychotherapists ought to proceed as physicians do with the diseased human body, that is, restrict themselves to repairing the particular psychic functions when they get out of order. Is there, however, anything more nonsensical and impossible than that? To take such a conception involving the belief in the occurrence of autonomous particular psychic functions and in their discrete susceptibility to psychotherapy, and to apply it to a patient, is not this also always and necessarily a highly philosophical proceeding and at the same time a very powerful interference with the human existence of the patient seeking help? Only, such a philosophical-existential interference would be based on a notion of man's being that yields but an incomplete and distorted picture of his nature and therefore could hardly ever be of any real therapeutic value.

However, it is not just a few foolish philosophers who do not want us psychotherapists to meddle in their handiwork. Also many theologians think they have to forbid our interest in our patients' religious phenomena that arise during treatment. They do not, however, show us how we could obey their prohibition without inflicting serious damage on our patients. If we instruct our patients not to say anything to us about their religious experiences and worries but to take them exclusively to their pastors, we violate the basic rule of psychotherapy which calls for unreserved truthfulness before the psychotherapist, and we do so in a way that gravely compromises the real chances of success for any psychotherapeutic treatment. In addition, we would expect of our patients nothing less than to allow themselves to be torn asunder, as it were, between a pastor and a psychotherapist. For this reason pastors have to concede that the religious sphere of human existence as well be disclosed in the psychotherapeutic treatment wherever and however it urges itself upon our attention. It goes without saying that when confronted by it the psychotherapist has to comport himself just as he does in the presence of all other human phenomena emerging in the course of treatment. In other words, he would have to confront it as well with due reverence and grant it the space it takes up in the totality of the existence of a patient.

Another question, and one which affects psychotherapeutic practice in detail, is in what way we can accompany our patients to the point of sharing, not only intellectually but by their whole being, those insights into their fundamental human nature that overcome all anxiety and oppression by guilt. Certainly the matter will never be allowed to rest with an appeal to reason and intellect or with an invocation of that modern catch-word "existence." That would mean a serious regress of psychotherapy back to the pre-*Freudian* era of persuasion. After all, it is not the head of our patients so much as their heart that is locked in. Therefore all mere words, even the most clever, remain for them empty sound and fury signifying nothing therapeutically. The most shocking proof of the senselessness, indeed the harmfulness of such a rational psychotherapeutic proceeding appealing to "reason" and "responsibility" only, can perhaps be encountered in India, in those neurotic Europeans who went over there and who sought to liberate themselves from the straitjacket of their Western neuroses by acquiring Hindu philosophy or who seek to gain their redemption in the Buddhist nirvana. The consequence of their attempts is the very contrary of any redemption and liberation, namely, lamentable, high-flown intellectualistic acrobatics. They do not know that the Indian path of salvation, if it is not to lead one astray, presupposes an entirely different state of mind from the neurotically restricted one that they took to the East with them. These poor souls remind one of a building contractor who would like to preserve a house that is decayed all the way into the cellar by a renovation restricted to the attic.

We as psychotherapists ought to refrain completely from the vainglorious practice of preaching any kind of maxims and dogmas to our patients. We have to content ourselves with clearing away a little stone here and there, an obstacle, so that what is already there and has always constituted the being of the patient can by itself emerge from its previous reserve into the open. The highest aim of all psychotherapy is and remains the opening up of our patients to an ability-to-love-and-trust which permits all oppression by anxiety and guilt to be surmounted as mere misunderstandings. Such trust can and may be fitly called the most mature form of human openness. However, our mentally disturbed patients can attain to it only in the way in which human maturing in general is possible. Normally this happens first of all by way of the physical, concrete experience of a sufficient, imperturbable bestowal of maternal love. Our patients would not be ill if they had not come off the losers in this primary experience. However, this business of coming off the loser and so becoming ill never depends solely on what the mothers were in a position to give in the way of loving support and strength but just as much on the highly variable need for love in the children, which sometimes is insatiably strong. In psychotherapy the important thing is to let the patients first make up for the missing but at bottom indispensable experience of the protective and unshakable bestowal of care and love suited to the individual nature of the patients.

Naturally, no psychotherapist can achieve this by turning himself into a kind of matron or by seeking to play the maternal role. However, there is a special way in which the psychotherapist can bestow sympathy and love on his patients, and it is not to be encountered anywhere in the world outside the psychoanalytic situation. This specific "psychotherapeutic eros" is different from the love of parents for their children, different from the love between two friends, different from the love of the priest for his flock, quite decidedly different from the extremely variable love between the sexes, as it is from the matter-of-fact indifference of purely conventional kindness. Certainly the nature of psychotherapeutic eros is far from having been described in the textbooks from a sufficiently scientific-phenomenological point of view. One will never be able to acquire it from books, anyhow. It will practically always be the case that one can grow into it only through the experiences of one's own training analysis. It was Freud, though, who already has depicted in terms of unequalled precision certain very essential features of this special kind of relationship which a psychoanalyst has to be capable of. He wrote that a psychoanalysis succeeds best if it occurs as though "unintentionally," void of all selfish ambition, of all deliberate aiming at any kind of therapeutic, educational or scientific success.[2] Also, Freud says the psychoanalyst must not derive any kind of personal advantage from the patient's relationship to him, no matter how willingly the patient may offer such advantages to him. Otherwise the analyst would be wholly responsible for the failure of the treatment.[3] The only exception to this rule is the return gift of an appropriate financial compensation which relieves the psychoanalyst from worry about his own physical needs and leaves him wholly free to devote himself to his patient in a manner that is right, balanced and imperturbable.[4] Genuine psychotherapeutic eros, in other words, has to distinguish itself by an otherwise never practiced selflessness, self-restraint and reverence before the partner's individuality and uniqueness. These qualities must not be shaken and perturbed either by cooperative, or by indifferent or by hostile behavior on the part of the patient. Psychotherapeutic eros has to go even somewhat beyond Christian humility in its selflessness and its triumph over egotism in so far as it must not even intervene in the interest of the therapist's own God and seek to guide the partner's life accordingly.[5] Only if the psychotherapist is capable of all this can the openness of such an interpersonal playground (Freud) allow our patients to get to the point where they again put out their antennae, as it were, and on their own independent responsibility gain admittance to ever freer and wider relationships with the phenomena of their world. Freud also knew very exactly that this was true. For this reason he expressly demanded of the practicing psychoanalyst—in crass contradiction, by the way, to his own severely deterministic theory—that he provide his patient in the doctor-patient relationship with an arena in which he, the patient, can in almost total *freedom* recognize without danger his previously buried impulses and tendencies, and in which he can try them out, appropriate them and integrate them in the formation of his own independent autonomous being. Freud, thereby, immediately added the warning that the doctor has to make sure only that he does not replace the eliminated neurotic distortions and constrictions with his, the doctor's, own emotional or intellectual prejudices. Then what occurs on the playground of the psychoanalytical situation based on genuine and selfless affection and sympathy is a gradual growth of the patients out of their childish self-centered reserve into ever richer possibilities of love, a growth that takes place as though spontaneously in so far as the patient's being is endowed at all with the corresponding potentialities for development.[6]

Only we shall in the future have to follow this basic therapeutic rule of Freud thus described by himself much more faithfully than Freud himself has ever been able to do owing to his entanglement in his naturalistic theory. We shall, for instance, be more Freudian than Freud in that we shall concede to the spiritual or religious experiences of our patients that emerge in treatment the same primariness, authenticity and reality as to the phenomena of the so-called drives. We shall be on our guard against demoting these experiences to merely derivative sublimation products of a drive libido, merely out of our prejudice in favor of the secondary psychoanalytic theory. On the other hand, of course, we should have to regard it as no less a blasphemy if our patients sought to condemn and deny their bodily and sensual nature as an impure invention of the Devil. In this way they meddle in God's handiwork no less than do the atheists in the wealth of human phenomena. Does not the Bible itself call the body the divinely endowed temple of the Holy Spirit? Therefore we have to question in detail and with the utmost patience all neurotic constrictions and distortions in whatever environmental, interpersonal or religious relationships these barriers may show themselves. Then we shall succeed in freeing very many patients from the torments of their neurotic anxieties and guilt feelings. It is precisely here, however, that we experience all the more impressively man's true underlying state of being-guilty and being-indebted.

A person can from childhood have a moral code forced upon him which essentially hinders and cripples the unfolding of his existence as it was meant to be as a whole. This moral code can, for example, have taught him to regard the bodily, physical, sensual potentialities to relate to his world as basically sinful and deserving of denial and suppression. Such a human being will become guilty of the brutal warding-off of very important spheres of reality. He closes himself to the appeal of so many phenomena which have an actual right to-be-able-to-appear in the light of his existence. Every person who is not constitutionally defective experiences such a refusal to exist wholly in the shape of monitory, gnawing guilt feelings and pangs of conscience. They summon him to become something better and something more complete. The summons is the more insistent the more he has been remiss in fulfilling all his life possibilities. However, a becoming-better can only be understood by such a crippled neurotic as a still more rigorous obedience to those familiar commandments and prohibitions burned into him from childhood, which are, however, alien to his nature and to what he is claimed for. He will thus endeavor even more radically to deny his possibilities of sensual relationships, which he mistakenly takes to be sinful. It is just in this way that he increases his true human guilt and indebtedness and becomes ever more profoundly remiss in the fulfilling of his custodianship. At the same time he can look for the origin of his guiltiness only in very peripheral, unimportant areas of his closed-in existence and moves farther and farther away from the possibility of the true discharge of his debt. Just remember the melancholic mentioned at the beginning who could only find the reason for all his moral misery in a kiss given twenty years before but had become blind to his central and present failure to realize his love potentialities.

Thus the guilt feelings of a neurotic are intensified ever more by the distorted, non-authentic inhibitions inculcated by alien mentalities. The greater the indebtedness and guiltiness become the more tormenting become his neurotic guilt feelings, which again drive him into still more guilty behavior. This gives rise to a vicious circle which not seldom leads to a short-circuit in the form of insanity or suicide, for the future of a person so entangled stares him in the face with increasingly horrible meaninglessness and emptiness.

A psychotherapy based on these insights into the fundamental constitution of man is often enough in a position to break such a vicious circle. It can happen that patients free themselves out of that entanglement of their neurotic guilt feelings, realize their genuine existential indebtedness, and accept it willingly. Then they experience their life really as an anxiety-free, fortunate and meaningful state of being-summoned to belong immediately to the luminating world-openness. Of course, it is not the business of a psychiatrist to determine in what special *way* such a healing experience in the psychotherapeutic treatment occurs at any given time and with any particular patient. In one patient it comes forth spontaneously out of his own being in the shape of a newly emergent religious encounter. In another it just as naturally takes the form of a liberating philosophical ability-to-think in the deepest sense of this word. In still a third patient it assumes the form of a meditative perception of his direct participation in the common ground of all beings. Most patients perhaps simply achieve the old Freudian goal of increased efficiency and capacity to enjoy life, except that these people too then have reached a basic attitude which allows them no longer to exercise their capacities merely in a *selfish* quest for power and pleasure. They too will rather work and enjoy themselves from a more or less articulated knowledge that they are being called on with all their possibilities of elucidating relationships to contribute their share to the world-openness into which whatever confronts them may succeed in shining forth and become one of the phenomena constituting our world.

NOTES

1 Freud, S., *Vorlesungen zur Einführung in die Psychoanalyse*. Ges. Schr., Vol. VII, p. 67, Vienna, Zürich. *Introductory Lectures on Psycho-analysis, The Standard Edition of the Complete Psychological Works of Sigmund Freud,* Vol. 15 (London: The Hogarth Press), 1963.

2 Freud, S., "Ratschläge für den Arzt bei der psychoanalytischen Behandlung," Ges. Schr. Leipzig, Vienna, Zürich, Vol. VI, p. 68, 69, 73. "Recommendations to Physicians Practising Psycho-analysis," in *Standard Edition,* Vol. 12.

3 Freud, S., "Bemerkungen über die Übertragungsliebe," *Ibid.*, p. 132. "Observations on Transference Love," in *Standard Edition,* Vol. 12.

4 Freud, S., "Zur Einleitung der Behandlung," *Ibid.*, p. 94 ff. "On Beginning the Treatment," in *Standard Edition,* Vol. 12.

5 Seguin, A., "Love and Psychotherapy—The psychotherapeutic eros." *Acta Psychotherapeutica et Psychosomatica, Vol. 10,* 1962,and this author's book on the same subject.

6 Freud, S., "Erinnern, Wiederholen, Durcharbeiten," *op. cit.*, p. 117. "Remembering, Repeating, and Working-Through," in *Standard Edition,* Vol. 12.

From Guilt-Feelings To Reconciliation: Images of Modern Man

JONATHAN S. WOOCHER

"Do you know that your case is going badly?" asked the priest. "I have that idea myself," said K. "I've done what I could, but without any success so far. Of course, my petition isn't finished yet." "How do you think it will end?"asked the priest. "At first I thought it must turn out well," said K., "but now I frequently have my doubts. I don't know how it will end. Do you?" "No," said the priest, "but I fear it will end badly. You are held to be guilty. Your case will perhaps never get beyond a lower court. Your guilt is supposed, for the present, at least, to have been proved." "But I am not guilty," said K.; "it's a mistake. And, if it comes to that, how can any man be called guilty? We are all simply men here, one as much as the other." "That is true," said the priest, "but that's how all guilty men talk."

Franz Kafka, *The Trial*

I

One of the most far-reaching effects of Western man's entry into the modern pluralist, secularized world has been the proliferation of "images of man" himself.[1] The Biblically-rooted, theologically focused world-view of pre-modern Western civilization[2] provided men with a clear framework within which to make sense of their psychic and social experiences. The structure of man's being and his place in the universe were both defined in terms of his relationship with a creating, revealing, and redeeming God whose reality was virtually unquestionable. For modern man, however, self-understanding has become more problematic. In place of a single fundamental image of his nature and destiny, he is confronted with a wealth of alternative frameworks within which to interpret his life experience. Alongside traditional religio-philosophic images, radically new pictures of man have emerged, drawn primarily from the province of the social sciences and, above all, modern psychology.

In view of this proliferation of images of man, widespread uncertainty about the nature and meaning of certain fundamental human experiences in the modern world is hardly surprising. One such experience which might well serve as a paradigm for an attempt to understand the problematic dimensions of the modern quest for a self-image is the experience of guilt.[3] As an imaging experience, guilt has in the past figured centrally in efforts to delineate both the internal structure and dynamics of the human person and the nature of the relationship between self and world. It is nearly impossible to speak seriously about guilt without speaking in *existential* terms;[4] and in life experience itself, how one actually deals with guilt-feelings is a crucial determinant of the character and meaning of his existence.

The existential significance of the experience of guilt has not escaped the attention of some of the modern world's most profound thinkers. We propose to focus on the work of three men—Martin Heidegger, Paul Tillich, and Martin Buber—for whom an understanding of existential roots and meaning of guilt-feelings provides a vital key to reconstructing an image of man in and for the modern world. This examination may have special import for those who believe that the classical Western religious tradition might yet reintegrate our diverse modern images of man if given the opportunity: if it is possible to formulate an understanding of guilt which resonates with our contemporary knowledge and experiences[5] and yet still reflects the central concerns and insights of that Biblically-rooted tradition, then it may be appropriate to re-examine the resources of that tradition and its claim on modern man's attention in other areas of life as well.

II

It is clear that modern man suffers no lack of guilt-feelings; indeed, the anxiety and neuroses arising from an acute sense of guilt provide psychotherapy with countless patients. What is unclear today, as we indicated above, is how to respond to these feelings within a coherent framework of understanding of the meaning of guilt as a defining dimension of human existence. Shall we respond to our experiences of guilt with a search for a therapy to regain a happy conscience; with a stoic shrug of the shoulders; with a contrite desire to confess misdeeds and be done with them; or with an effort to uncover the roots of an unrelenting conscience beyond psychological and social processes themselves? In essence, we are asking: what is the existential and ontological meaning of guilt as a human phenomenon? We know the *feeling* of guilt, but, we ask, does it mean anything to say that we *are* guilty, and if so, what?

For many of us, the traditional Western religious understanding of guilt has been left behind. In the Biblical image of man, the human potential for sin and guilt stands alongside that for righteousness and repentance in defining man's nature as that creature called upon to respond to God's presence and commands. Throughout most of Western religious history, a sense of guilt served as a clear sign of the need for expiation of one's sin, for altering the ontological state of guiltiness, through sacrifice, prayer, or confession. The acknowledgement of guilt, without excuse or justification, was a vital element in the life of faith. There could be no question in the mind of Biblical man, and in the minds of those whose self-definition has been Biblically oriented, that guilt is a real dimension of human existence, an ontological state resulting from disobedience to Divine Law and Command.

If modern man is unable to deal with guilt in these traditional religious terms (and relatively few seem so capable), it is no wonder that he must turn to the examination of his *sense* of guilt with some confusion and dissatisfaction.

The modern encounter with guilt-feelings is marked primarily by the endeavor to understand, explain, and thereby often eliminate these feelings as unwarranted intrusions upon our potential for happiness and peace of mind. This effort to contain and perhaps suppress guilt-feelings may well succeed in many instances. But the very possibility of such success may foreclose a confrontation with these feelings of guilt on another level: as signals pointing to guilt as an ontic reality in one's life, as the product of real events which have left not only psychic scars, but a residue of responsibility for altering one's personal being in the world. The attempt to control and eliminate guilt-feelings through an understanding of their roots in psycho-social processes alone often betrays an image of man which fails to locate the human person in a context of meaning or responsibility beyond that which can be studied and defined by the psychologist and sociologist. In the final analysis, such a man is the inhabitant of a biologically, neurologically, and culturally determined, even if manipulable, world.

The idea that guilt is merely the result of "a transgression, a crime, the violation of a specific taboo, boundary, or legal code by a definite voluntary act,"[6] and that all such taboos, boundaries, or codes are culturally relative human creations, makes guilt a socially and psychologically functional or dysfunctional phenomenon of considerable importance. But this psycho-cultural approach does not necessarily accord guilt existential significance for the individual unless it explicitly links this analysis to the meaning of humanness per se. The great virtue of the Freudian "depth psychological" understanding of guilt is that it does attempt to make this link. On the simplest level, Freud explains guilt-feelings as the products of the Oedipal complex and castration fears of childhood which result in the development of a harsh and punishing super-ego (through identification with the Father as model).[7] But Freud also goes further than this in claiming that guilt-feelings are the correlates of a universalized developmental pattern which unfolds within the human mind.

Modern man's sense of guilt, says Freud, is the psychic price he pays for living as civilized man. Consciousness of guilt is ultimately rooted in the instinctual war between Eros and Thanatos, the life and death instincts, within man. This struggle finds expression in an irreconcilable ambivalence in the sons' attitude toward the Father.[8] The sons want to kill the Father, but whether they do or not does not matter: guilt-feelings have been born.[9] These guilt-feelings, it must be noted, are *not* the products of real violations of an externally validated command, other than the generalized demand of all "civilization" to repress or sublimate libidinal and instinctual drives. Guilt-feelings define the human condition, for Freud, insofar as they reflect the tension man feels when confronted with the impossible dictates of his socially-derived super-ego. Excessive, "neurotic," guilt-feelings come from a patient's own early psychosexual experience. But guilt-feelings are not taken as signals to examine the actual conduct of the patient from any genuinely trans-psychical (e.g., ethical or religious) viewpoint. "Normal" guilt must be accepted as the result of living in a "sick" civilization; "excessive" guilt can be treated by a competent psychoanalyst.

The overall effect of the Freudian approach, even of the great importance accorded to guilt as a prime "discontent" of our civilization, is to feed that tendency in modern man which would divorce guilt-feelings from the realm of true personal accountability for conduct in the world. The connection which traditional Western religion sought to establish between action and feeling, between genuine transgression and conscience, has been ruptured. The act itself becomes merely a particular cultural violation; the feeling is a phylogenetically-rooted psychological condition. In the Freudian world, we may well accept culpability for actions in a legal or even "moral" sense. We may recognize the existence of deep feelings of anxiety and pangs of conscience as natural elements in our psychological makeup. But the Freudian understanding ultimately leads nowhere. Guilt-feelings may tell us who we are, but they help us little in deciding who we must be. Freud's meta-psychology, seeing in guilt the expression of an eternal struggle between Eros and Thanatos—the life and death instincts—in civilized man, does point clearly toward an understanding of guilt as a fundamental dimension of human existence. Yet it remains a dimension in which the individual is virtually powerless. His psychological structure is such that he cannot avoid feeling guilty if he lives in modern civilization. The clash of instincts and cultural norms is inevitable; the demands of the introjected super-ego transcend both the individual's actual conduct and any pretensions he might make towards alleviating his sense of guilt through more responsible living. The psycho-existential dynamic guilt for Freud is thus, in the final analysis, one that runs directly counter to any attempt to provide guilt with an ontological basis outside of the psyche—individual or collective.[10] Freud's analysis of the ultimate roots of man's sense of guilt certainly takes seriously the significance of guilt, but it strips the individual of the ability to make of the confrontation with his guilt-feelings an act of truly existential significance because there is ultimately nothing to confront but his own phylogenetically determined psychological processes.

A conventional psychoanalytic approach to guilt, even extended to its meta-psychological limits, ends either in a too facile evaluation of guilt as a psychological malady or a too abstract acceptance of guilt as an inevitable and essentially irremediable psychic effect of civilization as such. The person as a whole is, in either case, no longer responsible for his guilt-feelings; nor can he deal with them on the level of so-called responsible action in the world. Precisely insofar as guilt touches the fundamental levels of human existence, it is beyond the reach of the individual who seeks to confront it.

That there may well be something unsatisfying in this formulation of the problem of guilt is attested to by the fact that a number of important modern thinkers have tried to argue for a very different understanding of the existential status and significance of guilt and guilt-feelings. One of the most influential of these thinkers, a man whose phenomenology of human existence has influenced several psychotherapists both in Europe and the United States, is the German philosopher Martin Heidegger. For Heidegger, and those who accept his basic framework, man *is* guilty in a fully ontological sense (indeed his guiltiness helps to define him as man). Guilt is by no means merely a culturally nurtured psychological feeling in Heidegger's conception; but neither is it to be located in the traditional moral/ethical sphere, at least in its origins. In the Heideggerean understanding, "Dasein [equivalent for our purposes to "man"] as such is guilty." "Only because Dasein is guilty in the basis of its Being, and closes itself off from itself as something thrown and falling, is conscience possible." "This essential Being-guilty is . . . the existential condition for the possibility of the 'morally' good and for that of the 'morally' evil—i.e., for morality in general and for the possible forms which this may take factically."[11]

Heidegger thus insists that prior to any assumption by man of guilt in a moral sense or any "owing" (the root-meaning of the German word for guilt) in relation to others, there is a fundamental level of "Being-guilty" which must be recognized and explored. He begins with a formal definition of guilt as "Being-the-basis of a nullity," a lack.[12] In the inter-personal context, the root of our "owing" another person, of our guiltiness toward him, is our causing a lack in the other's existence. But much more importantly, Dasein (Man) is guilty because of a lack in its own being. This lack is the result of what Heidegger calls Dasein's "thrownness" into existence, its thrownness toward death in a way over which it has no original control. This "thrownness" constitutes a lack of full existence as long as it is not taken up by Dasein and actually directed towards its inevitable end. Existence in "thrownness" thus defines Dasein's very Being as Being-guilty according to Heidegger.[13]

"Thrown" existence is existence lived out as Das Man, as One in a Crowd. Das Man lacks its own self-being because it does not take up its "thrownness" into a real Self, a being in control of its own existence. As Das Man, Dasein is guilty (indebted) toward the Self which it might become were it to make the effort to escape from the negativity of the Crowd. Dasein owes it to its being to become such a Self; a Self is what it lacks, a full existence, a taking up of its own being.[14] All of these formulations are alternative attempts to express what Heidegger's phenomenology aims to demonstrate—that Dasein is defined in its very basis by a nullity, a lack, and hence is, in its very basis, guilty.

Dasein can, however, do something about its guiltiness. The call of conscience comes from and is directed to Dasein, calling it "*forth* to the possibility of taking over, in existing, even that thrown entity which it is."[15] Conscience (guilt-feeling) demands that Dasein overcome the lack of a Self which constitutes its existence as Das Man by becoming a real Self, by fulfilling its obligation to its own being. Dasein must "*be* 'guilty' *authentically,*" must listen to the "summons to Being-guilty" which signifies a "calling-forth to that potentiality-for-Being which in each case I as Dasein am already."[16] Understanding and responding to this call—understanding oneself in one's ownmost potentiality-for-Being and "projecting oneself upon one's *ownmost* authentic potentiality for becoming guilty"—is "resoluteness," "authentic Being-one's-self."[17] Resolute existence is no "escape" from guiltiness; rather it is, as the above formulations indicate, a full acceptance of one's Being-guilty and an assumption of responsibility for one's "thrown" (guilty) existence.

In all of this, Heidegger's primary reference point is the relationship of man to his own existence; it is there that both "guilt" and the possibility of "resoluteness" are defined. But in as much as Dasein is always Being-in-the-world alongside others, the confrontation of man with his guilt has clear implications for his life with other men. Resoluteness "brings the Self right into its current concernful Being-alongside what is ready-to-hand, and pushes it into solicitous Being-with-others."[18] "Real life together is the first thing to arise out of the real self-being of resolution."[19] The term which Heidegger uses to designate the interpersonal relationship flowing from resoluteness is "solicitude." As the word implies, solicitude is essentially a "helping" relationship—Dasein offering solicitous aid to another who stands in need of it. As such, it may perhaps help to overcome that guilt which arises in the interpersonal sphere, where Dasein is the cause of a lack in another, but it remains in Heidegger's[20] approach a correspondingly secondary, indeed dependent, aspect of Dasein's encounter with his guiltiness. "Resoluteness" in its own existence remains the central task for Dasein which wishes to transcend its condition as Das Man and takes up its "thrownness."[21]

The Heideggerean ontology of guilt clearly repudiates those tendencies in modern thought which would strip guilt of any existence-defining significance. In Heidegger's image of man, guilt does constitute a central dimension of humanness. What needs to be more fully explored, however, is how this understanding of guilt relates to both the human life-experience in which guilt is intimately connected with discrete acts in the "moral" realm and the traditional religious viewpoint which would refer human guilt ultimately to a source of obligation transcending the Self. It may, therefore, be worthwhile to examine the work of some of the psychotherapists who have tried to employ a Heideggerean model in treating the guilt-feelings of their patients and to see how they have adapted that framework in developing their own understandings of guilt as an existential phenomenon.

One of the leading proponents of Heideggerean psychotherapy is the Swiss analyst Medard Boss. Boss' understanding of guilt, like Heidegger's, begins with an assertion that particular guilt-feelings are rooted in a primal ability-to-be-guilty which is a "feature of man's very nature." ". . . Man's ability-to-feel-oneself-guilty as such is and remains in every guilt phenomenon as autochthonous Being-guilty, with its own autonomous origin and essential nature."[22] Boss asserts as well that the nature of human guilt can only be understood from the standpoint of what is lacking, of how a life misses "the fullness and fulfillment of human existence."[23] In explicating man's primal Being-guilty, Boss emphasizes another concept which emerges in the course of Heidegger's analysis of Dasein—man's role as world-discloser:

> Man's basic nature reveals itself to our immediate perception as that being that our world *needs* as the realm of lucidity necessary for the coming forth, the being-able-to-appear-and-to-be of its phenomena. However, it is just the allowing-oneself thus to-be-claimed and needed, and nothing else, which in his inner most recesses is what man owes to that which is and has to be. Thus all human feelings of guilt in general are rooted in this state of owing. *This* state of owing is, if you will, man's existential indebtedness and guiltiness. Consequently there is not a single phenomenon of the human conscience which would not have to and could not be understood basically as a summons and admonition to discharge the human duty to be a custodian and guardian of everything that has to appear, to be, and to unfold in the light of any given human existence.[24]

Man is in debt because he must accept and carry out "all the possibilities of relationships to the phenomena continually hurled upon him by his future" and allow "the emergence of the world which seeks appearance in the light of his existence."[25] "Man's existential guilt consists in his failing to carry out the mandate to fulfill all his possibilities."[26]

Within this context, Boss is able to recast the role of psychoanalysis in dealing with man's neurotic guilt-feelings, while at the same time emphasizing the need for a very different approach to the encounter with existential guilt. Existential guilt is a positive force in the broadest sense, if properly understood and willingly accepted.

> If [a man] freely assumes his being-guilty, his being indebted,over against his given existential possibilities, if he decides in this sense in favor of having-a-conscience and accordingly *wanting*-to-let-himself-be-used and engaged as the luminating world-openness, then he no longer feels the essential being-indebted and being guilty of human existence as a *burden* of guilt and an oppression by indebtedness.[27]

According to Boss the acceptance of one's existential guiltiness frees man from *neurotic* feelings of guilt. These neurotic feelings do not originate in the person, but rather reflect the imposition on him of alien modes of life which could not be shaken off. Neurotic guilt feelings add to the genuine existential guilt, since they work to prevent one from fulfilling his own existence. Unfortunately, the persistent voice of the conscience which seeks to call the individual to existential fulfillment is frequently misunderstood in narrowly moralistic terms as a demand for even greater fidelity to a way or life foreign to him. The result is a vicious circle.[28]

> A psychotherapy based on these insights into the fundamental constitution of man is often enough in a position to break such a vicious circle. It can happen that patients free themselves out of that entanglement of their neurotic guilt

> feelings, realize their genuine existential indebtedness, and accept it willingly. Then they experience their life really as an anxiety-free, fortunate and meaningful state of being-summoned to belong immediately to the luminating world-openness.[29]

Boss' indebtedness to Heidegger, in both language and fundamental conception, is clear. Yet so too should be some subtle shifts in emphasis. Boss' analysis of the onto-existential roots of human guilt is cast in a form which in most instances accords man's being-in-the-world a primary role and finds the ultimate source of guilt in failures of relationship. There is, to be sure, no consistent critique of Heidegger's essentially self-referential analysis in Boss' formulation, and, indeed, Boss' language sometimes points in the same direction by focusing on the fulfillment of the individual's possibilities as his primary existential responsibility. Still, one can see in Boss' understanding a more developed sense of the possibility of relating the structural foundations of man's guilt to his actual responsive and responsible life in the world where the apparent content of his guilt-feelings arises. This is evidenced not only in the goal which Boss establishes for his analysis—the "opening up of our patients to an ability-to-love-and-trust"[30]—but also in his understanding of the limits of therapy itself:

> The healing factor in psychoanalysis can never consist in . . . "living out," but consists, rather, in an increasing appropriation of all of one's life-possibilities as *possibilities*. Unless a human being has become aware of and acknowledged as his own all his possibilities of relating to what he encounters (whether they please him or his fellow man or not), no true self-knowledge, no authentic responsibility, is possible. The actual carrying out of these possibilities in one's relations toward partners outside the analytic situation, however, is—as must be made very clear to analysands—a completely different question, and must be in accord with the most productive unfolding of a patient's whole existence, including the welfare of those whom he encounters.[31]

Where Heidegger was clear in seeing both the guilt arising in the interpersonal situation and the changed relationship to the world involved in "resoluteness" as derivatives of Dasein's relationship to its own existence, Boss focuses on the appropriation of possibilities and the unfolding of one's existence in relationship to others. Yet—and here is where Boss' Heideggerean model becomes significant—we may well question how a formulation in these terms can come to grips with the concrete problem of responsibility in a specific situation of relatedness. In a sense, Boss, like Heidegger, has defined our existential guilt in terms of man's inevitable failure to fulfill an impossible task—namely, to carry out in life *all* the possibilities of relationship which he recognizes and accepts as his own. This may indeed be a fundamental limitation of human existence. But we must note that this centers guilt as such in the phenomenon of having to make choices, not, as the more traditional approach would have it, in making irresponsible choices.[32] The issue here should not be ignored. In practical terms, the follower of Boss, even if he comes to accept all of his possibilities as possibilities *and* recognizes that the never-ending summons to realize all of these possibilities leaves him always guilty, must still choose which possibilities to attempt to fulfill. Within Boss' formulation, there seems to be no basis for such a choice other than the individual's perception of that which best fulfills his own existence. It is true that Boss includes concern for the welfare of others as a dimension in this self-fulfillment. Yet, at the same time, he insists that moral standards extrinsic to the Self only make the perception of the "most productive unfolding" more difficult by loading the individual with neurotic guilt-feelings. Thus, the translation of concern for the welfare of others into precise behavioral norms remains subjective and subordinated to the impossible quest to fulfill the totality of one's own possibilities which is the source of our genuine existential indebtedness. Boss may indeed see a life of openness, love, trust, and responsibility growing out of the encounter with existential guilt as he defines it. There remains, nevertheless, a gap between the analytically derived structure of that guilt and the lived experience of guilt-feelings arising from a particular action or inaction which is perceived as deserving of self-condemnation.

In the context of our discussion there can be, of course, no "proof" of the validity of a given formulation. There is no doubt that the approach which sees existential guilt as rooted in a fundamental limitation belonging to man's nature as such, in every situation, constitutes a powerful response to the pervasiveness of guilt-feelings, often of a very diffused and amorphous kind, in our time. This is particularly so when the diagnosis is accompanied not by a Freudian resignation to the "discontent," but by a vision of an existence authentically and even joyfully led precisely through an acceptance of guilt. Heidegger's own reference point is perhaps uncomfortably self-centered, but others who have accepted his basic framework have placed far greater emphasis on the fundamental nature of the guilt arising in the interpersonal realm. In addition to Boss, one might look, for example, to the American psychotherapist Rollo May. In his formulation of the problem, May places alongside the denial, or locking up inside the self, of one's essential potentialities, another form of existential guilt, one which moves still further from the Heideggerean self-referential analysis:

> . . . Existential guilt against one's fellows [arises] from the fact that since each of us is an individual he necessarily perceives his fellow men through his own limited and biased eyes. This means that he always to some extent does violence to the true situation of his fellow, and always to some extent fails fully to understand and meet the other's needs.[33]

Even here, however, where existential guilt arises not merely from a failure to fulfill possibilities of relationship, but from an actual injustice done to the other, it is a human *condition,* not a specific *decision,* which is the root of guilt. Thus, May too asserts that:

> This is not a question of moral failure or slackness—though it can be greatly increased by lack of moral sensitivity. It is rather an inescapable result of the fact that each of us is a separate individuality and has no choice but to look at the world through our own eyes.[34]

A discontinuity still exists, therefore, between the claimed onto-existential root of human guilt and the realm of concrete *moral* conduct where guilt was traditionally believed to have its origin. Guilt is existentially definitive insofar as it is central to the fundamental structure and dynamics of human Being. But the specific admonitions and demands of the human conscience which expose this guiltiness do not enjoy the same onto-existential status. Even for May, though the structure of guilt is universal and existential, "the *content* of the guilt is given by the culture."[35]

III

In creating a modern image of man, Heidegger and his psychotherapeutic followers have unquestionably restored guilt to a central place. But they have failed to include at least two other dimensions of the traditional religious image of man—the direct link between guilt and a trans-personal, trans-cultural moral realm and the ultimate possibility of transcending one's existential guiltiness through the action of a forgiving and redeeming Deity. Even the possibility of an authentic existence free from neurotic anxieties may still leave some men groping for a way to escape the tension and problematic of existential guiltiness. Paul Tillich, perhaps the most influential existential theologian of the twentieth century, argues in his book *The Courage To Be* that, in the final analysis, the anxiety of existential guilt can be surmounted only through a man's faith in his being "accepted" despite the fact that in his guilt he sees himself as "unacceptable." Tillich's formulation of the nature of existential guilt and his prescription for a response to it deserve serious consideration, not least because they may lead us back to a full-fledged religious image of man which speaks authentically to the modern condition.

Tillich focuses his conception of existential guilt around the contention that within the limits of his finite freedom, man "is responsible for his own existence, he is required to answer if he is asked, what he has made of himself. He who asks him is his judge, namely, he himself, who, at the same time, stands against him."[36] For Tillich, man is always in need of self-affirmation, of efforts to actualize what he potentially is. This self-affirmation includes an explicit "moral" dimension: acting so as "to make of himself what he is supposed to become,"[37] is an integral part of man's existential task. (Thus far, Tillich appears to be working within a conceptual framework closely akin to Heidegger's.) In his actual existential Being, however, man is estranged from his *essential* Being, including his essential moral Being.[38] In moral terms, this estrangement is expressed in the fact that "however the norm is formulated man has the power of acting against it, or contradicting his essential being, of losing his destiny,"[39] and he does so act.

> A profound ambiguity between good and evil permeates everything be does, because it permeates his personal being. Non-being is mixed with being in his moral self-affirmation . . . . The awareness of this ambiguity is the feeling of guilt.[40]

Tillich sees the anxiety of guilt and self-condemnation, together with what he calls anxieties of fate and death and of emptiness and meaninglessness, as expressions of the basic threat to man's total self-affirmation posed by the power of non-Being which is part of him. In confronting his sense of guilt, man may, according to Tillich, attempt an impossible solution within the sphere of moral action alone:

> To avoid this extreme situation [of self-condemnation] man tries to transform the anxiety of guilt into moral action regardless of its imperfection and ambiguity. Courageously be takes non-being into his moral self-affirmation. This can happen in two ways, according to the duality of the tragic and the personal in man's situation, the first based on the contingencies of fate, the second on the responsibility of freedom. The first way can lead to a defiance of negative judgment, and the moral demands on which they are based; the second way can lead to a moral rigor and the self-satisfaction derived from it. In both of them—usually called anomism and legalism—the anxiety of guilt lies in the background and breaks again and again into the open, producing the extreme situation of moral despair.[41]

In such a situation it is also possible to build up a heavy load of neurotic guilt, to see guilt where there is none and to repress the awareness of real guilt. Neurotic guilt can make any responsible moral decision-making virtually impossible, and thus it must be treated through therapy.[42] But neurotic guilt is "not the existential experience of being guilty of a definite concrete act which expresses the general estrangement of our existence, an act for which responsibility cannot be denied in spite of the element of destiny in it."[43] Merely treating neurotic guilt, like seeking moral self-affirmation through anomism or legalism, cannot help us overcome the anxiety of our existential guilt. Here, Tillich is echoing a theme common to virtually all those thinkers who insist that guilt is rooted in more than mere psychic disturbance.

Tillich's own prescription for dealing with existential guilt, unlike the Heideggereans', takes us, however, clearly into the religious realm. Ultimately, he claims, we must move out of the sphere of moral self-affirmation entirely, for in our estrangement we come to doubt the validity of moral principles altogether.[44] What is needed is what Tillich terms the courage-to-be, the courage to accept acceptance despite one's consciousness of guilt, one's sense of being unacceptable and worthy of condemnation. This is not acceptance by oneself, because the Self is incapable of such an affirmation in the face of its own portion of non-Being. Rather it is acceptance by that Power which can serve as the source of the courage to take the anxiety of guilt into oneself, namely the Power of Being-Itself. We know this Power, in one manifestation, as the God who forgives us for our sins. But even if we come to doubt that such an Acceptor exists, there remains the power of acceptance itself which is implicit even in the act of final despair, the act of accepting the meaninglessness of everything. From such ultimate despair, according to Tillich, comes the breakthrough into the conscious acceptance of the power of acceptance which constitutes the only possible ultimate response to our existential guilt. Such acceptance constitutes an absolute faith, transcending both the mystical experience and the divine-human encounter of Biblical religion. Though this faith may be deprived by doubt of any concrete content, it can serve, nevertheless, as the source of the courage-to-Be, and, thereby, as a means of both accepting and overcoming our existential guilt. Tillich points, therefore, if not to the fact of forgiveness, at least to a faith in a transcendent Power which makes the experience of our existential guilt only penultimate, an expression of an estrangement which can be overcome even out of the depths of self-condemnation.[45]

IV

Tillich's ontology of existential guilt is not rooted simply in a phenomenological analysis of human existence in the world, as is Heidegger's. It rests as well on the assumption that there is an essential nature of man, including moral norms appropriate to that nature, from which we are existentially estranged. Heidegger, to be sure, recognizes that man is called to be himself fully, but he does not look outside the realm of lived existence for an understanding of the nature of that call or of the self toward which it points. In re-establishing a link between existential guilt, self-realization (or self-affirmation), *and* the explicitly moral dimension of human life, Tillich opens the way towards an encounter with our existential guiltiness that focuses upon the moral decisions of day to day life. For Tillich, unlike Heidegger, there is no question that guilt arises because of man's failure to live up to moral standards which he recognizes as appropriate to his essential nature, and thus we might well expect that moral reformation would serve as the focus for his prescription for dealing with that guilt (as it does not for Heidegger).

Yet, as the discussion above has made clear, Tillich himself rejects this path in favor of a religious answer to the problem of guilt which leaves the moral dimension essentially untouched. He pronounces man incapable of complete moral self-affirmation (as he undoubtedly is), and concludes that he must therefore turn to faith in order to maintain the courage-to-be in the face of self-condemnation. What he apparently ignores is the possibility that self-condemnation may also provide the spark for an effort at restitution and reconciliation in the moral realm itself, and that such an effort can itself be the mark of a courage-to-be no less powerful than that arising from the acceptance of acceptance. Within Tillich's framework, the failure to develop fully this possibility is perhaps understandable. Tillich approaches the moral dimension in terms of a Self seeking fulfillment of its destiny and realizing its essential nature, rather than seeing the moral sphere as the primary, inter-human realm in which a Self comes into being and *finds* its destiny. In this respect at least, he is really quite close to Heidegger. We should, therefore, perhaps turn to the question of the fundamental character of the moral realm itself and ask whether according conceptual primacy not to existential estrangement from an essential moral nature, but rather to estrangement and disruption of the *relationship between existing beings,* might not provide the key to still a third understanding of guilt, one which could stand alongside the formulations of Heidegger and Tillich and serve as the heart of a modern image of man. Just such an understanding can in fact be found in the work of a third great existentialist thinker: the Jewish philosopher Martin Buber.

In the simplest terms, Buber asserts that the choices we make and the actual injuries we commit in living our moral lives have a profound existential significance. These actions in relationship, and not human finitude in the rather abstract sense of the inability to fulfill all of our possibilities to understand fully another's needs or to affirm completely our moral nature, are the roots of our existential guilt. This alternative point of departure for the analysis of guilt thus takes seriously the specific content as well as the fact of guilt-feelings. If, however, it is to provide a truly universal image of man, it must be able to ground our so-called "moral" judgments in a truly existential, supra-cultural framework. A moral ontology which begins with a Self and its possibilities and demands simply the maximum self-conscious realization of these possibilities cannot—and indeed does not really attempt to—provide such a ground. The postulation of an essential human moral nature which reflects transcendent Being can do this, but requires a concession which many moderns are unwilling to make. Buber, however, offers an alternative ontological and philosophical anthropological approach which may provide that grounding without having to introduce prior essentialist assumptions.

Buber shares a number of fundamental positions with both the Heideggereans and Tillich. He is uncompromisingly critical of the reduction of guilt itself to a merely psychological condition or to a trespass against a taboo. Thus, he would join Boss in denouncing those psychotherapies which seek to "free" the patient from his guilt-feelings rather than teaching him how to respond authentically to the call of his conscience. For Buber, the Heideggereans, and Tillich alike, it is ultimately guilt, and not merely guilt-feelings, which must be confronted. In this insistence, at least, there is a link between all of these contemporary approaches and the religious tradition of the West.

The fundamental divergence between Buber and the thinkers we have examined thus far in the understanding of the phenomenon of guilt arises from

Buber's emphasis on the centrality of relationship, not self-realization or self-affirmation, in the life of man.

> Each man stands in an objective relationship to others; the totality of this relationship constitutes his life as one that factuality participates in the being of the world. It is this relationship, in fact, that first makes it at all possible for him to expand his environment (*Umwelt*) into a world (*Welt*). It is his share in the human order of being, the share for which he bears responsibility. An objective relationship in which two men stand to one another can rise, by means of the existential participation of the two, to a personal relation; it can be merely tolerated; it can be neglected; it can be injured. Injuring a relationship means that at this place the human order of being is injured[46]

"Existential guilt," writes Buber, "occurs when someone injures an order of the human world whose foundations he knows and recognizes as those of his own existence and of all common human existence."[47]

It might be objected that Buber's formulation, while certainly diverging from Heidegger's, is not far removed from those of Boss and May who place far greater emphasis on man's relatedness as a fundamental context in which guilt arises. Here, though, we must return to the distinction between guilt as a *condition* attributed to man *qua* man and guilt as the product, as Buber would have it, of a specific injury done to the human order of being in specific relationship.[48] It is not an inability to fulfill all possibilities of relationship, but a particular failure to respond with one's whole being in a particular situation of relatedness, which is the source of existential guilt.

> If I stand up to [the present beings before whom I am placed in the world], concern myself with them in a real way, that is,with the truth of my whole life, then and only then am I "really" there: I am there if I am *there,* and where this "there" is, is always determined less by myself than by the presence of this being which changes its form and its appearance. If I am not really there I am guilty. When I answer the call of present being—"Where art thou?"—with "Here am I," but am not really there, that is, not with the truth of my whole life, then I am guilty. Original guilt consists in remaining with oneself. If a form and appearance of present being move past me, and I was not really there, then out of the distance, out of its disappearance, comes a second cry, as soft and secret as though it came from myself: "Where were you?" *That* is the cry of conscience. It is not my existence which calls to me, but the being which is not I.[49]

Existential guilt is not the guilt of an abstract man; it is "guilt that a person has taken on himself as a person and in a personal situation."[50] The feelings of guilt that arise *in* oneself do not come *from* oneself.They are not the cries of one's potential or essential Self which has not been realized; they are the cries of others whom one has injured or slighted, not because one is inherently incapable of responding more fully, but because one has chosen not to. In so failing to respond, one injures the very foundation of human existence—the fabric of relationship between man and man.[51] That is the core of Buber's position.

To be sure, Buber acknowledges that existential guilt is intimately tied to our relationship to our own being. It is guilt "which arises out of [one's] being and for which he cannot take responsibility without being responsible to his relationship to his own being."[52] The voice of conscience *is* a recognition of the failure to be what we are called to become, and the failure to confront one's existential guilt is a sure way to miss one's destiny. In writing about the life history of a woman he calls Melanie, who under conventional psychoanalytic treatment was eventually "freed" from all of her guilt-feelings (including those rooted in a real existential guilt), Buber concludes that "the price paid for the annihilation of the sting was the final annihilation of the chance to become the being that this created person was destined to become through her highest disposition."[53] But this dimension of "self-realization" is itself intimately bound to the realm of relatedness to others. Melanie lost the chance to be what she was destined to become because in silencing her guilt-feelings she gave up "the possibility of reconciliation through a newly won genuine relationship to her environment in which her best qualities could at the same time unfold."[54] What Buber most vigorously rejects is the notion that existential guilt is ultimately rooted in the relationship of man to his own being, a relationship which Buber regards as only a partial one:

> Heidegger is right to say that all understanding of indebtedness must go back to a primal guilt. He is right to say that we are able to discover a primal guilt. But we are not able to do this by isolating a part of life, the part where the existence is related to itself and to its own being, but by becoming aware of the whole life without reduction, the life in which the individual, in fact, is essentially related to something other than himself.[55]

Buber affirms that the existential guilt which arises from a real injury to a relationship may well be mixed with a neurotic, groundless sense of guilt or with guilt-feelings arising from the violation of a purely cultural taboo.[56] But where existential guilt does exist—and Buber writes that "what I call existential guilt is only an intensification of what is found in some measure wherever an authentic guilt-feeling burns"[57]—it cannot be confronted through any therapy alone. Existential guilt arises when a man recognizes that the injury he has committed in the course of relationship in fact threatens the very basis of his own existence as a human being. It is rooted in the world of relationship, and only there can it finally be confronted. The conscience of the guilty man—a conscience which is grounded in man's ability to achieve distance from himself and judge his own deeds and omissions, his decisions and his failures to decide[58]—can point him towards the path of true reconciliation from which a misguided "psychotherapy" might lead him. The elevated conscience is, for Buber, no mere Freudian super-ego or introjection of the authority of society or religion (though its content may be partially determined by the commands and prohibitions of such authority).[59] It is a voice which calls a man to discover the being he is intended to become by establishing a genuine relationship to the world.[60] For the man who is existentially guilty—and that is, at some point, everyone, since no man, Buber asserts, may utter the words "I am completely guiltless" without presumption[61]—a true confrontation with his conscience should lead to a threefold response: self-illumination, perseverance, and reconciliation:

> From this position a man can undertake the threefold action . . . : first, to illuminate the darkness that still weaves itself about the guilt despite all previous action of the conscience—not to illuminate it with spotlights but with a broad and enduring wave of light; second, to persevere, no matter how high he may have ascended in his present life above that station of guilt—to persevere in that newly won humble knowledge of the identity of the present person with the person at that time; and third, in his place and according to his capacity, in the given historical and biographical situations, to restore the order-of-being injured by him through the relation of an active devotion to the world—for the wounds of the order-of-being can be healed in infinitely many other places than those at which they were inflicted.[62]

Self-illumination and perseverance, a radical acceptance of one's existential guilt and of the need to redirect one's own existence, are the vital first steps, but it is in reconciliation, the new relationship to the world, that this path finds its culmination.

> If a man were only guilty toward himself, in order to satisfy the demanding summons that meets him at the height of conscience, he would only need to take this one road from the gate of self-illumination, that of persevering. But a man is always guilty toward other beings as well, toward the world, toward the being that exists over against him. From self-illumination he must, in order to do justice to the summons, take not one road but two roads, of which the second is that of reconciliation. By reconciliation is understood here that action from the height of conscience that corresponds on the plane of the law to the customary act of reparation. In the realm of existential guilt one cannot, of course, 'make reparation' in the strict sense as if the guilt with its consequences could thereby be recalled, as it were. Reconciliation means here, first of all, that I approach the man toward whom I am guilty in the light of my self-illumination (in so far as I can still reach him on earth) acknowledge to his face my existential guilt and help him, in so far as possible to overcome the consequences of my guilty action. But such a deed can be valid here only as reconciliation if it is done not out of a premeditated resolution, but in the unarbitrary working of the existence I have achieved. And this can happen, naturally, only out of the core of a transformed relationship to the world, a new service to the world with the renewed forces of the renewed man.[63]

This transformed relationship to the world is the heart, not merely the by-product, of a genuine encounter with one's existential guilt. It does not follow from a self-referential commitment to "resolute" existence or from the endeavor to fulfill all one's possibilities and unlock one's potentialities. Transformed relationship is the key to self-renewal and the path into the realm of existence where guilt arises. The help that one can then offer in the course of reconciliation does not mark the summit or limit of human relationship, as does Heidegger's "solicitude." Rather, it serves as an expression of a new fundamental relationship between two beings, between man and man, the kind of primary existential relationship which the guilt-producing act injures.

The great strength of Buber's approach to the problem of guilt lies in its concrete, active character. Within the framework of the Heideggerean ontology of guilt, it is, as we have seen, difficult to translate existential guilt into terms recognizable as referring to specific, concrete actions in the world which may cause or which may meaningfully respond to that guilt. There is an abstractness not only in the identification of guilt as an inherent *state* in human existence, but also in the prescriptions for dealing with that condition even in the most "concrete" formulations of Boss and May. Guilt is recognized by Tillich as resulting from real moral failing, but the resolution of the anxiety caused by that failing is placed ultimately on a religious, not an active moral, plane. For Buber, the connection between existential guilt, both in its genesis and in our response to it, and our day-by-day lives in the world is immediate. There is a merely conventional or cultural dimension to human existence, but there is also a concrete, existentially rooted moral dimension of injury and reconciliation in which real guilt, tied to real decisions and real choices, arises. Buber's approach encompasses the aspect of self-realization, the becoming what we are called to be, and the element of Heideggerean resoluteness in perseverance and self-illumination. Because of his fundamentally different ontology, however, he is more successful than either Heidegger or his followers in placing these dimensions of the existential understanding of guilt in the context of man's relational and responsive participation in the human order of being. In so doing, Buber points the way to a confrontation with the moral *content* as well as the *fact* of our guilt-feelings, and in such a way that this content is itself of existential significance. We ought not, in Buber's view, abandon the therapeutic treatment of the component of our guilt-feelings which may properly be labelled neurotic (i.e., not corresponding to any real injury). But for those feelings of guilt which point back to genuine injuries committed through the failure to respond to another as the situation demanded, only the path of high conscience can lead to the possibility of reconciliation and Self-realization.

Buber would thus agree with Tillich that *Self-* affirmation is impossible for the individual. But, he would contend, *confirmation* of a man's Being in its unique worth and its possibilities grows out of concrete human relationships, and it is the possibility of such confirmation which the path of reconciliation holds out to us. Tillich's emphasis on the response of faith to the anxiety of existential guilt may run the same "danger" as does Heidegger's emphasis on resoluteness: because both seem inclined to regard guilt finally as a state of being expressing the Self's relation to its own "destiny," "possibilities," or "essential nature," rather than as a personal condition reflecting an individual's actual injuries to the human order of being, both approaches may deflect man from responding to his guilt-feelings with efforts toward restitution and rectification in his daily life with others. The Heideggerean and Tillichean understandings of guilt point toward a resolute acceptance or even a surmounting of one's guiltiness that may still anxiety. But could a "leap" into resoluteness or faith not also still the voice of conscience itself.

Buber does not claim that the threefold path of self-illumination, perseverance, and reconciliation will in any sense erase one's existential guilt, nor even that it will surely lead to the establishing of that new relationship to the world which the man of great conscience aspires to. He surely does not claim that such a path will readily provide the spiritual peace that may have come to believers who felt their transgressions forgiven and their guilt expiated. Yet he does not ignore the possibility of response to guilt in faith as well as in conscience. There is a sphere of faith, says Buber, where the guilty man responds in his guilt to his God and enters into relationship with Him, a sphere which corresponds to, and cannot be divorced from, the sphere of high conscience where man attempts his reconciliation with the human order of being.[64] What occurs in the sphere of faith is intensely personal and may be mysterious, but it is not an escape from the realm of the inter-human. It carries, in fact, an important lesson for the man of conscience:

> For the sincere man of faith, the two spheres are so referred to each other in the practice of his life, and most especially when he has gone through existential guilt, that he cannot entrust himself exclusively to either of them. Both,the human faith not less than the human conscience, can err and err again. And knowing about this their erring, both—conscience not less than faith—must place themselves in the hands of grace.[65]

Thus, our confrontation with the guilt-feelings of existential guilt may lead us finally to that contingency of human existence to which traditional religion has always responded. If Buber is correct, the authentic religious response of modern man to his sense of guilt indeed ought not to be merely a glance Heavenward searching for an act of mercy, but the path of high conscience and reconciliation. Here also grace is involved, but so too is a first step in the human world which each of us can undertake if he has the will. It is a step, Buber insists, which can be taken even by those who like Tillich's man in despair and so many contemporary men can acknowledge no transcendent, grace-giving Reality.

> It is not for me to speak in general terms of the inner reality of him who refuses to believe in a transcendent being with whom he can communicate. I have only this to report: that I have met many men in the course of my life who have told me how, acting from the high conscience as men who had become guilty, they experienced themselves as seized by a higher power. These men grew into an existential state to which the name of rebirth is due.[66]

V

Heidegger, Tillich, and Buber are, in the final analysis, united in affirming that modern man must not accede to the temptation to reduce guilt to guilt-feelings alone. Each contends that an image of man which does not take guilt seriously as a supra-cultural, super-psychic, existentially definitive phenomenon cannot do justice to the full meaning of humanness. For each of these thinkers, the identification of how and why man is guilty, and of how he can and should respond to that guilt, is central to the development of a full-fledged image of man. Heidegger, and those therapists who are indebted to him, depict man as a being whose true existence is not given to him, but must be taken over by him and directed toward authentic Self-hood. Tillich focuses on the interplay of man's being with the threat of non-being which is both the mark of his finitude and the ultimate source of his anxieties of guilt and self-condemnation. Tillichean man is estranged from his essential nature and cannot, therefore, affirm himself by himself. But he can open himself to the power of Being-itself which overcomes the threat of non-being and accepts man in spite of his guiltiness. Buber locates man in an order of being constructed out of inter-human relationship. The man who ruptures this order can also help to reweave it, and by restoring the fabric of relationship thereby becomes more fully the Self which only emerges from relationship.

Is there here an image of man which might serve as the focus for a new civilizational world-view? Do Heidegger, Tillich, and Buber point the way to a possible renewal of the traditional religious universe and its world-view? The Heideggerean image of man seems at best an invitation to *develop* a comprehensive world-view; its "openness" may well be both its greatest virtue and potentially its greatest danger for modern man (the compatibility in Heidegger's own mind between his thought and Nazi Politics ought to serve minimally as a warning). Buber and Tillich offer images of man which in the context of their own philosophies do serve as the centers of a broad picture of the world and the place of man within it. What is more, of course, this picture is for each derived in large measure from the Western religious tradition. In a sense, both Tillich and Buber are "translators" of that tradition: there is a genuine link between Tillich's "acceptance of being accepted" and the classical teaching of faith in God's forgiving grace, and similarly between Buber's path of reconciliation and the Jewish understanding of *t'shuvah,* the "turning" which constitutes true repentance.

The question, finally, is whether any translation is possible for modern man, and if so, how faithful to the original it can be. The great strength of the classical religious image of man lay, perhaps, in the very comprehensiveness of the picture of which it was a crucial part. The traditional religious world-view was able to locate man in a network of relationships which embraced everything from the dynamics of his personality to his destiny in the entire sweep of time and space. It is this kind of picture which modern secularized understandings of man and the universe seem so infrequently capable of providing. The response to this loss cannot in all probability be a wholesale return to the world-view of the past and perhaps not even the immediate affirmation of an equally comprehensive one in the present. Rather, it seems, we must try to build an ever more embracing picture through a continual confrontation with the reality we encounter in and around ourselves which mines each experience for its deepest and fullest existential significance.

It is in this context that modern man's encounter with his guilt-feelings might prove to be extraordinarily important.[67] The merit of Buber's understanding of the origins and place of guilt in human existence is that it points in its own right towards a comprehensive, multi-relational image of man. The experience of guilt, for Buber, can open the gate not only to a new relationship to one's Self and its potentials, nor even to one's Self in its essence and the ultimate power of Being which grounds all finite Being, but also to a new relationship to each and every form of Being which one encounters. Guilt, the rupture of the order of Being, and reconciliation, the repair of that order, are both parts of the life of dialogue. The very essence of this life is its recognition of the primacy of the concrete, its holding out to man the possibility of both Self-realization and faith, but only through the day by day effort to construct a world of genuine relationship between man and man.

If Buber is indeed correct in his understanding of the existential significance of our experience of guilt, we need not rush to embrace a new comprehensive world-view in order to make our lives meaningful—though we may in fact discover such a world-view along the way. What Buber suggests is that we do return to at least one crucial insight of Biblical man: that our guilt-feelings speak to us with the voice of one-who-is-present, a voice which calls us not only to concern for our own fate, but to a renewed life of action and trust in the world which is given to us and which we must at the same time continually recreate. If such a voice can indeed be heard, then guilt may once again become for us a profound imaging experience, one which in its very challenge to whom and what we are may help us envision and become what we are intended to be.

NOTES

1 The concept of an "image of man" as used in this paper is derived from the work of Maurice Friedman. It is intended to designate a picture of man which is both descriptive and exemplary, and which men utilize to help understand and become themselves more authentically. For a full discussion of images of modern man in literature, philosophy, and psychology, see Maurice Friedman, *To Deny Our Nothingness* (New York: Delacorte Press. 1967).

2 To speak of "the biblically-rooted, theologically focused world-view of pre-modern civilization" is, of course, to speak in vastly over-simplified terms. Great differences in world-view

certainly did exist among ancient and medieval Christians and Jews. Nevertheless, there were for nearly all such men and women certain common assumptions—belief in a living and revealing God, in the reality of the soul and of sin, in the immortality of man—which defined quite clearly the context in which human beings pursued their earthly ends. It is these widely shared assumptions which are meant by the world-view of pre-modern Western civilization.

3 In this paper "guilt" is used in its broadest sense as referring to the condition of human culpability without implying a specific cause of or reference point (society, God, the law, etc.) for that culpability. Thus, we will not distinguish, for example, between "guilt" and "sin," although such a distinction could be part of a particular approach to the problem of guilt (as it is, to cite one example, with Kierkegaard).

4 As we will use the term in this paper, that which is "existential" is that which relates to human existence in some *fundamental* way, that which tells us something abuot the structure or meaning of that existence which is important and definitive, not merely peripheral or transitory. "Guilt" per se may or may not be "existential" in this sense; a *conception* of guilt, however, even one which denies it existential significance in its own right, constitutes an important existential statement, if only by removing a previously significant phenomenon from the scope of our existential concerns.

5 This is an important consideration. We are asking how a conceptual understanding of guilt relates back to the actual feelings which constitute a specific experience of guilt. In everyday life and in our "common-sense" understanding, these guilt feelings arise from acts of wrongdoing related to a sense of moral responsibility and obligation. Any conception of guilt, no matter how rich in heuristic and analytic potential for the psychologist or the philosopher, must in some way deal with the relationship between the experience of guilt and the moral realm in which guilt is conventionally located.

6 Helen Merrell Lynd, *On Shame and the Search for Identity* (New York: Harcourt, Brace and World, Inc., 1958), p. 23.

7 Sigmund Freud, *The Ego and the Id,* Joan Riviere and James Strachey, trans. (New York: W. W. Norton and Co., Inc., 1960), pp. 42-47.

8 Sigmund Freud, *Civilization and Its Discontents,* James Strachey, trans. (New York: W. W. Norton and Co., Inc., 1961), pp. 79, 81.

9 *Ibid.,* p. 79. The status of all of Freud's meta-psychological "myths" is subject to considerable discussion. For our purposes we will simply consider them as descriptions of ostensibly universal psycho-social processes.

10 Unless, of course, one wishes to reestablish Eros and Thanatos as genuinely trans-psychic realities, although how this is to be done remains to be explored.

11 Martin Heidegger, *Being and Time,* John Macquarrie and Edward Robinson, trans. (New York: Harper and Row, 1962), pp. 331-332.

12 *Ibid.,* p. 331.

13 *Ibid.*

14 *Ibid.,* pp. 312-313.

15 *Ibid.,* p. 333.

16 *Ibid.*

17 *Ibid.,* pp. 333 ff., 343-344.

18 *Ibid.,* p. 344.

19 Martin Heidegger as quoted in Martin Buber, "What is Man?", Ronald Gregor Smith, trans., *Between Man and Man* (New York: The Macmillan Company, 1965), p. 169.

20 Cf. Heiddegger, *Being and Time,* pp. 157-159, 344.

21 Cf. *ibid.,* pp. 308 ff.

22 Medard Boss, "Anxiety, Guilt, and Psychotherapeutic Liberation," *Review of Existential Psychology and Psychiatry,* Vol. II, No. 3 (September, 1962), p. 182; Vol. XX, p. 80.

23 *Ibid.*, p. 186; Vol. XX, p. 84.

24 *Ibid.*, p. 188; Vol. XX, p. 86.

25 *Ibid.*, p. 189; Vol. XX, p. 87.

26 Medard, Boss, *Psychoanalysis and Daseinsanalysis*, Ludwig B. Lefebre, trans. (New York: Basic Books, 1963), p. 270.

27 Boss, "Anxiety, Guilt, and Psychotherapeutic Liberation," p. 189; Vol. XX, p. 87.

28 Boss, *Psychoanalysis and Daseinsanalysis*, p. 271.

29 Boss, "Anxiety, Guilt, and Psychotherapeutic Liberation," p. 194; Vol. XX, p. 92.

30 *Ibid.*, p. 191; Vol. XX, p. 89.

31 Boss, *Psychoanalysis and Daseinsanalysis*, p. 254.

32 It is true, of course, that there is a strand of the Western religious tradition which has always placed great emphasis on "original sin" as implying that man's condition of guiltiness is totally beyond his own power to alleviate. This interpretation of the Biblical teaching is not, however, definitive for all of Christianity or Judaism. More important, even this assertion of a primary guiltiness inherent in the very fact of being human did not prevent either Judaism or Christianity from developing quite specific catalogues of concrete actions which resulted in incurring guilt and which demanded specific acts of penitence or retribution. It is the fact that Heidegger and Boss lack a clear, trans-subjective set of criteria for defining guilt-incurring acts which most obviously separates them from the classical Western religious tradition.

33 Rollo May, "Some Comments on Existential Psychotherapy," *The Worlds of Existentialism*, Maurice Friedman, ed. (New York: Random House, 1964), p. 449.

34 *Ibid.*

35 *Ibid.*

36 Paul Tillich, *The Courage To Be* (New Haven: Yale University Press, 1952), p. 51.

37 *Ibid.*, p. 52.

38 This is where Tillich departs from the Heideggerean and orthodox psychoanalytic framework. For Tillich, what man is supposed to become is not defined in purely existential terms, nor the contents of the conscience purely psycho-social in origin. Man has, in his view, an essential structure of Being, from which essential norms and principles are derived. The voice of conscience is, therefore, a voice from something which stands over against our estranged existential Being as something actual, not merely potential: namely, our essential nature. This essential structure is rooted in transcendent reality, and thus, the estrangement of existence from essence which defines the human condition defines at the same time a religious situation—man estranged from transcendent Being.

39 Tillich, p. 52.

40 *Ibid.*

41 *Ibid.*, p. 53.

42 *Ibid.*, pp. 74-75.

43 Paul Tillich, "Existentialism and Psychotherapy," *Review of Existential Psychology and Psychiatry*, Vol. 1, No. 1 (January, 1961), p. 14; Vol. XX, p. 45.

44 Tillich, *The Courage To Be*, p. 54.

45 *Ibid.*, pp. 76-77, 164-165. Although our discussion has been based almost entirely on *The Courage To Be*, Tillich's treatment of guilt in his *Systematic Theology* would not seem to necessitate any alteration in our conclusions. Indeed, in the *Theology*, Tillich's approach to guilt is almost entirely devoid of concern for its explicitly moral character.

46 Martin Buber, "Guilt and Guilt Feelings," Maurice Friedman, trans. *The Knowledge of Man*, Maurice Friedman, ed. (New York: Harper and Row, 1965), p. 132.

47 *Ibid.*, p. 127.

48 This might be seen as a variant of the theological argument: do we sin because we are sinners, or are we sinners because we sin? For Buber, it is the latter which appears to be the case.

49 Martin Buber, "What is Man?" Ronald Gregor Smith, trans., *Between Man and Man* (New York: The Macmillan Company, 1965), pp. 166.

50 Buber, "Guilt and Guilt Feelings," p. 126.

51 This identication of relationship as the foundation of a fully *human* existence is, of course, the central theme of all of Buber's writing. For the most concise exposition of this position see Buber's essay "Distance and Relation," Ronald Gregor Smith, trans., *The Knowledge of Man*, Maurice Friedman, ed. (New York: Harper and Row, 1965), pp. 59-71.

52 Buber, "Guilt and Guilt Feelings," p. 135.

53 *Ibid.*, p. 129.

54 *Ibid.*

55 Buber, "What is Man?" p. 166.

56 Buber, "Guilt and Guilt Feelings," p. 127.

57 *Ibid.*

58 *Ibid.*, p. 134.

59 Buber does not deny the necessity of maxims and norms for continuity in human life, nor does he deny that the specific forms these may assume are in large measure shaped by a society and its culture. He would argue, however, that behind all such norms lie moments of real relationship in which these were first perceived, no matter how they were subsequently framed and transmitted. Further, and most crucial, in each new situation of genuine personal responding, these norms can and must be set aside in favor of true attentiveness to the call of the concretely existing other upon oneself. Thus, the conscience finally recognizes as the source for its demands not simply cultural norms which have been introjected, but a real and specific demand placed upon the person in the particular situation of relatedness. In this way, the contents of conscience are influenced by the culture (since we bring everything we are to the moment of meeting), but not created by or limited by that culture. Conscience, per se, is mostly certainly not, as far as Buber is concerned, a merely psycho-cultural phenomenon in any case.

60 Buber, "Guilt and Guilt Feelings," pp. 134-135.

61 *Ibid.*, p. 141.

62 *Ibid.*, p. 136.

63 *Ibid.*, p. 147.

64 *Ibid.*, p. 133.

65 *Ibid.*, p. 148.

66 *Ibid.*

67 The experience of guilt can be understood as a potential "touchstone of reality," to borrow Maurice Friedman's terminology. Even if we are unable to interpret the experience in terms of a pre-conceived world-view, the effort to come to grips with guilt-feelings may itself stimulate new insights into the nature of reality (including ourselves) which can be extended into other dimensions of human experience. For a full exposition of the concept of a "touchstone of reality," see Maurice Friedman, *Touchstones of Reality* (New York: E. P. Dutton and Co., Inc. 1974).

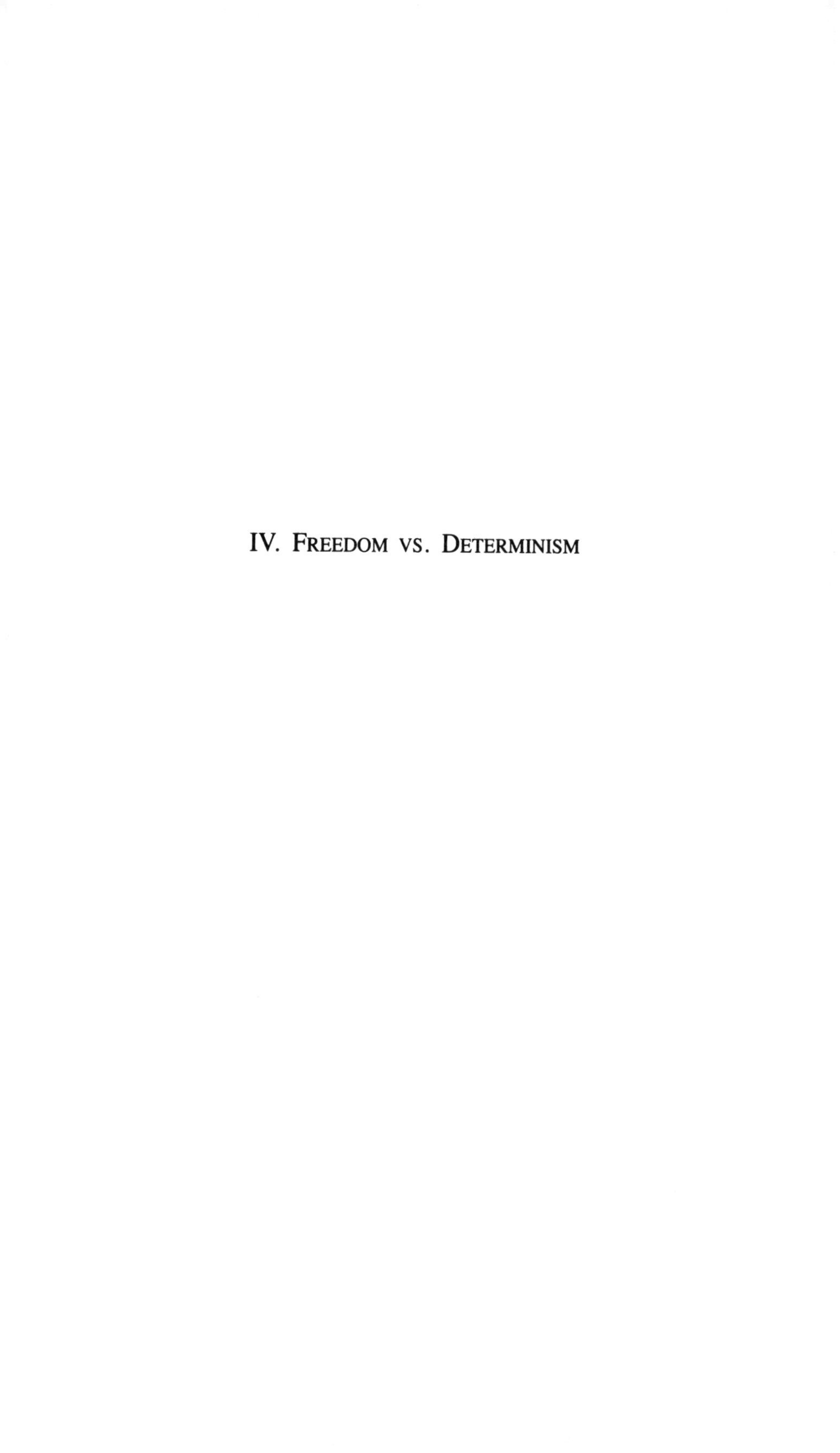

IV. Freedom vs. Determinism

Man's Freedom: Freud's Therapeutic Goal

MIGUEL ITURRATE

"The fact remains that I am free, not in spite of, or on the hither side of, these motivations, but by means of them." *Maurice Merleau-Ponty*

Psychoanalytic conceptions, and the obvious importance given to interpretation in their therapeutic applications, make us understand that human behavior is not only conditioned, but that it depends upon the *meaning* that men give to the things of the world. Consequently, human behavior cannot be understood when thought of as a mere mechanical process. It must be understood as depending upon the *constitution of meaning,* as a characteristic human process, according to which the human subject acts and behaves in the world. Constitution of meaning, on the other hand, cannot be explained on the basis of the blind and unchangeable necessity of nature, expressed by physical laws. Constitution of meaning, on the contrary, reveals that inasmuch as the subject is not confined by physical laws of nature, he is the one who, by means of his initiative, introduces variance and uncertainty into the world.

Free from the inexorable bond of physical laws, man as a subject is *free for* his self-realization in coming to be the meaning-giver in the unique structure which is accurately described as *dialectical situation* within the horizon of the life-world by some phenomenologists. Thus, in understanding man as meaning-giver, psychoanalysis reveals *man's freedom* too. Under this standpoint at least, Merleau-Ponty's idea that psychoanalysis and phenomenology complement each other, comes to be fully confirmed. [1]

TWO ANTIPODES: DETERMINISM AND INDETERMINISM

Merleau-Ponty's description of *scientism,* which distinguishes between scientism as a widely prevalent philosophy of science and science per se,[2] is dramatically confirmed by the scientistic stand on the question concerning man's freedom. Scientism denies man's autonomy vis-à-vis the fixed, determined and undeviating flux of events in nature. Scientism concludes that the answer to the question as to whether or not man is free must be negative: *There is no human freedom.* Scientism's reasoning is perfectly clear: if we want to enjoy the advantages of science, *we must assume* that man's behavior is determined, and *we must be prepared to adopt the* working model of behavior prescribed by science.[3]

Burrhus Frederic Skinner, one of the leading behaviorists of our time, proposes the foundations of *scientistic determinism* in unequivocal terms on the basis of these two assumptions. Science is characterized by him as a "set of attitudes" involving several decisions. One of them is the decision to deal with *facts* which means that any thoughts concerning a subject or subjective factors are to be excluded. Naturally, the only facts to be considered are those where we can find uniformities that confirm the existence of lawful relationships among events of nature. Thus science advances from the mere collection of laws to systematic arrangements that yield the "model" for its subject matter. The purpose of such a scientific system, which is also the purpose of the laws, is to enable us *to handle* the subject matter more efficiently. "By predicting the occurrence of an event we are able to prepare for it. By arranging conditions in ways specified by the laws of a system, we not only predict, we control: we 'cause' an event to occur or to assume certain characteristics."[4]

Starting from those premises, Skinner develops his ideas about a science of behavior, where man is pictured as a true robot whose conduct is to be completely determined by external conditions. The stimulus-response schema originated and perfected by reflexology has shown, according to Skinner, that the control of behavior "has passed from an hypothetical inner entity to the external environment."[5] Skinner's science of behavior turns out to be an attempt to establish the proper techniques to control and "cause" human affairs. Given Skinner's "set of attitudes," consciousness, meanings, the whole dynamism of intentional life, and the subject itself all recede into the field of unsubstantial speculation that has little or nothing to do with *the so-called scientific decisions and assumptions that pre-establish how the psychic life of man and man himself must be understood*. It is not necessary for us to prolong these comments on scientism. The scientistic point of view was presented here only in order to situate, in the contemporary scene, the question concerning man's freedom.

According to *indeterminism,* as opposed to determinism, man is free. Just as in presenting determinism we prescinded from its different historical forms and used only one influential contemporary theory as an example, in turning our attention to indeterminism we will consider only Jean Paul Sartre's radical affirmation of *absolute freedom*. Here again, the purpose is to situate the psychoanalytic disclosure of man's freedom and its philosophical implications vis-à-vis contemporary points of view.

Our examination of Sartre's notion of absolute freedom leads us to the theme of man as an I-subject. Sartre, the phenomenologist, begins by characterizing man as consciousness understood as consciousness of something different from itself. But for Sartre, this consciousness understood as self-presence, turns out to be *a for itself which*—in contrast with the *in-itself* which is not consciousness and which is full of it-self as being—is understood as a "decompression of being" because, according to Sartre, self-presence excludes identity and coincidence with self. Man is thus thought of as not being what he is.[6] Accordingly, man is at a distance from himself in his own immanence, which means "that an impalpable fissure has slipped into being."[7] The fact that human reality is characterized by a "lack of being" is made evident by *desire* which moves man beyond himself in search of something.[8] As we see, Sartre was unable to understand, first, that consciousness' self-presence can mean that the self is present to itself by identity, that is, without distance, and that the manner in which the body is present in consciousness reveals that not even man's body is at a distance from the subject. Secondly, Sartre was unable to understand that man's opening to the not-self through desire can be, rather than a perpetual lack in man, a means of fulfillment which, understood in terms of intentionality, enables man to assume his unique position in the world.

What is it, according to Sartre, that separates the subject, the for-itself- from itself? Sartre's answer to this question is plain and simple: an emptiness, the pure negative that, as a hole in being, is nothing but a negation of being. Thus, "human reality is being in so far as within its being and for its being it is the unique foundation of nothingness at the heart of being."[9] Consequently, as pure facticity, the for-itself *is* only in the manner of an event.[10] The for-itself is *nihilation,* the generation of not-being which is evident primarily in interrogation, destruction and negative judgment. As a matter of fact, in asking any question, Sartre contends, man actually nihilates the being about which he posits the question. This happens because through *interrogation* man situates that being in a neutral zone between being and not-being inasmuch as either a positive or a negative answer is possible.[11] Sartre contends that in assuming the attitude of interrogation, man is actually nihilating himself. Sartre contends that man is dissociating from being in asking any question: otherwise man would not be open to the possibility of the not-being which could be revealed by a negative answer.[12] Man's nihilation of the world is no less evident in *destruction* which is possible because man is aware of the possibility of a thing's possibility of not-being, and only because man is aware of this possibility.[13] According to Sartre, the *negative judgment* also reveals how man introduces nothingness into the world. If, for instance, I go to a cafe to meet Peter and I realize that Peter is not there, I acknowledge non-being in my judgment: Peter is not here.[14] In other words, non-being, nothingness appears in the world because there is man. *Nihilation is what enables man "to isolate and determine existents—i.e., to think them."*[15]

As pure facticity, i.e., as nihilating-nothingness, man, however, is not nothingness in general, but always the nothingness of a particular being, of *this* in-itself, upon which, it may be said, man depends, inasmuch as the for-itself "is in no way an autonomous substance."[16] Man is the "non-substantial absolute" that merely reflects a particular in-itself and thus makes it possible that appearing occurs, that is, so that it be actually appearing, *phenomenon.*[17] Now man, reduced to this "absolute lucidity," reveals himself *as freedom* as far as he is not what he is, as far as he is not the massive in-itself, as far as he is pure for-itself. By not being what he is, "in freedom the human being *is* his own past (as also his own future) in the form of nihilation."[18] Thus, free from the past that could influence him, man is *also free for* the future, because he is, precisely, nothingness between *his* action and whatever could be a motive, thus rendering any motive completely ineffective.

Sartre conceives of freedom not as a quality of man but rather as man's very essence or, better, as that because of which man's essence is in his own hands.[19] For Sartre, man is the one being in whom existence precedes essence,[20] which means that consciousness is in fact a lack of being *before* making itself by choosing, without any motive, between possibilities of being open to it. This seems to suggest that there are apparently some *limits* to man's freedom, derived from factual situations, birth, sexuality, death, etc., that man cannot escape.[21] Sartre, however, explains that situations decide nothing, but rather are only challenges to man to decide. Thus, for instance, the slave, even though in chains, is still free, because he can either accept his condition of slavery or decide against his fate and think of freedom. "The freedom which is *my* freedom remains total and infinite."[22]

Man's absolute freedom, however, does not mean the reign of caprice.[23] According to Sartre, every human action implies an original project—man's lack of being is basically a desire of being—and must be understood as a free choice attempting to attain a fundamental purpose through the mediation of the aims proper to particular actions.[24] Inspired by Freud, Sartre conceives an *existential psychoanalysis* as a way of understanding human behavior which seeks, in every instance of behavior, the manner in which that instance of behavior is an attempt to accomplish man's fundamental project,[25] namely, *to be the in-itself-for-itself,* that is a consciousness that would be the foundation of its own being-in-itself, "the *Ens causa sui,* which religions call God." Sartre finds this idea to be contradictory and finds man's fundamental project to be an absurd enterprise: "Man is a useless passion."[26] Thus in trying to demonstrate man's freedom, Sartre literally condemns man to absolute freedom. Between the horns of the determinism-indeterminism antinomy, Freud's psychoanalysis—going back to the things themselves—turns to man's lived experience in order to allow man's lived experience itself to reveal man's freedom.

THE PSYCHOANALYTIC DISCLOSURE OF MAN'S FREEDOM

Regarding the problem of man's freedom, Freud's personal philosophical convictions are clear: under the influence of his professors of medicine in the University of Vienna, Freud became persuaded, early in his career, that man was unconditionally ruled by the laws of nature, as any mere thing found in the world.[27] To admit any kind of breach in the absolute determinism of natural events would be tantamount to having "thrown overboard the whole *Weltanschauung* of science,"[28] declares Freud in keeping with the strict tradition of *scientistic determinism*. "You nourish the illusion of there being such a thing as psychological freedom, and you will not give it up. I am sorry to say I disagree with you categorically over this."[29] This theoretical conviction was supported, in Freud's mind, by the clinical experience dealing with mentally sick people and by what he called the psychopathology of everyday life. In either case, the obvious disaccord between an individual's conduct and concrete reality would appear, through psychoanalytic investigation, to be determined and imposed upon the individual by unconscious factors acting in the mind.

As Merleau-Ponty remarks, however, "Freud's genius is obviously not that of philosophical or exhaustive expression; it resides, rather, in his contact with things, his polymorphous perception of work, of acts, of dreams, of their flux, of counter coups, of echoes, of substitutions, of metamorphoses. Freud is sovereign in this listening to the confused noises of life."[30] And the noises of life that he attested to in his writings undermine the theoretical convictions inherited from his professors of medicine, even though Freud was unable to understand the philosophical dimensions of what he observed. In his essay *The Ego and the Id*—the last of his major theoretical works[31]—Freud states that the purpose of the psychoanalytical treatment of mental disturbances is not to attempt an impossible abolition of all pathological reactions, but rather to attempt "to give the patient's *ego freedom* to decide one way or the other."[32] He thus confirmed certain consequences which follow from his definite conception of the libido, which turns out to be, despite Freud's own philosophical convictions, the psychoanalytic affirmation of man's freedom.

Psychic energy is presented by Freud, in this metapsychological paper, as a basic *neutral energy* in the sense that it appears as an energy which is undetermined or indifferent by itself—*indifferente Energie* is Freud's characterization—in regard to any particular aims or objects.[33] Hartmann describes this indifferent energy as energy which belongs to the self as a whole, and constitutes the self in the state *of primary narcissism,*[34] energy which is the dynamic openness of the self—operative intentionality—thanks to which the self is in a context of respectivity with things found in the world. This indifferent energy, active as psychic life itself, is actually *libido*[35] which is employed by the three structural factors of the self, Id, Ego and Superego, and directed by them towards definite aims and objects in accord with the three levels that psychoanalysis distinguishes in psychic life.[36]

Understood as free and indifferent energy, *primary narcissistic libido* is, firstly, employed as *Id-libido* by the Id, which functions in such a way as to give psychic expression to the biological needs of the self as an incarnated-I. This Id-libido is the impulsive energy that appears in the form of *instinctual drives* which are determined in regard to aims and objects by the physiology of the body. Thus the source of a drive is always an organic process that, obeying the laws of nature, imposes upon the Id-libido its *sexual character*. This sexual libido, the purpose of which is to restore the homeostatic equilibrium of the organism, aims *necessarily,* under the rule of the *pleasure principle,* at securing pleasure in some part of the body by means of an object—the Id's object-choice—which represents, for the Id, nothing but pleasure to be attained or displeasure to be avoided.

There can be no doubt that *on the level of the Id we cannot speak of man's freedom*. All of the Id's drives are determined necessarily by the physiology of the body, ruled by the laws of nature. *Neither free from* its own physiological needs, *nor free for* acting differently, the Id, for instance, cannot but categorically demand fluids when they are required by the organic processes of the body: the self cannot but be thirsty. In this respect, from the standpoint of the psychic processes of the Id, we may say that man, just as is any mere thing found in the world, is *part* of the world.

The actual satisfaction of the physiological needs, however, and the concurrent sexual pleasure aimed at by the Id, necessarily require *the intervention of the Ego* because the Ego is the self's only structural factor that has direct access to real things found in the world. The Ego's intervention for the satisfaction of the Id's drives presents some characteristics that can only be understood if one affirms *a fundamental autonomy of the Ego* which shows man's freedom.

In the first place, the fundamental psychic energy of the self, *primary narcissistic libido,* must be employed now by the acting Ego as *Ego-libido* in its own processes of directing the Id-libido toward real objects. Thus, thanks to the intervention of the Ego, the Id-libido becomes *object-libido* inasmuch as it is now employed in such a way as to cathect a real object This indicates, first, that the Ego has its own libido, still indifferent and not sexualized like the Id-libido, as libido available to the Ego in the fulfillment of its proper functions; secondly, that the Ego determines such a libido to be employed in this particular function of providing the Id's drive with a real object; thirdly, that the Ego exerts control over the Id-libido as to perform its actual cathectization of a real object. All this reveals the Ego's autonomy in regard to the handling of its own libido, and the Id's necessary submission to the Ego in order to have access to real objects. Now, according to psychoanalysis, the Ego provides the Id-libido with a real object in three different ways: by direct, by substitutive and by indirect satisfaction, which are immediately related to the problem of man as the meaning-giver in the world.

In instances of *direct satisfaction,* the Ego satisfies the Id's drive with the real object that, producing pleasure in some part of the body, adequately satisfies the physiological need. Consequently, inasmuch as *the meaning "object of direct satisfaction,"* given by the Ego to a thing, depends on the physiological need that the Id's drive represents, as part of the subjective *a priori,* the Ego is *not free from* the requirements of the Id's drive in this case, although it is *free for giving* such a meaning to one object or another in a field of objects. Despite this inevitable submission to the Id, the Ego thus demonstrates another type of control over the Id, besides those previously indicated, and thus demonstrates another way in which it is autonomous with respect to the Id. Even though the Ego must obey the Id in giving an object the meaning "object of direct satisfaction," it has, nevertheless, the power to decide *which object* is to satisfy the libidinal demand directly. Furthermore, the Ego is also able to impose a postponement of the immediate satisfaction demanded by the Id. The reason for the postponement may be the fact that such an object is not available at the moment, or it may be the fact that other circumstances make the postponement advisable. In any case, this postponement indicates that, although directed by the Id to confer such a meaning, the Ego retains, however, a certain autonomy and control over the Id.

In instances of *substitutive satisfaction,* the Ego provides the Id's drive with satisfaction by means of an acceptable object that substitutes for the Id's own unacceptable object-choice. This manner of satisfaction displays the Ego's autonomy as regards the Id in a new fashion. The Ego is now able to exert, not only the controls indicated in the case of direct satisfaction, but also is able, first, to effectively oppose the Id's libido by actively denying the drive any access to consciousness by means of subjecting the drive to *repression,* and second, *to change the object* demanded by the Id even though the aim intended by the drive cannot be changed. The Ego is able to change the object demanded by the Id by means of the Ego's *defense mechanisms* which preserve the repression imposed upon the Id. This capability *to change the object* of the Id's drive, either on the basis of the Superego's norms, or on the basis of the requirements of external reality, or finally, on the basis of its own interests, clearly demonstrates an autonomy of the Ego which, in regard to the object, appears as *freedom from* the imposition of the Id's object-choice, and *freedom for determining the meaning of a thing as object for substitutive satisfaction* of the Id's drive. Now, if we consider the *why* of the Ego's substitution of one object for another, we realize that the Superego's norms, or the requirements of external reality, or finally, the Ego's own interests, *do not determine* the Ego, but are *only motives* for the Ego's decision, that is, although they are certainly antecedents to the substitution, they operate only by offering the Ego a meaning and *become effective only when* they are taken up by the Ego's own act.

Finally, in instances of *indirect satisfaction,* the Ego provides the Id's drive with satisfaction by means of an object that has nothing to do with sexuality, an object that belongs on the level of the Ego interests. The Ego's autonomy, in regard to the Id and its control over the Id are conclusively demonstrated by the process of *indirect satisfaction.*

By means of appropriating as Ego-libido the primary narcissistic libido, which by itself is indifferent as regards aims and objects, the Ego is able to relate to the kind of things found in the world which, as objects, serve as what psychoanalysis names *Ego-interests.* According to Freud, in giving the Id's drives one of these objects, the Ego performs a real transformation of the Id-libido.[37] First, the Id-libido is desexualized. Otherwise it could not be referred to a non-sexual aim. Second, the Id-libido becomes Ego-libido. Otherwise it could not be directed by the Ego towards the Ego's own interests. Thus the Ego *is able to change both the aim and the object* of the Id-libido, by subjecting it to the process of *sublimation*. This transformation of the Id-libido into Ego-libido is understood by Freud on the basis of the process of primal identification: By means of primal identification, the Ego "becomes" the object which is an Ego-interest. The process then proceeds as if the Ego were offering itself to the Id's drive as a lovable object: "Love me now, because I am the good object." The Id-libido then, abandoning the Id's object-choice, may be called *secondary narcissistic libido* because it becomes indifferent libido, desexualized, at the service of the Ego and its interests, just as the primary narcissistic libido is indifferent libido at the service of the whole self.[38]

This conception of indirect satisfaction and of the process of sublimation presents the Ego as not only *free from* the Id's impositions, but also *free for* changing the Id's own aims and objects, and thus signifies that *the Ego's freedom* does consist in its ability to change some factual situations within the internal reality of the self. At the same time, the Ego's freedom appears necessarily *conditioned* by all the factors that belong to the Id because it consists, precisely, in changing the flux of events that, otherwise, ought to develop by the rule of the laws of nature that determine the processes of the Id as the psychic representatives of physiological processes belonging to the I-body. Thus the Ego's freedom, such as psychoanalysis reveals it, is not absolute freedom, but *freedom in a situation, relative freedom, in so far as it is conditioned* by the whole constellation of factors that constitute the internal reality of the self as the subjective *a priori,* not to mention the factors that belong to external reality as the objective *a priori,* inasmuch as all such are the necessary *a priori* conditions for all possible experience. *Man's dialectical situation is the only horizon where man's freedom can be real freedom.*

If we consider the external reality with which the Ego deals in the process of primal identification, we realize that those factors that belong to the dimension of *culture of values,* mainly as norms of conduct that rule the relationships of men living in society, are particularly important. Strongly cathectized, because of the circumstances of the infantile development of the individual, these internalized norms of conduct, with which the Ego has identified, have the character of *commands and prohibitions* with which an external authority governed infantile behavior. This is the origin of the *Superego,* peculiarly conditioned by the parental images, that comes to exert influence upon the Ego in the form of *the motive force of what must be* at work in the constitution of meanings. Taking into consideration the external conditioning exerted by *the pre-given field of objects* belonging to the objective *a priori,* we recognize here another internal conditioning factor, besides those indicated by the examination of the Id's influences upon the Ego, that belongs to the subjective *a priori*. As an unconscious and preconscious mode of conditioning the constitution of meaning by the Ego, this influence on the Ego reveals that *the self is actually a bearer of intentions* that distinguish the individual's personal style and thus explain what we may call the *character* of a man, understood as his habitual manner of behaving. Once again, the factors that constitute the pre-given field of objects and those that characterize the individual as a bearer of intentions, are antecedents that only act upon the Ego as *motives* inasmuch as they do not determine the changes introduced by the Ego in the flux of the psychic processes. They may become effective in the determination of a meaning *only because and only when* the Ego takes up one of them in its own act of constituting the meaning of an object. It is the Ego which makes a determined object emerge from the pre-given field of objects as the Ego's own object, and it is the Ego which, by singularizing an object as its own, introduces a change in the self's internal reality by making an intention prevail among the intentions which constitute the self as a bearer of intentions.

Freud characterized the development of the human personality on several occasions by saying that it consists of the gradual predominance of the reality principle over the pleasure principle in human behavior.[39] This actually means that the individual's behavior is completely ruled by the pleasure principle until the Ego begins to differentiate itself from the Id and to develop its own proper functions. Secondary processes of the Ego are then distinguished from the primary ones that characterize the Id, and human action begins to appear as *rational* in so far as the Ego acts by considering different aims and means to attain them, side effects or consequences, and the relative merits of different goals in the light of both internal and external reality.[40] Ideally, the development of these processes would give the Ego complete control over the Id in such a manner that it would always be able to give the Id's libido either direct or indirect satisfaction by means of sublimation. Such an ideal development, however, is not accomplished. This ideal development is impossible because there are inborn constitutional limitations and because the concrete circumstances of the individual's development are never so favorable as to allow such complete control over the Id. The fact is that *internal conflicts* do appear and the Ego, in order to fulfill its synthesizing function, must develop its *defense mechanisms* and substitutive ways of discharging the Id's libido. This development helps explain how certain *constitutional limitations* and eventual *weaknesses of the Ego,* permit *irrational action,* characterized by being predominantly emotional and directed by actually unconscious instinctual purposes under the rule of the pleasure principle,[41] to break into human behavior at times and impair the functions of the Ego and the self's adjustment to reality. Accordingly, *in these circumstances,* the meanings given by the Ego to things in the world come to be not merely conditioned, but *determined by unconscious factors.* These meanings are unrealistic. They manifest themselves in human behavior in different degrees of inadequacy, from the common parapraxes of everyday life to the clearly pathological symptoms of mentally disturbed people. In the light of these considerations, we understand how Freud determined that the goal of psychoanalytic therapy is "to give the patient's *ego-freedom* to decide one way or the other" in fulfilling its role as meaning-giver, and thus to help the Ego master its natural controls over the Id.[42]

The point to be emphasized here, at the conclusion of our exposition of the psychoanalytic revelation of man's freedom, is that man's freedom, from the psychoanalytic standpoint, consists in the fact that *man is able to change some factual situations which—externally pre-given as a field of objects and internally sedimented as a field of intentions—offer him a variety of meanings which challenge him to take up one of them, as his own, by himself.*

MAN'S CONDITIONED FREEDOM

Considering man's freedom, Strasser points out that despite the fact that freedom is one of the important themes of phenomenological thinking, phenomenologists do not make any attempt to prove that man is free.[43] This is the case because human freedom is seen in phenomenology as one of the fundamental data manifest in our ordinary experience and, consequently, as not requiring any proof. We have the experience that we freely decide in some situations, just as we have the experience that we see things in the world with our eyes. Critical reflection upon this experience shows that freedom appears here with *apodictic evidence*.[44] The nonexistence of freedom is inconceivable because the denial of freedom involves unjustified assumptions and unwarranted decisions that distort and contradict the very experience that is to be clarified and understood.

To think of man as completely determined by the laws of physical nature, as *scientistic determinism* does, is to think of him as a mere thing in the world, as a mere result of forces that act of necessity with the same blind constancy as the laws of the physical sciences which register necessary relationships among events of nature. Accordingly, man should not be thought of any more as a subject. Subjective activity, consciousness, intentionality, meanings, etc., should be regarded as misleading words that express nothing real. As B. F. Skinner frankly proposes, we must recognize that scientistic determinism becomes a true matter of faith. Scientistic determinism is based upon the *assumption* that man's behavior must be determined. We must make this assumption if we want to be consistent with the *decision* of adopting the working model of behavior prescribed by physical causality. The worshiper of this faith must accept the validity of human knowledge as regards external experience, in order to found upon its apodictic certitude the constructions of sciences; but, at the same time, he must reject the validity of human knowledge as regards our own internal experience of freedom. For the scientistic faith, it is completely irrelevant that, in both cases, it is the very same perceiver who is aware of external phenomena and who is aware of himself and of his own internal phenomena by being conscious of both types of phenomena. The point is that a fundamental dogma of the scientistic faith commands that all phenomena in the world must be strictly explained by *physical causality,* which actually cannot be applied in the realm of psychic activity proper inasmuch as phenomenological reflection reveals that the relationship between man and things in the world is not a causal relationship but a *dialectical* one, actualized as the subject-object structure in the world.[45]

Freud's conception of the libido as a means of understanding human psychic activity, becomes especially doubtful and suspect in the eyes of the scientistic worshiper, because it implicitly contains the idea that physical causality has nothing to do with the realm of psychic phenomena. Furthermore, once psychic energy is conceived as essentially different from physical energy, the exclusive monopoly of physical causality as a means of understanding the whole of reality is fundamentally eroded in such a way as to make understandable—at least as a matter of principle—the old conception of *ontological causality* sustained by a respectable centuries old tradition.[46] The affirmation that man is an incarnated-I, mind-body, implies the recognition that there is no real obstacle to considering the possibility of two different types of causality at work in the world: physical causality *and* psychical causality. Man himself would thus display both types of causality. Freud's understanding of the libido at work in man seems completely coherent with psychical causality as a means of understanding psychic phenomena as actually *produced by the subject* in mental life. Accordingly, and beyond the physical realm, psychic life and freedom itself could be understood on the basis of causality in man. Thus the affirmation of freedom would not be the denial of causality as scientistic determinism contends, but rather the confirmation of causality as actually ruling the whole of reality, physical *and* psychical. If this is the case, the dichotomy determinism-indeterminism does not represent a real dilemma. First, man's freedom becomes a *special type of determinism* that, characterizing man as the real cause of his decision in the constitution of meaning, precludes indeterminism inasmuch as man, acting as a bearer of intentions, in a pre-given field of objects, determines himself by himself via a process of *self-determination* which involves the rational consideration of factors which contribute to the individual's situation. Second, man's freedom also turns out to be *a special type of indeterminism* inasmuch as the Ego is not determined, as the real cause of man's decision in the constitution of meaning, either by the Id, or by the Superego or finally by external reality. The Ego, as true psychical cause, is determined by *self-determination.* Nothing from outside the Ego determines the Ego causally even though the Id, the Super-ego, and external reality act upon the Ego.

Sartre understood the ultimate meaning of determinism as an attempt to establish that the motives, at work in any of our decisions, actually produce the act of deciding that we perceive in our ordinary experience, in the same way as the physical causes produce their effects.[47] Physical causality, however, is manifestly unable to clarify and explain our experience of deciding freely, and Sartre sees no other alternative than the recourse to the ontological dimension, where he conceives of absolute freedom as man's mode of being for itself. Without abandoning completely the basic notion of ontological causality, Sartre compares his own doctrine of freedom, based on existence, to Descartes', which is founded on reason. Descartes' freedom is understood by Sartre as pure freedom of thought, as freedom to think or not to think. The distinct and clear idea necessarily requires man's assent.[48] This notion of freedom, Sartre remarks, coincides with the traditional Christian conception of freedom, where man is conceived as free, but only for the evil and not for the good, as free for the error but not for the truth. Moreover, this conception attributes absolute freedom to God as the creator of all that is possible, of all truth and of all good. According to Sartre, Descartes has thus given God what actually belongs to man. "Two centuries of crises—crisis of faith, crisis of science—have been required to recover for man this creative freedom that Descartes placed in God."[49] Absolutely free, man becomes an actual creator responsible for the world and for himself as a way of being.[50] Sartre conceives of man, as the meaning-giver, as godlike, and thus man's constitution of meaning, as Merleau-Ponty observes, arguing against Sartre's conception, comes to be thought of as a purely *centrifugal* movement, "indistinguishable from the Kantian idea of a consciousness which 'finds in things only what it has put into them.' "[51]

Psychoanalysis and our own phenomenological reflection coincide in establishing, contrary to Sartre's conception of man's absolute freedom as meaning-giver, that *all constitution of meaning takes place in the dialectical situation where subject and object emerge in any experience*. This means that the constitution of meaning is a *centrifugal and centripetal movement* at the same time, required by the mutual exchange in which the self and the not self conform to each other as subject and object in the world. Man's freedom, therefore, revealed in the constitution of meaning, consists in the fact that man, conditioned and motivated by his own internal reality as a bearer of intentions and by external reality as an actual field of possible objects, is able to decide on one meaning-object. This is essentially how Merleau-Ponty understands Man's conditioned freedom.[52]

First of all, Merleau-Ponty thinks that man's freedom, in order to really be freedom, and to be recognized as such, must stand out against a background from which it is absent. Otherwise we would have absolute intentions immediately followed by real effects, as if the real were that which we think. According to Merleau-Ponty, we recognize freedom only where it comes into play in a decision which accounts for the fact that a particular chosen situation is actually a situation of freedom, that is, a situation which involves an act which contributes to but does not create the situation, and which, even though prepared and intended, is not necessitated by antecedent factors.[53]

In accord with the idea of man as a *bearer of intentions*, Merleau-Ponty describes an inclination or propensity of the kind which, as a manifold of *general intentions*, evaluates the potentialities of external reality as a field of objects in order to make possible the *expressed intention* incarnated by any decision in any concrete situation. Such general intentions have two distinguishing characteristics. First, they do not depend upon one's decision. They are rather the sediment of all the individual's experiences which, constituting the substratum of the unconscious, as Husserl said, act as motivating factors which condition our decisions. Secondly, these general intentions constitute a system in which all possible objects are simultaneously included. These general intentions thus signify an attitude and particular ways of dealing with things which, because of past effects in the individual's experience, have become preferred and favored as habitual modes of acting. This is the *character* of an individual which, once it is known as his personal style, permits us to determine which decision would most probably be made by him in a given situation. "Our freedom," says Merleau-Ponty, "does not destroy our situation, but gears itself to it: as long as we are alive, our situation is open, which implies both that it calls up specially favored modes of resolution, and also that it is powerless to bring one into being by itself."[54]

External reality as a field of objects and man as a bearer of intentions complement each other as perfect correlates. These complementary objects and intentions offer the individual subject a multiplicity of meanings. On the basis of his own decisions, the individual can take up any of these meanings into his life. The fact that things in the world are visible and touchable and the fact that we have eyes and hands to deal with them do not exhaust the relationship between things in the world and man. It is also the case that things in the world constitute the necessary condition for our own personal choices and decisions which transform a field of mere *a priori* dispositions—objective and subjective *a priori*—into an actual concrete situation of freedom.

"What then is freedom?" asks Merleau-Ponty. His answer is: "To be born is both to be born of the world and to be born into the world. The world is already constituted, but also never completely constituted; in the first case we are acted upon, in the second we are open to an infinite number of possibilities. But this analysis is still abstract, for we exist in both ways *at once*. There is, therefore, never determinism and never absolute choice, I am never a thing and never bare consciousness."[55]

NOTES

1 See "Phenomenology and Psychoanalysis, Preface to Hesnard's *L'Oeuvre de Freud*." in *The Essential Writings of Merleau-Ponty*, ed by A.L. Fisher (New York: Harcourt, Brace & World,

Inc., 1969), pp. 81 ff. Also in *Merleau-Ponty and Psychology,* ed. Keith Hoeller (Seattle: Review of Existential Psychology & Psychiatry, 1986), pp. 67-72.

2 See M. Merleau-Ponty: *The Visible and the Invisible,* trans. A. Lingis (Evanston: Northwestern University Press. 1968), pp. 14 ff.

3 Burrhus Frederic Skinner: *Science and Human Behavior* (New York: The Free Press. 1965), p. 6.

4 *Ibid.*, p. 14; see also pp. 12-14.

5 *Ibid.*, p. 49.

6 J.P. Sartre: *Being and Nothingness,* trans. H.E. Barnes (New York: Philosophical Library. 1956), p. 74.

7 *Ibid.*, p. 77.

8 *Ibid.*, p. 88.

9 *Ibid.*, p. 79.

10 *Ibid.*, p. 79.

11 *Ibid.*, p. 5.

12 *Ibid.*, p. 23.

13 *Ibid.*, p. 8.

14 *Ibid.*, p. 10.

15 *Ibid.*, p. 27.

16 *Ibid.*, p. 618.

17 *Ibid.*, p. 619.

18 *Ibid.*, p. 29.

19 *Ibid.*, p. 25.

20 Sartre: *Existentialism* (New York: Philosophical Library, 1947), p. 18.

21 *Being and Nothingness,* p. 548 ff.

22 *Ibid.*, p. 547.

23 *Ibid.*, pp. 452 ff.

24 *Ibid.*, p. 563.

25 *Ibid.*, pp. 568-569.

26 *Ibid.*, p. 615.

27 See E. Jones: *Sigmund Freud: Life and Work* (London: The Hogarth Press. 3 vols. 1956, 1955, 1957), vol. I, pp. 400-402.

28 Freud: *Introductory Lectures,* in *The Complete Introductory Lectures on Psychoanalysis* (New York: W.W. Norton & Company, Inc.), p. 28.

29 *Ibid.*, p. 49.

30 "Preface to Hesnard's *L'Oeuvre de Freud,*" op. cit., p. 82.

31 J. Strachey: Editor's Introduction, in Freud's *The Ego and the Id* (New York: W.W. Norton & Co., Inc. 1962), p. x.

32 Freud: *Ibid.*, p. 40, note 1. Freud himself underlined the word *"freedom."* See also *Analysis Terminable and Interminable,* C.P., vol. 5, pp. 325 ff.

33 *The Ego and the Id,* p. 34.

34 See H. Hartmann: *Essays in Ego Psychology* (New York: International Universities Press Inc., 1964), pp. 192, 287-288.

35 See *The Ego and the Id,* p. 34.

36 We refer here to the levels of the Id, the Ego and Superego with their proper and characteristic cathectizations.

37 See *The Ego and the Id*, p. 20.

38 *Ibid.*, pp. 35-36.

39 *Ibid.*, p. 15.

40 Hartmann: *Ibid.*, p. 49.

41 *Ibid.*, p. 49.

42 See *Analysis Terminable and Interminable*, pp. 325 ff.

43 S. Strasser: *The Idea of Dialogal Phenomenology* (Pittsburgh: Duquesne University Press, 1969), p. 100.

44 See Husserl: *Cartesian Meditations*, trans. D. Cairns (The Hague: Martinus Nijhoff, 1970), pp. 14-16.

45 See my essay "Man as the Meaning-Giver" in *Review of Existential Psychology and Psychiatry*, Vol XIV, No. 2, pp. 63-80.

46 We refer here to the Aristotelian and medieval traditions, where physical and psychical causalities were seen as modalities of ontological causality, exceeding the limits of purely physical causalty imposed by Galileo and reinforced by Humean tradition.

47 *Being and Nothingness*, p. 440.

48 Sartre: *Descartes* (Paris: Trait. 1940), pp. 42ff. This is a selection of Descartes' texts with an Introduction by Sartre.

49 *Ibid.*, p. 51.

50 *Being and Nothingness*, p. 553.

51 Merleau-Ponty: *Phenomenology of Perception*, trans. C. Smith (London: Routledge & Kegan Paul, 1966), p. 439.

52 *Ibid.*, p. 439.

53 *Ibid.*, pp. 436-437.

54 *Ibid.*, p. 442.

55 *Ibid.*, p. 453.

Skinner and Sartre: Towards a Radical Phenomenology of Behavior?[1]

STEINAR KVALE AND CARL ERIK GRENNESS

From a European point of view, the symposium "Behaviorism and Phenomenology: Contrasting Bases for Modern Psychology" (Wann, ed., 1964)[2] reveals some rather astonishing points. First, the opposition of behaviorism to phenomenology implies the latter as a renewed introspective psychology or "experientialism" (Koch). Phenomenology is limited to taking the verbal reports of experimental subjects seriously, or to the study of "pure experience" (see also Brody and Oppenheim, 1966). These views are rather strange, as precisely the radical development of phenomenology by Sartre and Merleau-Ponty has sought to bypass the contrast between "classical" behaviorism and introspectionism. Second, Skinner's radical behaviorism shows some remarkable similarities to Sartre's and Merleau-Ponty's views on psychology. This holds especially for the rejection of the dualistic philosophy inherent in much of contemporary psychological theorizing, and the emphasis upon behavior as the fundamental subject matter of psychology. Third, MacLeod and Rogers, who term their approaches "phenomenological" and "phenomenological-existential," seem rather out of touch with current European developments in this field.

The similarities of Skinner's and Sartre's views on psychology are not as astonishing as they might seem at first sight. Both are competent psychologists, but while Skinner's work is well known, Sartre's contribution to psychology is only now becoming known.[3] In popular thought the name of Sartre is usually associated with slogans as "free will," "choice," exhibited in literary work far removed from the stringent controlling techniques of a Skinnerian laboratory. We shall, however, note two developments which make a confrontation more likely. Of late years Skinner reveals an "extraordinarily libertarian" attitude (Koch) toward the classical behaviorist tenets. Skinner now willingly faces many of the fundamental philosophical problems of psychology, themes which have often been dismissed as "armchair psychology" by his colleagues. Less known is the fact that Sartre in his recent works goes beyond his earlier existentialism and approaches a more materialistic and deterministic position—though dialectically interpreted.

The current American interest in phenomenology and existentialism has mainly been limited to clinical psychologists, who give rather stressed idealistic, subjectivistic and voluntaristic interpretations of the older German phenomenology and existentialism. The radical French version of Sartre and Merleau-Ponty,[4] which we believe is more congenial to American psychology, has been conspicuously left out in the major American introduction to this field: *Existence: A New Dimension in Psychiatry and Psychology* (May, et al., 1958).

The aim of the present paper is to point to some similarities between the radical development of behaviorism by Skinner and the phenomenology of Sartre and Merleau-Ponty. We shall in this context largely bypass their more concrete *thematic* contributions to psychology as well as their specific *methods*, and limit the discussion to their *metapsychological* views on the nature of man's relation to the world. It is precisely regarding some of the fundamental philosophical problems of psychology that the similarities of radical behaviorism and phenomenology are most apparent.

THE ILLUSION OF THE DOUBLE WORLD

Skinner, as well as Sartre and Merleau-Ponty, strongly objects to what may be called "the illusion of the double world," inherent in most of contemporary psychology. It involves the assumption of an "outer," "objective," "physical" world and its "inner," "subjective," "psychological" copy.

This reduplication of the world is manifest in introspectionism, behaviorism, psychoanalysis, and Gestalt psychology. The introspectionists conceived of a kind of "box of consciousness" where sensations entered and were combined with previous images into percepts. The classical behaviorists replaced consciousness by the "black box," and confined themselves to the study of external behavior. Within psychoanalysis there grew up a complex mental apparatus by which the external world was "introjected" into an inner world, and inner complexes were "projected" to the external world, or "converted" to a mechanically conceived body. The Gestalt psychologists, who introduced phenomenology to American psychology, notoriously misunderstood, or were ignorant of, Husserl's intention of a phenomenological philosophy. They assumed the real nature of the inner world to be physiological, and searched for isomorphic copies of the external world.

The current representational theories of neobehaviorism are more sophisticated, but regardless of the ontological or epistemological status which they give the representational constructs, the latter obviously entail a doubling of the world.

> In fact, according to the representational theory, there is on the one hand the world of objective, observable things which transcends psychological activity; on the other hand, there is the psychological world of consciousness where the objective world is represented on an enclosed inner stage (Nuttin, 1955, p. 350).

Both radical behaviorism and phenomenology regard this doubling of the world as contradictory, and unnecessary for a scientific psychology. Logically, this model does not solve the problem it was supposed to answer—the nature of our perception of the world. The explanation of the outer world by an assumed inner world—mental, conceptual or neural—necessarily leads to an infinite regress. Who experiences the inner world? How is the picture on the area striata to be seen?

> The mental image of the psychologist is one thing; what the consciousness of that thing is must still be understood (Merleau-Ponty, 1965, p. 198).

> If the real world is, indeed, scrambled in transmission but later reconstructed in the brain, we must then start all over again and explain how the organism sees the reconstruction (Skinner, 1964, p. 87).

The common physiological explanatory models are radically discarded by Skinner and the phenomenologists. Suppose we were to find a copy of the visual stimulus in the brain, as e.g., indicated by Krech and Crutchfield, who even venture to draw a picture of the object seen in the area striata (1955, p. 169). To such an eventuality Skinner replies that then ". . . we should have to start all over again and ask how the organism sees a picture in its occipital cortex . . . " (op. cit. p. 87).

The explicit rejection of the doubling of the world in contemporary psychology is not whipping a dead horse. Hidden mentalisms as "percept" and "representation" are central terms even within the ranks of behaviorists (see e.g., Osgood, 1953). But they seem unwilling even to consider this a problem. Mowrer, in replying to Nuttin's critique of the doubling of the world in representational models, manifests a common attitude toward attempts at clarifying metapsychological problems "The issues here involved seem somewhat philosophical, i.e., without predictable consequences or testable implications, and therefore need not directly concern us here" (1960, p. 257). The critique against a model of consciousness which is as well illogical as empirically unverifiable, is thus dismissed by maintaining that the counter-argument is too philosophical!

Against the doubling of the world Skinner, Sartre and Merleau-Ponty maintain that perception is no duplicating of the outer world into an inner world. Perception cannot be separated from action. And just as action reaches the world directly, so does perception. The phenomenologists claim further that by discarding what Merleau-Ponty has termed "the prejudice of the objective world," to be discussed later, no inner reduplication is necessary to account for our perception of the world.

> By arguing that the individual simply reacts to its environment, rather than to some inner experience of that environment, the bifurcation of nature into physical and psychic can be avoided (Skinner, 1961a, p. 188).

> It is most convenient, for both organism and psychophysiologist, if the external world is never copied—if the world we know is simply the world around us (Skinner, 1964, p. 57).

> It is the thing itself which I reach in perception (Merleau-Ponty, 1965, p. 199).

> A table is not *in* consciousness—not even in the capacity of a representation. A table is *in* space, beside the window, etc. (Sartre, 1956, p. li).

THE FLIGHT TO THE INNER MAN

A parallel to the illusion of the double world is what Skinner has termed "the flight to the inner man" (1961b, p. 252). Just as psychology had to create an inner world to account for perception, it had to construct an inner man to account for action. This "inner man" is a rudiment of the now unacceptable "soul," but in a disguised form. To be found in many quarters of contemporary psychology, the inner man is especially distinct within psychoanalytic theory with its id-ego-superego conception of man.

Overt behavior is now to be accounted for by assuming an inner man, or to use an expression from the philosopher Ryle, by a "ghost in the machine" (1949). The machine is, of course, the organism. But the hypothesis of a consciousness, or a homunculus, enclosed in the organism and guiding behavior as a pilot guides his airplane, must eventually be discarded from a scientific psychology. On this point there is full agreement between Skinner and the phenomenologists. Just as with the "inner world," the "inner man" explanations lead to an infinite regress. The behavior of the inner man remains to be explained, this must be done by recourse to a new inner man, and so on indefinitely. At some point there must, however, be a subject acting in the world.

Merleau-Ponty thus states "Truth does not 'inhabit' only 'the inner man,' or more accurately, there is no inner man, man is in the world, and only in the world does he know himself" (1962, p. xi). Heidegger has used the term "being-in-the-world" to characterize man (1962); man exists and acts directly in the world. Being-in-the-world is simply man's concrete behavior in his world, his mode of relating to things and man. Behavior is no mere indicator of an inner state, man *is* his behavior to the world.

Skinner justly complains that one rarely finds behavior studied in its own right. Usually behavior is merely regarded as a manifestation or indicator of some mental or conceptual system, which is considered to be the primary subject matter of psychology. Rogers, for instance, talks of " . . . the behaviors which represent these inner variables" (1964, p. 131). Skinner, on the contrary, maintains that "Inner entities or events do not 'cause' behavior, nor does behavior 'express' them" (1961b, p. 253).

Several objections may be raised to such "explanatory fictions," or "mental way stations," as Skinner also calls them. For example, to explain emotional behavior as caused by an emotional state or impulse is meaningless. The only access we have to the emotion of another person is through his behavior—motoric, verbal or physiological. It makes no sense to explain behavior as caused by an emotional state when an emotional state cannot be investigated apart from emotional behavior. Skinner accordingly defines "emotion as a pattern of behavior" (1953, p. 168). Neither does Sartre consider emotions as states of consciousness, but talks of emotional behavior (1948). An emotion is a certain way of grasping the world. In emotions the body changes its relation to the world and the world changes its qualities to the bodily behaving subject.

The point of both radical behaviorism and phenomenology is that an adequate description and analysis of an individual's world and his behavior to the world make the recourse to an "inner man" superfluous. The phenomenologists' solution lies further in dismissing the mechanical conception of behavior, and in giving behavior an intentional interpretation, to be discussed later.

THE PREJUDICE OF THE OBJECTIVE WORLD

Intrinsically tied to the dualism of an outer and an inner world is the impoverishment of the "outer" world into the world of physics. The belief that the world as constructed by the physicist is more "real" than the world we perceive was termed by Merleau-Ponty "the prejudice of the objective world." His main theme was "The Primacy of Perception" (1964a).

My starting-point for believing in the reality of the physical world will always have to be my actual perception of the world as it appears to me.

> All my knowledge of the world, even my scientific knowledge, is gained from my own particular point of view, or from some experience of the world without which the symbols of science would be meaningless. The whole universe of science is built upon the world as directly experienced, and if we want to subject science itself to rigorous scrutiny and arrive at a precise assessment of its meaning and scope, we must begin by reawakening the basic experience of the world of which science is the second order expression. Science has not and never will have, by its nature, the same significance *qua* form of being as the world we perceive, for the simple reason that it is a rationale or explanation of that world (Merleau-Ponty, 1962, p. viii).

The scientist's world is an abstraction which would not be understandable without our basis in the intersubjectively perceived world—"Lebenswelt" as Husserl termed it. It becomes meaningless to assume that perceiving the world should be more subjective than constructing a world with abstract physical entities that we cannot even imagine, that do not have any reality at all, except as phenomena within our cultural world. Analogously, the geographer's map is an abstraction of the countryside where we have first learned what a forest, a mountain or a river is. The map would not be understandable without our primary knowledge of what a countryside is.

Skinner's attitude toward this point is ambiguous. He has seen sharply some of the problems inherent in the prejudice of the objective world.

> Such behavior seems to indicate that the 'perceptual' world—the world as the organism experiences it—is different from the real world . . .

> Thus I may "think" that an object in the sky is a plane only to see a moment later that it is a soaring bird. I may "think" that an object is a square only to find when I shift my position that it is not . . .
>
> There is no reason to regard the first of each of these pairs of reactions a 'perceptual' and the second as a form of contact with the real world. They are different responses made at different times to a common source of stimulation (1953, p. 138-139).

There are a multitude of different behavioral relationships to the world and it is meaningless to choose one as the correct objective approach to the real world. But still, Skinner's belief in the primacy of the physical world seems unshaken. He himself becomes the victim of the prejudice of the physical world when he talks definitely about "the world itself" and asserts that "we operate in one world—the world of physics" (*Ibid*, p. 139). Skinner must then assume that one reaction, namely, the physicists, is a reaction to the "real" world, and that every other perceptual reaction is an illusion, precisely the line of thinking he dismissed above.

To make sure, the phenomenologists in no way deny the existence of the physical world. But they consider the physicist's world as the result of a specific physical measuring, calculating behavior to the world. Correspondingly, our daily meaningful world, "Lebenswelt," appears through our practical actions, within our "natural attitude" (Husserl) toward the world. The phenomenologists see no reason to accord the physicist's world a primacy, or a more objective reality than our perceived world. On the contrary, the physical world is the working out of specific aspects of our perceived world, and is not understandable apart from our lived world (see also Holzkamp, 1965). An understanding of the physicist's concept of color presupposes our perceived world, where we have learned what a color is. The physical correlate of color is itself devoid of color. Interestingly enough, while contemporary physicists are approaching the view that the physical space is a purely theoretical construction, many psychologists still impute it an objective reality.

The world of the physicist and our daily perceived world are, to be noted, not two absolutely separate worlds. Precisely today, with the increasing popularization of scientific theories, our perceptual world becomes increasingly "scientific." Thus, we may not merely hear a sudden loud bang, but hear an airplane breaking through the sound barrier. Or the psychoanalyst may not "see" disturbed behavior in a patient, but "a conflict between the id and the superego."

The pointing out of the prejudice of the objective world makes some of the common objections to Skinner's system understandable. Koch and Rogers both reproach Skinner for replacing the rich inner experience with a simple external stimulus.

> This thinnest of all metaphors—'stimuli' . . . —now becomes all of experience (Koch, 1964, p. 162).

> The inner world of the individual appears to have a more significant influence upon his behavior than does the external environmental stimulus (Rogers, 1964, p. 125).

These objections to Skinner are to the point in that Skinner is systematically ambiguous when applying the term "stimulus," vacillating between a physicalist and a psychological interpretation. If the world is physically conceived, the replacing of our rich experience by stimuli is certainly an impoverishment of our world, and some inner construction may appear necessary to account for our world of daily experience. But by discarding the prejudice of the physical world, the "outer" world becomes our meaningful, lived world. The world, the meaningful stimulus, *is* our experience of it, and no mystical doubling of the world is necessary to account for our perceived world.

In this connection a point concerning the current American interest in phenomenological and existential philosophy may be mentioned. Rogers' position, manifested in the statement above, demonstrates a downright ignorance of a basic issue of phenomenology and existentialism—the overcoming of the dualism between an inner and outer world by Heidegger's characterization of man as being-in-the-world. Still, Rogers now terms his position "phenomenological-existential" (1964, p. 129).

Koch, although confusing phenomenology with "experientialism" (1964, p. 34) made some apt remarks to this issue.

> There are woolly revivalist overtones—a disposition to accept in advance an intellectual object the properties of which have hardly been cognized. And there are indications that existentialism is tending to be viewed, in some global sense, as an *external source of authority* for whatever ideas the viewer already owns that he feels to be unconventional. There is a marked parallelism here with the tendency of the neobehaviorists to seek support for attitudes which *they* had already embraced by a similarly global appeal to a prestigeful philosophical movement; in that instance, logical positivism (*Ibid.*, p. 36).

Incidentally, this attitude is conspicuously stated by Maslow in the title of his article "Existential Psychology—What's in it for us?" (1961).

There *are* relations of Rogers' client-centered approach and Maslow's concept of self-actualization to phenomenological and existential thought. But Skinner's radical behaviorism also contains important similarities to these lines of thought. To term either Rogers' or Skinner's approach as "phenomenological-existential" seems equally meaningless. We believe that phenomenology and existential philosophy may provide a sufficiently deep and comprehensive basis for integrating current psychological trends. This presupposes, however, that these lines of thinking are not merely used to support ideas one has already arrived at, but are taken seriously in their own right. For two such approaches, see Graumann (1960) and van Kaam (1966).

INTENTIONAL BEHAVIOR

Merleau-Ponty believed that Watson's rebellion against introspectionism in its start had the same intentions as the phenomenological movement. But the tendency to reduce behavior to muscular movements, the psychological to the physiological, made behaviorism a mere antithesis to instrospectionism, both neglecting man's primary directedness to the world.

The profound insight in Watson's uprising was, according to Merleau-Ponty " . . . the vision of man as a perpetual debate and 'explanation' with a physical and a social world . . . " (1965, p. 226). In a certain conception of behavior the phenomenologists agree that psychology is the study of behavior, namely, behavior understood as man's relatedness to a situation. Although notoriously ambiguous in his use of the term "behavior," Watson stressed behavior as a reaction to a total situation. In his own words:

> It has been claimed by some that behavior psychology is really physiology. That this is not the case appears from even a casual examination . . . nowhere in physiology do we get the organism, as it were, put back together again and tested in relation to its environment as a whole . . . . The physiologist *qua* physiologist knows nothing of the total situations in the daily life of an individual that shape his action and conduct (1929, p. 19-20).

Merleau-Ponty said about this conception:

> In our opinion, when Watson spoke of behavior he had in mind what others have called *existence;* but the new notion could receive its philosophical status only if causal or mechanical thinking were abandoned for dialectical thinking (op. cit., p. 226).

Merleau-Ponty's philosophy could be called a philosophy of the body as behavior. In *The Structure of Behavior* he stressed behavior as a fundamental psychological term, in itself neutral to the distinctions between the "mental" and the "physiological," as well as "inner" and "outer."

> It is not seen that, from the moment behavior is considered "in its unity" and in its human meaning, one is no longer dealing with a material reality nor, moreover, with a mental reality, but with a significative whole or structure which properly belongs neither to the external world nor to internal life (*Ibid.*, p. 152).

Within phenomenology, Husserl's assertion that consciousness is always consciousness of something has been a main theme. While Husserl and the older phenomenologists focused upon the intentionality of consciousness, Merleau-Ponty and Sartre have stressed the intentionality of behavior—man's basic relatedness to the world. The mental, which previously was encapsulated in a mind or a body, has now become a relation, namely, the body's relationship to the world, expressed through intentional behavior.

> Man and the world *are* relative beings, and the principle of their being *is* the relation (Sartre, 1956, p. 308).

> We thus arrive at a new localisation of the "mental," which is no longer interiority, but intentionality, in other words the relation of the subject and the situation. This does not imply that the relation unifies two strictly isolated poles, on the contrary, the me and the situation cannot be defined but in and by this relation (Lyotard, 1954, p. 55).

The phenomenologists unequivocally consider behavior as meaningful, human action. Intentional behavior is directed toward the world, it acts upon the world and reveals the world to man. Searching is "searching for something," running is "running away from something," looking is "looking towards something." A behavioral object is intrinsically tied to the object of the act.[5] The necessity of an "inner man" to guide behavior falls away when behavior is conceived as man's meaningful relatedness to the world. Behavior is a relation between man and the world, neither can be defined independent of the other. That is, world and man *can* be isolated and described independently, but they cannot be fully comprehended within this dualism.

When discussing the prejudice of the objective world, we saw that Skinner wavered between a physical and a "perceptual" conception of the world. The same ambiguity is reflected in his concept of behavior. On the one hand, Skinner conceives of behavior as mechanical movements: "Watching a person behave in this way is like watching any physical or biological system" (1961c, p. 206). He even applies his concept of behavior to microphysic particles when he compares the behavior of particles in a cyclotron to human behavior in a culture (1961d, p. 369). On the other hand, in practical examples, Skinner often considers behavior as meaningful human action, e.g., "the persistent behavior which we call teasing" (1953, p. 299).

Skinner explicitly denies the intentionality of the behavioral and consciousness aspects of man's relation to the world.

> We may regard a dream, not as a display of things seen by the dreamer, but simply as the behavior of seeing . . . . The heart of the behavioristic position on conscious experience may be summed up in this way: seeing does not imply something seen (1964, p. 88-89).

Skinner rightly dismisses the introspectionists' reifying of perception—considering a thing like content as the essential aspect of perception. "At some point the organism must do more than create duplicates. It must see, hear, smell, and so on, as forms of *action* rather than of *reproduction*" (*Ibid.*, p. 87). But Skinner goes to the opposite of introspectionism; by solely considering the behavioral aspect of perception, he comes to reify perceptual behavior. Perception then becomes isolated from that which it is directed toward, the things in the world. By accepting the separation between perceptual *behavior* and the *object* of perception, Skinner does not go beyond the introspectionists, but merely becomes their antithesis. Both approaches miss the unseparable unity of the perceiving act and the perceived object, as expressed by the phenomenological concept of intentionality. Even regarding imagination, Sartre avoids reducing it to an image or an act by focusing upon the imaginary act's intentional relatedness to its object "There are not, and never could be, images *in* consciousness. Rather, an image is *a certain type of consciousness*. An image is an act, not some thing. An image is a consciousness *of* some thing." (1962, p. 146).

KNOWLEDGE IS ACTION

With an enlarged conception of behavior, our knowledge of the world comes to be our behavior with respect to the world. Both Sartre and Skinner have developed an epistemology of action.

> What is needed, in a word, is a philosophical theory which shows that human reality is action, and that action upon the universe is identical with the understanding of that universe as it is, or in other words, that action is the unmasking of reality, and, at *the same time*, a modification of that reality (Sartre, 1949, p. 184). The point of view of pure knowledge is contradictory; there is only the point of view of *engaged* knowledge. This amounts to saying that knowledge and action are only two abstract aspects of an original, concrete relation (Sartre, 1956, p. 308).

Skinner puts the issue more briefly and concretely

> . . . knowledge is action rather than sensing . . . (1961e, p. 200). We "interpret" a stimulus as smoke insofar as we tend to respond with behavior appropriate to smoke . . .
>
> Our "perception" of the world—our "knowledge" of it—is our *behavior* with respect to the world (Skinner, 1953, p. 140).

We do not acquire knowledge of the world by creating duplicates within the organism. This "eating-epistemology," as Sartre has aptly termed it, builds upon a dualistic conception of man's relation to the world. While agreeing that it is by acting upon the world that we come to know the world, Skinner's and Sartre's concrete epistemologies of action sharply differ. This follows from their divergent conceptions of behavior, most important is the fact that Skinner misses the intentional world directness of behavior and consciousness.

Skinner does, however, sometimes come astonishingly close to a *dialectical* view of the interaction between man and the world. Sartre states that the dialectic interaction of the knower and the known has even become evident in modern physics. "The only theory of knowledge which can be valid today, is that which rests upon this micro-physic truth: the experimenter is part of the experimental system" (1960, p. 30). Discussing the relationship between the investigator and the object investigated, Skinner writes about the psychological experiment that "The subjects we study reinforce us much more effectively than we reinforce them" (1961f., p. 98).

In another context, Skinner states the dialectical relation of man to the world more generally: "Men act upon the world, and change it, and are changed in turn by the consequences of their action" (1957, p. 1). Sartre's view on this dialectical relationship has been summarized in this manner:

> For a man who freely starts by working upon matter is, by the dialectical next step, worked upon by the very matter which he has worked to produce. He starts by making objects, and the objects end by making him. They determine what he can do, and define his particular facticity (Warnock, 1965, p. 167).

The world is neither objectively given nor a pure subjective construction. The dialectical view maintains that the objectivity of the world can only be confirmed through praxis, by acting upon the world. Man creates and is created—in Skinner's terminology: controls and is controlled. The world is neither given nor created, it is a relation. Against this view the mechanical determinism as well as the popular "existential" free will becomes impossible to maintain.[6]

THE PRIMACY OF DESCRIPTION

The repudiation of inner entities and the focusing upon concrete observable behavior has led both Skinner and the phenomenologists to emphasize adequate descriptions in psychology. Skinner finds psychological theorizing most often a refuge from the data, and he repeatedly stresses: "But we must eventually get back to an observable datum" (1961g, p. 42). This demand is indeed close to Husserl's phenomenological slogan "back to the things themselves." If positive means being true to the immediately observable phenomena, we are the true positivists, Husserl asserted.

The phenomenologists maintain that it is a primary task of psychology to describe and analyze the concrete daily world of things and actions, "Lebenswelt," in common language. Skinner has mainly limited his observations to rats, pigeons, and, to a lesser degree, human subjects, in extremely narrow situations. It should here be noted that phenomenologists like Sartre explicitly recognize the value of such experimental studies of behavior: "The behaviorists were right in considering that the sole positive psychological study ought to be of conduct in strictly defined situations" (1956, p. 476).

The "descriptive" behaviorist Skinner would probably agree with the phenomenologists' claim that by elaborate descriptions of the immediately observable phenomena, the necessity of abstract theorizing recedes. Human behavior *is* understandable without recourse to speculative theoretical systems. Skinner posed the question "Are Theories of Learning Necessary?" (1961g), and he found the learning theories unnecessary to understand the concrete phenomena of learning. Although the different conceptions of behavior lead to obvious differences in the concrete descriptions, essentially the same point is made by existential analysts like Laing (1961) and Boss (1963). They find Freud's elaborate theoretical system of psychoanalysis unnecessary to understand the concrete behavior of their patients. They instead focus upon Freud's descriptions of neurotic behavior and his method of therapy, attempt to develop it further and to understand it within an existential frame of thought. Boss thus

> . . . limits the psychologist and the psychotherapist to the description and investigation of all the immediately observable modes of human behavior and their equally perceptible underlying moods, and to talking of them in everyday language (1963, p. 233).

UNREFLECTED AND REFLECTED CONSCIOUSNESS

The phenomenologists have made obstinate attempts at describing and analyzing our immediate experience of the world and our behavior to it. The uncovering of a primordial unreflected attitude to the world and ourselves has some important consequences for the understanding of consciousness and our living-our-body.

The introspectionist conception of consciousness is discarded by the phenomenologists as well as by Skinner.

> Here as everywhere else we assert that the state of consciousness is a pure idol of a positive psychology (Sartre 1956, p. 442). The subject need not be regarded as observing or evaluating conscious experiences (Skinner, 1964, p. 89).

Skinner further states that "It is not, however, seeing our friend which raises the question of conscious content but seeing that we are seeing him" (*Ibid.*, p. 88). The same point is made by the phenomenologists—it is first when reflecting upon our primary experience of the world that the problem of "objects in consciousness" is raised.

But while the phenomenologists describe and analyze both the unreflected and the reflected mode of consciousness, Skinner bypasses the primary unreflected mode of consciousness. Skinner also dismisses the intentionality of consciousness; to him "seeing does not imply something seen." To the phenomenologists, however, "It is a question of recognizing consciousness itself as a project of the world, meant for a world which it neither embraces nor possesses, but toward which it is perpetually directed" (1962, p. xvii).

On the unreflected level consciousness does not *have* any content, but *is* directed towards things in the world, it exists, resides with the things. We first acknowledge this, however, when a reflecting consciousness is directed upon the unreflected consciousness. And on this level consciousness may appear to have a thing-like character. When counting the cigarettes of a pack, the cigarettes are that to which any consciousness is directed, the act of counting is in itself unreflected. I may, however, in a new reflecting consciousness focus upon my activity of counting the cigarettes, making it the object of my reflective consciousness.

But consciousness has no content, reflected or unreflected. Where should content be located? The image we may find in a reflected consciousness is this consciousness' relation to the object (Sartre, 1961, p. 8). On all levels consciousness is a relation to the world or to itself. The reflecting consciousness is in itself unreflected, and if it is to be the object of reflection a new reflecting, and in itself unreflected, consciousness is needed, and so on indefinitely. In this connection Sartre cites Comte's remark "The eye cannot see itself." The reflecting consciousness entails in a way taking the attitude of the other to oneself, thus becoming an object to oneself, as G. H. Mead aptly has put it.

Consciousness is not primarily contemplating, as implied by the introspectionists, it is not something enclosed which cannot get out of itself. *Consciousness is primarily a relation to the world,* and this relationship is the presupposition which enables us to talk of a reflected consciousness with its "thinglike" character. Both introspectionists and behaviorists have neglected the unreflected consciousness with its intentional directedness toward the world. They have focused upon the reflected consciousness with its objectifying character, assuming it to be the only mode of consciousness. When the phenomenologists replace "states of consciousness" with intentional consciousness, actively directed to the world, and conceive of behavior as intentional acting upon the world, consciousness and behavior cease to be separate entities and become two aspects of man's intentional relatedness to the world.

The dismissal of the traditional "intellectualisation" of consciousness has some important consequences for the understanding of emotions. To Skinner a feeling is a reaction to a stimulus " . . . the stimuli we feel in pride or sorrow may not closely resemble those we feel in sandpaper or satin. But this does not mean that they differ in physical status" (1964, p. 86). But what about "the stimuli we feel" in sorrow? Skinner does not see that when we feel sorrow we *are* sorrow. Only in a reflected consciousness does our feeling sorrow become an object we can contemplate. And this reflection presupposes the sorrow already experienced unreflectedly. Feeling sorrow is primarily a mode of existence, a way of acting toward and experiencing the world, only secondary does it become a state we can analyse.

This issue is discussed by Sartre in connection with pain.

> Let us understand, of course, that pain "in the stomach" is the stomach itself as painfully lived (1956, p. 355).
>
> . . . for the unreflective consciousness pain was the body; for the reflective consciousness the illness is distinct from the body, it has its own form, it comes and goes (*Ibid.*, p. 337).

Only in a reflected attitude is pain *a state in me*. In an unreflected attitude the pain is the body's concrete mode of existence, we *are* our pain.

"Private" events as the experience of pain has usually been dismissed by the behaviorists, with their emphasis upon "public," intersubjective data. Skinner has here a divergent view, and stresses the public aspect of private experience.

THE PUBLIC AND THE PRIVATE WORLD

Methodologically oriented behaviorists generally consider immediate conscious experience as the basis of all science.

> . . . the data of all sciences has the same origin—namely, the immediate experience of an observing person, the scientist himself. That is to say, immediate experience, the initial matrix out of which all sciences develop, is no longer considered a matter of concern for the scientist qua scientist. He simply takes it for granted and then proceeds to his task of describing the events occurring in it . . . (Spence, 1948, p. 68).

However, neither Skinner, nor Sartre or Merleau-Ponty, conceive the data of science as events *in* the consciousness of the scientist, but explicitly refute this introspective solipsism (see also Straus, 1963). Neither do they follow the behavioristic tradition of drawing an absolute distinction between public and private events and rule the latter out of a scientific psychology.

An analysis of our unreflected attitude to the world reveals that we live primarily in an intersubjective world, and only secondarily do we distinguish something private. When sitting around a table, we do not usually conceive of our behavior as a reaction upon some subjective experience of that table. We all take for granted that the table and the other objects in the room are in *the* world and not only in *our* private world.

It is first by taking a reflecting attitude that this primary intersubjectivity is questioned—"Reflection suppresses intersubjectivity" (Merleau-Ponty, 1964b, p. 74). But a fundamental intersubjectivity remains a presupposition for the reflecting attitude. When posing the question of the "real" nature of, e.g., the table, we take it for granted that the table itself is an intersubjective phenomenon. If not, if the table were only our subjective experience, there would be no meaning in the problem posed.

To take another example, I have no means of ascertaining whether my experience of a certain red is identical with the others' experience of the same red. But notice here that this private aspect of my experience presupposes that the language we use has a common meaning to me and to the others—e.g., the words "the same red," and that the red we talk about is *the same*. If the red is not identical to itself when I look at it, and when the others look at it, there is no meaning in asking whether we have the same experience or not. Of course, the seen red may be different things to different observers, their experiences varying accordingly. However, only a primary public world makes the private interpretations possible. And this public world must be the basis of scientific research, not events "in" the private consciousness of the scientist.

What we intend is once more to avoid the doubling of the world. The early behaviorists threw the private world out of psychology, only to isolate it as another, scientifically irrelevant world. Skinner, on the contrary, states that behaviorism can only show its strength by also accounting for private events as imagination, dreams, "conscious content," thought processes, and so on; that is by making them a part of the public world. The private is not another world, but a difficult accessible part of the world.

Skinner makes the important point that since "inner states" are hidden from public observation, descriptions of these states will be more ambiguous than descriptions of events outside the organism. ". . . It is the private world which, if not entirely unknowable, is at least not likely to be known well" (1964, p. 84). Merleau-Ponty also made the same point: "our intersubjective confrontations bear only upon the intelligible structure of the perceived world" (1965, p. 211).

Skinner explains this phenomenon by discussing private experiences in relation to the development of language. Our descriptions of private events are determined by the history of reinforcements from the "verbal community," and

> Because the community cannot reinforce self-descriptive responses consistently, a person cannot describe or otherwise "know" events occurring within his own skin as subtly and precisely as he knows events in the world at large (*Ibid.*, p. 85).

A little child may believe that dreams and other "private" events happen in the world. Only gradually, by social reinforcement does the child learn to distinguish between something private and something public. In this way a private world develops and is given meaning, but always inside an already established public world.

Previously, we have seen how the spatialization of the private world to something "inner" and the public world to something "outer" lead to a series of inconsequences. Skinner explicitly rejects such a spatial localization of the public and the private world, and again stresses the social aspect of our world.

> The "boundary" for public-private is not the skin, but the line between the verbal community's being able to reinforce behavior differentially and its not being able to, or able to only with great difficulty (*Ibid.*, p. 107).

FIRST PERSON AND THIRD PERSON PSYCHOLOGY

Behaviorism has been the psychology of the other—a third person psychology. As such it has had substantial contributions to psychology. But it has neglected the study of the acting and perceiving *subject*—a psychology of the first person. How does the world appear to me as a perceiving subject, my actions to me as an acting subject, my body to me as a corporeal subject?

The behaviorist can account for the behavior of others, but not for his own behavior. Thus within behaviorist methodology a dualism between the psychologist and his subjects is advocated, e.g., by Mandler and Kessen who cite Bergmann, "*the behavior scientist and his subjects do not, in principle, speak the same language*" (1959, p. 36). This dualism is analogous to the behavioristic position that the immediate conscious experience of the scientist is the *basis* of all science, but not a legitimate *subject matter* for a scientific psychology.

Skinner rejects this behavioristic dualism and is, on the contrary, explicitly and repeatedly *self-referring*—what he says about others is also valid for himself. "He has found it 'useful' to regard himself exactly as he regards 'the pigeons, rats and other people' he studies" (1964, p. 99).

It is, however, when he applies the concepts he has developed from the study of others upon his own behavior that the limitations of his system become most apparent. For example, he writes "I observed events in myself which characteristically precede or accompany my going home" (1953, p. 262) and later on writes " . . . a self is simply a device for representing *a functionally unified system of responses*" (p. 185).

How does Skinner conceive of a system of responses that observes responses? Has the response got the power to reflect upon itself? Skinner must here either choose mentalistic conceptions or end in an infinite regress, which closely parallels the infinite regress he so convincingly demonstrated as a consequence of the physiological explanations of perception. Skinner is brought in the same position when he has to observe events in himself to find out if he is going home. This observation must then again be verified by another observation, and so on indefinitely.

The dilemma can be solved by distinguishing between first person and third person sentences, as suggested by Malcolm. He criticizes Skinner on this same point and argues that a verification depends on observations that cannot be verified, but must be presupposed.

> I can verify that the animal in the field is a brown cow. I cannot verify, in addition, that I see a brown cow. In the case of another person I can verify both that there is a brown cow in the field and that he sees it (1964, p. 150).

Why is this so? I can observe how another person's eyes are directed toward the spot where I see the cow. By observing the other person's behavior I can verify that he sees a cow by comparing my observation of the cow with my observation of his eye movements.

I cannot, however, apply this method to my own observations. I cannot observe how my own eyes follow the cow and thus deduce that I see a cow. To be sure, I could maybe verify my own observation of the cow by an ingenious system of mirrors, but then this verification would require another system of mirrors, and so on. *At some point there must be a primary observation of something seen.* Consciousness is always consciousness *of* something.

The implications of this argument are that all relationships verified by third-person-sentences are relative, that is, their validity presupposes first-person-sentences which validity cannot be related to an observed relation. This point is central to Sartre, who writes about " . . . the error of the psychologists, who define *my senses* by the Other's senses and who give to the sense organ as it is for me a relativity which belongs to its being-for others" (1956, p. 341).

The relativity is the above discussed infinite regress. In short, the error consists of considering a third-person-relation—and not a first-person-relation—to perception as primary. The relevant point was also implied when discussing consciousness—a reflecting consciousness requires a primary unreflected consciousness to reflect upon. And as with regard to verification, the primary and in itself unverifiable relation has been overlooked.

A main theme in the discussion of the relation of radical behaviorism to phenomenology has been the refutation of the common dualistic conceptions of man in psychology. There are two ways of depassing this dualism: reduction to one of the dualistic aspects or a new solution to the whole issue.

Malcolm concluded his critique of Skinner that "perhaps the best way to sum up behaviorism's shortcomings as a philosophy of psychology is to say that it regards man as *solely an object*" (1964, p. 154). This is also an important aspect of the phenomenological critique of behaviorism. Its mechanical conception of behavior is not broad enough to account for man's concrete relations to the world.

A phenomenological psychology does not attempt to reduce man to a subject or an object, as introspectionism and behaviorism with their first person and third person reductions. We cannot here argue for a philosophy of man which tries to solve this problem, we would then leave Skinner's behaviorism completely. In concluding, we will merely hint at the possibility that a fully worked out *psychology of the body*—the body as expressing man's intentional behavior to the world—may give an alternative to the reduction of man to either an object or a subject. Within both subjectivistic and objectivistic psychologies, the body as lived and acted has been a strangely neglected theme. To phenomenologists like Sartre and Merleau-Ponty, however, man's bodily being in the world has been a central theme.

Man *is* neither object nor subject, but his bodily being in the world with other men entails his being an object in the world *and* a subject for whom the world exists. The traditional reductions of man to either a "material" object or an "ideal" subject may be depassed, we believe, by focusing upon man's concrete bodily behavior to the world.

SUMMARY

This article has attempted to demonstrate that current European phenomenology is in no way a revival of introspectionism. On the contrary, we have found some basic similarities between Skinner's radical behaviorism and the phenomenology of Sartre and Merleau-Ponty. At the metapsychological level, we have depicted an intrinsic harmony in their refutation of the many forms of dualism inherent in modern psychology. This holds for the dualism of inner and outer, private and public, as well as the dualism between the psychologist and his subject.

Sartre and Merleau-Ponty also agree with Skinner in stressing behavior as the fundamental subject matter of psychology, in conceiving knowledge as action, and in emphasizing adequate descriptions in psychology. However, Skinner's ambiguous and mainly mechanical conception of behavior leads to several inconsequences, especially when applied to his own behavior, which may be bypassed by the phenomenological concept of intentional behavior.

We hope to have indicated that Skinner's metapsychological views, which are commonly dismissed by American colleagues, as, for example, Koch and Rogers, may be better understood—in their force and weakness—on the basis of Sartre's and Merleau-Ponty's more comprehensive discussions of the philosophical foundations of psychology. In conclusion, we maintain that "behaviorism and phenomenology" are not "contrasting bases for modern psychology," but that the positive aspects of behaviorism may be developed further on the basis of a radical phenomenology, focusing upon man's behavioral relatedness to the world, as revealed by his body.

REFERENCES

Boss, M. *Psychoanalysis and daseinsanalysis*. New York: Basic Books, 1963.

Brody, N. and Oppenheim, P. Tensions in psychology between the methods of behaviorism and phenomenology. *Psychol. Rev.*, 73, 295-305, 1966.

Graumann, C. F. *Grundlagen einer phänomenologie und psychologie der perspektivität*. Berlin: Gruyter, 1960.

———. Subjektiver Behaviorismus? *Arch. Ges. Psychol.* 117, 240-251, 1965.

Heidegger, M. *Being and time*. New York: Harper & Row, 1962 (German ed. 1927).

Holzkamp, K. Zur Problematik der realitäts-verdoppelung in der psychologie. *Psychol. Rundschau,* 16, 209-222, 1965.

Koch, S. Psychology and emerging conceptions of knowledge as unitary. (See Wann), 1964.

Krech, D. and Crutchfield, R. S. *Elements of psychology*. New York: Knopf, 1958.

Laing, R. D. *The self and others*. London: Tavistock, 1961.

Laing, R. D. and Cooper, D. G. *Reason and violence. A decade of Sartre's philosophy 1950-1960*. London: Tavistock, 1964.

Lyotard, J-F. *La phénoménologie*. Paris: Press. Univ. France, 1954.

Malcolm, N. Behaviorism as a philosophy of psychology. (See Wann), 1964.

Mandler, G. and Kessen, W. *The language of psychology*. New York: Wiley, 1959.

Maslow, A.H. Existential psychology —-what's in it for us? In May, R. (ed.) *Existential psychology*. New York: Random House, 1961.

May, R., Angel, E. and Ellenberger, H.F. (eds.) *Existence—-a new dimension in psychiatry and psychology*. New York: Basic Books, 1958.

Merleau-Ponty, M. *Phenomenology of perception*. London: Routledge and Kegan Paul, 1962 (French ed. 1945).

———. *The primacy of perception*. Northwestern Univ. Press, 1964a.

———. *Le visible et l'invisible*. Paris: Gallimard, 1964b.

———. *The structure of behaviour*. London: Methuen, 1965 (French ed. 1942).

Mowrer, O. H. *Learning theory and the symbolic processes*. New York: Wiley, 1960.

Nuttin, J. Consciousness, behavior and personality. *Psychol. Rev.*, 62, 349-355, 1955.

Osgood, C. E. *Method and theory in experimental psychology*. New York: Oxford Univ. Press, 1953.

Rogers, C. Toward a science of the person. (See Wann), 1964.

Rubinstein, S. L. *Prinzipien und wege der entwicklung der psychologie*. Berlin: Akademic-Verlag, 1963.

Ryle, G. *The concept of mind*. London: Hutchinson, 1949.

Sartre, J-P. *The emotions: outline of a theory*. New York: Phil. Library, 1948 (French ed. 1939).

———. Materialisme et revolution. In *Situations III*. Paris: Gallimard, 1949.

———. *Being and nothingness*. London: Methuen, 1956 (French ed. 1943).

———. *Critique de la raison dialectique*. Paris: Gallimard, 1960.

———. *The psychology of imagination.* New York: Citadel Press, 1961 (French ed. 1940).

———. *Imagination.* Ann Arbor: Univ. Michigan Press, 1962 (French ed. 1936).

Skinner, B. F. *Science and human behavior.* New York: Macmillan, 1953.

———. *Verbal behavior.* New York: Appleton-Century-Croft, 1957.

———. *Cumulative record.* London: Methuen, 1961.
a) A critique of psychoanalytic concepts and theories (1954).
b) The flight from the laboratory.
c) What is psychotic behavior?
d) The design of cultures (1961).
e) Psychology in the understanding of mental disease (1957).
f) A case history in scientific method (1956).
g) Are theories of learning necessary? (1950).

———. Behaviorism at fifty. (See Wann, 1964). Spencer, K. W. The postulates and methods of "behaviorism." *Psychol. Rev.*, 55, 67-78, 1945.

Straus, E. *The primary world of senses.* New York: Macmillan, 1963.

van Kaam, A. *Existential foundations of psychology.* Pittsburgh: Duquesne Univ. Press, 1966.

Wann, T. W. (ed.) *Behaviorism and phenomenology—Contrasting bases for modern psychology.* Chicago: Chicago Univ. Press, 1964.

Warnock, M. *The philosophy of Sartre.* London: Hutchinson, 1965.

Watson, J. B. *Psychology from the standpoint of a behaviorist.* Philadelphia: Lippincott, 1929.

NOTES

1 This study was supported by grants from the Norwegian Research Council for Science and the Humanities and from the Alexander von Humboldt-Stiftung, Germany. The authors would like to thank psychologist Finn Tschudi for calling the "metapsychological" Skinner to their attention.

2 Contributors to this symposium were the psychologists Koch, MacLeod, Skinner, Rogers, and the philosophers Malcolm and Scriven.

3 Among Sartre's psychological works which first appeared about 25 years ago, are "The psychology of imagination" (1961) and "The emotions: outline of a theory" (1948). His main philosophical works "Being and nothingness" (1956) and "Critique de la raison dialectique" (1960) also treat psychological and sociological problems.

In a recent interview project, sponsored by the National Science foundation, with "outstanding contributors to psychology," Sartre as well as Skinner were included. The others were G. Allport, E. Fromm, A. Freud, A. Luria (*Am. Psychol.* 1964, p. 79).

4 Merleau-Ponty was a more academic colleague of Sartre, first professor of child psychology and later of philosophy at the Sorbonne. His major psychological works, which first appeared about 20 years ago, were "The structure of behaviour" (1965) and "Phenomenology of perception" (1962)

Although taking different views on many problems, Merleau-Ponty and Sartre took a common stand on the metapsychological issues discussed here.

5 Regarding the relation of the phenomenological conception of behavior to Tolman's purposive behaviorism, see Graumann (1965). Confer also the emphasis upon action as well as the thesis of the unity of behavior and consciousness in Soviet psychology (Rubinstein, 1963).

6 For an exposition of dialectical thought, see Laing and Cooper's (1964) account of Sartre's "Critique de la raison dialectique."

V. Imagination and Myth

The Role of Imagination in Phenomenological Psychology

JEFFNER ALLEN

Although there are a myriad of perspectives from which one may come to an understanding of phenomenological psychology, its distinctive character may be brought to light in a definitive manner by examining the methodological role of imagination. To understand the significance of the imagination for the development of a method for studying human being and being-in-the-world is to grasp the unique character of phenomenological psychology itself. We propose, in consequence, to engage (I) in a general clarification of the nature and task of phenomenological psychology, (II) in a detailed analysis of the function of the imagination in defining of phenomenological psychology and in bringing its task to fruition and (III) in several critical reflections on the problematics that our approach presents for the theory and practice of phenomenological psychology.

Our approach will be specifically Husserlian in character, for it is Husserl's philosophy and phenomenological psychology that has, either directly or indirectly, laid the foundations for subsequent phenomenological and existential psychology. Present-day phenomenological and existential psychologies may be either anti-Husserlian, or even silent with respect to their relation to Husserl. If such psychologies, however, are to discover the source of their approaches to the understanding of the human being they must, at least in part, return to Husserl's work and, in particular, to Husserl's conception of phenomenological psychology and the role that the imagination plays in the articulation of its nature, task and problematics.

PHENOMENOLOGICAL PSYCHOLOGY: THE SCIENCE OF PSYCHIC PHENOMENA AND THEIR ESSENCES

Let us turn first to a general clarification of the nature of phenomenological psychology. Within this context we propose that it may be defined as *the science of psychic phenomena and their essences*. An elucidation of the various terms of our definition will lead us to an initial understanding of phenomenological psychology itself.

As a particular form of *science*, phenomenological psychology is an *a priori*, intuitive discipline directed toward the phenomena and structures of the life-world. Our discipline is an *a priori* one, for it "aims first of all at all those essential universalities and necessities without which psychological being and living are simply inconceivable."[1] It is intuitive in that it discloses the *a priori* structures of human existence through an inner seeing of their necessity and universality. All subsequent analyses and pure descriptions of such structures must proceed in conformity with what is intuitively seen. Our psychology is a science of the life-world, and not a transcendental science, for it presupposes the existence of the human psychic world in which we live, a world of personal meanings, and seeks to explore that lived reality in a natural human manner.

As a science of the *psychic,* phenomenological psychology views the human *Geist* (mind, spirit, or even, psyche) as that which forms a unitary internal nexus *[Zusammenhang],* whose content is our lived experience *[Erlebnis],* and whose fundamental structure is that of intentionality.

Since the psychic may be disclosed as a *Zusammenhang,* a single internal nexus, or coherent whole, its moments are not to be considered as self-sufficient elements which are separate from, or external to, one another. To even speak of a single psychological datum—a perception, a mood, etc.—is to abstract that datum from its meaning context in the unity of its all-inclusive psychic milieu. To artificially single out and isolate any one moment of our psychic life is to ignore and distort the very nature of the human psyche. Instead, the psychic may be considered phenomenologically as being composed of internally interwoven states-of-mind which are given, directly or indirectly, along with any particular mental state that may be under consideration. Of course, we may also ask: How is the unity of psychic life disclosed and made intelligible? Our response to this question must wait until we have further examined the nature of the psychic.

Phenomenologically speaking, the content of our unitary psychic life is the *Erlebnis,* or lived experience. The lived experience has as its moments the single perceptions, recollections and anticipations, fearing, dreading, and willing, etc., which together form the unbroken unity of a human life. The experience flows on constantly. It encompasses my own stream of experience, to which I have immediate access, as well as those experiences of other individuals and of the social community at large, experiences to which I have access indirectly.

The fundamental structure of our unitary lived experience is that of intentionality, which Husserl calls, ". . . the most universal essential characteristic of being and living."[2] To call our psychic life intentional is to say that it is always a consciousness *of* something, a being directed at something, e.g., a perception of x, a hoping for x, a fearing of x. In our usual unreflective being-in-the-world we do not explicitly recognize our awareness as intentional. Nevertheless, if we view reflectively the nature of our consciousness, we find it to always be intentional. We see that we are constantly undergoing subjective experiences in which we are directed, projected, pointed toward, or are conscious *of,* those phenomena, or objects, which appear to us. To grasp the nature of the psychic we must eventually examine all aspects of the intentional structure of awareness—our subjective acts and those phenomena which are given as their correlates.

Having briefly delimited the basic dimensions of the psychic we may again step back and reexamine our proposed definition of phenomenological psychology, this time with an emphasis on our discipline as the science of psychic *phenomena and their essences*. Here phenomenological psychology appears as a science that attempts to see the *a priori* meaning, rationality, or essences immanent in all personal, or mental, phenomena. The phenomena are neither isolated self-sufficient elements, nor raw material devoid of meaning in themselves, nor merely quantitative data obtained by empirical induction. The essences are neither arbitrary constructions derived from hypotheses and inferences, nor subjective data arrived at by private introspection, nor the product of a mere description of our experience without any insight into its meaning structures. On the contrary, the phenomena are simply that which is given to consciousness; the essences are nothing other than the *a priori* meaning structures disclosed in a phenomenological intuitive seeing. The psychic phenomena and their essences are symbiotically bound together in the life-world of human existence such that "Husserl's essences are destined to bring back all the living relationships of experience, as the fisherman's net draws up from the depths of the ocean quivering fish and seaweed."[3]

Thus our elucidation has shown that phenomenological psychology is an *a priori* intuitive science of the life-world. It is a science of the psychic, that is, of the unitary nexus of our lived experience, whose fundamental structure is that of intentionality. In short, it is the science of psychic phenomena and their essences. Its task is to bring to light the psychic phenomena and essences of the life-world, *and* to do so in a scientific manner. But how is phenomenological psychology to bring forth the full sense of our lived experience without doing violence to it? How are we to uncover the meaning of our psychic life without imposing on it our own prejudices and distortive abstractions?

THE IMAGINATION: THE DISCLOSURE OF PSYCHIC PHENOMENA AND THEIR ESSENCES

Implicit in our description of the nature of phenomenological psychology is the issue of the role of the imagination in a phenomenological study of human being-in-the-world. What is the imagination? How is it relevant to the task of the phenomenological psychologist? Or, in other words, how is it involved in disclosing the fundamental structures of all psychic phenomena?

In most general terms, we may define the imagination as that modality of consciousness which liberates us from the world of naively accepted fact so that we can see what is given to consciousness *as* it is given to consciousness. The imagination frees us from our customary face value acceptance of everyday opinions and beliefs, from every form of prejudice, including that of our usual unquestioning adherence to the scientism of the medical model. In so doing, the imagination fulfills its function by helping us to grasp more clearly the basic structures inherent in that which is present to us.

If we are to deepen our understanding of the specific role of the imagination in phenomenological psychology we must observe the imagination in operation. We must examine in succession the three methodological levels on which the imagination has relevance for phenomenological psychology: (A.) The epoché: the psychologist's initial liberation from the world of fact, (B.) The eidetic variation: the unfolding of the phenomenological psychologist's proper domain, (C.) The liberated seeing of psychic phenomena and their essences: the culmination of the phenomenological psychologist's task.

The Epoché

Before we can engage in phenomenological psychology proper we must free ourselves from the world of "fact," that is, of empirical actuality.[4] Indeed, Husserl's first demand is that we set aside our naive straightforward immersion in the intuitively pre-given world of experience. We must epoché—bracket, suspend—our natural attitude in which we simply accept the world as it is actually and factually experienced; we must abstain from upholding our usual reductive prejudices and preconceptions.

But what clues do we have for the accomplishment of this most desirable, although seemingly impossible, activity? Husserl writes:

> Every felt necessity is an indicative sign of an a priori in the sense of an unconditional so-called apodictic universality, which can be seen as such. Showing it is the test whether the felt necessity is a genuinely apodictic one, and not a confusion with a merely empirical indication.[5]

Accordingly, we must focus on the "felt necessities" which inhere in our daily experience, while at the same time probatively examining them so as to determine their genuineness, their degree of liberation from all presuppositions. Any "felt necessity" or universal essence which comes into prominence in that which is given to us empirically is to be scrutinized, purified and thereby liberated from any contingencies that may adhere to it.

While such a clue may offer us some guidance, the specific matter of how the phenomenological psychologist is to perform the epoché must still be clarified. Certainly the psychologist would lose everything if the carrying out of the epoché involved a giving up of one's world of experience, or a skeptical denial of that world's very existence. On the contrary, the psychologist's epoché seeks to retain all phenomena of the life-world while at the same time enabling one to attain to a clear viewing of their meaning. It is in light of this goal that the epoché requires that,

> 'With one blow' he [the phenomenological psychologist] must put out of effect the totality of his participation in the validities explicitly or implicitly effected by the persons who are his subjects; and this means all persons.[6]

Or, in other words, we as phenomenological psychologists must not take up any position of our own, must not allow our validities to be operative for ourselves qua psychologists or for others. By virtue of such an epoché we can attain to the standpoint of the "disinterested spectator,"[7] one who neither argues with or denies, neither questions or doubts, the validities of oneself or of others.

Upon performing the psychologist's epoché we find that all factual actualities are to be treated solely as possibilities among other possibilities.[8] The factual world is no longer the preferred world. Although the existence of the life-world remains unquestioned, the phenomenon of the *Lebenswelt* serves only as "an exemplary beginning for the style of free fantasies which I shape from it . . . ."[9] From this perspective the issue of whether or not an experience concerns something that is actual, or whether an experience is itself factually actual, is cancelled out, is completely irrelevant. Factual actuality no longer serves as the limiting standard according to which psychic experiences are to be judged.

With the epoché we have completed the propaedeutics necessary for the exercise of the pure imagination. The full implications of the epoché will, however, not be evident until we enter the domain of the imagination, which is likewise the proper domain of the phenomenological psychologist.

The Eidetic Variation

As we enter into a further level of methodological concern we find ourselves engaged in the eidetic, or imaginative, variation. It is here that the imagination plays the determinant role in liberating us from the realm of the factual and in generating eidetic variants which reveal the fundamental structures of the manifold of psychic phenomena.

We can begin the eidetic variation by starting with a given, for example, with a lived experience or with that "felt necessity"[10] which we previously suggested might lead us to the *a priori* structure of a particular state of affairs. Since the epoché transforms every fact into fiction, the given may be either an objectivity that has actually been experienced, or one that is simply imagined. Our initial example—which may be composed of the *Erlebnis* of a single individual—then takes on the character of a model: it guides our investigations; its horizon prescribes a style for our reflections on it; it serves as the point of departure for the formation of an infinite multiplicity of variants.

How do we produce variants of our initial example? We do so by an act of volition in which we drop the identity of the individual phenomenon—together with its determinate and indeterminate horizons of meaning, or intentional nexus—and imaginatively change it into other possibilities. Precisely which variants are produced remains a matter of indifference. In fact, there is an arbitrary, or optional, character *[Beliebigkeit]* to the entire process. Any number of variations may be formed, precisely as one wishes, without restriction. There is no objective criterion for the type or number of variants that must be generated in order that the structure of our example can be disclosed. It is the same whether we engage in a long process in which we attempt to actually produce all possible variants or whether we discontinue the process at some arbitrary point. To engage in the former, longer process, is to obey a nonsensical demand, "as if only then could we be sure that the eidos apprehended at the end actually conformed to all the possibilities."[11] Since the possible variations of our initial model are inexhaustible, we need not and cannot actually produce all of them. In the end we must arbitrarily settle upon an incomplete series of variants whose number and kind will remain infinitely open.

Yet if we begin with a given lived experience and then arbitrarily produce variations of it, how does the unitary structure of our initial datum reveal itself in the variants? As we run through the multiplicity of variants how is it that we find that they overlap, or coincide, so as to disclose their synthetic unity? According to a Husserlian explanation, the unitary bond between the variants is always already there; it is passively constituted. We can come to see those structures which are always implicitly operative in our initial *Erlebnis only* by retaining in view the entire multiplicity of variations. To see a structure is not simply to hold on to the last variation, identifying that with the essential form of the subject matter under consideration. On the contrary, if we are to see an eidos the entire multiplicity of imaginings must be present as a plurality that is never let completely out of our mental grasp. The synthetic unity, or eidos, is a "hybrid unity,"[12] a unity of images, some of which may even nullify and/or exclude one another. Indeed, the depth and richness of a structure may be attributed in large part to the fact that it is *hen epi pollon,* one over many, having no meaning without the many[13]: ". . . the universal . . . appears as something standing out *in* them [the multiplicity], as a concept dwelling in them."[14]

While we must on the one hand retain the manifold of images within our mental grasp, it is also true that we must at the same time look toward that which is congruent and purely identical in the manifold. Only in this way can we grasp what agrees as the eidos At this stage we actively identify the congruent over against the discordant which often tends to obscure the visibility of the eidos. We view the differences among the many in light of their involvement with an identically common structure; we see the eidos as that which is given to us immediately and intuitively.

The Seeing of Essences

We have said that the phenomenological psychologist's task comes to fruition in the seeing of the essences of psychic phenomena, and that such a seeing is the outcome of the methodological employment of the imagination. Yet what an essence is needs further clarification. It should be noted that for the phenomenologist the essence is not to be treated as a traditionally metaphysical notion. It is seen; it is not constructed or invented. The eidos is the unity which becomes evident as we run through the imaginative variations. It is an invariant structure which we retain as that necessary universal form without which our initial phenomena could not be imagined as such. The eidos is, as it were, the *a priori* condition for the possibility of a phenomena, and logically precedes all factual actualization of that phenomena. Moreover, the eidos may be taken as an example, or model, which may itself be subject to an eidetic variation, thereby giving rise to a hierarchy of essences.

It should also be clear that for the phenomenological psychologist the seeing of essences is not an end in itself. Rather, once we have tested the genuineness of our initial "felt necessity"[15] and have seen its validity, we must remember that such seeing is for the sake of an understanding of human being-in-the-world and requires a constant return to the world of lived experience. Or as Merleau-Ponty writes when discussing Husserl's seeing of essences:

> . . . we cannot subject our perception of the world to philosophical scrutiny without ceasing to be identified with that act of positing the world, with that interest in it which delimits us, without drawing back from our commitment which is itself thus made to appear as a spectacle, without passing from the *fact* of our existence to its *nature*, from the Dasein to the Wesen. But it is clear that the essence is here not the end, but a means, that our effective involvement in the world is precisely what has to be understood and made amenable to conceptualization . . . The need to proceed by way of essences does not mean that philosophy takes them as its object, but, on the contrary, that our existence is too tightly held in the world to be able to know itself as such at the moment of its involvement, and that it requires ideality in order to become acquainted with and to prevail over its facticity.[16]

CRITICAL REFLECTIONS

It may be noted that we have claimed that phenomenological psychology is the science of psychic phenomena and their essences. In light of this claim one may ask: In what sense is phenomenological psychology—a mode of reflection based on the use of the imagination as a methodological device—a science?

It is not a science in the usual sense of the word, according to which science is commonly defined as knowledge that seeks to understand, to predict and to control. Indeed we have said nothing at all about prediction and control of the human being—precisely because the method and goals of our science exclude both of these from its domain. But, then, might our phenomenological psychology still be a science in that it endeavors to understand our being-in-the-world?

Certainly our phenomenological psychology does not seek to "understand" in any way that would ordinarily be considered to be scientific. Its understanding results directly from the foundational role that it gives to the imagination—

something that most psychologists would consider to be absolutely unscientific. Due to the function of the initial guiding example, or model, with which the eidetic variation begins, it suffices for our discipline to have as its content the lived experiences of a single individual, if desired. Again, owing to the arbitrary character of the variation, phenomenological psychology has no objective criterion for the number or kind of possible variants that it must consider before arriving at a "conclusion." Such procedures can in no way qualify as scientific in any customary sense of the word. Moreover, the phenomenologist focuses on essences, "intangibles" which the innate naturalism of contemporary scientist—usually assigns to the unscientific realm of the "mystical."[17] A further consequence of our psychology's use of the imaginative variation is that it does not employ the inductive method frequently typical of the natural sciences.[18] For phenomenological psychology the application of an empirical inductive methodology to the science of the psyche is a reductive naturalistic prejudice that must be reflected.[19] Finally, perhaps what may most alarm the scientist in the usual sense of the term is that the phenomenological discipline seems to violate even the dictates of "good sense"—it arrives at conclusions without being obliged to engage in experiments. The "unscientific" nature of such non-experimental psychology has been challenged since its beginning. In this regard we need only note Moritz Geiger's report on the unfavorable response to his paper in phenomenological psychology, "On the Essence and Meaning of Empathy," presented to the IV. Kongress für experimentelle Psychologie in Innsbruck, 1911. Part of Geiger's report is recounted to us by Husserl:

> . . . his [Geiger's] efforts were not well received by the gathering. Amid loud applause Ms. Martin said: "When I came here, I expected to hear something about experiments in the field of empathy. But what have I actually heard? Nothing but old—very old—theories. Not a word about experiments in this field. *This is no philosophical society*. It seems to me that it is high time for anyone who wants to introduce such theories here to show whether they have been confirmed by experiments."[20]

In sum, a psychology based on the method of imaginative variation, instead of empirical experiment, is not commonly considered to be a science or to understand its subject matter properly. It is held to be "armchair psychology"[21] at best and, at worst, mere "philosophizing."

Yet might there not be another sense in which phenomenological psychology could be said to be a science and to give us scientific understanding? Clearly insofar as the methodological role that phenomenological psychology gives to the imagination allows it to go "To the things themselves," to the lived experience *as* it is itself, it can also be said to give us an understanding of the highest sort, i.e., scientific understanding. Its scientific understanding is none other than that of the pure *a priori* grasping of the phenomena and structures of psychic life.

We can now distinguish the sense in which our *a priori* intuitive science of the life-world is and is not a science. It still remains for us to put our methodological theories into practice, to open ourselves to new possibilities by applying the phenomenological method of the epoché, eidetic variation, and seeing of essences to an understanding of the unitary internal nexus that constitutes the intentional structure of our lived experience. Although our methodology is, in theory, applicable everywhere, " 'applicable' does not yet signify applied.' "[22]

NOTES

1 Husserl, *Phenomenological Psychology: Lectures, Summer 1925 [Phänomenologische Psychologie: Vorlesungen Sommersemester 1925]*, trans. John Scanlon (The Hague: Martinus Nijhoff, 1977), p. 46. In the subsequent citations of this work the title of the book will be abbreviated *PP* and only the German pagination will be given.

2 *PP*, p. 47.

3 Merleau-Ponty. *The Phenomenology of Perception*, trans. Colin Smith (London: Routledge & Kegan Paul, 1962) p. XV.

4 *PP*, p. 71.

5 *PP*, p. 70.

6 Husserl, *The Crisis of European Sciences and Transcendental Phenomenology: An Introduction to Phenomenological Philosophy*, trans. David Carr (Evanston: Northwestern University Press, 1970), p. 239.

7 *Ibid.*

8 *PP*, p. 71.

9 *Ibid.*

10 *PP*, p. 70.

11 Husserl, *Experience and Judgment: Investigations in a Genealogy of Logic*, trans. James S. Churchill and Karl Ameriks (Evanston: Northwestern University Press, 1973), p. 342.

12 *Ibid.*, p. 345.

13 *PP*, p. 105.

14 Husserl, *Experience and Judgment*, p. 328.

15 *PP*, p. 70.

16 Merleau-Ponty, *op. cit.*, pp. XIV-XV.

17 Husserl, *Phenomenology and the Crisis of Philosophy: Philosophy as Rigorous Science*, trans. Q. Lauer (Harper & Row, 1965), p. 110.

18 *PP*, p. 141-143.

19 *PP*, p. 143.

20 Husserl, *Phenomenology and the Crisis of Philosophy*, p. 121.

21 *Ibid.*, p. 92.

22 *PP*, p. 92.

The Meaning of the Oedipus Myth

ROLLO MAY

Our thesis is that symbols and myths are an expression of man's unique self-consciousness, his capacity to transcend the immediate concrete situation and see his life in terms of "the possible," and that this capacity is one aspect of his experiencing himself as a being having a world. We shall inquire how symbols and myths do this through the myth of Oedipus.

The story of Oedipus is a myth rather than a symbol, but the two are very closely related. *Symbols* are specific acts or figures, while *myths* develop and elaborate these symbols into a story which contains characters and several episodes. The myth is thus more inclusive. But both symbol and myth have the same function psychologically; they are man's way of expressing the quintessence of his experience—his way of seeing his life, his self-image and his relations to the world of his fellow men and of nature—in a total figure which at the same moment carries the *vital meaning* of this experience. The myth of Adam is thus not just a tale of a man in paradise who eats an apple in disobedience to a command, but a story by which we confront the profound problem of the birth of human consciousness, the relation of man to authority, and moral self-knowledge in the sense symbolized by "the *tree* of the knowledge of good and evil." Thus true myths and symbols, so long as they retain their original power, always carry an element of ultimate meaning which illuminates but reaches beyond each individual man's concrete experience.

The Oedipus myth is particularly useful for our inquiry since it is central both in psychoanalysis and literature. It is basic to the thinking and theoretical system of Freud, and is present in practically all other schools of psychoanalytic thought as well. Freud took it as a picture of the sexual attraction between the child and the parent of the opposite sex: the child experiences guilt thereby, fear of the parent of whom he is the rival, and, illustrated most clearly in the situation of boys, he then suffers castration anxiety. Other schools, like Adler's, deny the instinctual aspect of the Oedipal conflict and see it rather as a power struggle between child and parent; the neo-Freudian cultural schools likewise tend to view it, as does Fromm, in terms of the conflict with authority vested in the parent. In general, it is accepted in American thought along the lines made popular by Freud, that the little boy wants to have sexual relations with and marry his mother, has concurrently the desire to kill and put out of the way his rival, the father, and experiences all the conflicts of repression, anxiety and guilt inherent in such a situation.

But there is a radical and very important difference between the approach of Freud to this myth and this meaning it is given in this country, including that by most orthodox psychoanalysts. Freud presupposed a view of the infant as destructive and driven by cannibalistic desires; the "innocence of the child consists of weakness of limb." For Freud, therefore, the Oedipus myth was genuinely tragic. But in this country we have an almost opposite attitude toward the infant, a Rousseau-esque attitude, as Dr. Ramon Sarro pointed out at the Barcelona Conference. The baby is essentially social, is called an "angel" by doting parents and viewed at least potentially, as an angel if only society—and these all-important mothers and fathers who, in the hey-day of this attitude, tried to discharge their impossibly heavy task by tiptoeing around on pins and needles when they weren't frantically reading books on childcare—does not frustrate the little angel's needs for nourishment too much. The significant point here is that Freud's emphasis on the genuine tragedy in the Oedipus myth was wiped out; the external form of the concept was kept, but its central meaning was lost. Recently one of the leading theorists of the orthodox psychoanalytic school remarked that the Oedipus myth only showed the "vicissitudes of the family relationship." Certainly it shows much more than that. This illustrates how the tragic aspects of Freud's theories—aspects which saved Freud from succumbing to the mechanistic implications inherent in his dynamics—are the first things thrown overboard when Freudianism crosses the Atlantic.

We believe that Freud's tragic view was closer to the truth, but that he was in error in interpreting the myth literalistically. One consequence of this literalistic interpretation was that the healing aspects of the myth are left out. We propose to demonstrate here that the myth transcends the literalistic problems of sex and aggression. Its tragic locus lies rather in the individual's self-consciousness, his struggles with his fate, in self-knowledge and self-consciousness.

When we read the actual drama of Oedipus, let us say as it comes to Freud and to us from the pen of Sophocles,[1] we are surprised to see that it has nothing to do with conflicts about sexual desire or killing the father as such. These are all done long in the past when the drama begins. Oedipus is a good king ("the mightiest head among us all," he is called) who has reigned wisely and strongly in Thebes and has been for a number of years happily married to Queen Jocasta. The only issue in the drama is whether he will recognize what he has done. The tragic issue is that of seeing the truth about one's self; it is the tragic drama of the passionate relation to truth. Oedipus' tragic flaw in his wrath against his own reality.

Thebes is suffering under a plague as the curtain rises. Word has been brought from the oracle that the plague will be lifted only when the murderer of King Laius is discovered. Oedipus calls the old blind seer, Tiresias, and thereupon proceeds a gripping and powerful unfolding step by step of Oedipus' self-knowledge, an unfolding replete with rage, anger at the truth and those who are its bearers, and all other aspects of man's most profound struggle with recognition of his own reality. Tiresias' blindness seems to symbolize the fact that one can more insightfully grasp inner reality about human beings—gain insight—if one is not so distracted by the impingement of external details.

Tiresias at first refuses to answer Oedipus' questioning as to who is the guilty one with the words,

> "How terrible it is to know . . .
> Where no good comes from knowing! Of these matters I was full well aware, but let them slip me . . . ."

In response to Oedipus' new demands and threats, he continues,

> "Let me go home; . . .
> So shalt thou bear thy load most easily."
> "Ye
> Are all unknowing; may say, in any sort. I will not say, lest I display my sorrow."

The drama then unfolds as the progressive revelation of Oedipus to himself, the source from which the truth proceeds being not Oedipus himself but Tiresias, as Professor Paul Ricoeur of the Sorbonne has indicated. The whole gamut of psychoanalystic reactions like "resistance" and "projection" are exhibited by Oedipus as the closer he gets to the truth, the more violently he fights against it. He accuses Tiresias of planning to betray the city; is this why he will not speak? The seer replies,

> "I will not bring remorse upon myself
> and upon you. Why do you search these matters?"

Then in a burst of angry projection Oedipus accuses Tiresias of having killed Laius himself. And when Oedipus is finally told the truth by the goaded seer, that he himself is the murderer of his father, Oedipus turns upon Tiresias and Creon with the charge that these words are inventions, part of their strategy to take over the state. These forms of behavior termed "resistance" and "projection" are an understandable part of every man's bitter struggle against the impossibly heavy and painful burden of responsibility in learning the truth about himself and of enduring the revolutionary impact on his self-image and identity. The former, resistance, is an acting-out of the conviction "I cannot bear to admit it is I, so I will not see it!" The latter, projection, is a way of crying out. "If it is true, it is somebody else; not I! not I!"

Jocasta tries to persuade Oedipus not to place any weight on the seer's accusation,

> "Listen and learn, nothing in human life Turns on the soothsayer's art . . .

But then, as he begins to sense that some portentous mystery surrounds his birth, she, the mother whom he has married, now herself becomes aware of the terrible knowledge that awaits him. She tries desperately to dissuade him;

> ". . . But why should men be fearful,
> oer whom Fortune is mistress, and fore-knowledge
> Of nothing sure? Best take life easily.
> As a man may. For that maternal wedding,
> Have no fear; for many men ere now
> Have dreamed as much; but he who by such dreams
> Sets nothing, has the easiest time of it."

When he still proclaims his resolve to face the truth whatever it may be, she cries,

> "Don't seek it! I am sick, and that's enough . . .
> Wretch, what thou art O mightst thou never know!"

It is fascinating to note here that Jocasta, in saying one should not take dreams—or myths or symbols—too seriously, is sharing the viewpoint we see in many textbooks of psychology. Her words above also express the concept of "adjustment" in psychotherapy, an emphasis which tends always to creep into psychology and psychoanalysis precisely because of the anxiety and radical upheaval that goes with pursuing fully the truths about one's self. Jocasta here enunciates the principle of acceptance of reality *without* the passionate, tragic relation to truth.

Interestingly enough, this emphasis in this myth and many others is identified with the *feminine* principle. The mother or wife, the conserving biological function, is blamed for the tendency to hold the man back from the creative breaking through to truth. This tendency for the man to see the woman as the bearer of the temptation to "take life easily as a man may," the temptress leading him to turn against the possibilities of his emerging "better self," has been commented upon by C. G. Jung and Otto Rank in their depth-psychological studies of creativity. The most fruitful single line of explanation of this, in my judgment, is Rank's idea that all growth is a series of birth experiences and that every new view of truth or the creative act in life is a step in breaking out of the womb and gaining greater individuation. I would add that, since the original breaking out is from the actual womb of the mother, every subsequent act is a reenactment both of fighting against the mother who now represents one's own fear of moving ahead, and an expression of anger and hostility at her for having ejected one in the first place.

Oedipus is not dissuaded, but insists that he must know what he is and where he came from. He must know and accept his own reality and his fate.

> "I will not hearken—not to know the whole,
> Break out what will. I shall not hesitate . . . "

The old shepherd who rescued the infant Oedipus from death on the mountain-side is finally brought, the one man who can provide the final link in the fateful story, "O, I am at the horror, now, to speak!" the shepherd cries. And Oedipus answers, "And I to hear. But I must hear—no less."

When Oedipus does learn the final, tragic truth, he cuts out his eyes. It is significant that he is not *castrated* nor does he castrate himself; he cuts out his eyes, the organ of *seeing*. (The tendency to call this a "symbolic castration" would miss the whole point, and would be another example of using a theory, e.g., the primacy of sexual prototypes, as a procrustean bed on which to force the data). His punishment is then *exile*, first self-imposed but later, as in Colonus, imposed by Creon and the state. The tragedy has now come full circle: he was originally exiled when he was a few days old on his father's order; and his life at last ends again in exile. The exile is a fascinating symbolic act from our modern psychoanalytic viewpoint, for we have much data to indicate that the greatest threat and greatest cause of anxiety for Western man in the middle of the twentieth century is not castration but *ostracism*, the terrible situation of being thrown out of the group. Many a contemporary man castrates himself or permits himself to be castrated because of fear of being exiled if he doesn't. He renounces his power and conforms under the greater threat and peril of ostracism.

We now turn to the drama which follows and which reveals the healing, integrative aspects of the Oedipus myth, namely *Oedipus in Colonus*. So far as I know, this drama is never mentioned in psychoanalytic literature at all, an amazing fact in itself. One reason for its neglect is that discussion of the integrative functions of myths in general tends to be omitted in psychoanalysis. But, more specifically, a consequence of the literalistic interpretation of the myth as having to do with sex and killing the father requires that we stop when these are worked through, punishment meted, and the situation accepted as at the conclusion of *Oedipus Tyrannus*. But viewing the myth as the presentation of man's struggle in self-knowledge to know the reality about his own being, we must indeed go on, as Sophocles does, to see how a man comes to terms with the meaning of these acts. This subsequent drama is Oedipus' stage of reconciliation with himself and with his fellow men in the persons of Theseus and the Athenians, and it is a reconciliation with the ultimate meaning in his life. "For the gods who threw you down sustain you now," as his daughter Ismene phrases it. In some ways this drama is more significant than the first; and since it was written by Sophocles when he was an old man of eighty-nine, it can be supposed to contain the wisdom of his old age as well.

One theme we find in the old Oedipus' meditation at Colonus is *guilt*—the difficult problem of the relation of ethical responsibility to self-consciousness. Is a man guilty if the act was unpremeditated, done unknowingly? In the course of his probing old Oedipus has come to terms with his guilt. He defends himself indignantly against the brash accusations of Creon,

> "If then came into the world—as I did come—
> In wretchedness, and met my father in fight
>
> And knocked him down, not knowing that I killed him

Nor whom I killed—again, how could you find
Guilt in that unmediated act? . .

As for my mother—damn you, you have no shame,
Though you are her own brother,—

But neither of us knew the truth: and she
Bore my children also—. . .
While I would not have married her willingly
Nor willingly would I ever speak of it."

Again, about his father he cries out that he has

"A juist extenuation.
This:
I did not know him; and he wished to murder me.
Before the law—before God—I am innocent!"

It is clear that Oedipus accepts and bears his responsibility; but he insists that the delicate and subtle interplay of conscious and unconscious factors (as we could call them) always makes any legalistic or pharisaic imputation of guilt inaccurate and wrong. It is a truism since Freud that the problem of guilt is as much within the heart as within the act. The play holds that the sins of meanness, of avarice and the irreverence of Creon and Polyneices are "no less grave than those sins of passion for which Oedipus was punished; that in condemning them to the merciless justice soon to descend, Oedipus acts thoroughly in accord with a moral order which his own experience has enabled him to understand."

In angry, vehement words, Oedipus refuses the tricky proposal of the cruel Creon, the present dictator of Thebes, who tries to get the exiled king to return by using Antigone as hostage; and Oedipus refuses likewise the entreaty of his son, Polyneices, though he knows the destruction of Thebes will result. Oedipus' maturity does not at all include the virtue of forgiveness of enemies, a later Christian idea he would no doubt have scorned. Nevertheless, the play does point toward a conclusion emphasized by modern existential psychologists that because of this interplay of conscious and unconscious factors in guilt and the impossibility of legalistic blame, we are forced into an attitude of acceptance of the universal human situation and recognition of the participation of every one of us in man's inhumanity to man. The words to Oedipus from the hero, King Theseus, who exhibits no inner conflict at all, are nevertheless poignant.

". . . for I
Too was an exile . . .
I know I am only a man; I have no more
To hope for in the end than you have."

Another theme in this integrative drama is the power of Oedipus—now that he has suffered through his terrible experiences and come to terms with them—*to impart grace.* As he himself says to the natives who find him with his daughter in the grove at Colonus,

> "For I come here as one endowed with grace,
> By those who are over Nature; and I bring
> Advantage to this race . . . ."

Theseus accepts this: "Your presence, as you say, is a great blessing." This capacity to impart grace, assumedly, is connected with the maturity and other emotional and spiritual qualities which result from the courageous confronting of his shattering experiences. Says Oedipus,

> "One soul, I think, often can make atonement
> For many others, if it be devoted . . . ."

But there is also a clear symbolic element to make the point of his grace unmistakable: the oracle has revealed that his body after death will ensure victory to the land and the ruler which possess him. The mere "presence" of his body has this power.

A last emphasis we mention in the outworking of the myth is *love.* The messenger who came back to the people to report the marvelous manner of Oedipus' death states that in his last words to his daughters he said

> ". . And yet one word
> Frees us of all the weight and pain of life:
> That word is love."

But Oedipus does not at all mean love as the absence of aggression or the strong affects of anger. His sharp and violent temper, present at the crossroads where he killed his father years before and exhibited in his sharp thrusts with Tiresias, is still much in evidence in this last drama, unsubdued by suffering or maturity. The fact that Sophocles does not see fit to remove or soften Oedipus' aggression and his anger—the fact, that is, that the "aggression" and the "angry affects" are not the "flaws" he has old Oedipus get over—lends support to our thesis above that the aggression involved in killing the father is not the central issue of the dramas. Oedipus' maturity is not at all a renouncing of passion to come to terms with society, not at all a learning to live "in accord with the reality requirements of civilization." It is a reconciliation with himself, with special persons he loves, and the religious meaning of his life.

Love, thus, is not the opposite of anger or aggression. Old Oedipus will love only those he chooses to love: his son, who has betrayed him, asks for mercy and remarks, "Compassion limits even the power of God," but Oedipus will have none of it. The love, rather, he bears his daughters, Antigone and

Ismene, and the love they have shown him during his exiled, blind wanderings, is the kind of love he chooses to bless.

Robert Fitzgerald, translator, writes in his notes to the play, "It should be remembered that one of Oedipus' distinguishing qualities was, in the first place, his intelligence. He saved Thebes once by solving the riddle of the Sphinx. He saved the city again by solving with furious persistence the riddle of his own birth. And in this play we see once more the working of that intellect, driving this time toward a transcendence of the purely human." I think Fitzgerald is wrong here in calling this "intelligence," though obviously he is right in his general emphasis. This saving quality of Oedipus goes quite beyond intellectual functions; his solving the riddle of the Sphinx (the word "Sphinx" means "one who binds fast") is much more what we would call "insight" and sensitivity than it is the purely rational functions. I believe the term, "self-consciousness" in the special way we have used it in this paper to refer to man's capacity for self-knowledge and self-transcendence (rather than in the strictly Cartesian sense of consciousness) is what Fitzgerald is referring to. It is, incidentally, an intriguing psychological implication in the dramas as a whole that *that particular man* who lives through his aggressive potentialities, who does not shrink from standing against his father and consummating the sexual drives in his assertive way, is just the man who solves the riddle and knows the answer "man" and the one who, experiencing his tragic fate, goes on to be a bearer of grace and salvation for others.

Finally, describing Oedipus' miraculous death and burial, the messenger says,

> "But some attendant from the Atrain of Heaven
> Came for him; or else the underworld
> Opened in love the unlit door of earth.
> For he was taken without almentation,
> Illness or suffering; indeed his end
> Was wonderful if mortal's ever was."

This touching and beautiful death of a great character is magnificent as Sophocles presents it dramatically. As *Oedipus Tyrannus* is the drama of "unconscious," the struggle to confront the reality of the dark, destructive forces in man, *Oedipus in Colonus* may be said to be the drama of consciousness, the aspect of the myth which is concerned with the search for meaning and reconciliation. Both together comprise the myth of man confronting his own reality, a confronting that is possible and inevitable by the unique structure of self-consciousness.

NOTES

1 To the argument that we are taking Sophocles' "drama," and that the myth itself does have the "content" of killing the father and marrying the mother, I would rejoin that the myth of Adam has the content of eating an apple against a commandment. Than Anatole France could rightly remark. "Tant de bruit pour une pomme" (So much noise over one apple). But everyone would agree that such a literalistic, fundamentalistic interpretation does not at all do justice to the profound truths and meaning of the Adam myth. If we are to take the Oedipus myth literalistically, as a portrayal of the growing boy's attachment to his mother, Oedipus would precisely *not* have had this toward Jocasta: for he was thrown out on the hillside to die as an infant before he scarcely saw his mother; his "Oedipus" would have expressed itself with the Queen of Corinth, who raised him. I wish by this illustration of the "reductio ad absurdum" of the literalistic interpretation to indicate that we must always go beyond such interpretations and ask the meaning of the myth. Sophocles does this, and I think in a way faithful to the inner consistency and truth of the myth.

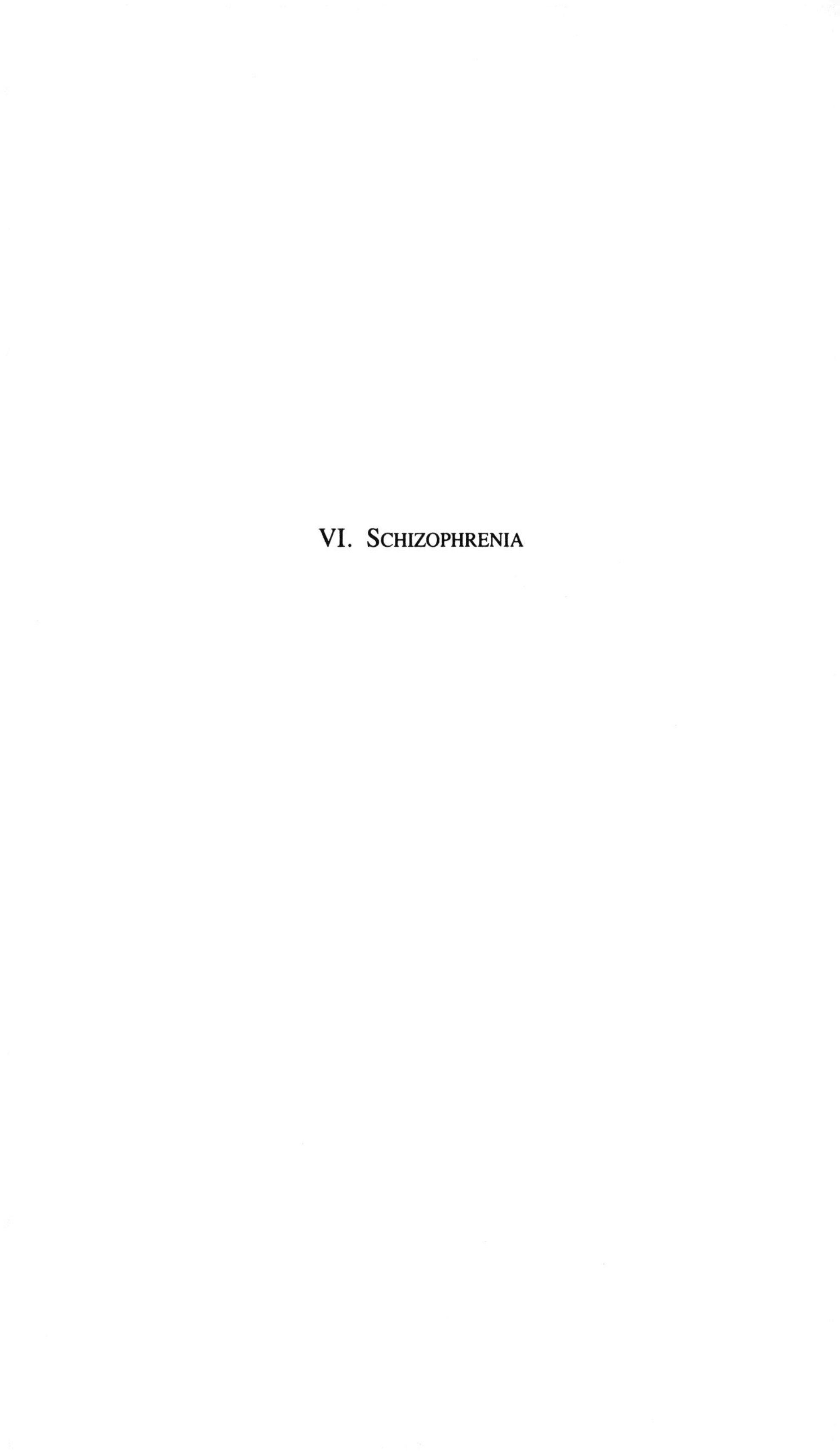

VI. Schizophrenia

Schizophrenia: Problems and Methods of Psychotherapy

EUGENE T. GENDLIN

I

Later in this paper, I will state five principles for psychotherapy with schizophrenics. First, I want to discuss several problems which schizophrenics, in particular, pose for the therapist. It is really more true to say that these were problems for us, as a group of therapists, in working with schizophrenics. Looking back, we see now that the same problems arise also with parents, with children, and with people who do not have a well worked out sense of what therapy is. They arise also with the externalized defensive, non-inward-looking client who isn't ready to sit down and engage in therapy. In the last analysis, the same problems arise with everyone. Still, I will term these "special challenges in working with schizophrenics."

First, silence. Over and over again we met hours of silence. This was not the kind of silence that we like and are used to in therapy: the kind of silence in which the individual deeply, inwardly explores himself, or feels something relevant and important. That kind of silence is not only easy to stand; it seems important and valuable to us. If the individual talks all the time, then he is *not* deeply engaged in therapy. Only when he stops to let something "sift down" or "seep in" (whatever you choose to call this inward process), he is really doing therapy.

The silence we met in working with schizophrenics was a different kind. It was a silence of emptiness, of resistance. Sometimes the patient did not know what this—to us a therapy relationship—was. It was an unwilling, not knowing what to do in, kind of silence. Sometimes it stretched for twenty or thirty interviews. There would, perhaps, be one hour in which something did happen, and then, next time, silence again.

Second, whether silent or not, these patients did not develop a sense for the exploration process of therapy. They were not *set* to ask questions of themselves, to inquire into themselves, work on themselves, come to know themselves, or struggle through what was bothering them. The assumption (which we have not yet formulated well) that is usually shared between the therapist and the client—"I have a problem," or "I have lots of problems," or "I don't like my life," or "I'm not happy with me . . . *what can we do about it?"*—was missing with these patients. If, for a little while, it seemed as if the patient were talking about something of importance to him in the direction of understanding, or exploring, or improving, or struggling with his person, a little while later that would be gone again. It would be as if it had never happened. There was no continuing exploration set.

Third, the self-propelled process that we were used to did not occur with these patients. Usually this process arises after a certain initial period. At first, I have a sense that I, as the therapist, am "pulling" the process. It is my responses that are bringing the client's attention to his feelings, to something relevant. Then, after a while, as I respond repeatedly to the level of felt meaning or feelings, *it* moves. The client finds that he is now looking at a new feeling, and he says, "Oh, there is this other aspect." He finds arising in him something that he has always felt, yet never really looked at before. Soon both he and I are *following* whatever feeling comes up next. When that process stops temporarily, he "scans inwardly," or "sifts inwardly" for a while, and then says, "Oh, and another thing is. . . ." The process becomes self-propelled. *It* pulls both of us. This, too, did not occur with these patients.

Fourth—and this was a phenomena that happened with great regularity—the patient would reject the therapist. The rejection was not just the give-and-take of interview encounter as we are used to it from therapy. Rather, it was a total rejection of the whole prospect of a relationship with this therapist, seeing this therapist, coming to interviews. It was a more or less total "go away and leave me alone" from the patient, pointed both at the therapist and at the idea of continuing interviews. If these patients had not been hospitalized, and if it had not been possible (and in a sense required) for the therapists to *force* themselves on the patients, in most cases therapy would have stopped at one time or another.

I was the first therapist in this group to take a patient, and the first to be rejected. I was not, at least then, accustomed to seeing someone who did not want to see me. It had always been the other person's need that was my excuse for being there, for living, for working. *He* needed me and I had nothing to do with it. Even my specific responses, what I said in therapy, occurred because of what *he* just said. I was quite used to (and quite spoiled by, as I see it now) the fact that my foundation was always provided by *his* need. But here was a person who said, "Leave me alone. Go away. I don't want to talk. I talk to *some* people, but I don't want to talk to *you*. Aren't there other patients you can see?" Here was a person who did not even want to enter an office with me, let alone have some tense, mysterious, and probably phony thing called "therapy" or "let me help you."

Yet he was our first research patient. He was of the right age, sex, social class and degree of disturbance, and had been matched with a control on all of these points. The whole research would be skewed if we began dropping people who were not cooperative. We would have a group of only those patients who wanted therapy and were outgoing and cooperative. Our findings would mean very little. As a result, when the patient did not want to see me I felt and surely conveyed a great deal of pressure. He *had* to see me. I very much felt the need to tell him somehow that there was no choice—neither he nor I had any choice. The research design had selected us for each other. There was no way out. But I wasn't used to this. Both as a therapist and as a person, I did not then have any ability to force myself into a situation where I was not welcome.

I slowly learned that there is another reason why I might go to see someone. It might not be because he needs me, which makes it very easy. Instead, it might be because I want to, because I decide to. The space I take up is in some sense mine, and I can say that I am here because I decided to be here. I know you don't want me to be here, but you stand *there,* I stand *here*. This space I take up because I want to. It took me a while to learn that. During this period I would go to see him for just a few minutes, just as much as I could bear—*I* could bear—and then I would leave again.

This happened repeatedly to almost every one of the therapists. And it is invariably a painful experience. It isn't just that you blame yourself for things you did that may have brought it about. The patient is ill, afraid, and withdrawing. You know that, but it's still painful—particularly painful not to be *able* to reach out to him for such a long period, when you want to (and not to be able to give up either). And it is painful in another sense: I find that I have a great deal of warmth for the person I am trying to make contact with, and the warmth gets turned back by this rejection. It then has to accumulate again and overcome this feeling.

A fifth special characteristic of these patients is that they are isolated, or disconnected, or out of interaction in a way that is worth talking about separately. It isn't just that they have "this problem" or "that personality content," or "this conflict," or "that difficulty." They are somehow as people cut off. I am becoming increasingly convinced that we should approach this kind of patient from the beginning with a thrust to reconnect him. I now say, at the beginning, something like, "I will get you out of here." "I will do something about this." "There can be a job for you after a while. You'll work here and then we'll get you a job on the outside. You don't have to go back where you came from." I know that where he came from is where he got sick, and the people he lived with are the people he got sick with and became isolated from. I want to bring this message—even though I know it can't be heard completely at the beginning (I think it is heard on some level). The message is: I'll reconnect you to the world and to me, and in a different way than you were before because that failed—there you were isolated.[1]

I think it is characteristic of these people that there is not only this or that specific difficulty. It is not only *what* the trouble is. As whole persons, they have become isolated, cut off, dampened, shut in, silent inside, dulled, and separated from living. Some kind of reconnecting them to us and to the world is needed. For this reason, I think that all our efforts to define schizophrenia—to classify it as a disease entity—will probably fail. Schizophrenia is something that *isn't*. Interaction *isn't*. Being alive toward other people inside *isn't*. Certainly there must be all kinds of chemical imbalances and organismic reactions as a result of this. If we can find chemical means to alleviate these, the individual may be more able to become reconnected. I doubt, however, that there can be a chemical or any other kind of cure without interaction. I think the *not* being, the absence, the cutoffness of interaction constitutes what we call schizophrenia.

In summary, the special characteristics I mentioned were: a long and empty kind of silence, the absence of an exploration process and the absence of a set towards exploration, the absence of a self-propelled therapeutic process, the rejection of the therapist, and the disconnectedness.

II

In the face of these challenges, a typical therapist reaction would be to try just about everything. Preconceptions and favorite methods that don't work are very quickly discarded. This, more than anything else, has moved us away from a concern with technique, a concern with being "client-centered" or being any other particular way—even from being "therapeutic[1]" to the extent that the word implies a particular method. We have shifted from talking about the optimal response behavior to much more basic and global factors: the attitudes of the therapist, the approach that as one person he takes toward the other person, how to make interaction happen where it isn't happening. We now see these as much more fundamental variables.

This trend began even before we began working with schizophrenics. Rogers presented a theory of basic "conditions" or therapist attitudes some years ago. *Conceptually,* this was what I have just described: Rogers proposed that the personal attitudes of the therapist toward the client are basic, rather than "reflection of feeling," or "interpretation," or some other method. But for some years, despite this theory, we continued discussing and practicing quite definite kinds of behaviors. For example, whatever the client said, I would try to sense the felt meaning of what he said and I would respond to that. We held theoretically that there might be any number of other behaviors which would manifest understanding, but in practice we remained within this fairly narrow band of response behavior. Working with schizophrenics taught us a much wider vocabulary of behavior, a much wider range of what one might do, what one might be pushed into doing by one's own feelings and own needs, in order to reach a person not being reached.

I think, and will try to show, that the basic principles are the *same* as they were. If you look, not at the specific technique or behavior that we earlier asserted, but at *why* that technique seemed so important, the *why* is the same for the different behaviors today as it was then.

For example, we felt then that the therapist should not add interpretations, extraneous material, or expressions of his own feelings. Why? Because these are likely to get the client off *his* track. It is, after all, *his* process of experiencing, working through, and focusing on himself that makes therapy. Opinions and extraneous deductions distract the client from his inward attention, and, as a result, therapy will not move. For this reason, such responses did not seem to fit into therapy.

However, here is a client who is not on any therapeutic track. In order to *make something happen,* a therapist can use not only what the client is expressing and going through, but also what he himself, as a therapist, as a person in this moment, is going through. While the client may give me very little to go on, I have all the events going on in me to use in order to make something happen. As I will discuss in more detail later, I still also have the important responsibility to respond to *him,* especially once I do make something happen.

We also felt that it was not good to answer questions. If a client asked a question, it was typical for the client-centered therapist not to answer it, but instead to pay attention to why he was asking it or to try to reflect the feeling that underlay the asking. Why? Because very often a question would be only indirectly related to what the individual was concerned about. Answering the question would shut off the process before the real point of the question could appear. For example, a client who did not feel understood by the therapist in some important way might ask, "How old are you?" This was relevant only in the sense that it meant: "How can a young person like you understand me, particularly as you just didn't?" If the therapist answered the question, he often shut off the important process which develops from this underlying concern. For the same reason we did not express opinions. The therapist's opinion would get in the way of the further process which often leads to quite different concerns than appear at first.

With these patients, however, I find that I want to and need to bring myself in much more. I need to show the patient where I am. I don't want subverbal cues alone to determine his imagination of what I might be thinking. My tendency now is flatly to answer *all* questions, showing what is going on inside me, and then very quickly I add, "But why are you asking?" or "Are you asking because of this?" This may seem like the opposite behavior, but the basic principle in both is to bring out *his* track, to enable him to express where *he* is. Similarly, I now very often express quite flatly what my opinion is. I then make *sure* I say after that, "But I don't really know, and besides, I have a feeling that you think something entirely different, and what I just said doesn't fit." I tell him why I think that the opinion I have just presented is probably miles away from what he is concerned about and perhaps *must* be concerned about *before* anything else will fit or be pertinent or helpful. I sometimes flatly ask, "Now tell me, why doesn't that fit?" As a result, we then attend to where his concern is and why my opinion doesn't fit. Again, the principle of getting to his process, or enabling him to express *his* perceptions and work with *his* feelings, stays the same.

We used to wait for the client. We did this because the client's ongoing process is well worth waiting for. For example, even if I know he will have to talk about a sexual difficulty which he has hinted at, I can wait, because the process is moving. What he is working on *now* is next; that is what he is now feeling and is now up against. When that is resolved, something else will be next, and then something else. Soon he may be where I have guessed he has to go, and it is now the next step in *his* process.

With these people, however, it did not work that way. So often there is no ongoing process of this sort. The patient's hints are quite often desperate beggings that someone help him talk about "this thing." If, in the middle of an incoherent jumble, a patient says to me, "I feel like a prostitute," I will respond to that. If I don't respond to it at that moment because I'm not able to or don't want to, *I'll* come back to it. I need not wait for the patient to raise it again. I will respond not only to this one phrase but to a whole problem area it implies. What I make of it is, of course, my own construction, and I'll tell him that. I might say, "I imagine that you have some kind of important sexual mess there that you're afraid to talk about and that you don't like yourself for. That's what I imagine. I don't really know because you didn't tell me very much. But I wish you would. And if not today, then some other time." And *I* will bring it up again.

What is the principle of this? Earlier, as now, the principle is: even though I intellectually conclude that he must soon talk about sex, that does not mean that bringing it up now, while he's working on something else, will enable him to deal genuinely with the sexual matter. What will happen? We won't really be working on anything. He will *cognitively* discuss the correctness of my guess, and eventually we will have to go back to what he was genuinely working upon and work there again. But it is quite different when someone half-helplessly asks please to be responded to on this, which he can hardly stand to talk about, but which, nevertheless, is there for him. It does not hurt such a person to talk about it openly. It is not as though *you* have "dredged it up" and it might harm him because he is not yet ready to hear it. He already has it. It is not true that he would not have to deal with it had you left it alone. Nor will he deal with it only intellectually. He *is* dealing with it, and in an intensely painful and lonely way. The question is: will you leave him to deal with it alone, or will you respond to him on it?

Finally, as an underlying client-centered principle (this is only one of the many ways of stating it): we have always wanted to respond to the *felt meaning*. (I term it the "felt meaning." More commonly it is called "the feeling," though we do not only mean any emotion such as "You're angry" or "You're afraid." Rogers termed it the felt concrete "personal meaning" implicit in what an individual says). For example, someone may tell you a story about what happened to him. He is working in some sense on himself. This situation that happened is important, and upsetting, and that is all he knows clearly. He tells the whole situation in great detail: "He said this . . . and I said this . . . and then this happened . . . and how could that happen?" Then you respond. What do you respond to? Not to all the details of the situation, but to what that whole situation is for him—what it amounts to for him, how he is in it, what the personal implicit felt thing he is struggling with is—in so far as you get that. Your words point to that, whether you are accurate or inaccurate. You may say, "You felt helpless in that situation, and yet you wanted very much for it to be all right, but you couldn't convince yourself or something." He may say, "No, it's not quite that. It's more like this. . . ." He is focusing his attention on how that feels.

Contrast this with a deductive response. Instead of trying to grasp the individual's felt sense of the reported situation, you use it to deduce what you can about him. From his description of himself or the situation you can tell that he is a given *kind* of person, and that, under different circumstances, he would react in various given ways. He has deducible general traits. You can correctly deduce many generalized traits of this sort.

I draw this distinction as a horizontal and a vertical axis. *Horizontally,* from what the individual now says, you can deduce many things he is *not now* saying (is not now concerned with). Such things are true *in general* of people who say the kind of thing he is saying. *Vertically,* the dimension is the depth with which you can point to the felt sense of what he *is now* looking at. This model will fit any type of therapy, though it would not necessarily be expressed in these terms. Psychoanalysts would say that the interpretation for which the patient is ready, the proper interpretation for now, is one which helps what is *just now* under the surface, about to "break through." Any other interpretation may be correct, but the patient is "not ready for it" now. Though we use different ways to describe it, we all try to respond to the felt, now ongoing, concrete, momentary process of experiencing. The present implicit felt meanings can thereby be spoken and interacted with.

Again, this principle has stayed the same. However, often with these clients this type of process is not now ongoing. The therapist has to do something to *make* it happen.

III

With this emphasis on the therapist's use of his own experiencing, some rules or principles are necessary. I will state some of these, though we have not yet formulated enough such rules. We need to differentiate, define, and make much more explicit what we do as therapists, so that we can discuss it, institute research and train people in it. We do not have enough defined words with which to talk about what we do as therapists. Thus the differentiations I will draw are in an area we know well but in which we have no socially standard words.

First, I will describe three levels on which I might respond to another person. I might respond, as I have just discussed, to the very specific felt meaning implied in what he just now says. This is the narrowest level on which I might respond: what he just now says or indicates is going on in him. (If he says nothing, I may still respond to what I sense might be occurring just now.)

On a broader level, I can ask myself, "What is *all this* about? Where are we? What is this?" (I might mean by "all this" what has happened in the last few minutes, the whole hour, or even the last several interviews.) I can respond to all of this that has happened or that he has been trying to do.

There is a third and even wider source of response, and that is I. I can ask, "What is *my* response, as a person, to this other person?" We are taught to look least at *ourselves,* to look least at our personal response to this person in this moment. Usually, our own personal response must be quite strong before we feel it at all. By then it has usually become something upsetting or wrong: "How can I get across?" or "Why doesn't he talk about something important?" or "Why doesn't he talk?" or "Why are we stuck?" At such a well advanced stage of trouble I first become aware of a riot going on *in me*. Otherwise, as long as he is doing something therapeutically relevant, my attention is comfortably settled on *him*.

To illustrate these three levels: here is a person saying something to which my response might be, "You feel all alone." This is a response on the first level: a response to what he is just now saying, what is now occurring in him. Then I have a sudden realization that, "Oh, yes, that seems to be the point of *all of this*. He's *been* sitting there the whole hour, isolated, alone, looking away, talking in his own autistic space, as if I weren't even here, yet in some way reaching out for someone to come and pick him up and take him, touch him, or be with him." That is the second level. Finally, on the third level, there is *my* reaction of wanting to take him by the shoulders and make him aware that I am here, my wanting to take him out of this autism in some way. I find that these three response levels are always available.

A second principle: there is almost always a *positive* way of responding to another person's troublesome behavior. *In the world,* the given behavior is self-defeating. It pushes people away, makes them angry, and defeats what he is trying to do. Yet there is a way of looking at the behavior such that there appears in it the implicit *positive* attempt to live, to reach another person, to express a feeling, to be real, to be a warm, enjoyed person, to satisfy needs. I may not be able to see it that way at first, but I can assume it is there. I can assume that this person who is now pushing me away is, in some sense, reaching for someone. This may seem like my stubborn assumption, but it is a helpful one. I find at the next moment that I can respond to the fear of me that is involved in his pushing me away. Or I may find that I can respond to a way in which we *are* related which is implicit in this angry pushing me away. Perhaps he is angry at me because I will not stay longer. The hour is over. Initially, it bothers me that he is angry at me. I don't like it when people are angry at me. Now the whole hour seems spoiled. He can't stand limits and refuses to accept my need to go. With a few seconds of attention, however, I can see, in addition to this, that his anger means we have the kind of relationship in which it is important that I stay. It suddenly strikes me that his anger is also an expression of closeness toward me. I now have a very different reaction than my initial one: "I am glad that you very much want me to stay!" I find this powerful reaction only a few seconds later. This kind of reaction fits the patient's experiencing process in a way which carries it forward as a successful interaction.

By positive, I do not mean "good" or "nice" (in my example, it was anger). Rather, I mean *completed as an interaction between two human beings*. A great many things these people do (as well as a great many things we all do) are not successful as efforts to interact as persons. However, there is (probably always) the possibility of responding to these behaviors so as to make a completed interaction. Only sometimes do I find this response. Yet, it is extremely powerful when I am occasionally able to make a successful interaction out of one of these self-defeating relationship moves.

Third, I find that it is necessary to go through a few steps of looking at and differentiating my own feelings. At first I may have only a painful, stuck, embarrassed, frustrated feeling that something is wrong. That, by itself, gives me very little with which I can do anything. When I look at it, however, I find in the next second that: "Oh, yes. Why isn't he talking more about something important? *That's* really what is bothering me." With another moment of attention I then find: "I wish he would." At the first moment I was simply tense and frustrated, and I had nothing to say. A moment later I could have said, "Why don't you ever say anything you really feel? Why do you give me only this junk?" At the third instant, however, I can say, "Why don't you let me hear more from you? I have a strong wish to hear from you. I feel like inviting you to come in much further than you have been doing." It is really the same feeling at all three points, but a few seconds of attention are needed to allow it to unfold. When I can allow myself to attend to the stuck, embarrassed feeling of: "I don't know how to do anything useful here with you," I almost always find in it a whole reservoir of responses, most of them towards the other person.

A fourth principle, and I think this should be a formal rule: It Is Permissable For Me To Be Foolish. I have discovered that there is only one person in the world who really deeply and strongly cares whether I am very effective and marvelous or whether I am foolish, and that person is I. It does not matter so much to anyone else. Therefore, I do not really need to care so much about it either. I can risk not doing well, or seeming as though I am not doing well. I can afford to take this kind of chance.

This specific rule involves a broader principle: I find it helpful to separate my concern *for the other person* from my concerns and fears *for myself*. Once I realize, for example, that I am afraid I will do the wrong thing and be an incompetent therapist, then I can see that I also care for him quite separately from this. My care *for him* has a different quality. My fear for me constricts me. My care for him is an expansive, freeing feeling. Thus when I find myself hurt, stuck, and constricted, I know I am concerned for me, and I spend a few seconds untangling my own concerns. If I allow these room, I then find: "Oh, yes. *He's* still there and he's important to me." He is *another* person. We are not "grown together" in such a way that *he* has to get well so *I* can be comfortable with myself. That, it is true, is my concern, but above and beyond that, there *he* is, a separate person.

Especially in a situation where you are rejected and where, no matter what you do, you sometimes feel foolish or incompetent, it is quite important to let the separateness of the patient emerge in this way. It is a freeing discovery that, because he is separate, I don't really *have* to get him well. All these felt pressures are really just for me.

I admit these pressures which, I realize, I feel *for me*. They do not drop away. But, when I realize they are for me, they lose their seemingly great importance. As long as my fears for me and my concern for him are mixed together, the mixture carries all the importance and worth of my professional and personal concern for this human being. I feel I *must* give such concerns weight. They are my indicators of when I do a responsible job. I am not easily careless or foolish with other people's lives. When I realize the part of my felt pressure which is for me, that part loses its importance. I can afford to play with it, to incur it, to be foolish. Above and beyond these pressures there is left my concern *for him*. How what I do will affect him, that *is* important, that isn't something I can be careless about—but, as usually happens, my concern for him doesn't feel constricting and pressured. It feels expansive and freeing. *He* suddenly emerges as a separate person and I can really care for him.

For these reasons, I think, it is a very important principle to try to distinguish between the feelings and concerns I have for me, and those I have for him. It is this distinction which allows me to be or seem foolish as only my self-image is at stake.

Finally, I want to state a rough formula to summarize all these considerations. By being *more* expressive, by bringing *more* of ourselves, we can be even *less* imposing than we were before. Years ago the principle that we did not want to impose led us to keep ourselves secret. However, we did impose assumptions, pressures, expectations, and preconceptions which we left unstated. The client remained in a half-lonely condition, while we, also in a half-lonely way, kept to ourselves what was going on in us.

The principle of non-imposition still stands. We try to keep separate what is he and what is I. If I can sense something happening in him, a statement of what I feel is going on *in him* is still the most powerful response. But just as I try to say what is occurring in *him,* without imposing on it my own feelings and interpretations, so also can I say what is in *me* separately, without confusing it with him or forcing it on him. I can say it clearly as *me*, as a statement about myself. I may not be at all sure what he feels. I leave that space empty for him to fill purely as him. By not imposing on his space, I can also say what I feel as *me*, in my space.

NOTE

1 This runs counter to the policy of some hospital systems, e.g., Wisconsin. With only a few exceptions, the patient must be signed out by, and go back to, the people who signed him in. However, in different hospitals customs vary a great deal in this regard. For example, the policy of VA hospitals is not always to send a patient back to the relatives who brought him. By "disconnected" I do not mean that the patient feels separate—very often he lives all his reactions within his bad, closed, hurtful relationship to someone. But that is a relationship in which interaction is largely missing and his inward living is shut down to a large extent.

Minkowski and Schizophrenia

R. D. Laing

Minkowski's major contribution to psychiatry is his work on schizophrenia. The phrase by which he is best known in Britain and America, "the loss of vital contact with reality," gives only a hint of the nature of his views. As no adequate account of this work is available in English, the following is a somewhat belated exposition and critique of its main features.

SCHIZOIDICITY VERSUS SYNTONICITY

The prevailing theory about schizophrenia on the Continent in the 1920s was the same as today: namely, that schizophrenia was a hereditary-genetic disease, the core of which was a hypothetical schizophrenic "process," that tended to be progressive. One tried to unravel signs of the process and signs deriving from attempts to adapt to the process. "Schizoid" was variously used in the literature to denote

(i) all persons presumed to be genetically linked with schizophrenics;
(ii) phenemona presumed to be consequence of a schizophrenic process;
(iii) patients presumed to have a genetic link with known schizophrenics and presumed to be subject to the schizophrenic process, although not psychotic: i.e., who exhibited what would be regarded as a mild form, or a "forme fruste" of schizophrenia, or latent schizophrenia. (If a schizophrenic illness could have stricken the organism in utero, or in very early childhood, the schizoid might be post-psychotic.)[1]

Manic-depressive psychosis also had its companion concept of cycloid, modified by Bleuler to syntonic.

For Minkowski, schizoid and schizophrenic are two distinct concepts.

> "Schizoid and schizophrenic remain as concepts, clearly separated from each other. The one refers to a constitutional factor and this is in principle unchangeable in the same individual. The other is an illness which tends to progress."[2]

In this, Minkowski follows Bleuler's later formulations, in regarding the "schizoid" and "syntonic" as two principles of life which are not specifically "morbid." In schizophrenia, the syntonic factors seem to become more and more effaced. Deprived of the counterbalance of this regulating factor, the schizoid factor comes to dominate the psyche, and in so doing gives birth to the monstrous forms of which manifest schizophrenia is composed.[3]

In the manic-depressive psychosis, on the contrary, the schizoid "radical," whereby the human personality is supposed to affirm itself as such in and through the continued interaction with the world, no longer intervenes. Psychic life in its absence becomes stripped of depth and has only one dimension. The manic-depressive, as a person, no longer exists; he has disappeared. He is all words and gestures.[4]

But, Minkowski points out, if we say that the schizophrenic becomes more and more schizoid and less and less syntonic, we cannot say *mutatis mutandis* that the manic-depressive becomes more and more syntonic, even though he may become less and less schizoid. If we say that the syntonic faculty consists of understanding one's fellows, of feeling "with" them in their suffering and in their joy, of being at one with them and at one with things, how can one say of the manic-depressive, with his flight of ideas and his lability of mood, that he is more syntonic than the normal syntone. As Bleuler and others have said, the manic avidly absorbs the external world and is continually occupied by it. There is a sense in which, in contrast to the agitated schizophrenic, he remains in contact with the world. His "contact" is a very imperfect one, however. It exists only for the moment, it has no duration, and for this reason is far from representing greater syntonicity: compared to the full and harmonious syntonia of the normal syntone, it is empty and dissonant. The maximum of syntonicity is thus found in the normal, whereas it seems that one must seek for the maximum schizoidicity in the pathological.

In applying the concept of schizoidicity and syntonicity diagnostically, Minkowski became one of the first to make explicit the use of inter-personal disjunction or conjunction as a diagnostic instrument.[5]

Every psychiatrist knows, according to Minkowski, that instinctively he bears himself in quite a different way when he is face to face with a case of manic-depressive psychosis from when he has to deal with a schizophrenic. Since Bleuler, the psychiatrist now uses his own reactions as a criterion in trying to assess where there exists affective contact (Affektiver Rapport of Bleuler) between him and his patients.

The psychiatrist uses his own response to the other (the patient) to gauge the degree of schizoidicity or syntonicity: the "countertransference" thus becomes one of the principle criteria, if not *the* principal criterion, for distinguishing between the schizophrenic and the manic-depressive.

Bleuler himself was obliged to recognise that there did not exist a negative pathognomonic sign permitting the exclusion of schizophrenia. However, Minkowski feels that we are now able to say that there is a sign which if present absolutely excludes schizophrenia. Where syntonic factors are "prevalent," there can be no question of schizophrenia.

It is of immense value that this should be brought clearly out into the open. There is an oral tradition in psychiatry that is only partially put into the textbooks. It is perpetuated through the clinical conference. Here, the young psychiatrist is taught to get the "feel" of schizophrenia. Bleuler and others, in the early 1900s, had been speaking of "Gefuhls" diagnosis. Minkowski speaks of diagnosis by "sentiment" and by "penetration." On the basis of the psychiatrist's sense of rapport with the patient (or more accurately the psychiatrist's sense of the patient's rapport with him), the patient is sensed to be a true schizophrenic or a pseudo-schizophrenic, a schizoid melancholic or a melancholic schizoid, an early involutional depressive with schizoid features, or a late schizophrenic with depressive hypochondriacal features, and so on.

However, Minkowski should not be held responsible for these still current absurdities. He, although partially entangled in this clinicism, succeeds, as well as anyone who has not emancipated himself from it, in shedding some light on the nature of autism.

AUTISM IN SCHIZOPHRENIA

We shall now examine this further. For Bleuler, the phenomena of dream and reverie serve as the prototypes in normal life to make more clear the mode of being of schizophrenics.

This concept of Bleuler's was influenced by Freud, and a similar idea is developed by Jung in his polarity of introversion and extraversion. Autism, as a turning inward away from others, as a decathexis of objects, has even been regarded as *the* essential mechanism of schizophrenia; while a cathexis of external objects has been associated more with so-called normality, or with manic-depression.

Neither view can be supported by the evidence. There are many people who are dreamy and who do not "cathect" others much, without being taken to be schizophrenic. Not all schizophrenics are withdrawn. Not all schizophrenics tend to be inactive. Minkowski emphasizes the nature of schizophrenics activity, which may be intense and tireless. But he sees in this activity the imprint of something profoundly morbid, and it has this imprint even if we do not see it necessarily and always as an expression of hidden complexes. Such activity by itself can show the autistic disturbance which to Minkowski is pathognomonic of schizophrenia.

In Minkowski's view, Bleuler's concept of the schizophrenias moves appreciably away from Kraepelin's approach in the direction of a phenomenological orientation, but remains caught within the doctrine of atomistic associationism.

Minkowski believes that it is clinically feasible to subsume all the essential manifestations of schizophrenia under a single basic disturbance—the loss (or as he later wishes to put it, the "rupture") of vital contact with reality. Although this idea is foreshadowed in Bleuler's concept of autism, for Bleuler, autism was one symptom among others; for Minkowski, the loss of vital contact with reality is presupposed by all the other disturbances.

Minkowski's elucidation of his concept of autism is a significant contribution to the understanding of schizophrenia. His mature exposition (1953) of his concept of autism is as follows.

> It is very easy to geometricise the notion of contact with reality by thinking of it as a single line linking self and world. Autism thus becomes a turning away from the world, turning in on oneself and one's complexes. Many authors have gone so far as to think of the schizophrenic as a sort of waking dreamer. Imagine a hole in a pane of glass caused by a bullet; around the hole are radiating cracks on all sides. It is not so much that the individual loses vital contact with reality, but that reality loses its vitality—the reality of the self as much as the reality of the world. Our morbid rationalist does not turn himself away from reality of the world. On the contrary, he is constantly at grips with reality outside himself, but this reality has become shorn of vitality. He sees the external world in terms of the internal model that he carries with him. Thus, what he lacks in himself he experiences as lacking in the world.[6]

This is very different from Bleuler's concept of autism, which was essentially a turning inward, a withdrawal.

Minkowski reasons that all personal action requires the capacity to have a scale of values which must be constantly open to rearrangement. If one is hanging a picture on a wall, one will give up doing this if someone cries out for help. The act in itself is not autistic, but the act may become so if one persists in it because one's system of values is, as it were, congealed. He describes acts "without tomorrow," acts which are congealed, acts which do not aim for fulfillment, acts which short-circuit themselves. These actions need not, in Minkowski's view, be any more or less unconsciously determined in a Freudian sense than ordinary actions. They are not particularly dissociated from the rest of the personality. Minkowski sees in them the expression of the essential character of the deterioration to which the person succumbs when he loses vital contact with reality. Minkowski points out that often schizoids and schizophrenics do not understand the meaning of rest and relaxation. But, though they may be constantly in action, this does not mean that they are driven by "unconscious forces," any more than that their activities are the expression of syntonicity. Quite the contrary. It is a complete mistake to equate autism with drawing away from the world in the sense of becoming inactive and absorbed in day-dreams.

> Let us cite an example. In a small, modestly furnished flat there lives in straitened circumstances the family of a public servant. The father's income barely meets their current needs. One day the mother announces that she would like a piano so that the children can continue the music lessons which they had formerly been given when the family were in better circumstances. The father tries to dissuade her, producing valid arguments to the effect that their budget would not let him dream of such a thing. But in vain. She wants a piano and she will have one. She knows how to do dress-making and she finds a job. She has sleepless nights. She no longer mentions what it is she wants, but one day the father, on returning from the office, discovers to his complete surprise a brand new piano. The piano is there. It conflicts with the rest of the furniture, with all the life of the family, it is like a stranger, like a dead thing without a future. It serves particularly the elder son, who has just been through a serious, schizophrenic illness, who is certainly not a bad musician, but who now feels the need to play late into the night, thus provoking complaints from the neighbours.

> For whoever is accustomed to these questions there can be not the slightest doubt that we are dealing here with a schizoid manifestation. The purchase of the piano in these circumstances casts a glow over all the behaviour of a personality in relation to its surroundings. However, there is no question here of interiorisation. The wife of our public servant does not content herself with imagining that she has a piano, in a magnificent apartment where she receives princes and statesmen. She no longer executes stereotyped movements as if she were playing a piano. Finally, we do not believe that her desire must have some symbolic meaning and must be motivated by a complex, for example, a romantic feeling, formerly repressed, for a music teacher. That is possible, but it is not necessary if we have to understand the particular behaviour which we have before us. She wishes to have a piano and we find nothing incomprehensible or morbid in this desire. She wants it at any cost and achieves her ends. One would almost like to congratulate her for her perseverance. However, it lacks something most essential. It lacks life. The piano is only a nuisance in the given circumstances. In its haughty majesty it strikes a discordant note in the modest interior, and the act, accomplished with so much tenacity, has no future and dies of an excessive and blind rigidity.[7]

Now, in taking up the phenomenological stance one suspends all judgment of one's own, and undertakes simply to enter into the other person's perspective. Minkowski has not developed a genuine suspension of his own position. When he is describing the purchase of the piano he does not state from whose point of view it is a "nuisance," or a "stranger," or a "dead thing." To whom has it "haughty majesty," or for whom does it die of "an excessive and blind rigidity"?

It is just this *rigidity* of perspective that we need to loosen. Unless we can see the *inter-experience* of different persons, we shall not be able to understand *one person's experience*.

In order to understand one perspective, we have to be able to see it in the perspective of multiple perspectives that interpenetrate with one another as much as actions interpenetrate.

Minkowski distinguishes an autism which is rich in inner content and an autism which is poor in inner content. Just as normal men have more or less imagination, so with these patients. All schizophrenics do not turn entirely from external reality to seek refuge in the "castles of Spain" of the imagination. But when they act, they act without intuition in Bergson's sense. The schizophrenic is like a door which has come off its hinges. He is "unhinged," rather than locked up.

It is an autism which is poor in content which shows us the schizophrenic disorder in its pure state. The schizophrenic who is a dreamer is not a schizophrenic because he is a dreamer, but he is a schizophrenic first, and a dreamer afterwards. The schizophrenic founders in the void. His dreams are used to fill his emptiness—the emptiness which is a consequence of loss of a living relation with realness, inner or outer. His capacity to dream is in fact one of the more nearly normal aspects of his personality.

SCHIZOPHRENIC ATTITUDES

Minkowski's theory of schizophrenic *"attitudes"* follows from his theory of autism. The schizophrenic founders in the void. He clings desperately, therefore, to any fragments of vital reality, internal or external, past or present. The tenacious clinging on to something "real," be it an image, a memory, an emotion, involves the schizophrenic in striking an "attitude." Minkowski's development of this concept of schizophrenic attitudes is another major contribution, and another advance on Bleuler's position.

Minkowski notes that schizophrenics commonly adopt certain "attitudes." These attitudes are "psychic stereotypes." He does not believe that these attitudes are an indispensable attribute of every case of schizophrenia. They are sometimes entirely lacking. They sometimes give to the otherwise rigid personality of the schizophrenic a nuance of plasticity and allow us, therefore, to distinguish between plastic and aplastic forms of the disease. He separates schizophrenic attitudes provisionally into two groups—ideo-affective and purely intellectual. These attitudes conserve in the subject a certain human aspect, and if we understand them they can help us to get better contact with the patients.

The attitudes described by Minkowski are morbid reverie, sulking, morbid regrets and the attitude of interrogation. Each is seen as an effort to avoid "the void" opened by the loss of vital tone to reality.

Thus, as indicated above, the person plunged in "morbid reverie" is seen not as ill because of his engrossment in his reverie, but as engrossed in it because of his illness. However, Minkowski sees this reverie as possibly also "morbid" in itself, because, although an attempt to compensate for the basic phenomenological deficit, it is not itself immune from the schizophrenic process. Thus, in ordinary day-dreaming there is always a latent awareness of reality. We would not call Archimedes or Pasteur autistic because they were so absorbed in their work. Both are types of syntonic scholars. In the schizophrenic, however, reverie, and other attitudes, tend themselves to become marked by the stigmata of autism—sterility, immobility, and rigidity. Yet a day-dream, a mood, sulks, a tenaciously held memory, etc., may be what has been saved, albeit in modified form, from the schizophrenic disintegration, and it is to this, therefore, that the patient will cling as the most intact, least devitalised area or fragment of his experience, to prevent himself from falling into total nothingness.

THEORETICAL MODIFICATIONS

Minkowski has not fundamentally changed his original systematic presentation of his views on schizophrenia, but he has modified these views in certain ways since 1927.

In this original study of schizophrenia, Minkowski followed Bleuler in seeing schizoid and syntone as the two basic principles of life. Subsequently, however, he became more and more impressed by the evidence for an epileptoid constitution or type, in addition. The epileptoid constitution, according to Minkowski, is bi-polar; it is adhesive on the one hand, and explosive on the other. This particular type of "affective contact" with the world that characterises the epileptoid is only a sign or symptom of the epileptoid mode of being in general. In his latest position, Minkowski wishes to make the basic distinction between schizoid and epileptoid, and to put the syntone on the side. The provisional classification now becomes rational-schizoid type and sensorial-epileptoid.

The rational is involved in the abstract, in the immobile, in the solid and the rigid. Movement and intuition elude him. He thinks more than he feels: he grasps nothing in an immediate way: his abstract world is "cold," and he himself is cold inside as well. He discerns and separates objects. He sees cutting contours and precision of form. The sensorial type, on the other hand, lives in a concrete-hyper-concrete world. He cannot detach himself: he feels more than he thinks: he allows his attachment to things, through his feelings, to guide him. He sees the world in movement, not movement as simple displacement of objects in space, but in terms of elementary dynamism. He tends to lose in this a sense of precision. He tends to see the world in images.

Minkowski characterizes three types of man: the rational, the affective, and the sensorial. The rational is orientated toward the object, toward the thing. It is completed in the immobile, its realm is that of the anonymous, of extension, of universality. The affective has to do with our neighbour and all that goes on in human encounter, of intimacy, of union, of vibrating together with, etc. Sensoriality has its realm in depth of penetration into the world (e.g., Van Gogh). A man caught in one of these types will always be to that extent limited: the preponderance of one or the other will determine the structure of his life, his essential mode of living and seeing the world. The rational works his perspective toward the abstract. The sensorial is orientated toward the cosmic aspects of life, he feels everything in all its implications.

In this classification, "affectivity," in the strict sense of the term, loses any meaning: also, the old opposition of extra- and introversion. Much of the evidence for this comes from the drawings of infants and from Rorschach material.

Schizoid-rational and epileptoid-sensorial are not mutually exclusive types, but can be associated in the one individual. What matters to Minkowski is not the one category fixed once and for all, but the play of different factors which co-exist.

After discussing the complexity of classifications he asks:

> . . . can one, in view of this complexity, still speak of constitutional types? One should not forget in this respect that whatever be the variations in our behavior, our unity still remains. We retain in the course of our life the same psychological profile . . . The pure case, although much less frequent than mixed cases, can still be our criterion and guide.[8]

In a reaction away from associationism and the classical triad of functions or faculties (thought, feeling, will), Minkowski had emphasised autism and saw dissociation, disintegration of thought and everything else as only the consequence or expression of loss of vital contact with reality.

However, with his new contrast of schizophrenia and epilepsy, he feels it no longer adequate to speak of a good or bad affective contact which is arrived at by the diagnosis of "sentiment" or by penetration, but must now give greater weight to Bleuler's "splitting" ("Spaltung") and contrasts it to the concept of links (liens).

He quotes Françoise Minkowska as follows:

> These differences emerge very clearly in the Rorschach, on condition that one does not content oneself with a simple selection of responses, but attaches a suitable importance to *basic expressions,* that is to say, to those which recur frequently in the responses of the test subject. It is thus that we can ascertain, in testing schizophrenics, the relative frequency of expressions such as cut, separated, parted, divided, fragmented, jagged, slashed, gnawed, dissolved, while in epileptics, on the contrary, the predominant responses are those such as fastened to, attached, linked, sewn together, approached, sealed, suspended, crouching, leaning, clinging to. Prepositions such as: on, between, with, which aim at establishing a link between apparently separate parts, play the same role. Let us note, further, the frequency among them of verbs, which one meets much less often among schizophrenics who, as we have seen, prefer the immobile and static.[9]

According to Minkowski, Spaltung, autism, and dissociation are not synonymous. Bleuler saw Spaltung in the majority of early manifestations of schizophrenia, but he contrasted the splitting of the personality into complexes (so that the patient, as he said, could have as many personalities as he had complexes) with what he called "Zerspaltung," which referred to a primitive loosening of associations. Autism is seen as a direct consequence of splitting. Autism is a global concept; Spaltung is a more atomistic concept, at least in Bleuler. But as they are developed in Wyrsch, there does not seem to be any incompatibility between the concepts of autism and Spaltung. At first view, the facts in question do not seem to be the same, in that the concept of loss of vital contact with reality is linked to those phenomenological facts discussed under rationalism and morbid geometricism, whereas Spaltung makes its appeal to those facts whose motif is in intra-psychic separation, fragmentation and disintegration.

Spaltung refers more to an activity of the subject; autism more to a state of affairs generally characterising the person's relation to the world.

Apart from true splitting, Minkowski describes interestingly a mechanism he calls *denudation* (see also *L'Évolution Psychiatrique,* 1956) which he discusses with particular reference to language. He sees language as a system of references which can reveal to us the structure of life in general and that of the human being in particular. But there is need of an existential semantic. Denudation is apparent through language when language becomes a mere verbalisation empty of content. He gives an example of denudation in Rorschach responses, where everything is stripped of its life: instead of flowers and houses, there are lines and points. There is a tendency to see the skeleton in everything. The person who denudes this world schematises everything: for such a person the skeleton can become the most important part of a man because it is that which gives him indispensable support. But in seeing the skeleton or the skeletal schemata of things everywhere, he may lose his relation to flesh and blood, to life and reality (p. 245).

If we do not denude reality of all its vitality, we will find much more actuality in the world than we often suppose there to be. If we consider a tree or a bridge in terms of what they actually are, in terms of the relationship which they do, in fact, have to the rest of the world, we will not need to take the quite denuded notion of what a tree or a bridge is as a symbol for something else, when so often what the denuded tree or bridge is supposed to symbolise is rather another aspect of its own nature, from which we have estranged it by our original act of denudation.

As a further example, he considers how denuded of vitality is our usual way of thinking of depth. Again, we take our physical weight to be literal weight. But when one speaks of a weight on one's heart, or says that one is falling deep into depression, it is supposed that this is metaphorical weight and metaphorical depth: that is to say, that the existential use of these words is derived from their external physical application, whereas the truth of the matter may be quite the converse. It may be that we understand the world, and are able to orientate ourselves and find our way about in it, because the weight of a stone and the depth of the sea are really metaphors for existential depth and weight,[10] or that each form of weight or depth is equally "literal." The task before us is to study all the manifestations and all the activities and all the movements of the soul, where their variety and nuances are caught by and expressed in language.

A CRITIQUE OF MINKOWSKI'S POSITION

It is not difficult to point out various limitations to Minkowski's position.

The fabric or "tone" of "reality" appears for Minkowski to be constitutionally determined in the first place, and is then possibly modified by pathological process. Change in the basic texture of reality sets the scene for all subsequent changes. This texture may lose its "tone" and may "tear," and delusions, attitudes, hallucinations appear functionally to patch up the gap in the fabric. He appears to neglect the close similarity his view has with one of Freud's various views on schizophrenic symptomatology.

Minkowski never entirely extricates himself from clinicism. His schizophrenic patients move from a schizoid constitutional condition to a schizophrenic disease. For the later Minkowski, as we have seen, the distinction between constitution and disease may have lost some acuity; but it has certainly not gained in clarification. What is the testable, observable difference between constitution and disease? By what "intuition" or "sentiment" does the one end and the other begin?

His types appear to be intuitive syntheses of a lifetime of clinical observation. Their value for him appears to be that they are magnetic poles, as it were, around which many diverse facts can be ordered. However, when Minkowski shifts from phenomenology to classification, whether quasi-nosological or quasi-typological, the result is not a happy one. He appears to try to develop, by intuitive grasp of essentials, a type of typology or nosology that cannot be worked out without recourse to a statistical treatment of variables, whose reliability and validity have been established, etc. Minkowski has apparently never undertaken research of this kind.

Minkowski makes no original contribution to ontogenetic study in psychiatry. The most that can be said is that he does not regard it as irrelevant. He quotes Morel (1860) with approval.

> For my part I have observed many nervous conditions change into psychosis (aliénation mentale), and I have noted on many occasions the justifiability of the observation by the relatives of a patient when they affirm that *the insanity is nothing more than an exaggeration of his usual character* . . . But if in many cases the neuropathic state may be considered as the incubation period of the psychosis, it is incontestable that a great many persons suffer all their lives from a similar state without ever crossing the line of demarcation, sometimes so difficult to define, which separates sanity from insanity . . . It is impossible in medicine to define these simple states of suffering otherwise than by a general designation: nervous temperament, nervous state.

He does not appear to have passed beyond this position. He refers to Meyerson (*Identity and Reality,* Paris, 1912) to justify the seeking in the past for some light on the present symptoms. Following the general principles of science, psychiatric research, he says, is orientated towards the past of the patient. It tries to find in preexistent particularities of character, the essential traits of the actual psychosis. In this way, "nervous temperaments" may be differentiated analogously to the clinical differentiation of nosological categories. In Minkowski's view, the possibility of checking these broad clinical categories with differences of temperament provides evidence to support the belief in the relative autonomy of these clinical categories. Ontogenesis could thus begin to play an important rôle in the classification of psychosis, as prognosis did with Kraepelin.

In the above respects there is nothing in Minkowski which has not been overshadowed by psychoanalytic research.

Two further areas may be noted in which Minkowski (in common indeed with almost all the psychiatrists of the first half of this century) appears from our present perspective to be somewhat naïve. These are his idea of "volition," and his understanding of human interaction.

Minkowski ridicules the idea that schizophrenics retreat from the surface encounter with a frightening world into the depth, and hence are withdrawn. This concept, he says, easily leads to the idea that schizophrenics flee voluntarily from the world—a conception that, he says, is much more literary than clinical. We have to deal, he says, with patients that cannot be otherwise than patients.

> The loss of tonality to reality, or if we attribute this loss to the activity of our subject, it is suppression, can be only the result of something approaching an act of violence, like a punch as it were. The verb 'to split,' however, cannot be used to mean a willed and conscious act. There is a complete difference between the state of affairs we are describing and an act of putting one's head in the sand.[11]

In discussing a patient of Morel's who showed intense morbid sulking, he says that just as with day-dreaming, he hesitates to make sulking the "primum Movens." Sulking cannot be the essential mechanism behind all the other troubles. If this were so, one might be forced to the view that sulking, dreaming, and all the other forms of inactivity and stereotypes, even mutism and apparent dementia, were voluntary, at the beginning at least. While, he says, being a partisan on all other facts from a psychological point of view, he cannot follow Morel in this.

These voluntary manifestations can only arise when the entire personality has undergone in the first place a profound deformation (p. 145).

The problem raised here is still a very open one. Some psychoanalysts would agree with Minkowski that it is necessary to presuppose structural changes to understand some of the experiences of schizophrenia. However, psychoanalysis has also familiarised us with the possibility that one can act intentionally on one's own experience without fully admitting or realising that one is so doing. Accepting the metaphor for the moment, we do not know how tough the ordinary fabric of experience is, for the "ordinary" person does not "punch" at his experience in this way.

It seems to us that he does not give sufficient weight to his own reports of what his own patients tell him in this connection.[12]

> *I suppressed feeling as I suppressed all reality. I dug a moat around me. I became insensible.* I exist as a body, but no longer have any internal sensation of life. I no longer feel things, but this does not trouble me, as all feeling is dead in me. I no longer have normal sensations, and it is only with difficulty that I experience heat and cold. Nor do I any longer know mental suffering, the death

> of my mother leaves me indifferent. It is true that I fill this emptiness of sensation with reason by telling myself in this or that circumstance one should experience this or that feeling, but this is not the same thing. My feelings are not entirely dead, they are only numbed. If I lose a friend, I do not experience suffering. I only know that I now lack that friend, but I also know that I will experience this loss with pain when I am once again able to feel.

This patient states plainly that at one time he intended nothing else than the devitalisation of the reality of self and world.

Minkowski does not pursue the question of why someone should want to attack his feelings and perceptions in such a way.

Our criticisms of Minkowski are directed, therefore, to the fact that he did not go further in his own direction. Such criticisms are ungrateful and ungracious unless we bear in mind that his accomplishment is considerable. He is the first figure in psychiatry to bring the nature of phenomenological investigation clearly into view.

In our view, he is correct in his estimation of Jaspers. In the *General Psychopathology* of 1913, Jaspers distinguished phenomenology both from the psychological methods that study the external signs of illness, or measure "objective" performances of functions (e.g., intelligence tests), and from genetic dynamic understanding. He defined phenomenology as the study of the subjective experiences of the patient, as we intuitively realise or represent them to ourselves, through the study of his spoken and/or written testimony, his gestures, expressive movements, and actions generally.

In our sense of the term, however, Jaspers was not fully a phenomenologist, since he continued, as Minkowski points out, to itemise the patient's experience according to his own preconceived categories. In his pathographies of Strindberg and Van Gogh, it becomes apparent how entrenched Jaspers remains in a non-phenomenological clinicism.

Minkowski's own phenomenology is still entangled in clinicism, in two major respects. He does not entirely succeed in describing—he introduces his own judgments and attributions into his description of the other. Secondly, he is unable to see and does not describe the schizophrenic within a social system. The changes of experiential texture in the one person that he describes remain, therefore, unintelligible.

Yet he makes the first serious attempt in psychiatry to reconstruct the other person's lived experience. His carefully documented phenomenological investigations are an important contribution to psychiatry, and one which has by no means yet been adequately assimilated.

REFERENCES

Laing, R. D. *The Divided Self.* London: Tavistock Publications. Chicago: Quadrangle Press, 1961.

Kahn, E. *Psychopathic Personalities.* (Trans. H. Flanders Dunbar), New Haven, Conn.: Yale University Press, 1931.

Minkowski, E. "La realité et les fonctions de l'irréel (Le Troisième Monde)." *L'Évol. Psychiat,* 1950, 59-99.

Minkowski, E. *La Schizophrénie,* Paris: Desclée de Brouwer, 1953.

NOTES

1 E. Kahn, *Psychopathic Personalities,* (Trans. by H. F. Dunbar), New Haven, Conn., 1931, pp. 326-329.

2 E. Minkowski, *La Schizophrénie,* Paris, 1953, p. 46.

3 *Ibid.,* p. 51.

4 *Ibid.,* p. 52.

5 R. D. Laing, *The Divided Self.* London, 1961.

6 Minkowski, *La Schizophrénie,* pp. 212-213.

7 *Ibid.,* pp. 115-116.

8 *Ibid.,* p. 206.

9 *Ibid.,* p. 209.

10 *Ibid.,* pp. 248-250.

11 *Ibid.,* pp. 212-213.

12 *Ibid.,* p. 246.

VII. Suicide

Ellen West—And Loneliness

CARL R. ROGERS

This chapter has a long history. Rollo May's book *Existence,* a presentation of an existential point of view, was published in 1958. It contained a chapter by Dr. Ludwig Binswanger on a famous case in which he and Dr. Eugen Bleuler were involved, which was first reported in German (Binswanger, 1944–1945). Obviously, the treatment methods were in the early days of psychiatry and psychoanalysis.

In the autumn of 1958, a conference was held by the newly formed American Academy of Psychotherapists, which included both psychiatrists and psychologists. Dr. May organized a symposium at the conference to discuss the case of Ellen West. Taking part in the symposium were three psychiatrists, two psychologists (I was one), an anthropologist, and a social historian. The meeting was an all-day session, and the case was discussed from many angles. It has never been reported in full.

As I studied the case in preparation for the symposium, I became more and more angry at the many and serious "mistakes" that were made in the treatment of Ellen. I felt she was dealt with by her parents, her various physicians, her psychiatrists, and her two analysts in ways that could not possibly help her—ways that would, in fact, certainly worsen her psychological health. Intellectually, I could forgive these errors, knowing that Ellen had lived many, many years ago and that psychotherapy and psychiatric treatment were in a primitive stage. But my forgiving thoughts did nothing to change the anger I felt.

Consequently, in my presentation at the symposium I not only presented the dynamics of the interactions as I saw them, but I also speculated on what the dynamics would be if Ellen entered my office, or that of any client-centered therapist today, seeking help. The outcome, as I saw it, would have been very different.

Some years later I expanded the paper, presenting the major events in Ellen's life, summarizing Binswanger's account, and relating Ellen's life to the isolation and loneliness that exist in modern society. The expanded paper is able to stand alone; it is not just one commentary in a symposium.

Even though the initial commentary was written long ago and the expanded paper is far from new, I still stand by it, and am pleased to present it as illustrating additional facets of a client-centered, person-centered approach to a human being in distress.

I would like to give my own view of the basic isolation felt by modern man. I will then indicate the way in which I see Ellen West as an illustration of the development of this loneliness to a tragic point.

There are many ways of looking at loneliness, but I wish to focus on two elements of the sense of aloneness which we so often see in our clients and in others. The first is the estrangement of man from himself, from his experiencing organism. In this fundamental rift the experiencing organism senses one meaning in experience, but the conscious self clings rigidly to another, since that is the way it has found love and acceptance from others. Thus we have a potentially fatal division, with most behavior being regulated in terms of meanings perceived in awareness, but with other meanings sensed by the physiological organism being denied and ignored because of an inability to communicate freely within oneself.

The other element in our loneliness is the lack of any relationship in which we communicate our real experiencing—and hence our real self—to another. When there is no relationship in which we are able to communicate both aspects of our divided self—our conscious façade and our deeper level of experiencing—then we feel the loneliness of not being in real touch with any other human being.

Is this loneliness contemporary only? Perhaps. In earlier times the individual also distrusted or ignored his experiencing in order to keep the regard of significant others. But the façade he adopted, the meaning he now felt he had found in his experiences, became a unified and strongly supportive set of beliefs and meanings. His whole social group tended to perceive life and experience in the same way, so that while he had unwittingly given up his deepest self, at least he had taken on a consistent, respected, approved self by which he could live. An early Puritan, for example, must have experienced much inward strain as he denied vast areas of his organismic experiencing. It is doubtful, however, if he experienced as much isolation and aloneness as our clients today.

Modern man, like the members of earlier and more homogeneous groups, deserts his own experiencing to take on the way of being which will bring love. But the façade he adopts is taken over only from parents or a few others, and he is continually exposed to the knowledge that although that façade is approved by some, others see life in very different fashions. There is no security in any single façade. Hence, to a degree probably unknown before, modern man *experiences* his loneliness, his cut-off-ness, his isolation both from his own deeper being and from others.

In the remainder of this paper I will discuss this very fundamental present-day type of isolation, using as an example the highly informative history of a young woman known as Ellen West.

I am pleased that this case was chosen as the basis of this symposium. First, Ellen West's diaries and letters add much personal richness to the account. There are also included observations and reports by physicians, therapists, and diagnosticians, further adding to the completeness. Second, the full account of the case is available in both German (1944–1945) and English (1958). Finally, the case illustrates the way in which some of the best-known persons in the psychiatric and psychotherapeutic field thought and worked as of a generation or more ago.

I cannot possibly give the whole tragic history of Ellen West—which in its published form covers more than thirty closely packed pages—but I shall choose and comment on a few of the crucial events of her life.

First, her youth. Up to the age of twenty I see her as being as whole, as integrated, as the average person. It is easy for clinicians to read pathology into a history, especially with the advantages of hindsight, but I do not see pathology here. Ellen is a girl who is lively, headstrong, sensitive, defiant, questioning, competitive, emotional, expressive, variable—in short, a living person. She is devoted to her father. She wants very much to be a boy—until she meets a boy she likes. She wonders what life is for. She has idealistic dreams of great achievement for herself. None of these characteristics necessarily portends a black future. On the contrary, she seems to be a richly variable and sensitive adolescent, with much promise.

"Her twentieth year is full of happiness, yearning and hopes." (quotations from Binswanger, "The Case of Ellen West," in *Existence*). She is eager to find a vital, serious, loving man. She takes pleasure in eating and drinking. But during this year there occurs a significant estrangement from herself. "She becomes engaged to a romantic foreigner, but at her father's wish breaks the engagement." Our facts are meager, but I suspect, from the lack of any protest on her part, that she adopts her father's feelings as if they were her own. If we put this episode in schematic form, her realization would be something like this: "I thought my feelings meant that I was in love. I felt I was doing the positive and meaningful thing to get engaged. But my experiencing cannot be trusted. I was not in love. My engagement was not a meaningful commitment. I cannot be guided by what I experience. To do so would be to act wrongly, and to lose my father's love."

Within a few weeks of this time she is eating too much and growing fat—the first appearance of what was to become her major symptom. It is perhaps indicative of the beginnings of her lack of trust in herself that she begins to diet only when teased by her companions. She feels an increasing need to live her life in terms of the expectations of others, since her own impulses are unreliable.

It is not difficult to see why she begins to despise herself shortly after this time, and even to perceive death as "a glorious woman." After all, she is an untrustworthy organism, a misleading cluster of experiencings, deserving to be despised. Her diary reports "shadows of doubt and of dread," which soon translate into a dread of getting fat. Nor is it surprising that she is frightened at the "evil spirits" in her—the unaccepted and denied feelings which haunt her.

I am sure this was not the first real estrangement between her self and her underlying feelings, but there seems little doubt but that it was a deeply significant one. It went a long way in destroying her confidence in herself as a being capable of autonomy. Even though her good spirits return, and she has happy periods, she has given up a part of her self, and introjected as her own the feelings of her father.

During this period she is full of fluctuations. She wants to do something great; she hopes for a social revolution; she works very hard as a student; she establishes reading rooms for children. But at times she is "a timid, earthly worm"; she longs for death and has her tutor reread the sentence, "The good die young." Occasionally, "life has triumphed again." She has an "unpleasant affair with a riding teacher." She has a "breakdown." She is very overconcerned with her weight.

When she is twenty-four, there is another point at which she even more fully loses confidence in herself. Though she still is unsure enough of herself to need her old governess with her, she is nevertheless happy in her studies. "The diary breathes joy of life and sensuality." She falls in love with a student. This was evidently a deep commitment, judging by its lasting and pervasive qualities. She becomes engaged, but again her parents insist that her experiencing is erroneous. They demand a temporary separation. So to her it must seem that the relationship is not real, is not wise, is better given up. Once more she distrusts and disregards her own experience, and introjects her parents' feelings. She gives up the relationship and, with it, any trust in herself as capable of wise self-direction. Only the experience of others can be trusted. At this time, she turns to her doctor for help.

Had she rebelled at this point, had she possessed the strength to fight for her own experiencing of her own world, she would have been true to her deeper feelings, and would, quite literally, have saved her potentially autonomous self. But instead of rebellion there is only a terrible depression, and a hatred of her body, which is obviously a totally untrustworthy organism for dealing with life. The extent to which she has surrendered her self is indicated by her terrific dieting. As she says later, "Something in me rebels against becoming fat. Rebels against becoming healthy, having plump red cheeks, becoming a simple, robust woman, as corresponds to my true nature."

In other words, if she were to trust her own feelings, desires, experiences, she would become a robust, plump, young woman, and marry the student she loves. But her feelings have been proven completely unreliable, her desires and experiences totally untrustworthy guides. So she must not only deny her feelings for her loved one, but must also starve and coerce her body into a form approved by others, but completely opposite from her own tendencies. She has lost, completely, her trust in her own experiencing as the basis for living.

I shall comment briefly on one other episode. She finds her cousin to be a possible mate, and this choice is approved by her family. They plan to marry. But for two more years, until age twenty-eight, she vacillates between her cousin and the student she loved. She goes to see the student, and breaks off with him, leaving, in her words, an "open wound." We know nothing of the content of this most crucial interaction, but I would speculate that her psychological life hung in the balance here. Should she trust her own experiencing and choose the person she loves, or should she choose her cousin? Her own feelings are cooler toward the cousin, but for him she *should* feel all the approved feelings she is supposed to feel. I suspect that she realized dimly that if she chose the student, she would be choosing the uncharted path of autonomous selfhood. If she chose her cousin, she would be living the life expected of her by others, but it would be a safe and approved pretense. She chose her cousin and married him, thus renouncing still further any trust in her self. (To show how differently the same episode can be viewed, here is Dr. Binswanger's comment, as he contrasts the struggle she feels between the "ideal" and the "real" parts of herself. He compares "the blonde beloved who is part of the ethereal (ideal) world and the other (the cousin) who stands with both feet firmly on the ground. . . . Life on the earth wins out again." I fear this indicates—both for Dr. Binswanger and for me—that our values show through even when we are trying to make "objective" observations!)

By the age of thirty-two, she is totally obsessed with the idea that she *must* make herself thin. To this end she starves herself and takes sixty laxative pills a day! Not surprisingly, she had little strength. She tries psychoanalysis but feels she is not helped. She says, "I analyzed with my mind, but everything remained theory"; and, "The analyst can give me discernment, but not healing." However, when the analysis is broken off by circumstances, she becomes worse.

During this period she speaks of her ideal love, the student. She says to her husband in a letter, "At that time you were the life I was ready to accept and to give up my ideal for. But it was . . . a forced resolve." She appears to be trying desperately to have the feelings that others want her to have, but she has to force herself.

From here on, the estrangement within herself leads to more estrangement and to more and more feelings of isolation from others. It is not surprising that her first attempt at suicide comes at a point when her second analyst, working with her in the hospital to which she was sent, repeats the now familiar pattern. Her husband wants to be with her in the hospital—and she wants him to be with her. But the father-figure, the analyst, knows better, and he sends the husband away. He destroys still further any lingering confidence she might have in herself as a self-directing person.

From this point on, the isolation is ever greater, and the tragedy closes in. She goes to more doctors, to more psychiatrists, becoming increasingly an object in the eyes of those dealing with her. She is finally placed in Dr. Binswanger's sanitarium, where she remains for a number of months.

During this period there are continuing differences over her diagnosis. Emil Kraepelin, the noted psychiatrist, diagnoses her during one of her depressed periods as a victim of melancholia. Her second analyst diagnoses her as having a "severe obsessive neurosis combined with manic-depressive oscillations." A consulting psychiatrist says that her problem is a "psychopathic constitution progressively unfolding." He says she is not schizophrenic, because there is no intellectual defect. But Drs. Bleuler and Binswanger are in agreement that her situation is "progressive schizophrenic psychosis ("schizophrenia simplex)." They see little hope for her and say, "It was clear that a release from the institution meant certain suicide."

Since Ellen was aware of a number of these discussions, she must have come to seem to herself not a person but some strange abnormal mechanism, completely out of her control, going its own way to destruction. One looks in vain through all these "diagnoses" for any trace of recognition that the doctors were dealing with a human person! It is not hard to understand Ellen's words: "I confront myself as a strange person. I am afraid of myself." Or, at another time: "On this one point I am insane—I am perishing in the struggle against my nature. Fate wanted to have me fat and strong, but I want to be thin and delicate." Indeed, she is perishing in the struggle with her nature. Her organism wants to be healthy and strong, but the introjected "I"—the false self she has taken on to please others—wants to be, as she says at one point, thin and "intellectual."

The wise doctors, in spite of the risk of suicide, come to the following conclusion: "No definitely reliable therapy is possible. We therefore resolved to give in to the patient's demand for discharge." She left the hospital. Three days later, she seemed well and happy, ate well for the first time in years, and then took a lethal dose of poison. She was thirty-three. Her epitaph might well be her own words: "I feel myself, quite passively, the stage on which two hostile forces are mangling each other."

What went so fatally wrong in the life of Ellen West? I hope I have indicated my belief that what went wrong is something which occurs to some degree in the life of every one of us, but which in her case was exaggerated. As infants, we live in our experience; we trust it. When the baby is hungry, he neither doubts his hunger nor questions whether he should make every effort to get food. Without being in any way conscious of it, he is a self-trusting organism. But at some point parents or others say to him in effect, "If you feel *that* way, I won't love you." And so he feels what he *should* feel, not what he *does* feel. To this degree, he builds up a self which feels what it should feel, only occasionally seeing frightening glimpses of what his organism, of which the self is a part, is actually experiencing. In Ellen's case this process operated in an extreme fashion. In some of the most significant moments of life, she was made to feel that her own experiencing was invalid, erroneous, wrong, and unsound, and that what she *should* be feeling was something quite different. Unfortunately for her, her love for her parents, especially her father, was so strong that she surrendered her own capacity for trusting her experience, and substituted theirs, or his. She gave up being her self. This observation, made by one of her doctors during her last year, is no surprise: "Though as a child she was wholly independent of the opinion of others, she is now completely dependent on what others think." She no longer has any way of knowing what she feels, or what her opinion is. This is the loneliest state of all, an almost complete separation from one's autonomous organism.

What went wrong with her treatment? Here is an intelligent, sensitive young woman, seeking help. The prognosis, by modern standards, would seem very favorable. Why such complete failure? I am sure opinions differ, but I should like to state mine.

The greatest weakness in her treatment was that no one involved seems to have related to her as a *person*; a person worthy of respect, a person capable of autonomous choice, a person whose inner experiencing is a precious resource to be drawn upon and trusted.

Rather, she seems to have been dealt with as an object. Her first analyst helps her to *see* her feelings, but not to experience them. This only makes her more of an object to herself, and still further estranges her from living in and drawing upon her experience. Wisely, she says that the "analyst can give me discernment, but not healing." The analyst points out to her that she is an individual with such and such dynamics. She agrees with him, though surely not on the basis of experiencing these dynamic feelings. She is simply following the pattern which has already isolated her—distrusting her own experiencing and trying to believe and feel what she should feel, what the expert tells her she feels.

Then comes the comic-tragic argument over her diagnosis, of which she was evidently quite aware. The doctors disagree as to what type of object she is: She is manic-depressive. She is obsessive-compulsive. She is a case of melancholia. She is treatable. She is not. Then comes the final, incredible decision: She is suicidal, schizophrenic, and hopeless for treatment; therefore we will discharge her, and let her commit suicide. This at least was one prediction that was fulfilled.

"I scream but they do not hear me." Ellen's words ring in my ears. No one *did* hear her as a person. Beyond her childhood years and perhaps not even then—neither her parents, nor her two analysts, nor her physicians ever seem to have respected her enough to hear her deeply. They did not deal with her as a person capable of meeting life, a person whose experiencing is trustworthy, whose inner feelings are worthy of acceptance. How, then, could she listen to herself, or respect the experiencing going on within her?

"I am isolated. I sit in a glass ball, I see people through a glass wall. I scream, but they do not hear me." What a desperate cry for a relationship between two persons. She never experienced what Buber has called "healing through meeting." There was no one who could meet her, accept her, as she was.

Reading this tragic case angers me (as will have been evident) but it also encourages me. I feel angry at the tragic waste of a human being, encouraged because I feel that we have learned enough during the intervening years that if

Ellen West came today to my office, or to the offices of many therapists I know, she would be helped. Let me try to sketch this possibility. To do it most vividly, I will assume that she came to my office at about the age of twenty-four. This is the time when she did seek medical help, so it is reasonable to assume that today she would have sought psychological help. It is just after she has separated, at the insistence of her parents, from the student whom she loves.

Even from just a reading of the case I feel sure I would find no barrier to feeling acceptant toward this depressed, unhappy, emaciated, self-starved young woman. I would sense both what she is and what her potentialities are, and I would be willing for her to be both, or either.

I feel sure that our contacts would start with themes such as the following. "I am very depressed, with no reason for my depression." "I can't bear to be alone, but I don't know why." "I hate myself when I'm fat, and I *have* to be thin, but again I don't know the reason for this." "I did love this student, but I don't believe it would have been a wise match. My father and mother felt he was not the man for me." As I understood each of these feelings and accepted her right to *be* these feelings, other attitudes would tentatively and fearfully appear: Her disappointment at the separation from her fiancé; the strong feelings that she had, and still has for him; her resentment (a very frightening feeling) toward her father. Slowly, gradually, she would discover that she could experience and be both love and resentment toward her father, both love and resentment toward me, both fear of independent living and eagerness for independent living, both the desire to be a man and the desire to be a woman, both the desire to be a plump, robust, contented wife and the desire to be a slim, brilliant, competitive achiever of social reform. She could experience both her hunger and desire to eat and be plump and her fear of being fat, ugly, and disapproved of by friends. She could say, as she did say, "I am afraid of myself, of the feelings to which I am defenselessly delivered over every minute." Little by little, she could freely experience all of these feelings, all of these elements of herself.

She would discover that some of these feelings are very frightening indeed. To explore and to *experience* both the risk and the excitement of being an independent person is one of those fearful elements. Another person, a client of mine, expressed this realization in a statement which Ellen would be likely to make. She said:

> *I have all the symptoms of fright. . . . It really seems like I'm cut loose and very vulnerable. . . . Still, I have a feeling of* strength. . . . *I'm feeling it internally now, a sort of surging up, or force . . . something really big and strong. And yet at first it was almost a physical feeling of just being out* alone, *and sort of cut off from a support I have been carrying around. . . . (pause) . . . I have the feeling that now I am going to begin to* do *more things.*

This is an example of what I mean by experiencing a feeling fully and acceptantly, in a safe relationship. It represents, in my judgment, a moment of change—probably physiological, irreversible change. As Ellen experienced, in a similar way, these different hidden facets of herself, she would find herself changing. This time the changed self that emerged would be based on her organismic reactions, her inner experiencing, and not on the values and expectations of others.

She would find that she did not have to struggle against her nature, against her feelings. Rather, she would find that when she could be open to all her experiencing—both her inner experiencing, and her experiencing of the demands and attitudes of others—she would have a basis by which to live. She would discover that her experiencing, if she could be open to it and could listen sensitively for its meaning, would provide a constructive guide for her behavior and for her life.

This is not to say that the process would be smooth or comfortable. To be a person—sometimes opposing her parents, sometimes standing against social pressures, often choosing to act even though uncertain of the outcome—this would be painful, costly, sometimes even terrifying. But it would be *very* precious: to be oneself is worth a high price. It would also have many other valuable aspects.

In the therapeutic relationship, where all of herself was accepted, she could discover that it was safe to communicate her self more completely. She would discover that she did not need to be lonely and isolated—that another could understand and share the meaning of her experience. She would discover too that in this process she had made friends with herself—that her body, her feelings, and her desires, were not enemy aliens, but friendly and constructive parts of herself. It would be unnecessary for her to utter those desperate words, "I am perishing in the struggle against my nature." Her two essential estrangements would have been assuaged. She would be in a good and communicative relationship with herself. She would also have found it safe to *be* her full self in a relationship. As a consequence, she would find herself relating with more of herself to others, and again discovering that it is not dangerously unsafe, but rather far more satisfying, to be one's real self in relating to others.

It is by such a process, in my judgment, that the glass wall would have dissolved. She would have found life adventurous, often painful. It would be a never-ending puzzlement to discover the behavior that would best harmonize with her complex and contradictory feelings. But she would be vital and real and in relationship to herself and others. She would have resolved for herself the great loneliness of contemporary man.

I cannot apologize for having stated with confidence and optimism the probable outcome of therapeutic events for Ellen, had she had the opportunity to participate in person-centered therapy. My experience justifies no other conclusion. I am not sure she would move as far as I have indicated, but that she would move in this direction I have no doubt, providing I had been able to create a person-to-person therapeutic relationship.

For myself, I draw certain lessons from this case of Ellen West. The first is that in every respect in which we make an object of the person—whether by diagnosing him, analyzing him, or perceiving him impersonally in a case history—we stand in the way of our therapeutic goal. To make an object of a person has been helpful in treating physical ills; it has not been successful in treating psychological ills. We are deeply helpful only when we relate as persons, when we risk ourselves as persons in the relationship, when we experience the other as a person in his own right. Only then is there a meeting at a depth which dissolves the pain of aloneness in both client and therapist.

REFERENCES

Binswanger, L. Der Fall Ellen West. *Schweizer Archiv für Neurologie und Psychiatrie,* 1944, *53,* 255–277; *54,* 69–117, 330–360; 1945, *55,* 16–40.

Binswanger, L. The case of Ellen West. In May, R., Angel, E., & Ellenberger, H. F. (Eds.), *Existence: A new dimension in psychiatry and psychology.* New York: Basic Books, 1958.

May, R. Angel, E., & Ellenberger, H. F. (Eds.) *Existence: A new dimension in psychiatry and psychology.* New York: Basic Books, 1958.

Despair and the Life of Suicide

LESLIE H. FARBER

INTRODUCTION

Gabriel Marcel has written ". . . the fact that suicide is always possible is the essential starting point of any genuine metaphysical thought."[1] It might equally be said that the possibility of suicide will always oppose psychiatry's efforts to rid itself of metaphysical concern. For once that possibility disrupts the civilized and ordinary boundaries of psychotherapy, every technical category loses its ordered place in our thinking and must be questioned with a new urgency or exploited in a manner which robs it of whatever truthful meaning it may have earned. What I have chosen to discuss here is—if I may be permitted this irony—the life of suicide, as distinguished from the act itself.

Martin Buber once remarked: "The act of suicide—it is a trapdoor which suddenly springs open. What else can one say?" Well, one can say a great deal, to judge from psychiatric literature. But it is my impression that while to the man who kills himself the act of suicide may be a trapdoor suddenly sprung, to the analyst it seems rather to resemble a psychological staircase, leading step by logical step to an inescapable culmination. Although I don't wish to force the image, I must remark that whether this staircase goes down or up it must always be traveled backwards. Confronted with the fact of suicide the analyst must construct his explanation in reverse, laying motive upon motive (hostility is favored here), and strategy upon strategy, until he reaches some final necessity. Having arrived at the end of his staircase, he may then retrace his steps forward, issuing those kitchen prescriptions for the heading-off of the act with which we are all familiar.

I would suggest that this staircase, though a far more reassuring and manageable structure than the suicide's own trapdoor, exists principally in the analyst's head, not in the real world. On the other hand, the world is full of trapdoors, even though the only ones we can be sure of are those which have already sprung open. The invention of the staircase is hardly surprising; a trapdoor offers very little to an investigator bent on explanation, and, by extension, recipes for prevention. But it is my suspicion that the staircase leads us not to greater understanding but merely away from the issue. It prevents us, after all, right at the outset, from even considering the possibility that the act of suicide is not the final move in a chain of causation—that perhaps it is not *caused* at all, in a psychological sense. Naturally this is not an agreeable proposition to the psychologist, who tends, understandably, to feel somewhat panicked if suddenly robbed of his basic tenet and tool, causation. Be that as it may, I feel that there is a more fruitful approach, even for psychiatrists, to the issue of suicide than the construction of causes out of motives. And that is: to leave aside, for the moment, the act itself, and to contemplate what I have called "the life of suicide"—which must be seen not as the situation or state of mind which leads to the act, but that situation in which the act-as-possibility, quite apart from whether it eventually occurs or not, has a life of its own.

It is part of our most profound—or metaphysical—awareness of ourselves, as Marcel has pointed out, to acknowledge that the possibility of suicide belongs to the human condition. We know this and must live with it, in much the same way as we know and must live with the fact that sin and evil are no strangers to our nature. But the awareness that it is possible for us to kill ourselves does not lead us to embrace suicide, any more than does the awareness that we are sinners prompt us to go forth and sin. For the man who is caught up in what I have called "the life of suicide," however, the possibility of being the author of his own death exercises a demonic and seductive fascination over him. This fascination takes different forms. There is a certain kind of person for whom the idea of suicide is a secret and cherished solution to any difficulty life may throw across his path. Suicide is the ace up his sleeve (revealed to no one), the secret possession of which shapes his response to any and every problem. Such a man confronts his life whispering to himself, "If I can't find a better job I'll kill myself. If my son won't confide in me, if my daughter flunks her final exams, if my wife forgets my birthday just one more time—I'll kill myself." This man, although caught up in one form of the life of suicide, is not, I think, in despair. Despair, which arises only in someone capable of some seriousness toward his life and himself, is literally beyond such a person. His secret scheming with the concealed trump of suicide altogether robs any event in his life—and quickly enough his entire life—of meaning, but without imposing upon him the necessity of acknowledging or dealing with meaninglessness. And, because concealment is so vital to his "advantage," as he conceives it, and therefore his deviousness and dishonesty so virtually impossible to penetrate, he is, I believe, the most difficult of all potential suicides to treat—or help in any way. Though not suffering the estrangement of true despair, this man is actually more separated from the world and his fellows than the despairer in his worst agonies of despairing isolation. I will return to this question of estrangement, but at this point I would like to contrast this form of the life of suicide that I have described with a form that we more commonly encounter: the suicidal preoccupation of the man who *is* in despair.

THE LANDSCAPE OF DESPAIR

Suicide finds no more fertile soil for its intrigues than despair—that "sickness unto death" in which, as Kierkegaard observed, we long to die and cannot. It is the middle years which are most vulnerable to the claims of this sickness of spirit, which now radically questions all we have been, at the same time scorning the solace formerly sought in the future, making who we are to become the most oppressive of questions. As both the workings and visages of the flesh falter and wither, all crude preconceptions of immortality are shattered, giving way to a brooding—and equally crude—apprehension of the finitude of our earthly stay. Gradually—or even suddenly—there emerges the realization, "For better or worse, that was it. There never was a second chance." Time past now isolates itself as an alien, often perverse accomplice, sometimes accepting but more often refusing memory's overtures. What cannot be remembered robs us of goods which seem rightfully ours, so that memory turns feverish and willful in its pursuit of the past—the past we thought we owned when it was the present, and assumed we would continue to own in the future. What we would remember eludes us; what we would forget we now remember with a fresh and painful clarity we never before knew. All those cruelties, deceits, betrayals which we inflicted on the human order disclose themselves as wounds which would not and cannot heal. Of such real guilt Martin Buber wrote:

> A man stands before us who, through acting or failing to act, has burdened himself with a guilt or has taken part in a community guilt, and now, after years or decades, is again and again visited by the memory of his guilt. Nothing of the genesis of his illness is concealed from him if he is only willing no longer to conceal from himself the guilt character of that active or passive occurrence. What takes possession of him ever again has nothing to do with any parental or social reprimand, and if he does not have to fear an earthly retribution and does not believe in a heavenly one, no court, no punishing power exists that can make him anxious. Here there rules the one penetrating insight—the one insight capable of penetrating into the impossibility of recovering the original point of departure and the irreparability of what has been done, and that means the real insight into the irreversibility of lived time, a fact that shows itself unmistakably in the starkest of all human perspectives, that concerning one's own death. From no standpoint is time so perceived as a torrent as from the vision of the self in guilt. Swept along in this torrent, the bearer of guilt is visited by the shudder of identity with himself. I, he comes to know, I, who have become another, am the same.[2]

THE ESTRANGEMENT OF DESPAIR

As despair deepens, what had meaning now seems meaningless, what seemed meaningless is fraught with meaning. There develops an ever widening rift between the despairer and the person he was, between him and the world in which he lived. Though estranged from the world, and the self who formerly dwelt in that world, he is at the same time—out of his craving for reconciliation—now wholly absorbed with that world and that self. Envy and pride conspire to increase the rift. Strangers passing him on the street appear to him transfigured by their thoughtless possession of just what he has lost: the sheer, taken-for-granted ordinariness of life. In the misery of the envy they incite in him he isolates and exalts that quality of life which can flourish only in disregard: a sense of belonging to whatever worlds one lives in that is both concrete and casual. Finding himself outside his own world, he discovers that he is unequal to it, and he yearns to sever whatever ties still bind him to this world to which he no longer belongs. Fitfully he contemplates other worlds—the simple job, the monastery, the tropical island, the sick room. But he flinches as he imagines addressing himself to the machinery of preparation, explanation and farewell that such a flight requires, and he realizes further that no haven offers a promise of honoring his passport on arrival. Though he may believe himself the most miserably humbled of men, it is not humility but pride which rules his imagination in this enterprise. His visions of escape from his tormenting world are apt to be rather grand in scope, and turn about such possibilities as remote lands and the monastic life. Taking a job as a shoe clerk does not occur to him—though it might be more in keeping with the humility he ascribes to himself. Within him pride and despair, which since the earliest stages of his affliction have found themselves natural and powerful partners, each encouraging and supporting the claims and strategies of the other, now discover in the despairer's yearning for escape merely one more invitation to exercise their formidable collaborative gifts and assume command. Inspired by his despair, his pride now invents in its own image the possible alternatives to the world that surrounds him, excluding him. It may happen that he perseveres, and reaches his island, or the disturbed ward of some closer-by institution, thus shutting out the world that had shut the door on him. Yet what he cannot shut out, what accompanies him on any journey he makes, is his own despair. And, with his despair, his overweening pride. His despair is not in the possession of the world, nor can he abandon it as he can abandon a city, a job, a marriage, and flee to some uncontaminated place. His despair is his alone; it travels with him and lives where he lives; and whether he stays or flees he must eventually discover that it responds—in any significant sense—as little to geographical as to stylistic change. Its indifference to maneuvers is absolute.

Because intercourse with his fellows only reminds him of what he no longer has, he slowly loses the power to be with other human beings—even as their physical presence grows ever more essential. To some degree he is conscious that his mounting self-absorption is accompanied by a dwindling perception of others. What concern he manages he must will: thus does he leap from his reveries to arrange his features in some imitation of interest and animation, to open doors, light others' cigarettes, to "participate"—usually in some stilted, feverish way, which constitutes the best performance to which his will alone can move him—in "the scene," in "a social situation," where his presence in a group of people seems to require certain ordinary capacities he finds he now suddenly and totally lacks. Dreading that others will recognize what he already knows, and abandon him, he feels compelled to declare some disability which will legitimize his distracted self-absorption in the eyes of those about him, in the hope they will extend the same tolerance toward him that any invalid may rightfully expect. Like the sinner in *The Fall,* by Camus, the despairer knows that "the essential is being able to permit oneself everything, even if, from time to time, one has to profess vociferously one's own infamy."[3] In this state he experiences an overwhelming longing to confess—but what he confesses is not his wickedness, which would be a proper subject for confession and which might involve him in some redeeming attitude toward both his confession and his life. Instead, what he wishes to confess is his worthlessness—his infirmity. Such a confession is spurious, of course; it does not touch on issues of forgiveness or repentance which are relevant to his condition. In "confessing" infirmity what the despairer would coerce—and here his willfulness is quite brutal—is an acknowledgement of his disease in terms which are almost physical. I find no mystery in the eagerness of those in despair to secure a physical diagnosis—say depression—and then offer themselves to pills or electric shock or lobotomy—anything which will spare them real contrition. But more mysterious to me is the willingness of those of our calling to accept the more demonic terms of despair, to conspire to relieve the despairer of his humanity through chemical, electrical or surgical means.

A VAUDEVILLE OF DEVILS

Even in such a brief account of the landscape of despair, it must be clear that despair—potentially at least—is both destroying and renewing. With this double potentiality in mind, T. S. Eliot has addressed himself to the despairer in this manner:

> I said to my soul, be still, and wait without hope
> For hope would be hope for the wrong thing; wait without love.
> For love would be love of the wrong thing; there is yet faith.
> But the faith and the love and the hope are all in the waiting.
> Wait without thought, for you are not ready for thought:
> So the darkness shall be light, and the stillness the dancing.[4]

While we may not share the author's rather Eastern reliance on the waiting itself as the way out of despair, still we must acknowledge how difficult it is for the despairer to still his soul—or his mind. While despair means literally the loss of hope, the movements of despair are frantically directed toward hope; but the hope born of despair may turn to the prescriptions of the isolated will. Spurning the self-illumination arising from true humility, despairing hope concerns itself pridefully with certainties—even the certainty of hopelessness may paradoxically appear as a form of hope, promising to make reasonable what is unreasonable, namely hopelessness itself. The despairer may, at this opaque moment, be utterly convinced of the clarity of his vision, condemning the world which preceded his despair as no more than a sentimental insanity, a silly fabrication created by his own unwillingness to discern the harsh truth about this existence. It is as if his imagination, in its fullest sense, had abdicated, and now his will could apply itself to the task of reducing what is most human, to pursuing ever further the inevitability—and therefore the essential absurdity—of all that has been and all that will be. He now seems to himself, despite his melancholy, the most reasonable and forthright of men. Like Kirilov in Dostoyevsky's *The Possessed*, he proclaims, "I am just such a scoundrel as you, as all, not a decent man. There's never been a decent man anywhere . . . all the planet is a lie and rests on a lie and on mockery. So then, the very laws of the planet are a lie and the vaudeville of devils."[5] This is the realism of a truly macabre predictability. And a "vaudeville of devils" accurately describes the stale, repetitious, lifeless routines from which the despairer yearns to escape. Surprise and mystery have vanished from his view, if not from his experience. If he contemplates a visit with friends he can no longer imagine the casual, the unexpected moment which might offer even momentary relief. No, instead he writes both scripts and concludes from his authorship that since he knows what would happen there is no reason for making such a visit. But if life itself should provide a casual moment, even with a stranger, which quite cuts through his self-absorption, wholly transforming his mood, he has no capacity to celebrate this moment. In fact, he will disown or conceal the moment rather than allow it to question his dismal certainty, and he thus learns cagily to protect his state from life's interventions. Even the rational or logical steps to his conclusions, which strike him as utterly convincing, may turn shabby if exposed to the light of discourse. So, pride urges him to keep to his own counsel, even though it mean his death. Thus does the despairer appear before us to ask that most extraordinary and truly diabolical question—especially when addressed to a psychotherapist—"Is there any good in talking?" After this, we may recover our composure and succeed in engaging him imaginatively, so that real talk, does, after all, begin to come about. Despite his absolute certainty of a few moments before that even momentary relief from the torment of despair was no longer possible, his despairing self-absorption may yield to forthright interest in the subject at hand, a yielding which goes beyond mere distraction. Relief has, in spite of everything, actually been granted him; his despairing certainty has been exposed to the real world of discourse and proved false. We might even say that a minor miracle has occurred. What are we to answer then, when, as the hour nears its end, our patient or friend, preparing to take his leave, turns to us and asks, "But haven't you something *useful* to say to me—something I can use after I leave here?" If there is an answer to this question, it has not occurred to me. I wish to comment only on one of its most curious aspects: the man who spoke these words was one who had recently been in despair and would, very likely, soon be in despair again. Yet by this question, which could occur only to a despairing mind, despair reasserted its claim on him, still without forcing upon him the anguish which is its customary companion. Contained within his question is the reminder that such fleeting moments of relief are all very well, but after all truth is truth and logic is logic, and by truth of course he means despairing truth and by logic he means despairing logic.

This is to say that what he wishes to take with him to counter his despairing certainties are other certainties, maxim-like morsels, prescriptive in nature, which, like pills, will offer him some comfort when the pain returns. Almost while still celebrating the wonder of his renewal, he has with his question submitted himself again to despair.

KIRILOV: THE CASE OF SUICIDE

The fascination of suicide to a despairing mind lies in the fact that it offers a demonic solution for every anguished, humbling, and potentially renewing claim which despair may make. As Marcel has written, the possibility of suicide may provide the beginnings of metaphysical thought. However, when an absorption with suicide possesses the despairer, it becomes—as Marcel has said—"the expression of another much more profound and more hidden possibility, the possibility of a spiritual denial of self, or, what comes to the same thing, of an impious and demonic affirmation of self which amounts to a radical rejection of being."[6] We have, I think, no more desperate illustration of the manner in which suicide violates every human claim which may exist in despair than Kirilov's explanation of his suicide:

> Man has done nothing but invent God so as to go on living, and not kill himself . . . I can't understand how an atheist could know there is no God and not kill himself on the spot. To recognize that there is no God and not to recognize at the same instant that one is God oneself is an absurdity, else one would certainly kill oneself. If you recognize it you are sovereign, and then you won't kill yourself but will live in the greatest glory. But one, the first, must kill himself, for else who will begin and prove it? So I must certainly kill myself, to begin and prove it. Now I am only a god against my will and I am unhappy, because I am *bound* to assert my will. All are unhappy because all are afraid to express their will. Man has hitherto been so unhappy and so poor because he has been afraid to assert his will in the highest point and has shown his self-will only in little things, like a schoolboy. I am awfully unhappy, for I'm awfully afraid. Terror is the curse of man . . . But I will assert my will, I am bound to believe that I don't believe. I will begin and will make an end of it and open the door, and will save. That's the only thing that will save mankind and will recreate the next generation physically; for with his present physical nature man can't get on without his former God, I believe. For three years I've been seeking for the attribute of my godhead and I've found it; the attribute of my god-head is self-will! That's all I can do to prove in the highest point my independence and my new terrible freedom. For it is very terrible. I am killing myself to prove my independence and my new terrible freedom.[7]

This quotation is a combination of two speeches of Kirilov's which occur close together in the course of a dialogue several pages long, a series of assertions which seem to me to constitute an excellent example of certain aspects of the suicidal despair I have been discussing. As I examine Kirilov's declarations I will try to make clear my own understanding of what is happening in this passage, and what significance it may have for our consideration of despair and the life of suicide.

WILL AND REASON IN THE SERVICE OF DESPAIR

As Kirilov expounds on the purpose and necessity of his suicide, the voice we hear seems hardly to belong to a person. Or if we can imagine a person to be present, it must strike us that this person's singular life as human being is almost wholly submerged in a sea of generalizations about the human condition and the existence of God. Both the tone and the substance of these generalizations exhibit the certainty of a creature with godlike pretensions, while at the same time testifying, by the forced nature of the logic, that this certainty is constantly assailed by fear and doubt. And, further, that uncertainty is unnaturally frightening to such a mind; in its fear of any sort of question it leaps to answer the wrong questions. Again Eliot's lines come to mind: Kirilov is precisely a man unable to still his soul—or his mind, which, indeed, has become merely the reasoning function (however impaired its power to reason) of his sovereign will. The very thing he cannot do is wait. Willfully he hopes, and inevitably his hope is hope for the wrong thing. Bereft of faith yet lusting for faith, willfully he invents his own creed and embraces it with willful belief. He is indeed "not ready for thought," yet thought seems to be the only response his mind can imagine making to the despair which overwhelms it.

We should note that at no point—in this passage or in the course of the entire scene—does Kirilov admit, or indeed even begin to recognize, his own despair. This is the worst of all despairs in which, as Kierkegaard has written, the despairer does not know he is in despair. With that variety of logic which is born only in despair, he reasons that even though he might live on and on in "greatest glory" as God, he must be the first to kill himself in order to "prove" his divinity—or, more accurately, his immortality. Usually the despairer, as I mentioned earlier, learns to mask such demonic logic as this out of his prideful apprehension that any explicit exposure might reveal it as foolish, even absurd. But Kirilov, ignorant of his despair, fails to experience such apprehension; although not altogether confident of the truth of his assertions, neither his doubts nor his pain suggests to him the nature of his condition. What intervenes between the plentiful evidence of despair and his notice of such evidence is, of course, his will, which cunningly blocks his vision at every turn.

And, in this willed blindness toward his state of mind, he is incapable both of imagining and certainly of contending with such a real issue as guilt. There is little suggestion in his discourse of a human soul suspended in anguish and guilt over its own particular injuries to the human order. Being beyond remorse, all Kirilov can do is to call himself and all other men scoundrels, at the same time declaring the entire planet to be a mockery. That there might potentially be guilt, were he able to pursue real self-illumination, is suggested by his wish to save—not himself, but "mankind," even though all men be scoundrels. Out of his loss of faith he perpetrates a familiar psychologism, strangely similar to Freud's view of religion: namely, that men have invented God in order to stay alive. Untroubled by any memory of other times when he must have deceived himself with other certainties, he now decrees without hesitation that if there is no God then he must be God.

Not only is there no suggestion of guilt in Kirilov's proclamations, neither is there any intimation he may have wrestled with—or even acknowledged—the terror roused in him by the idea of his own death. What we hear instead is the rather plaintive statement that he is unhappy and afraid. And even the possibilities for self-illumination that might lie in this limited admission—were he able to hold himself still in the presence of such unhappiness and fear long enough to perceive some hint of their nature and meaning—are quickly dissipated in the generalization that "terror is the curse of man."

At only one point in this passage does Kirilov seem perilously close to an encounter with the real nature of his condition—an encounter which might force him to abandon his despairing logic. His abrupt assertion that his suicide is "the only thing that will save mankind and will recreate the next generation physically; for with his present physical nature man can't get on without his former God, I believe," contradicts the primary assumption on which his entire argument has rested up to this point: namely, that man could get on without God perfectly well if it were only proved to him once and for all that God didn't exist. He seems suddenly to have stumbled upon an alarming and utterly unmanageable truth: man's need for God is contained in his very physical nature—his mortality, his helplessness to alter the absolute necessity of death. The fact that such a truth could have penetrated the fortifications that will has erected on every side of his awareness must mean that, despite his claims to omniscience, Kirilov has failed to convince himself with his own despairing reasoning. In the moment of his realization of this failure, and faced with the truth he has just perceived, his despair would seem to be on the brink of a crisis of exposure and self-illumination. But his will, rather than accept such a defeat, commands avoidance of this crisis, and presses him instead to outwit the moment with the most extreme and bizarre assertion he has yet made: since man's "physical recreation" is necessary to liberate him from his need for God, such "physical recreation" is precisely what Kirilov's suicide is designed to achieve.

The principal attribute of his godhead, he has discovered, is "self-will," by which he means the naked will directed toward the self—an unconditional Nietzschean will, which we might term willfulness or perhaps pride, and which suggests the "demonic affirmation of self" of which Marcel has spoken. Kirilov will not entertain the possibility that such "self-will" might have landed him in his suicidal despair. Instead he asserts the demonic principle that man has been unhappy because he has been afraid to be willful enough. Therefore he will prove his independence and his "new terrible freedom" through the "supreme" act of "self-will," namely suicide. This is to say that if, out of cowardice, he has failed himself and others, he will now prove his courage, not by contending in fear and trembling with the tumultuous questions of his existence and thus finding his life, but by ending his life. What never occurs to him is that by means of this very concept of "self-will" his whole argument has—perhaps not in terms of its own peculiar logic, but certainly in relation to truth—turned itself on its head. Instead of seeing "self-will" as his affliction, he conceives it as his godhead, and the instrument of his self-realization. Instead of seeing that his sovereign "self-will" enslaves every human aspect of his intelligence, he imagines it as the key to his "terrible freedom." Instead of recognizing "self-will" as the unmistakable clue to his demonic despair, he finds in it—by virtue of the extraordinary demands it imposes—the supreme heroism of his calling, justifying and explaining whatever fear, doubt or pain may have threatened to shake his resolve. Instead of calling into question his manner—and, along with it, all his reasoning, the idea of "self-will" arrives in his mind as a sort of deus-ex-machina of logic, clarifying and confirming all that has gone before, setting upon the ordered whole its seal of authority and exaltation.

Having thus established the necessity of his suicide, Kirilov shoots himself. While perhaps a literary necessity, this is not really characteristic of the life of suicide, which may or may not terminate in the suicidal act itself.

SELF-WILL AS MANIA

Even before plots of suicide have begun to invade and absorb the despairer's subjectivity, his "self-will" may be exerted in destructive ways other than the "supreme" act of suicide. In an effort to breach his growing sense of estrangement, he may explode into a mania of self-assertive activity in which he would seem to be trying to over-power his anguish by exalting those more headstrong aspects of his nature which have brought him at last to despair. Alcohol or drugs may offer brutish assistance to this euphoric surge of personal motion, by means of which he tries to force his way back into the world. Of all the movements of despair, this clatter of the spirit is the most deafening and the most defeating, convincing no one, least of all himself. Deprived by this rush of will of the capacity for quieter moral discrimination, he now exposes himself to more and more opportunities for guilt which must also be overridden. Desperately hungry for reconciliation, he becomes increasingly estranged from those loved ones who might conceivably offer some relief, were it not being demanded of them. At this stage in his deprivation he may turn unhappily to the task of documenting his estrangement by becoming a self-appointed though miserable expert on those deficiencies of his fellows which render them incapable of love particularly the love toward him which would lighten his despair. While dimly conscious that his hectic state makes him unlovable, he maintains in the midst of his fever a wavering hope that the other will overwhelm his isolation with a burst of affection which will lighten his anguish and effectively dispute his despairing certainties. Naturally he hesitates to reveal his perceptions of the manner in which the other has failed him, out of fear he will make himself even more unlovable in the other's eyes. Nevertheless, his need may provoke him into an angry encounter in which despite admissions of his own state he still manages to list his charges. When love—or the inability to love—is examined in this objective manner as still another article of knowledge, every human being must acknowledge his failure. To defend one's capacity to love is a spiritual impossibility; it forces the loved one to objectify and therefore lose that which cannot be objectified, namely love itself. Often enough the consequence of such an encounter is mutual despair. Even if the loved one manages not to fall into despair himself, he may still feel himself charged with the responsibility to love, so that in a self-conscious way he attempts to will what cannot be willed.

HOW CAN I LIVE DECENTLY IN SUICIDE?

This phase of explosive activity will persist until the despairer's excesses become so outrageous to himself that a sudden—and shocking—perception of his own behavior plunges him into real self-loathing. In this state he can no longer escape—or postpone—an acknowledgement of his despair, and by virtue of this very acknowledgement he may—still within despair—find his way toward the beginnings of self-illumination and renewal. But should the possibility of such renewal elude him, he will now discover that this self-loathing has landed him in the bleakest, most naked realm of despair. The rush has subsided, leaving his despairing mind increasingly at the mercy of suicidal machinations. It is as though the will which formerly asserted itself in activity, now turns to the invention of the details of one's self-destruction. At this stage the body grows heavy and alien, so that the most ordinary physical tasks seem like monstrous obstacles, making the despairer wonder how he could ever have taken these matters for granted. He experiences his body as a ponderous affliction to which he longs to put an end. Yet, at the same time, his physical vanity is offended by this new imposition, so that often, in the midst of his suicidal ruminations, he will leave his chair to inspect his face in the mirror for any new wrinkles which may have appeared. At one moment he may have decided on the exact date for his demise, while in the next he finds himself considering the purchase of a new and fashionable jacket. Such an outlandish mixture of the profound and the trivial—so characteristic of the life of suicide—does some disservice to his view of himself as a tragic figure. Increasingly he comes to charge himself with duplicity, shallowness, even frivolity, and now it appears that the act of suicide is necessary to prove his seriousness. The absurdity and pathos of the life of suicide stem from the despairer's will to achieve—through suicide—his status as a moral human being. In a sense he asks, "How can I live decently in suicide?" Referring to the "radical rejection of being" which follows upon the "demonic affirmation of self" in the contemplation of suicide, Marcel adds, "that rejection is the final falsehood and absurdity; for it can exist only *through* someone who is; but as it becomes embodied it develops into perverted being."[8] As a demonically constitutive symbol, suicide invokes every human concern. Inevitably the issue of courage is raised—not the courage to live in spite of despair, but the courage suicidally to put an end to all those cowardly hesitations which prevent the despairer from consummating his death. Brooding over the manner of his suicide, he searches again and again for the considerate way—the way which will make manifest his continuing solicitude for those who would be most damaged by his death. Timing becomes a weighty problem: it would be cruel to spoil the Christmas season for his family, selfish to disturb office business at this particular moment. (Let us note that this intricate solicitude toward others is, in truth, merely an absurd imitation of—or substitute for—his real guilt toward them and toward the whole human order, a guilt he is incapable of contending with directly.) The suicide note, since it must justify what cannot be justified, becomes a formidable and frustrating document as it is composed and recomposed in the despairer's mind, each new version suggesting the possibility that perhaps no note would be preferable to an unconvincing one: particularly since any note, depending on its imaginative adequacy, may expose to the despairer the essential absurdity of all he seeks to prove.

THE LOGICAL FLAW: ENDURANCE AND CHOICE

Even the extent of his suffering must be witnessed and authenticated by suicide. Repeatedly he announces to himself that his state is unbearable. But should he be challenged on this score—that is, how is he to know what is and what is not bearable for himself; in other words, what gives him this godlike certainty?—his answer, to himself at least, is that it must be unbearable, otherwise he would not be thinking of suicide. In solitude this answer appears unassailable to the despairer. In fact, it may happen that the act of suicide seems to have become necessary to demonstrate how unendurable his pain is, in which case he commits suicide in order to prove it unendurable. Here the despairer takes his own life to prove that he is not responsible for taking his own life. By definition what is unendurable cannot be endured; therefore his suicide is not a matter of choice but an externally determined response to a situation which has deprived him of choice. The flaw in this logical construct, of course, is that his definition of his condition as unendurable is very much a matter of choice, and thus, obviously, so is his suicide. What is interesting here is the despairer's effort to deny the fact of choice and, by extension, to deny responsibility for his suicidal act. He does not say: "I am in great pain; I do not know how much longer I can contend with it; I do not know if I will be permitted some relief, or how much, or how soon, or if it will afford me any more than momentary comfort. But I choose to bear these uncertainties no further. I prefer to end my life of my own will and by my own hand. I choose this act and accept full responsibility for it." Though such a declaration contains a fairly accurate description of his situation, the despairer goes to some trouble to avoid such an acknowledgement of choice and responsibility. He must believe his suicide to be an inescapable fate imposed on him from without. Why? Is it perhaps possible that even in the grip of his despair he has not lost contact with his more human self, and the human truths his despair strives to deny—has not lost contact to such a degree that he no longer conceives suicide as a demonic act? Indeed, because he *does* recognize its nature he shrinks from confronting the actual role of choice in his act. Even his despair will not allow him such an unholy embrace of moral grotesquerie as suicide. Were he capable of acknowledging the nature of this unholy embrace, and his responsibility in submitting to it, his despair—and his despairing estrangement from the world of the human—would be complete. The fact that instead of prompting this acknowledgement his despair labors to deny it altogether, to persuade him of his role as helpless, therefore blameless, victim, this fact suggests that in an important sense despair by its very nature is incapable of wholly fulfilling itself. As I remarked earlier, despair seems to afflict only those whose relation to life is a serious and potentially responsible one. It seems to me that those who are vulnerable to the worst torments of despair are also those who—because of what they were before falling into despair, and still, in the clutches of despair, potentially are—are seldom able quite to reach the demonic affirmation of self and the radical rejection of being toward which their despair strains. In some sense the despairer moves hazardously, despite distractions and entrenchment, toward a tragic, often excessively tragic, position in regard to the inauthentic in his life and in his relations with others. In other words, through his objectifications he may arrive at an extreme and radical concern over the very center of his being, creating in this way an abyss too wide and too deep for easy bridging. The very strategies of despair, and especially the logical strategies involved in the contemplation of suicide, reveal that there is some connection still linking them to life-outside-despair—perhaps only imagined, but imagined still—that despair is unable to sever. Despair would not be so anguished a condition as it is were it as wholly and hopelessly estranged as it believes itself to be.

THE BARGAIN WITH DEATH

There is one last clause to the pact suicide makes with despair: suicide appears to offer a means of contending with the necessity and all the attending uncertainties of one's own death. What Buber has written of guilt applies equally to the person in despair: potentially he is permitted "the real insight into the irreversibility of lived time, a fact that shows itself unmistakably in the starkest of all human perspectives, that concerning one's own death." Opposing this insight, suicide promises through an act of will to resolve the terrors of mortality which in despair are so overwhelming. Death itself is certain; but how, when, where, in what manner, under what conditions, with what serenity or wild ravings, and *how soon*—this knowledge is not granted us. There is, however, one way in which a man may attain it, and by so doing "cheat" death, become its master by mastering its uncertainties—and this way is to stage and execute his own death, at the time, place, and in the manner of his own choosing. But once embarked on this enterprise—or the contemplation of this enterprise—he becomes absorbed in the scene itself. As though carelessly overlooking the inevitable climax of the action: death, *his* death, he focuses his attention upon the staging of the act; he reviews and evaluates the methods available to him; in his imagination he lives and relives the discovery scene—at which in reality he can hardly expect to be present. And yet in effect he must expect to be present, if through suicide he intends to master the terrors of death, because such terrors belong to life. Although the strategies involved in the attainment of this mastery can succeed only by luring his attention away from the real issue of his own death, their success is almost always incomplete and intermittent. Since his death is, after all, a detail of action inescapably necessary to his scenario—the single act about which his entire dramatic construction turns—its ultimate significance is not likely to remain safely hidden behind his busy concern with an endless variety of production problems; from time to time it rudely assaults his awareness, and in those moments he realizes all too clearly that the mastery suicide seemed to offer him was a cheat and a fake. But each time this dreadful moment arrives he wrenches away from it and fastens his imagination again on the fictional representation of his death, in which what absorbs him is not his actual death but the possibility for self-expression that the drama affords. And why should an opportunity for self-expression—so strikingly, almost farcically, inappropriate to his particular situation—tempt him so? We need but briefly remind ourselves of his condition, and the extraordinary vulnerabilities common to it, to guess that the explanation for his response lies in what he believes is being promised him in return for the cooperation he so wholeheartedly supplies. What can this promise be but that self-expression, given free reign in this exceptional enterprise, will produce for him the dramatic representation of some uniqueness, some singularity of self with which life has seemingly so far failed to provide him, and of which his natural—un-self-engineered—death threatens to rob him? What I wish to point out here is that all this is a dream of the will—a despairing attempt to affirm the self in a form in which the self has never *been* and can never be. The uncertainties—and even the terrors—of death belong, as Kirilov almost discovered, to life and to our nature. Living the life of suicide a man struggles to deny this truth, and should the trapdoor spring open beneath him, he will die proclaiming his denial. But it is a redeeming paradox of the life of suicide that it does not always—and need not—make its exit from life via the trapdoor. The despairing man can return to life—alive. Many have done so, and some have left their accounts of that treacherous passage to remind us that salvation is never wholly out of reach, even in the farthest country of despair.

NOTES

1 Gabriel Marcel. *The Philosophy of Existentialism*. New York: The Citadel Press, 1961, p. 26.

2 Martin Buber. "Guilt and Guilt Feelings," *Psychiatry,* 1937, 20, 114-129, p. 116.

3 Albert Camus. *The Fall*. New York: Alfred A. Knopf, 1957, p. 141.

4 T. S. Eliot. East Coker. *Four Quartets*. New York: Harcourt, Brace, 1943, p. 15.

5 Fyodor Dostoyevsky. *The Possessed*. New York: The Modern Library, 1936, pp. 625-629.

6 Gabriel Marcel. *The Mystery of Being: 2. Faith, & Reality*. Chicago: Henry Regnery, 1960, p. 194

7 T. Dostoyevsky, *op. cit.*, pp. 629-630.

8 Gabriel Marcel, *op. cit.*, p. 194.

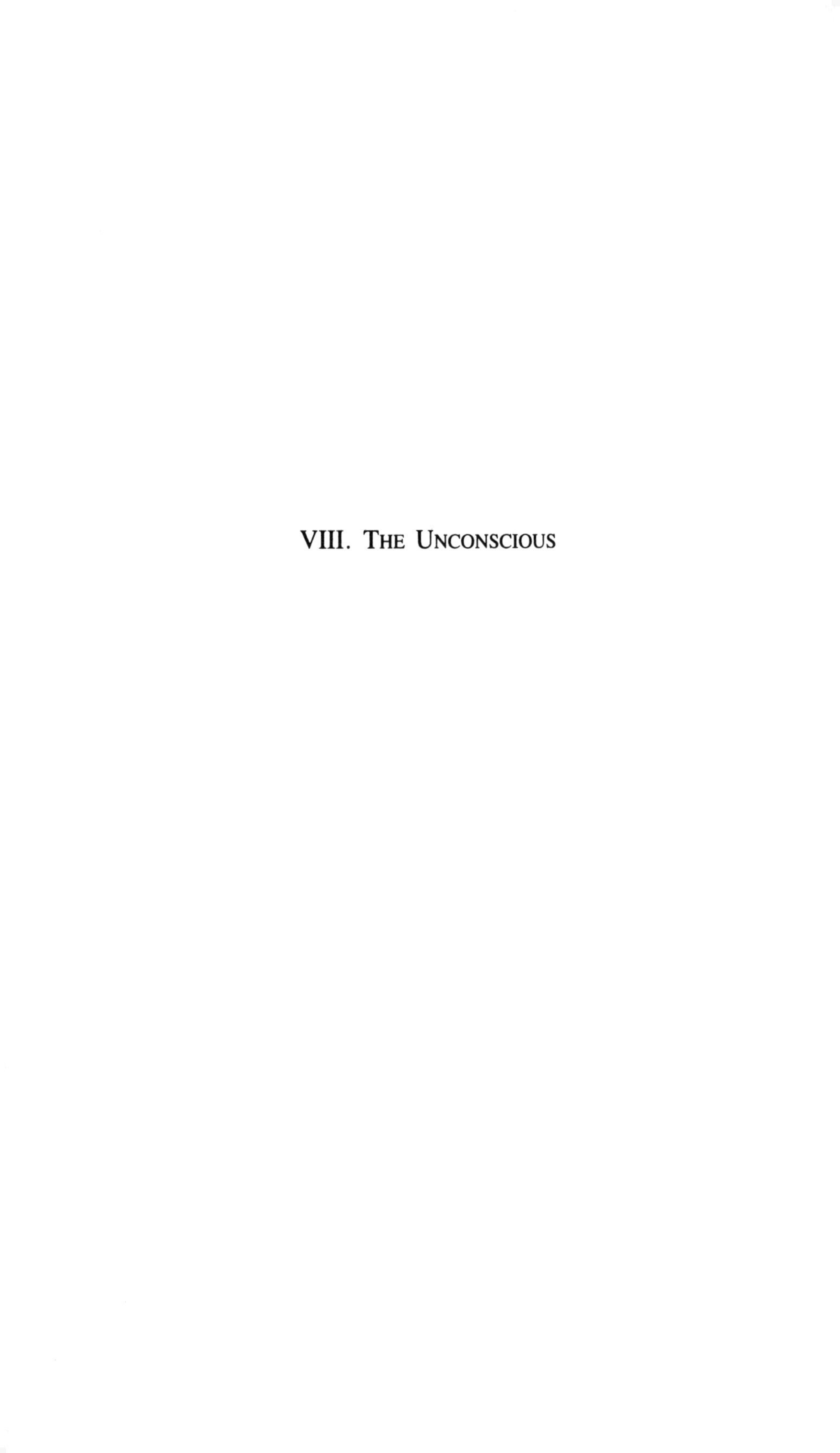

VIII. The Unconscious

The Unconscious—What Is It?

MEDARD BOSS

Translated by E. S. Goodstein

"The unconscious" is a central concept in Freud's psychoanalysis, so much so that Freud would not allow those who did not believe in the actual presence (*Vorhandensein*) of an "unconscious" the right to call themselves psychoanalysts. To review Freud's harsh verdict adequately, we must consider that the noun "psychoanalysis" refers to two completely different things. First of all, Freud gave this name to a very concrete, practical therapeutic procedure. His Viennese colleague Breuer had brought to his attention the fact that many human ailments can only be made to disappear permanently if one allows the patients in question to talk about the secret meaning of their symptoms and how these came about in the course of their lives. At the outset, Freud called in the help of hypnosis for this purpose. Soon, however, he changed over to the method of "free association." He imposed upon his patients the duty of being unconditionally, ruthlessly and unrestrainedly honest with themselves and with their analyst. They were to say aloud everything that occurred to them during the session, no matter how painful or embarrassing it might seem. This duty became a fundamental rule of psychoanalytic *praxis*.

But then Freud felt the need to give a scientific foundation to the concrete therapeutic procedure he had discovered in praxis. For this purpose, he constructed a splendidly self-enclosed theory that he also called "psychoanalysis." Freud designated this theoretical psychoanalysis a mere secondary superstructure and in general permitted that all of its parts which should subsequently prove unusable be let go. The central concept of the "unconscious" belongs entirely in the realm of "psychoanalysis" as a psychological theory, or psychoanalytic "metapsychology," as Freud also referred to his theory.

For a long time, Freud himself was somewhat uncomfortable with his theoretical concept of an "unconscious." He had come across the word in the German philosopher Lipps, but had immediately filled it with "a new content"[1] (II/III, 616ff.; XVII, 147). He therefore reserved for himself the right to have discovered the "unconscious" for psychology. At first thought, Freud's concept of the unconscious depended only on a single "characteristic of certain psychical structures. . . ." The unconscious, he wrote, "appeared to us at first to be simply the enigmatic quality of a certain process." However, soon this was supplemented by a fundamentally new linguistic usage, one which became more important than the original descriptive-qualitative meaning of "unconscious." In the course of the same article, Freud writes "but now it (the unconscious) means more. . . . The value of the unconscious as an index has left its significance as a quality far behind . . . . We use the name 'the unconscious' for a system that makes itself known to us via the characteristic that the individual events of which it is composed are unconscious. This is the most important meaning which the expression 'unconscious' has acquired in psychoanalysis."[2]

In Freud's metapsychology, therefore, the concept "unconscious," something represented initially as an adjectival characteristic of an intrapsychic reality, itself unexpectedly became a thing, present in and for itself as a psychic "locality" or system. The most diverse qualities and regularities were henceforth attributed to the "unconscious," as to an independent thing. For example, now the "unconscious" was said to exhibit a sovereign disdain for the fundamental principle of thought: the law of contradiction. One of the first qualities Freud ascribed to the unconscious, before it was metapsychologically hypostasized into an object, was that a special sort of "thought processes" took place in it. By labelling these initially as "primary processes," Freud differentiated them from the conscious trains of thought, the secondary psychical processes. The "primary process" in the "unconscious" was, according to Freud, distinguished especially by an incomparably looser mobility of its free psychic energy. As a result of this mobility, representations which did not belong together would condense into a single one, and the forces of many representations could be shifted onto a single one in the unconscious. Further, the "unconscious primary process" was said to behave without consideration for time or for the logical principle of contradiction. Thus it would replace external by psychical reality, within which the events in the psyche were subordinate solely and immediately to the regulation of pleasure-unpleasure.[3]

However, it is permissible to ask what actually befell Freud's thinking in the formation of this theory. Our answer: nothing less than that philosophy now took a terrible revenge on the man who, in all of his work, had nothing but scorn and contempt for philosophers. For example, in one of his most important works, Freud makes fun of the philosophers in the following way:

"I am not at all in favor of fabricating world views. I leave this up to philosophers, who by their own admission find the journey through life impracticable without such a Baedecker to provide information about everything. Let us humbly accept the scorn with which the philosophers look down upon us from the standpoint of their higher neediness. Since we cannot deny our narcissistic pride, we will seek comfort in the consideration that all of these guides to life quickly age, that it is precisely our myopically limited detail work which makes a new edition of theirs necessary, and that even the most modern of these Baedeckers attempt to replace the old comfortable and complete catechism."[4]

Philosophy's revenge on Freud consisted in making him, though he never noticed this in the least, fall victim to that genus of her species, the thinking of which is as inappropriate to human existence as possible. How could Freud possibly have avoided running into theoretical dead ends?

That philosophy was Rene Descartes', the French mathematician in whose head the primordial unity of the world was torn into two radically different realms. This had the most serious consequences for the subsequent history of the west, for with this thinker's approach as premise it was never again possible to reconstitute that unity. The first Cartesian domain was that of the *res cogitans,* the human spirit, the human consciousness. The other comprehended all things outside of the *res cogitans.* Descartes designated it the realm of the *res extensae,* since the fundamental property of the things present in it was their extension. Through this train of thought Descartes enthroned the human consciousness as the single thing which underlies all other entities, as the sole subject, as *hypokaimenon.* From then on all other being could only become meaningfully real if a human subject set it in opposition to itself and thus made it into an object. In Descartes' thinking, the *res extensae,* the objects of an outer world, were reflected in an enigmatic way in the inside of a human consciousness, itself represented in a primarily capsule-like fashion. Once there, these objects became representations of this subject with some meaning or other. The unavoidable consequence of this was that the fundamental character of all that which lay outside of the *res cogitans,* that is, human thinking, feeling, and judging, became its representedness by human subject.

Only a single essential trait (*Wesenszug*) was left to be shared by the *res cogitans* and *res extensae,* the things of these two deeply severed realms of the world. That was their character of being object-like and present-at-hand someplace in the world-cavity thought already to exist. In Descartes' thought, every human mind, every *res cogitans,* every subject, consciousness, psyche, every *cogitare* with all its contents, thoughts, wishes, attitudes, and judgements, also experienced such an objectification and definition as something present at hand somewhere.

This Cartesian philosophy, then, fell upon Freud and forced him to hand himself over to it blindly and unquestioningly. In delivering himself up, he did not at all suspect its purely philosophical character, that is, its nature as a purely axiomatic anticipation of the determination of the essence of what is encountered. In truth, however, it is an anticipation, the appropriateness to the encountered or objectivity of which cannot at all be proved, least of all scientifically. Nevertheless, Cartesian thinking remained the unquestioned background for Freud's subsequent encounters with the phenomena of healthy and sick fellow human beings.

At first, Freud considered the banal observation that at a given moment a person can, for example, ascend the Corcovado mountain entirely in thought, and then, in the next moment, be just as completely filled by an entirely different thing, for example, contemplation of a bouquet of flowers standing before him on the table. But right after this his thinking can return to Corcovado. So Freud asked: Where was the representation of Corcovado in the meantime? It cannot have been annihilated, for how could it then have turned up again so rapidly. The representation must have remained latently present in consciousness. But where? In a typically Cartesian manner, Freud had already hypostasized everything immeasurable, immaterial, and unobject-like in human existence to a "physical apparatus" present somewhere. Although at first Freud knew and even italicized that this conception was merely a *fiction,* he soon afterwards began to speak of it as of something really present (*Vorhandenem*). Freud could only conceive of that into which the mountain Corcovado, for example, temporarily disappeared as a sort of sublocality within this "psychical apparatus." He called this "the unconscious" . . . the representation of Corcovado, so Freud now thought, spent the interim time "in the unconscious."

An "unconscious" is merely the negation of: "consciousness." As such, it remains constantly related to the latter. At this point, therefore, one might have expected a thoughtful illumination of consciousness from Freud. However, he is so comfortably settled into Descartes' definition of what thinking is that he modestly states: "We need not elucidate what conscious means for us: it is beyond all doubt."[5] Further on he writes: "This investigation (of the unconscious) departs from the unique fact of consciousness, which frustrates all explanation and description. If one speaks of consciousness, one nevertheless knows immediately, out of one's ownmost experience, what is meant."[6]

Only in his early work, *The Interpretation of Dreams* (1900), does Freud still reflect on the nature of this consciousness. He answers the question about its role simply: "None other than that of a sense organ which perceives a content given elsewhere."[7] In Freud's opinion, then, consciousness is nothing other than a perceptual organ, analogous to the external sense organs. The "external world" is given to consciousness via the mediation of the latter, but consciousness immediately perceives the "inner world," that which is thought as intrapsychically present-at-hand data.

But then the phenomena of parapraxes in everyday life, dream images, and neurotic symptoms begin to claim Freud's attention. Among other things, Freud mentions the example of the president who misspeaks at the outset of a meeting. The following sentence escapes from him while opening the assembly: "I declare this meeting *closed.*" Freud concluded from this occurrence that the thought "this business bores me; if only this meeting were already over, then I could go home," must have been present somewhere in the man. But since the latter had not an inkling of any such thought, it could be at hand only in that subrealm of the psychical apparatus which merits the name "the unconscious."

Yet Freud saw himself compelled to distinguish between the "unconscious," in which he had placed the aforementioned representation of Corcovado, which returned rapidly and spontaneously, and "the unconscious," which in his opinion harbored the assembly leader's wish for the quickest possible end to the session. For in contrast to the representation of Corcovado, this wish remained inaccessible to the president's consciousness: it was and remained "repressed" out of consciousness into the unconscious. The man who committed the president's slip would probably have resisted mightily if one had attributed any such secret meaning to that slip. On the contrary, he would have wanted to persevere in the self-deception that he was enthusiastic about the meeting over which he was presiding. Thus Freud distinguished "the unconscious" which contains that which is repressed for reasons of self-love or for moral motives as the "genuine unconscious," from the temporary shelter of any representation that would be accessible again without further ado. The latter received the name "preconscious."

Thus Freud obtained the concept of the "genuine unconscious" from the theory of repression. He wrote, "for us, the repressed is the prototype of the unconscious."[8] By this he meant that repressing was a "tendentious" forgetting, the basis of which was not that that which had been forgotten was too insignificant to be remembered, but rather that it was not supposed to, or not allowed to be, remembered.

Such a forgetting is much more an active doing than a mere occurrence; in Freud's opinion, repression is a means of banning a certain content from consciousness. That which cannot be reconciled with a person's "conscience" is banished. According to Freud, the conscience, to which he gives the technical term "superego" (*Überich*), consists of nothing other than the internalized commandments and prohibitions of the society in which the individual grew up. Repressing is a peculiarly human way of relating to oneself, insofar as the human being is basically a social being. The fundamental reliance on recognition by one's contemporaries (*Mitwelt*), arises from an interest in hiding one's own nonconformity. The so-called unconscious can thus be more precisely defined as that which a person by *himself* has concealed, and that the concealed is concealed *from himself* because of a nonconformity. To conceal something from oneself through oneself amounts to self-deception.

In this ambiguity, the expression "self-deception" precisely captures the circumstance out of which Freud abstracted his theoretical concept of the unconscious. In 1975 Holzhey commented correctly on this: "In self-deception it is not only the case that the psychical subject errs *with respect to* itself; rather, it is at the same time deluded and deceived by itself, not by another. The unconscious is something concealed which I conceal from myself. In self-deception the deceiver and the deceived are one."

Freud has the task of positively illuminating this phenomenon. How is self-deception possible? He solves the puzzle by combining, as it were, two persons in one. He writes: "We designate a psychical process as unconscious when we conclude from its effects that we must assume its existence though we know nothing about it. We are then in the same relation to it as to a psychical process in another human being, except that this process is our own."[9]

My own unconscious, then, is removed from me in the same way as is the inside of other people, which is closed to me insofar as I have no power of my own to bore into it. I only discover what the other shows me: he can open himself to me or not; he can even intentionally mislead me.

If this is also to be true for the relation between conscious and unconscious, then there must be an authority to decide whether something unconscious should become conscious or not. Freud calls it the censor. It is often personified as a "watchman" in accompaniment to the projection of the following picture of the human soul:

"We may compare the system of the unconscious to a large anteroom in which the stirrings of the psyche roam about as individuals. Adjoining this anteroom is a second, narrower one, a sort of salon in which consciousness, too, is present. But on the threshold between the two rooms a watchman executes his duties, inspecting the individual stirrings of the psyche, censoring them, and not admitting them into the salon if they incur his displeasure."[10]

However, Holzhey correctly countered Freud's speculation with this compelling critique: "The relation between unconscious and conscious is determined by the censor. If one asks what the nature of the censor must be for it to exercise this function, the attempted solution proves to have foundered already, for the censor itself can be only an unconscious consciousness; the assumption of censorship brings back the difficulty (*aporia*) that was supposed to be overcome."[11]

As has already been noted, Freud himself was of two minds regarding his attempt to elucidate the phenomenon of self-deception and with it the slips, dreams, and neurotic symptoms. He wrote for example: "Where, in which domain, shall proof be brought that there is knowledge of which the person knows nothing? . . . That would be a self-invalidating fact . . . a contradiction *in adjecto*."[12] On the other hand, he also admitted that he had gone beyond experience with the assumption of an "unconscious." Finally, he even conceded the rough character of his visualization of that which at bottom cannot be viewed, the "unconscious."[13] Yet again he continues: "I want to assure you that these rough assumptions . . . must signify a very far-reaching approximation of the real state of affairs."[14]

Soon after the discovery of the "unconscious," it was proved by no less a personage than Jean-Paul Sartre that Freud's concept was condemned from the outset to fail to provide an explanatory basis for slips and neurotic symptoms. In his early work, *Being and Nothingness,* he wrote: "When I lie, I myself know the truth, which I distort; yet at the same time, as the deceived one who I also am, I do not know this same truth. As the deceiver, I also know of my intention to deceive. However, if I know that I want to deceive myself, I can no longer let myself be deceived, for I can only be deceived where I want to know the truth."[15]

Freud's own subsequent development of his notion of the "psychical apparatus," which led from topical ideas to dynamical and economical ones, is no more help. The inadmissible objectification of human existing and its reduction to energy processes are not in the least overcome in this development.

Therefore, we have no choice but to have our own look into the phenomena which Freud believed could not be comprehended without the introduction of "the unconscious."

There were, to recapitulate, the following four points:

1. One can be completely absorbed by something either in beholding it or simply "in thought." In the next moment, however, something entirely different may completely engross one. Then immediately afterwards one devotes one's attention to the first thing again. Freud could not think of the time in-between except as a span in which "the representation" of the first thing had disappeared by being thrust into "the unconscious" of a psyche, or more precisely into its "preconsciousness." Otherwise, how would it have been able to resurface forthwith in "consciousness"?

2. There are doubtless a great number of parapraxes in everyday life, in which one does or says something which one did not at all knowingly want to do or say. Must there not be a corresponding slip of thought (*Fehlgedanke*) present in the "unconscious"?

3. Most dreams consist of "images" (*Bilder*); if they are to be understood, they must be reinterpreted in terms of something which heretofore lay in the "unconscious."

4. According to Freud, it is possible to make sense of psychoneurotic symptoms as well only if one explains them by representational or affective contents enclosed in an "unconscious" in the narrower and genuine sense.

The question is: do all these phenomena in themselves really compel all these suppositions? Do they not do so only if one has previously subscribed to another, prior supposition, namely, the "fiction" of the presence-at-hand of a "psychical apparatus" conceived as an object. Only one who had accepted this could imagine a "psychical unconscious" as the sub-container in which "psychical garbage" might be lain aside.

This question may be settled without further ado if we concern ourselves with a Daseinsanalytical or phenomenological access to the disputed facts of human existing. This immediately turns many things, the presence of which Freud considered to be evident, into enormous uncertainties.

For example, when I gaze upon the mountain over there, and it claims my entire attention, is it really just in the form of a "representation" in my consciousness? And when I look away from it and no longer think of it, but instead am fully concentrated on the bouquet of flowers before me, then is there really only a "representation" of it in a psychical sub-container of my psyche-capsule called the "preconscious?" Or does not the reality of our relations to something we have once perceived include the peculiarity that the perceived (*das Vernommende*) is always retained, held fast in the place in our world in which it belongs, even if it has a much less explicit presence than just before? It is the same with all of the things which now surround me. If in this moment I am explicitly directed entirely towards my listeners, the podium before me and the wall behind me nevertheless remain what they are and where they are, in my world, albeit in an inexplicit way. If this were not the case, I would constantly bump into the podium before me and stagger into the wall behind me. Just because they have remained present (*anwesend*) in their places in my world, thus their implicit presence can very easily be transformed back into an explicit one.

Though we have just said of these actualities (*Gegebenheiten*) that they lay before us in a merely "inexplicit way" at any given moment, the same things can be distinguished as "not-expressly-thought." This would likewise be a much more humanly adequate description than the spatial specification "in the preconscious."

And how do the parapraxes look when we approach them Daseinsanalytically or phenomenologically and cease all unsubstantiatable speculations?

As an example for parapraxes, Freud had introduced the assembly leader who made the mistake of saying "I pronounce this meeting closed" during the opening ceremonies. Did an "unconscious thought" about the quickest possible end to the session really haunt his "unconscious" before this event? But can anyone even explain how "a thought" and especially an "unconscious thought" is supposed to be in me, intrapsychically present-at-hand? When I say: now the thought comes to me that such and such is the case, then this always means just that something which speaks to me in its meaningfulness out of the openness of my world, is given up into its light, and appears (*zum Vorschein kommt*).

The parapraxis of the man in our example, who opened a meeting with the phrase for closing it, is not a mysterious effect of a thought supposedly preexisting in his "unconscious." Rather, this parapraxis arose immediately from a negative mood that was anything but inaccessible and that held sway over the man's entire existence at the time of his slip. This would be the case even if the session leader was not specifically concentrating on his momentary mood, if it were the case that he had obstinately sought to look away from it. One may be completely engaged in looking away from a painful matter, for example, by turning to others all the more intensively—that which he is so concerned to look away from has by no means therefore evaporated into a mere "representation" and been cast into an intrapsychical subdistrict. On the contrary, that which so intensively compels him to looking away then truly concerns him from its place in his world. That which is shoved aside, "the repressed," remains so very present where it is, that there is especially strong pressure on him from it in the place in which it is in the world.

This describes the phenomenon for which Freud, in order to give a causal-genetic explanation, came up with the speculation of a "repression" of thoughts and feelings into the "unconscious," in the narrower and genuine sense, in a more humanly adequate fashion. The *aporia* of the further supposition—also necessary to Freud's theory—of a censor on the border between his "unconscious" and consciousness has already been sufficiently exposed above.

However, two more things must be added. First, the "having-to-look-away" emphasized in the so-called "repressing into the unconscious" does not consist of a looking away from some sort of "affects" or likenesses of intrapsychically present representations, but of looking away from the thing "repressed" and from its place in the surrounding world (*Umwelt*). Second, this looking-away is anything but a free and autonomously determined action. On the contrary, here it is a matter of "not-being-able-to-do-otherwise," and indeed in consequence of a person's mentality being dictated by the person's early upbringing. The "repressor" is still so much in their power that he is capable of existing only non-autonomously through their behaviors. However, in his non-autonomy he cannot at all become specifically aware of how much he still exists as one "driven from the outside."

But even *having*-to-look-away and not-*being-allowed*-to-take-cognizance is only possible with regard to something that is not in an intrapsychical container called the "unconscious," encapsulated in the form of representative images and affects, but which exists in the world of the "repressor" and is present out "there" in its place. But it is first necessary to realize that something can be present (*vorliegen*) in the most diverse modes of presence (*Anwesenheitsmodi*) and thus be. Among other things, there is also being in the mode of the presence of something that "actually" is not allowed to be, from which one has to look away. But that which is to be repressed is no less in the world-realm than is something immediately present and sensibly perceptible.

Since the details of how a "repressing" constituted in this way proceeds in the concrete neurotic phenomena have been presented at length in the author's *Grundriss der Medizin und der Psychologie* (*Existential Foundations of Medicine & Psychology*),[16] it need not be repeated here.

Likewise, there is no need again to indicate how the existential occurrence called dreaming is commonly misunderstood today. In two books, the author has already pointed out at great length that an essentially more appropriate understanding of dreams is possible without the unsubstantiatable speculation of an "unconscious" and without assuming that distortive activities take place inside it.

But for all of the pressingly necessary corrections to "depth-psychological" theories up to now, the need for a radically new understanding of human being is evident. Thinking this out cannot be the task of medical or psychological scientists. For their research would never have been able to begin, had they not already embraced a certain philosophical understanding of human being, even if they had never considered it specifically. Procuring foundation-laying essential insights into a matter is the business not of dilettantish, but of professional, thinkers. Since ancient times they have been called philosophers.

The soundest foundation of this sort thus far found by the author was in the philosophical insights into the fundamental constitution of the human being, his world, and its congruity as Martin Heidegger knew how to express them. He brought these under the heading of a phenomenological or Daseinsanalytical fundamental ontology.

Becoming able to understand these all-supporting insights demands of us "solely" an ever-sharper regarding of nothing other than ourselves and our being-in-the-world itself. Then that which is shows itself to us of itself. Right away it becomes clear that what occurs in human existence is anything but the presence of a primary "psychical apparatus" encapsulated in itself. Rather we find ourselves as human beings always already placed in this or that relationship to something that speaks to us from its place in our world as this or that meaningful something. But our existing would not be remotely capable of being engrossed in any relationship to something had not the fullness of meaning of this something in each case revealed itself to us just as primordially from there where it is. Thus, of itself, our existing reveals itself to be that in the most literal Greco-roman sense of this verb. This means that our being-in-the-world reveals itself as the holding open (*Ausstehen*) of a primary *Ek-stare*. This consists of holding open a realm of openness to the world, of the ability to perceive the significances of that which encounters us spreading out world-wide. *Thus* is the essence of our primary being-in-the-world revealed to us, if we do not make any pretences.

However, it is not for private pleasure that our existing is endowed with such a fundamental constitution. On the contrary, thanks to this fundamental constitution, all of that which is supposed to be lays claim to our existing from afar as the abode for appearing and unfolding. How could anything at all be, be present, and come to appear, if a perceiving world-openness like human existing did not always already stand at its disposal? Without an openness, there is no coming-to-be (*An-wesen*) in somewhere, and thus no being; without shining (*Scheinen*), no being-able-to-come-to-appearance of anything.

However, lightness, illumination, openness always only exist together with darkness, concealedness, closedness. The one conditions the other. As a remaining open to the world, human existing wrests from concealedness, that means, the inaccessibleness that surrounds us, now a wider, higher, now a narrower and darker realm of remaining open to the world. In each case, its momentary mood determines the sort of concrete world-openness or closedness of an existence. Every single psychologically describable mood (*Bestimmung*) is a definite way of fulfilling the fundamental having-a-mood (*gestimmtsein*) of human existing. But having-a-mood is itself an essential trait of human existence, one that is never missing. Spoken Daseinsanalytically: Being in a mood as such is one of the ontological characteristics of that existence, one of its "existentialien." As one of the possible ontical ways of fulfilling the fundamental, ontological essential trait of "being attuned," the concrete mood in each case determines the breadth or narrowness of an existence present then; it thus also determines which actualities find admittance into this existence's openness to the world (and how) and which do not. An existence upset (*verstimmt*) by panic, for example, offers entry into its world only that which is threatening in all that is encountered. One who has fallen prey to panic mistakes every shrub in the dark woods as a potential murderer.

Departing from René Descartes' old understanding of human being, which served as godfather to Freud's metapsychology, an intrepid mental leap is required to reach the ground of the more adequate, Daseinsanalytical understanding of human being. With this as a foundation, however, Freud's notion of a psyche-capsule primarily present-at-hand somewhere cannot ever even arise, much less the suppositions of all of the intrapsychical forms represented as thinglike and supposed to fill this capsule. The phenomenological view admits no more talk of the likenesses of intrapsychically present representations of the things of the outer world, of feelings and affects, or of drives and primary thought processes. In the light of phenomenological insights into the fundamental constitution of human existence, the latter consists (according to its essence and therefore always already) of the holding open of a worldly realm of openness with an ability to perceive through which the fullness of meaning of that which is encountered in each case emerges and addresses the existing one.

For this reason, in an incomplete execution of human holding-open, but little can reveal itself and find entry into its light, and even this generally only in distorted form. Precisely the most authentic thing in human existence here remains unrevealed in concealedness. But not in a concealedness represented as an intrapsychical container—such as Freud's "unconscious"—but in a concealedness in the sense of something "overhuman," "prepsychical," an obscurity inaccessible to us, out of which everything that ever is, including the human being in his being, is let free into its revealedness. At the same time, however, as long as this is a givenness, it remains constantly permeated by being as such.

From this point of view, Freud's fundamental concept of an "unconscious," thought as intrapsychically present-at-hand, appears to be anything but nothing. It now appears, however, merely as a maximally narrowed, psychologized, and objectified abstraction from a phenomenon that truly occurs, namely, the "great concealedness" just mentioned.

Therefore, a Daseinsanalytically oriented therapy no longer strives to haul up any thoughts, representations, wishes and feelings (supposedly hidden out of vanity or shame in a special intrapsychical locale called the "unconscious") into consciousness (a higher-lying intrapsychic locale). Besides, no psychologist can explain what these thoughts, representations, and wishes, conceived as intrapsychically present-at-hand, are supposed to be, as independent structures present somewhere, although these concepts are constantly on their lips.

A Daseinsanalytical therapy, then, does its best by solicitously leaping ahead for a suffering human being, to broaden and illuminate as much as possible that openness to the world as which he had previously existed and which had been largely veiled and limited in its execution. The analysand is to be freed for an opening of the luminous realm of his existence so that the full truth of the encountered in its entire plenitude of meaning can unfold within it. This freedom is not only for that which does not belong to the person's existence, but also for all of those specific possibilities of behaving with respect to the encountered which constitute the existence of the person in question.

A curative method which calls itself a mere "free association" misunderstands itself. A more adequate designation would be the method of "breaking in freely" (*der freien Einfalle*). However, to repeat, that which breaks in does not consist of intrapsychically present thoughts, representations, likenesses. Nor does it break into an intrapsychically present-at-hand locale. Rather the actualities themselves (and as such) can appear and be revealed from where they are and can come to their being in the luminous realm of the broader and freer openness to the world (*Weltoffenständigkeit*) as which the former patient is now able to exist. During a session, this coming to being at first happens mostly only in their being present in the mode of being brought to mind (*Anwesenheitsmodus der Vergegenwartigung*).

The surgeon who with his specialized knowledge uses steel pins and plates to bring a broken thighbone back in order renders a small service toward such a liberation of a fellow human being. The highest purpose, however, of work on a suffering human being can be indicated through Martin Heidegger's own words. It would be achieved if a former patient "was able to attune himself" in a "cheerful composure towards things" that had become profoundly unshakable "and enter in openness into the mystery of the hidden meaning of our current epoch."[17]

However, the aforementioned highest purpose of all therapies must never be misunderstood as a seduction to the passivity of a self-satisfied, selfish, purely contemplative life. On the contrary: it is the attunement just mentioned which first frees a human being for the highest and most comprehensive ability possible for him of seeing and hearing that which speaks to him out of the openness of his world. At the same time, he must perceive the challenge to him of being adequate to that which he perceives, of helping it—actively and with the full devotion of his existence—to become that as which it is essentially meant [to be].

NOTES

1 Sigmund Freud, *Gesammelte Werke,* Bd. II/III (London: Image Publishing Ltd, 1942), pp. 616 ff.; *The Standard Edition of the Complete Psychological Works of Sigmund Freud,* Vol. 5, *The Interpretation of Dreams II* (London: The Hogarth Press, 1953), pp. 611 ff.

2 *Ibid., G. W.,* Bd. VIII (1943), pp. 438-39; Freud, "A Note on the Unconscious," *Collected Papers,* Vol. 4 (London: The Hogarth Press, 1925), p. 29.

3 *Ibid., G. W.,* Bd. X (1946), p. 285 ff.; Freud, *Collected Papers,* Vol. 4, p. 118ff.

4 *Ibid., G. W.,* Bd. XV (1940), p. 92; Freud, *New Introductory Lectures on Psycho-Analysis,* New York: Norton, 1933).

5 *Ibid., G. W.,* Bd. XV (1940), pp. 76-77.; Freud, *New Introductory Lectures,* p. 70.

6 *Ibid., G. W.,* Bd. XV (1940), p. 79.; Freud, *Ibid.*

7 *Ibid., G. W.,* Bd. II/III (1942), pp. 149/270.; Freud, *Standard Edition,* Vol. 5, *The Interpretation of Dreams II.*

8 *Ibid., G. W.,* Bd. XIII (1940), p. 241.; Freud, *Standard Edition,* Vol. 19 (1961), "The Ego and the Id," p. 14.

9 *Ibid., G. W.,* Bd. II/III (1942), p. 690; Freud, *Standard Edition,* Vol. 5 (1953), *The Interpretation of Dreams II.*

10 *Ibid., G. W.,* Bd. XI (1940), p. 305; Freud, *Standard Edition,* Vol. XV (1963), *Introductory Lectures on Psychoanalysis.*

11 A. Holzhey, "Das sogenannte Unbewusste" ["The So-called Unconscious"], *Zeitschrift für psychosomatische Medizin und Psychoanalyse,* Gottingen/Zurich: Vandenberg & Ruprecht, Vol. 21 (1975), p. 287.

12 Freud, *op. cit., G. W.,* Bd. XI (1940), p. 100. *Standard Edition,* Vol. 15 (1963).

13 *Ibid., G. W.,* Bd. X (1946), p. 265; Freud, *Collected Papers,* Vol. 4 (1925), "The Unconscious," p. 99.

14 *Ibid., G. W.,* Bd. XI (1940), p. 306.

15 Jean-Paul Sartre, *L'Etre et le Neánt* (Paris: Gallimard, 1943), p. 91. *Being and Nothingness,* trans. Hazel E. Barnes, (New York: Philosophical Library, 1956.)

16 Medard Boss, *Grundriss der Medizin* (Bern: Hans Huber, 1971); *Existential Foundations of Medicine and Psychology,* trans. Stephen Conway and Anne Cleaves (New York: Jason Aronson, 1979).

17 Martin Heidegger, *Gelassenheit* (Pfullingen: Neske, 1959), p. 22; *Discourse on Thinking,* trans. John M. Anderson and E. Hans Freund (New York: Harper & Row, 1966).

Sartre's Refutation of the Freudian Unconscious

MARK CONKLING

I

Our culture has reached the point where the phrases "unconscious impulse," "unconscious motivation," and "unconscious *cause*," have become commonplace in ordinary language. In a word, Freud's message has profoundly reached the man on the street.

The concept of the unconscious mind has tremendous force. In the penal system, for example, the concept may decide the fate of a man's life. People change occupations "because" of it, they choose a new spouse "because" of it, they maim their children "because" of it, they worship their God "because" of it, they fight wars "because" of it. In short, the existential eye sees the avoidance or acceptance of all forms of responsibility being explained and described via the underlying dark region of the mind called the unconscious. In the face of this, one may significantly ask, "does such an entity exist?" The force of this question alone should dispense with any argument which suggests that the philosopher should not deal with the matter.

In Lecture XVIII of his *Introductory Lectures on Psychoanalysis* (1917), Freud remarked,

> We challenge anyone in the world to give a more correct scientific account of this state of affairs [referring to hypnosis], and if he does we will gladly renounce our hypothesis of unconscious mental processes. Till that happens, however, we will hold fast to the hypothesis; and if someone objects that here the unconscious is nothing real in a scientific sense, is a makeshift, *une façon de parler*, we can only shrug our shoulders resignedly and dismiss what he says as unintelligible.[1]

Since Freud's challenge in 1917, the reality of the unconscious has been assumed and the psychoanalytic community has proceeded with few alterations of Freud's formulations of the notion. Philosophy has scarcely dealt with the concept, except as a parallel movement which resulted from the studies of consciousness in phenomenology and American pragmatism (namely, Brentano, Husserl, and William James). [One very notable exception is Eduard von Hartmann's *Philosophy of the Unconscious*, 1869 (New York: Harcourt, Brace & Co., 1931).] More recently, however, the existence of the unconscious has become a significant issue in the realm of existential psychology. Pioneered by Heidegger's *Being and Time* [*Sein und Zeit*] (1927), the philosophers of the Here and Now have directed their interests to all phases of man's being-in-the-world. Psychology as a discipline has responded with phenomenological methods of analyzing the human psyche which can most clearly be seen as contradictory to determinism.

One of the first existential philosophers to stimulate interest in the unconscious was Jean-Paul Sartre, whose *Being and Nothingness* [*L'Etre et le Néant*] (1943) directly answers Freud's challenge. Sartre's phenomenology expressly denies the existence of the unconscious, and, in place of the notions of repression, suppression, and the unconscious, he offers the concept of "self-deception" or "bad faith" *(mauvaise foi)*.[2] Our task will be to analyze the arguments Sartre sets forth in arriving at his claim.

II

In a sense, the term "unconscious" acquired a greater scope of meaning as Freud's formulations progressed. Initially Freud used "unconscious" in a *descriptive* sense, that is, as describing a particular quality of a certain mental state. This use of the term was predominant in *The Interpretation of Dreams (1900),* although there were implicit references to an added *dynamic* meaning which appeared explicitly in Freud's "A Note on the Unconscious in Psychoanalysis" (1912). In addition, then, to "unconscious" being used as a descriptive term, it was (1912) also being used as a dynamic term in that a particular function was attributed to a mental state. Among the explanations of the use of the term was yet another meaning couched in Freud's topographical imagery, that is, the concept of the unconscious being a *system* among other mental systems. Freud's diagrams, although "not to be taken literally," afforded evidence for his use of "unconscious" as being a system in the mind. Although it appears at times that Freud subsumed the dynamic meaning under the phrase "the system Ucs.," such as in his metapsychological paper on "The Unconscious" (1915), it is relatively clear that the three meanings of the term are used extensively in his later works. This can be shown to be the case in his *New Introductory Lectures* (e.g., Lecture XXXI, 1933).

Given these three meanings (descriptive, dynamic, and system), we can say that Freud made a discovery in terms of ordinary language. The term "unconscious" becomes, after Freud's usage is made clear, "*the* unconscious." This usage is somewhat more than an extension of the term in that it becomes a new term with a newly prescribed meaning. As Alasdair MacIntyre has observed,

> . . . he [Freud] uses "unconscious" in a way that it is never used in ordinary language, as a noun, and not as adjective or adverb.[3]

Furthermore, in adopting the term "the unconscious" Freud is making an implicit existential claim. Even though he cautions against literal translation of his topographical language, the dynamic and systematic sense of his term testifies to this claim. In effect Freud has stated that the world contains an entity hitherto undiscovered. The unconscious is a place in the mind, a locale which affords descriptions, "displays" functions, and can be seen as a system. There can be little doubt that *at least* Freud is offering a hypothesis about a new existent reality. Freud can be said to have discovered the unconscious mind, as Stephen Toulmin states,

> . . . in a way strictly comparable to Columbus' discovery of America or Harvey's discovery of the circulation of the blood.[4]

In his "A Note on the Unconscious in Psychoanalysis" (1912)[5] Freud draws distinct lines between unconscious, preconscious and conscious. Conscious activity is restricted to those ideas of which we are aware, the preconscious denotes ideas which may pass into consciousness with relative ease (such as easy recollections), and unconscious activity refers to that which remains cut off and distinct from consciousness. It is not impossible for an unconscious idea to become conscious; however, a great deal of effort is required along with the overcoming of a "feeling of repulsion" which exists when the attempt is made. This feeling of repulsion is the correlate of the phenomenon of resistance which Freud says occurs when an analyst attempts to bring a patient's unconscious ideas into a conscious state. Thus,

> . . . we learn that the unconscious idea is excluded from consciousness by living forces which oppose themselves to its reception, while they do not object to other ideas, the preconscious ones.[6]

We can see that unconsciousness is more than a characteristic or quality of a mental act, that is, it is an indicator of something greater—a mental category—which can be seen as a system involving a certain *kind* of mental acts. It is in this respect that Freud defines the unconscious:

> The system revealed by the sign that the single acts forming parts of it are unconscious we designate by the name "The Unconscious," for want of a better and less ambiguous term.[7]

Ideas and emotions exist in the unconscious. Moreover, unconscious affects and ideas strive toward expression in the consciousness of the individual; yet some ideas are destined to remain in the unconscious because of the phenomenon of repression. In this respect a mental act goes through two phases:

> In the first phase the mental act is unconscious and belongs to the system Ucs.; if upon the scrutiny of the censorship it is rejected, it is not allowed to pass into the second phase; it is then said to be "repressed" and must remain unconscious.[8]

In other words, *the unconscious is a world of its own.* An idea in the unconscious is unknown to consciousness and it proceeds without conscious intention. This is what has led MacIntyre to observe that Freud,

> . . . in calling a piece of mental activity unconscious is suggesting *both* that it is carried on without conscious intention, that it is unknowing, *and* that it is such that it is unknown to the agent.[9]

In his *New Introductory Lectures* (1933), Freud substitutes the term "id" for the phrase "system Ucs." His terminology is designed to indicate that the characteristic of being unconscious is not restricted to the "system Ucs." Portions of the ego and super-ego are also unconscious, and, for that reason, the new term "id" is invoked to denote the mental region which is foreign to the ego. The id is a realm, region, or province of mental apparatus, as are the ego and super-ego. We have the same relation to our id as we have to a psychic process in another person. In other words, we do not know it in the strict sense. We can only approximate it through the analysis of dreams and neurotic symptoms. The id is the inaccessible part of ourselves; as such it has no organization, no sense of time, no external reality, and does not conform to the law of contradiction. Contradictory, that is, in the sense of contrary impulses existing side by side and pushing toward discharge in order to fulfill the demands of the pleasure principle. The id is the driving force which is at the base of all mental life, and, as such, is at odds with the ego and super-ego.

> Thus the ego, driven by the id, confined by the super-ego, repulsed by reality, struggles to master its economic task of bringing about harmony among the forces and influences working in and upon it; and we can understand how it is that so often we cannot suppress a cry: "Life is not easy!"[10]

Thus we can conclude that when Freud uses the term "unconscious" he is using it to describe "the unconscious" or the id which is a dynamic and functional system. When he uses the term "the unconscious" he is *explaining* behavior in terms of a dynamic process. The unconscious is the realm outside of consciousness and the area of the primary process. Via the phenomenon of repression, some pieces of behavior can be said to be unconscious, and, further, can serve to explain the resistance put forth against a conscious experiencing of unconscious wishes. Also the unconscious is the link between the psycho-sexual development and the adult behavior manifestations—there is a *direct* causal influence of the infantile on the adult. There is no time when the unconscious does not causally influence conscious life; that is, there resides an inherent determinism between the infantile and the adult, the unconscious and the conscious, the instincts and the ego. Finally, entailed in the term "the unconscious" is an existential claim. The unconscious is a place or an arena in the mind. The human organism is inherently constituted in terms of drive-reduction. Unconscious wishes, ideas, and impulses *cause* behavior. Repressed ideas in early childhood have a causal efficacy on adult life. A painful memory in the unconscious *causes* resistance in therapy. I *know* my ego but I *do not know* my id. The unconscious is a place in the mind: to make this hypothesis is *at least* an existential claim. It is an entity, it has contents, it causes behavior, and it contains the energy of the personality.

What sort of justification does Freud offer for his hypothesis of the unconscious? The evidence, warrant, or backing for his assumption takes many forms. In different phases of his writing the following phenomena are offered as backings for the hypothesis: failures of memory, dreams, parapraxes, hypnosis, repression, and resistance. Also Freud speaks of the "utility of the assumption" in terms of, say, prediction, as being a sort of justification. That is, it becomes "necessary" to assume the existence of the unconscious in order to both explain and progress in the studio of psychoanalysis. In this respect, Patterson has observed that there is no reason to postulate an unconscious. He feels, rather, that one's expressed values and opinions are more indicative in terms of prediction than are projective techniques. A treatment of this point of view, however noteworthy, is beyond the scope of this study.[11]

III

Sartre's program of philosophy is the very antithesis of the determinism which we observed in Freud. Sartre's main interest throughout all his writings has centered upon the twin notions of freedom *(pour-soi)* and Being *(en-soi)*. His *Being and Nothingness* (1943) reveals that phenomenology is his method, intuition is his criterion of knowledge, and Cartesian rationalism is his preoccupation.[12]

Sartre's earlier phenomenological studies *[The Transcendence of the Ego* (1936), *The Emotions: Outline of a Theory* (1939), *The Psychology of Imagination* (1940)] illustrate his interest in human consciousness. This interest comes to fruition in *Being and Nothingness* and places him in opposition to Freud on the nature of consciousness itself. In terms of the arguments Sartre advances against Freud, the meaning of the term "consciousness" requires careful clarification.

Sartre's concern with consciousness throughout his earlier works is best seen as a resolute project intending to empty consciousness of all things and to advocate a pure and free spontaneity. In *The Psychology of Imagination* he enters into a phenomenological study which offers the phenomenon of imagination as *prima facie* evidence for the freedom of consciousness. The imagination cannot be reduced to causal forces, that is, it entertains whatever it wants and is hence highly selective. Further Sartre challenges the belief that an image is *in* consciousness. The misconception of thinking in terms of space in regard to the mind he calls the "illusion of immanence." The term "image" is seen to denote nothing more than the relation of consciousness to an object. That is,

> . . . it means a certain manner in which the object makes its appearance to consciousness.[13]

Consciousness is always related to something other than itself, it is always consciousness *of.* Sartre's notion of the intentional nature of consciousness is somewhat stronger than Husserl's, and he uses it for the basis of his argument against realism and idealism.[14]

Consciousness is seen to have a double character, that is, it is consciousness of objects and at the same time conscious of itself being conscious. In Sartre's words,

> . . . every positional [cognitive] consciousness of an object is at the same time a non-positional consciousness of itself.[15]

Pre-reflective consciousness is the immediate relationship of consciousness to the world. This aspect of consciousness is manifest whenever one is involved in something but not reflecting upon the involvement. If I am counting or writing, my pre-reflective consciousness is manifest. When I reflect upon my action, however, my consciousness is of a different sort. In pre-reflective consciousness I am conscious at once of the object and of myself being conscious of it. I may perceive a menacing object directly in front of me—yet for an instant there is no fear. The fear reveals itself only when I take a reflective stance in regard to my pre-reflective consciousness of the object, that is, when I reflect upon my situation. Moreover, I cannot be conscious of an object without at the same time being conscious of the fact that I am *not* that object. This is true of both the reflective and pre-reflective aspects of consciousness.

Knowledge is a function of reflective consciousness, and, hence, not coextensive with consciousness. In other words, consciousness is more than knowledge, and it is the prereflective consciousness which is the condition for knowledge. Pre-reflective consciousness makes knowledge possible and serves as the basis for Decartes' *cogito.* The reduction of consciousness to knowledge is not accepted because of the resulting introduction of the subject-object dualism. Moreover, to say "to know is to know that one knows" is seen as an infinite regress and untenable. The phrase should read, "to know is to be conscious of knowing," or "all knowing is consciousness of knowing." For Sartre, then,

> . . . there must be an immediate, non-cognitive relation of the self to itself.[16]

It is with this conception and meaning of the term "consciousness" that Sartre enters into his argument with Freud and elaborates on the notion of self-deception.[17]

IV

In "Lecture XIX, Resistance and Repression" (1917), Freud discusses the phenomenon of resistance and offers a spatial analogy for clarification. First, resistance is seen as a type of behavior which is common to all patients in therapy. The analyst offers an interpretation and the patient denies it vehemently: he offers opposition "at any price." In Freud's terms,

> If we are on the point of bringing a specially distressing piece of unconscious material to his consciousness, he is extremely critical; he may previously have understood and accepted a great deal, but now it is just as though those acquisitions have been swept away . . .[18]

Secondly, repression is explained analogously in the following fashion. Consider an image in which the system of the unconscious is a large hallway filled with active mental impulses. The hall leads to an adjoining room in which consciousness is found. At the doorway stands a censor who examines the mental impulses and admits only those which please him. Mental impulses in the unconscious hallway are not visible to consciousness and are destined to remain unconscious unless allowed to pass by the censor. Those impulses which are pushed back are called "repressed." Some of the impulses that are allowed to pass are still not conscious, that is, they exist in the pre-conscious and can only become conscious "if they succeed in catching the eye of consciousness." The censor or watchman,

> . . . is the same watchman whom we get to know as resistance when we try to lift the repression by means of the analytic treatment.[19]

Repression occurs, then, when desires are in conflict with enforced standards of conduct. The impulses or desires, along with their affective counterparts, are thrust back into the unconscious. If a painful conscious experience is unbearable, it too can be thrust into the unconscious. The repression is automatic and the repressed impulses remain active and determine behavior and neurotic symptoms. Repression is sharply distinct from suppression, which is a conscious and voluntary dismissal from consciousness of painful thoughts, memories, and desires. Resistance becomes manifest when the analyst attempts to bring a repressed impulse to consciousness.

Sartre accepts the phenomenon of resistance but challenges the explanation by asking, "what part of the self does the resisting?"[20] It cannot be the ego because the ego's relation to the meaning of his own reactions is like that of the analyst. Moreover, the ego is involved in a conscious pursuit of therapy and is considering all interpretations as probable in hopes of arriving at a cure.

The resistance cannot be explained in terms of the unconscious because it knows no external reality. Further,

> The complex [the one the analyst is trying to bring to light] as such is rather the collaborator of the psychoanalyst since it aims at expressing itself in clear consciousness, since it plays tricks on the censor and seeks to elude it. [BN, p. 52]

Thus, the only explanation has to be in terms of the censor, the watchman. The censor is the only part of the subject which can comprehend the interpretations of the analyst, because "it alone *knows* what it is repressing." The censor must know what it is repressing in order to be selective and to discriminate among impulses. But, explains Sartre, this is not enough:

> The censor must also apprehend them *as to be repressed,* which implies in it at the very least an awareness of its activity. In a word, how could the censor discern the impulses needing to be repressed without being conscious of discerning them? [BN, pp. 52-53]

Hence, the resistance of the patient implies that the censor has an awareness of the thing repressed,

> . . . a comprehension of the end toward which the questions of the psychoanalyst are leading, and an act of synthetic connection by which it compares the *truth* of the repressed complex to the psychoanalytic hypothesis which aims at it. These various operations imply that the censor is conscious (of) itself. But what type of self-consciousness can the censor have? It must be the consciousness (of) being conscious of the drive to be repressed, but precisely *in order not* [to] *be conscious of it*. What does this mean if not that the censor is in bad faith? [BN, p. 53]

By showing that the censor is in bad faith, Sartre feels he has dispensed with the notions of repression and the unconscious. Given the constitution of the censor, he could simply not function as he does in Freud's schema. The tasks which the censor performs imply that he must have a cognitive and conscious disposition toward the unconscious impulses. His selectivity implies at least awareness, if not cognition. Rather than operate within a paradox, Sartre feels that repression and the unconscious can be sufficiently explained in terms of self-deception or bad faith. That is, the patient *is* aware of what has been repressed, but *refuses* to notice it until the analyst persists.

Bad faith or self-deception is the act of lying to oneself. A person is aware of the truth but tries to hide it from himself. He is the deceiver and the deceived simultaneously and knows that he has deceived himself. He believes the lie he has created and hides from himself the fact that he is the creator of the falsehood. He is fleeing from the truth, but he is not totally unaware that he is fleeing.

For Sartre, then, Freud has substituted for self-deception a lie without a liar, namely, the unconscious. The liar, which I myself am, is replaced by the concepts of repression, suppression, and the unconscious. This is tantamount to saying, "I *am* my ego, but I *am not* my id." I am not that unconscious instinct or impulse which compels my act.

A question arises when one asks of the logical meaning of self-deception. It appears that to deceive onself entails believing p and not-p at the same time in the same person and in the same respect. In resolution of this apparent violation of the law of contradiction, Raphael Demos comments on the two usual hypotheses offered concerning self-deception. On the one hand, it can be said that the believing and disbelieving occur at different times; on the other hand, it can he said that the agreeable belief remains conscious and the unpleasant one is repressed into the unconscious. Both explanations solve the apparent contradiction, but neither, observes Demos, is true to experience. For example, I may be convinced that I am a true Don Juan, yet I am constantly haunted by a nagging doubt. The evidence indicates that

> . . . both the belief and the disbelief are simultaneous and both exist in the consciousness of the person.[21]

The solution is exactly that of Sartre. There are two levels of awareness: one is simple (like the pre-reflective consciousness), the other involves attending or noticing (like the reflective consciousness).[22] In this way I can be aware of something without at the same time attending to it. For example, I am aware of sitting before my desk, but I am not attending to that fact. As Demos states,

> This comes about because I may be distracted by something else, or because I may *deliberately ignore it,* or because I may *not wish to think* about it.[23]

Self-deception is possible because a person may yield to one belief by lying to himself and by failing to notice or by ignoring the truth of the matter. In addition to being logically possible, this account conforms to the way in which people talk of such matters in ordinary language.

> Thus they would say of the mother who has come to believe that her son is a fine fellow, that she knows all along *in some corner of her mind* that he is not much good.[24]

For further clarity and backing for Sartre's point, let us consider his example of the young woman out with a particular man for the first time. She treats the man's compliments as literal and removes all sexual connotation from them. She is aware of the desire that she provokes, but does not apprehend the desire for what it is. Rather, she apprehends it in terms of admiration and respect (or other refined forms) and refuses to acknowledge the desire per se. Then he holds her hand and the situation changes. His act demands a decision on her part. To leave the hand there would be an engagement, to withdraw it would break the evening's charm. She avoids this dilemma by leaving the hand there and *not noticing* that she has done so. She becomes all intellect and talks of lofty things like her life.

> And during this time the divorce of the body from the soul is accomplished; the hand rests inert between the warm hands of her companion—neither consenting nor resisting—a thing. [BN, p. 56]

In terms of the phenomenon of repression, Sartre feels that Freud did not adequately account for neurotic symptoms. Repressed drives are said to be realized consciously in different forms. A symptom, such as an unusually frequent washing of the hands, is said to be the symbolic representation of an impulse repressed in early childhood. I *know* the hand washing ritual, but I *do not know* that which it symbolizes. I am conscious of performing the act, but I am not conscious of what my act represents.

Sartre comments that Freud is speaking of "disguised" impulses and asks how an impulse can disguise itself if it does not include

> . . . (1) the consciousness of being repressed, (2) the consciousness of having been pushed back because it is what it is [a displeasing impulse], (3) a project of disguise? [BN, p. 53]

Hence Sartre concludes that his careful description of the process of disguise renders Freud's description of the unconscious contradictory and untenable.

In a similar manner Sartre claims that Freud failed to account for pleasure or anguish adequately. The symbolic and conscious satisfaction of a drive necessarily entails *at least* an obscure consciousness of the end to which the drive is aiming. And further it entails that there must be a consciousness of the desired and forbidden object beyond that of the consciousness of the censor.

Sartre's final argument rests on the unconscious-conscious dichotomy and is a variation of his first argument. After the analyst has "overcome the resistance" the patient recognizes the interpretation of the analyst as being the truth. The patient sees himself in a mirror, so to speak. The analyst takes this testimony as *both* evidence for the existence of the unconscious *and* evidence that the therapeutic goal has been reached. Freud doesn't admit of the very possible alternative, that is, the patient may be resisting because the analyst is *wrong*.

Sartre maintains that the analyst has no justification for utilizing the patient's testimony, that is,

> If the complex is really unconscious—that is, if there is a barrier separating the sign from the thing signified—how could the subject *recognize* it? Does the unconscious complex recognize itself? But haven't we been told it lacks understanding? And if of necessity we granted to it the faculty of understanding the signs, would not this be to make of it by the same token a conscious unconscious? [BN, p. 573]

Again we find Freud's explanation ending in paradox. It cannot be the patient who recognizes the interpretation because in order to compare it with the truth he would, in principle, have to be conscious of that which is unconscious. If the patient does come to believe the interpretation of the analyst, it is a simple belief and no more. The patient has no privileged access, he is like a third party or the analyst himself. In a final relinquishing gesture, Sartre comments,

> The psychoanalyst doubtless has some obscure picture of an abrupt coincidence of conscious and unconscious. But he has removed all methods of conceiving of this coincidence in any postive sense. [BN, p. 574]

V

Has Sartre made a decisive case against Freud? The problem in weighing this question obviously concerns the term "consciousness." If the ploy of imposing a new meaning of consciousness upon Freud's theory is decisive, then Sartre has made his case. This sort of argument may be highly presumptuous, however, and to call the argument decisive on this basis alone would be ludicrous.

On the other hand, a case can be made for the claim that Sartre's analysis of consciousness is a discovery, and, as such, serves as an equally valid explanatory principle. Sartre parsimoniously claims less presuppositions than Freud, and his treatment of bad faith or self-deception is phenomenologically attested to in experience. Sartre seems to be appealing to "experience" in a way as profound as Freud. Also Sartre's analysis dispenses with the troublesome notion of psychic determinism and allows for a view of human freedom which, although viewed by some as extreme, does justice to the personal predilections of all who consider themselves fundamentally free. Sartre's existential psychoanalysis, although it "has not yet seen its Freud," suggests a view of man that in many cases elicits a nod of approval from orthodox Freudian analysts. Admittedly though, in regard to particularly aberrant behavior, it is difficult to think in terms of the Sartrean "original project of being."

Further, if the argument had been limited to Freud's narrow definition of consciousness, then the hypothesis of the unconscious would escape Sartre's attack except on the significant point of repression, If we grant the ambiguity of the terms "consciousness" and "know" in both Freud and Sartre, there still appears to be no logical way that repression can be understood, given Freud's definitions. That is, in the ordinary sense of knowing, there is simply no way a person would not know, at one time or another, what he had repressed *(not* suppressed). Also the problem still remains in regard to the pleasure-seeking activity of the person. Unconscious desires are not known to consciousness. How, then, does one know what objects to seek? That is, in some sense, one would have to know what objects were simultaneously desired and forbidden in order to experience remorse or pleasure.

Sartre is correct in maintaining that experiences cannot be repressed without first being aware of or knowing the experience. To say, as does Freud, that unconscious impulses are not allowed into consciousness, and are therefore repressed, is a meaningless statement. We do not know the unconscious. We do not know the impulse. We do not know what we have repressed. But we know the painful impulse and recognize it when it has been pointed out in analysis. It is curious that this "knowledge" would be trusted as evidence by the therapist because in terms of meaning Freud could have just as easily talked of the "forces of evil" or some other such vacuous notion. Given the constitution of the censor, he could not perform the function Freud assigns to him and still remain consistent with the theory in which he is couched. Metaphors notwithstanding, the process itself it not consistent. It would be hard to conceive of a meaningful foundation of repression which was not inordinately mechanistic and relied on viewing man as a peculiar kind of robot. In other words, in extreme mechanism like, say, Freud's drive-reduction theory, the more one reduces behavior, the more abstract it becomes. In such a case the existing human being eludes the theory at every turn. The essential concern should be meaning-*for* the patient rather than meaning-*on* the patient. The understanding *(Verstehen)* of meaning-*for* is the precondition for any objective psychology. Utilizing extreme objectivity in behavior analysis could be viewed as a form of escape from the true existential conditions, and hence a divesting of the significance of human attitudes. These attitudes, such as pride, shame, passion, sympathy, boredom, despair, joy, and ecstasy are meaningful human phenomena. To immerse them in extreme objectivity results in seeing them, in many cases, as pathological rather than essentially human.

In terms of the unconscious, it is noteworthy that we need not come as far as existentialism to find dispute with the psychoanalytic notion. The Adlerian school of psychology, which is close in many respects to Sartre's ideas,[25] has offered alternative explanations to Freud's formulation. For example, Demetrios Papageorgis maintains

> . . . the same observations which have been used as evidence for the unconscious and repression can be dealt with, meaningfully and parsimoniously, without recourse to these concepts and solely on the basis of conscious and intentional functions.[26]

Failures of memory, he claims, can be sufficiently accounted for by reference to the qualitative losses and changes over a period of time. Also, parapraxes can be explained simply by realizing that they are momentary intrusions of a competing thought process.[27]

A case may be argued that in reality Freud and Sartre merely have a verbal battle going between what one calls pre-reflective consciousness and the other calls unconsciousness. It can be shown, however, that this is not the case at all. The dispute represents the pitting of theory against theory, tradition against tradition, and phenomenology against determinism. To claim a mere verbal dispute is to miss the point. Although the terms may be ambiguous in both writers, the argument encompasses the explanation of *all human behavior* and cannot therefore be reduced to the statement: "Well, somehow, Freud and Sartre are talking about the same thing."

In a sense both writers have involved themselves in a peculiar sort of circularity. If you deny Sartre's position and enter into the "spirit of seriousness" by believing that consciousness is constituted by causal forces, then you are commiting an act of bad faith or self-deception. You are not realizing your fundamental freedom and are hiding behind theories of man which deny the responsibilities you are plagued with. You are not being true to the phenomena.

If, on the other hand, you deny that you are constituted by causal forces and advocate your freedom, i.e., "the ego is the master in his own house," then Freud would say you are resisting because of the tremendous blow to your primary narcissism. Your self-love will not allow you (affectively) to believe otherwise. This was Freud's thesis in his paper "One of the Difficulties of Psycho-Analysis" (1917).

What are we to conclude about these circular statements? Only this: if Sartre's analysis of consciousness and bad faith is correct and is as true to our experience as it seems to be, then Freudian psychoanalysis as a theoretical structure is untenable without revisions. This is not to say, however, that Sartre's analyses are clear and efficacious to the point of replacing Freudian psychoanalysis. It is simply to say that the existentialist posture offers an alternative to Freud that purports to be a truer explanation of man and his human condition. The existential psychoanalysts are theoretically young, but Sartre's arguments add an undeniable impetus to their reformulations, in both theory and therapy, of how and why men behave as they do. It is either paradoxical or profound that the existential analysts (e.g., May, Binswanger, Frankl, Boss, *et al.)* show results in therapy just as Freud did. In terms of philosophy, however, their accomplishments lie in their parsimony and economy of explanation and their non-deterministic constitution of man. If Sartre's arguments have done nothing else, they have *at least* demonstrated the fact that man is free to constitute theories about his behavior. This fundamental freedom is undeniable. The assessment of the value of a particular theory, however, is a different matter. Our attempt has been one of showing how Freud's formulation of the unconscious has been assessed as inconsistent by Sartre. Also we have attempted to show how the Freud-Sartre dispute is no small matter: the implications are of ubiquitous importance in any project of attempting to understand the human psyche.

NOTES

1 Sigmund Freud, "Lecture XVIII, Fixation to Traumas—The Unconscious," in *Introductory Lectures on Psychoanalysis* (1915-1917), in Sigmund Freud, *The Complete Introductory Lectures on Psychoanalysis,* ed. and trans. by James Strachey (New York: W. W. Norton and Co., Inc., 1966), p. 277. The James Strachey compilation will hereafter be referred to as CIL.

2 Walter Kaufman [*Existentialism From Dostoevsky to Sartre* (New York: Meridian Books, 1956) p. 222] feels that *mauvaise foi* is best translated as "self-deception" rather than "bad faith." In terms of our treatment, both translations will be used for purposes of clarity.

3 Alasdair MacIntyre, *The Unconscious* (New York: Humanities Press, 1959), p. 44.

4 Stephen Toulmin, "The Logical Status of Psycho-Analysis," in Margaret MacDonald (ed.), *Philosophy and Analysis* (Oxford: Basil Blackwell, 1954), pp. 132-133.

5 Sigmund Freud, *General Psychological Theory, Papers on Metapsychology* (New York: Collier Books, 1963).

6 *Ibid.*, p. 53.

7 *Ibid.*, p. 55.

8 *Ibid.*, "The Unconscious" (1915), p. 122.

9 MacIntyre, *op. cit.*, p. 42.

10 CIL, "Lecture XXXI, Dissection of the Personality," p. 542.

11 C. H. Patterson, *Counseling and Psychotherapy: Theory and Practice* (New York: Harper, 1959).

12 In regard to Sartre's rationalism, see Iris Murdock, *Sartre: Romantic Rationalist* (New Haven: Yale University Press, 1953).

13 Jean-Paul Sartre, *The Psychology of Imagination* (New York: Citadel Press, 1966), p. 8.

14 For a detailed study of Sartre's phenomenology, see Herbert Spiegelberg, *The Phenomenological Movement,* II (The Hague: Nijhoff, 1960), pp. 445-513.

15 Jean-Paul Sartre, *Being and Nothingness,* trans. Hazel Barnes (New York: Philosophical Library, 1956), p. liii, hereafter referred to as BN.

16 BN, p. liii.

17 For a careful conceptual analysis of *Being and Nothingness,* see Jacques Salvan, *To Be and Not To Be, An Analysis of Jean-Paul Sartre's Ontology* (Detroit: Wayne State University Press, 1962). For further clarification and critical comments on Sartre's theory of consciousness see Wilfrid Desan, *The Tragic Finale* (New York: Harper Torchbook, 1960).

18 CIL, "Lecture XIX, Resistance and Repression" (1917), p. 293.

19 *Ibid.*, p. 296.

20 Sartre's arguments are found in BN. Quotes given in the development of his argument will be cited parenthetically.

21 Raphael Demos, "Lying To Oneself," *J. of Philos.* Vol. 57, No. 18, Sept. 1, 1960, p. 592.

22 The correlations with Sartre are mine and do not reflect the stated opinions of Demos *(supra.* ftn. 21).

23 Raphael Demos, *op. cit.*, p. 593 (italics mine).

24 *Ibid.*, p. 594.

25 In this respect, see Paul Rom and Heinz L. Ansbacher, "An Adlerian Case or A Character by Sartre?" *J. Indiv. Psychol.*, Vol. 21, No. 1, May, 1965, pp. 32-40; A. Stern, "Adler and Sartre: Comment," *J. Indiv. Psychol.* Vol. 21, No. 2, Nov., 1965, p. 202.

26 Demetrios Papageorgis, "Repression and the Unconscious: A Social-Psychological Reformulation," *J. Indiv. Psychol.*, Vol. 21, No. 1, May, 1965, p. 29.

27 For other examples of the Adlerian's debate with psychoanalytic concepts, see G. Ichheiser, "On Freud's Blind Spots Concerning Some Obvious Facts," *J. Indiv. Psychol.*, Vol. 16, 1960, pp. 45-55; R. M. Collier, "A Figure-Ground Model Replacing Conscious-Unconscious Dichotomy," *J. Indiv. Psychol.*, Vol. 20, 1964, pp. 3-16,; Arthur Nikelly, "The Adlerian Concept of the Unconscious in Psychotherapy," *J. Indiv. Psychol.*, Vol. 22. No. 2, 1966, pp. 214-221.

IX. Will

Will, Decision and Responsibility

Rollo May

INTRODUCTION

There is no better area in which to inquire into the distinctive character of existential psychotherapy and what distinguishes it from orthodox psychoanalysis than that of our present theme. One of Freud's great contributions—if not his greatest—lay in his cutting through the futility and self-deceit in Victorian "will power," conceived by our nineteenth century forefathers as the faculty by which they "made resolutions" and purportedly directed their lives down the rational and moral roads the culture said they should go. I say possibly Freud's "greatest" contribution not only because in this area of "wish" and "drive" lay Freud's profound power as the formulator of a new image of man that shook to the very foundations our emotional, moral and intellectual self-image in Western history, but also because it was *the* exploration of this area that made possible Freud's formulation of what he called the "unconscious." He uncovered the vast areas in which behavior and motives are determined by unconscious urges, anxiety, fears, and the endless host of bodily drives and instinctual forces. Under his penetrating analysis Victorian "will" did indeed turn out to be a web of rationalization and self-deceit. He was entirely accurate in his diagnosis of this morbid side of Victorian "will power."

But along with this emphasis there went an unavoidable undermining of the functions of will and decision themselves and similarly an unavoidable emphasis upon man as determined, driven, "lived *by* the unconscious," as Freud, agreeing with the words of Groddeck, put it. This reflected, rationalized and played into the hands of modern man's pervasive tendency—which has become almost a disease in the middle of the twentieth century—to see himself as passive, the willy-nilly product of the powerful juggernaut of economic forces (as Marx on the socio-economic level demonstrated with a brilliant analysis parallel to Freud's). Of late years this tendency has spread to include contemporary man's conviction that he is the helpless victim of scientific forces in the atom bomb, about the use of which the citizen in the street feels powerless to do anything. Indeed, a central core of modern man's "neurosis" is the undermining of his experience of himself as responsible, the sapping of his willing and decision. This lack of will is much more than merely an ethical problem: the modern individual so often has the conviction that even if he *did* exert his "will" and capacity for decision, his efforts would not make any difference anyway.

Now it was against precisely these trends that the existentialists like Kierkegaard and Nietzsche took their strongest, most vehement stand. And it is in the light of modern man's broken will that the existential emphases of

Schopenhauer with his world as "Will and idea," Bergson with his "elan vital," William James with his "will to believe," are to be understood.

The protest of the existentialists was violent and at times desperate (as in Nietzsche), at other times noble and courageous (as in the resistance movement of Camus and Sartre), even if it seemed to many observers to be ineffectual against the on-moving lava of conformism, collectivism, and the robot man. The existentialists' central proclamation was this: No matter how great the forces victimizing the human being, man has the capacity to *know* that he is being victimized, and thus to influence in some way how he will relate *to* his fate. There is never lost that kernel of the power to take some stand, to make some decision, no matter how minute. This is why the existentialists hold that man's existence consists, in the last analysis, of his freedom. Tillich has phrased this view beautifully, "Man becomes truly human only at the moment of decision" (Tillich, pp. 39-47).

EFFECTS OF DETERMINISM

The implications of this problem for psychology are, of course, profound. In general in our academic psychological tradition we have tended to accept the position, no matter what individual psychologists themselves believed about their own ethical actions, that as psychologists we were concerned only with what is determined and can be understood in a deterministic framework. This limitation of perception, of course, tended inevitably to make our man into the image of what we let ourselves see.

In psychoanalysis and psychotherapy the problem of the undermining of will and decision became more critical, for the theory and process of psychoanalysis and most other forms of psychotherapy inevitably played into the passive tendencies of the patient. As Otto Rank and Wilheim Reich in the 1920's began to point out, there were built-in tendencies in psychoanalysis itself that sapped its vitality and tended to emasculate not only the reality with which psychoanalysis deals but the power and inclination of the patient to change. In the early days of psychoanalysis, when revelations of the unconscious had an obvious "shock value," this problem did not come out so much into the open; and in any case with hysterical patients, who formed the bulk of those Freud worked with in his early formative years, there does exist a special dynamic in what Freud could call "repressed libido" pushing for expression. But now when most of our patients are "compulsives" of one form or another, and everybody knows about the Oedipus complex, and our patients talk about sex with an apparent freedom which would have shocked Freud's Victorian patients off the couch (and, indeed, talking about sex is perhaps the easiest way of avoiding really making any *decisions* about love and sexual relatedness), the problem of the undermining of will and decision can no longer be avoided. The "repetition compulsion," a problem that has always remained intractable and insoluble within the context of classical psychoanalysis, is in my judgment fundamentally related to this dilemma about will and decision.

Other forms of psychotherapy do not escape the dilemma of psychoanalysis, namely, that the process of psychotherapy itself has built-in tendencies which invite the patient to relinquish his position as the deciding agent. The very name "patient" proposes it. Not only do the automatic supportive elements in therapy have this tendency, but so does also the tendency to search for everything else as responsible for one's problems rather than one's self. To be sure, psychotherapists of all stripes and schools realize that sooner or later the patient must make some decisions, learn to take some responsibility for himself; but the theory and the technique of most psychotherapy tends to be built on exactly the opposite premise.

A NEW APPROACH

The existential approach in psychology and psychotherapy holds that we cannot leave will and decision to chance. We cannot work on the assumption that ultimately the patient "somehow happens" to make a decision, or slides into a decision by ennui, default, or mutual fatigue with the therapist, or acts from sensing that the therapist (now the benevolent parent) will approve of him if he does take such and such steps. The existential approach puts decision and will back into the center of the picture—"The very stone which the builders rejected has become the head of the corner." Not in the sense of "free will against determinism"; this issue is dead and buried. Nor in the sense of denying what Freud describes as unconscious experience; these deterministic "unconscious" factors certainly operate, and the existentialists, who make much of "finiteness" and man's limitations, certainly know this. They hold, however, that in the revealing and exploring of these deterministic forces in his life, the patient is orienting himself in some particular way to the data and thus is engaged in some choice, no matter how seemingly insignificant, is experiencing some freedom, no matter how subtle. The existential attitude in psychotherapy does not at all "push" the patient into decisions; indeed, I am convinced that it is only by this clarification of the patient's own powers of will and decision that the therapist can avoid inadvertently and subtly pushing the patient in one direction or another. The existentialist point is that self-consciousness itself—the person's potential awareness that the vast, complex, protean flow of experience is *his* experience—brings in inseparably the element of decision at every moment.

We are, of course, using the terms "will" and "decision" in a way that does not at all refer exclusively to the momentous and life-shaping decisions only; the words have infinitely more extensive and subtle meaning. And though perception always involves decision (the act, for example, of electing what you are going to attend to), decision and perception must not at all be identified.

Decision always brings in some element that is not only not determined by the outside situation but not even *given* in the external situation; it involves some element of leap, some taking of a chance, some movement of one's self in a direction the ultimate outcome of which one can never fully predict before the leap. This "leap" is obviously involved in the big decisions of life, but my point here is that qualitatively it is present in some degree or other in experiences as simple and non-world shaking as any new idea I find myself entertaining, or any new memory that pops up in a seemingly random chain of free association. This is part of the explanation of the fact that anxiety arises in free associations and the birth of new ideas: I am then in a "new place," I see myself and my life in a slightly different way and must re-orient myself accordingly. The mature human being (i.e., one who is not rigidly constricted and determined by neurotic compulsive patterns) generally takes this anxiety in stride and is then ready to make the new orientation and the new "decision" in the place in which he now finds himself.

WILL AND DECISION IN EXISTENTIAL THERAPIES

It is these and similar considerations which have led the existential psychotherapists to be concerned with the problems of will and decision as central to the process of therapy. But when we turn to the endeavor to understand will and decision themselves, we find our task is not at all easy. Our problem hinges upon the terms "will" and "wish" and the interrelation between the two. The word "will," associated as it is with "will power," is dubious to say the least and perhaps no longer helpful or even available. But the reality it has historically described must be retained. "Will power" expresses the arrogant efforts of Victorian man to manipulate nature and to rule nature with an iron hand *(vide* industrialism and capitalism); and to manipulate himself, rule his own life in the same way as an object (shown particularly in Protestantism but present in other modern ethical and religious systems as well). Thus "will" was set over against "wish" and used as a faculty by which "wish" could be denied. I have observed in patients that the emphasis on "will power" is often a reaction formation to their own repressed passive desires, a way of fighting off their wishes to be taken care of; and the likelihood is that this mechanism had much to do with the form will power took in Victorianism. Victorian man sought, as Schachtel has put it, to deny that he ever had been a child, to repress his irrational tendencies and so-called infantile wishes as unacceptable to his concept of himself as a grown-up and responsible man. Will power was then a way of avoiding awareness of bodily and of sexual urges or hostile impulses that did not fit the picture of the controlled, well-managed self.

CLINICAL APPLICATION

Speaking now of the concrete individual clinically, the process of using will to deny wish results in a greater and greater emotional void, a progressive emptying of inner contents which must ultimately impoverish intellectual experience as well. If I may speak epigrammatically, the more such an individual *succeeds* in developing his will-power, that is, the more he becomes able to make up his mind, the less sure we are that he has any mind to make up. Woodrow Wilson once remarked speaking of this type of post-puritan man, "I take leave to believe that the man who sets out to develop his own character will develop only that which will make him intolerable to other men." And we could add, intolerable to himself. For no one needs to remind us now of the great stores of resentment, inhibition, hostility and inability to love, and the related clinical symptoms which can develop as a result of this repressive kind of will power.

In attacking these morbid psychological processes, Freud produced his far-reaching emphasis on the *wish*. The term "wish," let us hasten to say in view of the fact that in our post-Victorian day we still tend to impoverish the word by making it a concession to our immaturity or "needs," may be seen as related to processes much more extensive than the residue of childhood. Its correlates can be found in all phenomena in nature down to the most minute pattern of atomic reaction, for example, in the context of what Whitehead and Tillich describe as negative-positive movements in all nature. (Tropism is one form in its etymological sense of the innate tendency in biological organisms to "turn toward.") If, however, we stop with "wish" as this more or less blind and involuntary movement of one particle toward another or one organism toward another, as Freud did, we are inexorably pushed to Freud's pessimistic conclusion of the "death instinct," the inevitable tendency of organisms to move back toward the inorganic. Thus in human beings "wish" can never be seen without relation to "will."

Our problem now becomes the inter-relation of "wish" and "will." I shall offer some suggestions which, though not intended to make a neat definition, show us some of the aspects of the problem that must be taken into consideration. "Wish" and "will" may be seen as operating in polarity. "Will" requires consciousness, wish does not. "Will" implies some possibility of freedom of choice, "wish" does not. "Wish" gives the warmth, the content, the child's play, the freshness and richness to "will." Will gives the self-direction, the freedom, the maturity to "wish." If you have only will and no wish, you have the dried up Victorian, post-Puritan man. If you have only wish and no will, you have the driven, unfree infantile human being who as an adult may become the robot man.

I propose the term "decision" to stand for the human act which brings both will and wish together. Decision in this sense does not deny or exclude wish but incorporates it and transcends it. Decision in an individual takes into the picture the experiencing of all wishes, but it forms these into a way of acting which is consciously chosen. Despite the fact that the word "decision" lost much of its usefulness for those of us in New York when Billy Graham came to town, it nevertheless remains in many ways the most useful and viable term for the uniting of wish and will.

THERAPEUTIC DIMENSIONS

The process of therapy with individual patients involves bringing together these three dimensions of wish, will and decision. As the patient moves from one dimension to the next in his integration, the previous level is incorporated and remains present in the next. We shall now show more fully the meaning of our problem by describing practical therapy on three levels.

The first dimension, wish, occurs on the level of *awareness*, the dimension which the human organism shares with all nature. The experiencing of infantile wishes, bodily needs and desires, sexuality and hunger and all the infinite and inexhaustible gamut of wishes which occur in any individual, seems to be a central part of practically all therapy from that of Rogers on one wing to the most classical Freudian on the other. Experiencing these wishes may involve dramatic and sometimes traumatic anxiety and upheaval as the repressions which led to the blocking off of the awareness in the first place are brought out into the open. On the significance and necessity of unmasking repression—dynamic aspects which are beyond the scope of our present discussion—various kinds of therapy differ radically; but I cannot conceive of any form of *psycho*therapy which does not accord the process of awareness itself a central place. The experiencing of these wishes may come out in the simplest forms of the desire to fondle or be fondled, the wishes associated originally with nursing and closeness to mother and family members in early experience, the touch of the hand of a friend or loved one in adult experience, the simple pleasure of wind and water against one's skin; and it goes all the way up to the sophisticated experiences which may come, for example, in a dazzling instant when one is standing near a clump of blooming forsythia and is suddenly struck by how much more brilliantly blue the sky looks when seen beyond the sea of yellow flowers. The immediate awareness of the world continues throughout life, hopefully at an accelerating degree, and is infinitely more varied and rich than one would gather from most psychological discussions.

From the existential viewpoint, this growing awareness of one's body, wishes and desires—processes which are obviously related to the experiencing of identity—normally also brings heightened appreciation of one's self as a being and a heightened reverence for Being itself. Here the eastern philosophies like Zen Buddhism have much to teach us.

The second level in the relating of *wish* to *will* in therapy is the transmuting of awareness into self-consciousness. This level is correlated with the distinctive form of awareness in human beings, consciousness. (The term *consciousness*. coming etymologically from *con* plus *scire*, "knowing with," is used here as synonymous with self-consciousness.)[1] On this level the patient experiences I-am-the-one-who-has-these-wishes. This is the level of accepting one's self as having a world. If I experience the fact that my wishes are not simply blind pushes toward someone or something, that I am the one who stands in this world where touch, nourishment, sexual pleasure and relatedness may be possible between me and other persons, I can begin to see how I may do something about these wishes. This gives me the possibility of *in-sight,* of "inward sight," of seeing the world and other people in relation to myself. Thus the previous alternatives of repressing wishes because one cannot stand the lack of their gratification on one hand, or being compulsively pushed to the blind gratification of the wishes and desires on the other, are replaced by the experience of the fact that I myself am involved in these relationships of pleasure, love, beauty, trust and I hopefully then have the possibility of changing my own behavior to make these more possible.

On this level *will* enters the picture, not as a denial of wish but as an incorporation of wish on the higher level of consciousness. To refer to our example above: but the realization that I am the person who lives in a world in which flowers are yellow and the sky so brilliant, and that I can even increase my pleasure by sharing this experience with a friend, has profound implications for life, love, death, and the other ultimate problems of human existence. As Tennyson remarks when he looks at the flower in the crannied wall, " . . . I could understand what God and man are."

The third level in the process of therapy is that of *decision* and *responsibility.* I use these two terms together to indicate that decision is not simply synonymous with will. Responsibility involves being responsive, *responding.* As consciousness is the distinctively human form of awareness, so decision and responsibility are the distinctive forms of consciousness in the human being who is moving toward self-realization, integration, maturity. Again, this dimension is not achieved by denying wishes and self-assertive will, but incorporates and keeps present the previous two levels. *Decision* in our sense forms the two previous levels into a pattern of acting and living which is not only empowered and enriched by wishes and asserted by will, but is responsive to and responsible for the significant other persons who are important to one's self in the realizing of the long-term goals. This sounds like an ethical statement, and *is* in the sense that ethics have their psychological base in these capacities of the human being to transcend the concrete situation of immediate self-oriented desire and to live in the dimensions of past and future and in terms of the welfare of the persons and groups upon which one's own fulfillment intimately depends. The point, however, cannot be dismissed as "just" ethical. If it is not self-evident it could be demonstrated along the lines of Sullivan's interpersonal theory of psychiatry, Buber's philosophy and other viewpoints, that wish, will and decision occur within a nexus of relationships upon which the individual himself depends not only for his fulfillment but for his very existence.

INTERRELATION OF WISH, WILL AND DECISION

May I now illustrate the interrelation of the levels of wish, will and decision with a personal example. I have for some time had the practice of never making an important decision without analyzing my dreams the night before. Not because the dreams will determine the decision, although I believe every dream has an element of decision in it, every dream pushes toward some act, but because the dream will assumedly present my archaic and wish levels bearing upon my act. Indeed, I may then decide just the opposite to the tendency or desire shown in the dream. The dream may show anxiety, fear of making the decision and a wish to flee to the Sahara Desert and join the Foreign Legion or to take some other easier way out, or it may predict dire doom for me if I make the decision. Or the dream may show that the decision I have in mind is being made on the basis of self-deceitful, hypocritical motives. I seek to be as fully aware as possible of all these more primitive levels within me in making the decision; otherwise the decision will be wrongly made. Or assuming I believe it is the right decision and I make it but without awareness of my buried wishes, I will be sabotaged by some unconscious elements within me in my acts that carry out the decision. I want, rather, to take my dream along with me, reluctant companion though it may be. One cannot give over oneself to the dream; but not to be aware of what it is telling one is just the way to turn it into a compulsive drive. The decision hopefully will be made responsive to these inner tendencies as well as responsive to one's conscious relationship to the other persons involved and the future welfare of one's self and them. The decision then occurs on a level that incorporates wish and will, even though one knows that he will still have to make the decision despite anxiety and *against* some aspects of himself. This points toward the important existential concept of commitment, the rich and profound implication of which goes beyond our present discussion.

If decision and responsibility thus include previous levels, as we have been pointing out, the usual concepts of "self" and "ego" in psychology are inadequate. I propose a concept borrowed from Paul Tillich: *the act of the centered self.* Actions that proceed from an integration of the levels of awareness and wish with will and consciousness, and ensue in behavior which is responsible, are acts of the centered self.

CONCEPTS OF EGO PSYCHOLOGY

Let us turn our attention for a brief caveat to the concepts of "ego" and what is called ego psychology, since it is often argued that the problems of will, decision and responsibility are encompassed in psychoanalytic ego psychology. In the last few years, in response to contemporary man's great need for autonomy and a sense of identity, considerable interest has swung to "ego psychology" in the psychoanalytic movement. But what has resulted has been the handing over to the ego of the functions of autonomy, sense of identity, synthesis of experience and other functions, more or less arbitrarily arrived at, which were suddenly discovered as functions the human being had to have. The result in the orthodox analytic movement is that many "egos" now appear. Karl Menninger speaks of the "observing ego," the "regressive ego," the "reality ego," the "healthy ego," et cetera (1928). A Freudian colleague and friend of mine congratulated me after a speech in which I had attacked this concept of a horde of egos by remarking that I had a good "synthetic ego"! Some psychoanalysts now speak of "multiple egos in the same personality," referring not to neurotic personalities but to the so-called normal ones. To my mind, "multiple egos" is a precise description of a neurotic personality.

In this picture of many different egos, where has the principle of centeredness vanished to? If you have this multitude of egos, you have by definition lost the center of organization, the center of unity that would make any centered act possible. If it is countered that this picture of the multitude of egos reflects *the* fragmentation of contemporary man, I would rejoin that any concept of fragmentation presupposes some unity of which it is a fragmentation. Rapaport writes an essay entitled "The Autonomy of the Ego" as part of the recent development we are referring to; Jung has a chapter in one of his books entitled "The Autonomy of the Unconscious"; and someone could write an essay, following Cannon's "Wisdom of the Body," entitled "The Autonomy of the Body." Each would have a partial truth; but would not each be fundamentally wrong? For neither the "ego" nor the "unconscious" nor the body can be autonomous. Autonomy by its very nature can be located only in the centered self.

In our inquiry for a new concept which will do justice to the intricate problems of wish, will and decision, the concept of "the act of the centered self" has several merits. It includes the act. In the emphasis upon the *centered* nature of the self, it takes into consideration that there are three aspects of what is loosely called self, three aspects of this centeredness. The "ego" as Freud used it, the "swivel" with the real world, the organ of perception by which the individual sees and assesses and relates to the outside world, is one aspect. A second aspect is the "subjective self," which is what most people mean when speaking untechnically about the self, the capacity to be aware that I am the one who sees the world in such and such ways, that I am the one who behaves in such and such ways. The third aspect is what William James called the "self" and Jung the "personal," the social roles the individual plays, the self as reflected in social and interpersonal relations.

ACT OF THE CENTERED SELF

Now the centeredness of a given self must be presupposed if these three aspects are to have meaning. At this point our European colleagues would use some form of the term "being," which unfortunately remains still almost unusable in English. They speak of *Dasein* as the individual who experiences himself as here and now, present at this given instant in history, accepting the fact that he is thus present—which means being to greater or lesser degree responsible. Our phrase *the act of the centered self* has both this subjective and objective meaning; and thus the concept of "being" must in some form or other be presupposed.

This being, or centered self, comes into existence *at the point where one is able to commit one's self.* The unity occurs at the moment of putting one's self on the line and accepting the risk unavoidably connected with this commitment. We see now more of the underlying meaning in Tillich's sentence quoted earlier in this paper, "Man becomes truly human only in the moment of decision."

REFERENCES

Menninger, K. *The Theory of Psychoanalytic Therapy*, New York: 1928.

Tillich, P. "Existentialism and Psychotherapy," *Review of Existential Psychology and Psychiatry,* 1961, 1, pp. 8-16. *See also* this volume, pp. 39-47.

NOTE

1 I have developed relationships of awareness to self-consciousness elsewhere, "The Existential Bases of Psychotherapy," in *American Journal of Orthopsychiatry,* October, 1960, Vol. XXX, No. 4. Strictly speaking, "self-consciousness" is redundant: consciousness already implies relation to the self.

Will and Anxiety

Leslie H. Farber

The last half century has been a propitious one for the development of psychological theory, particularly of the psychoanalytic variety. And without this development our preoccupation with anxiety would be inconceivable, however impressed we might be by the peculiarly disruptive nature of our present human predicament. It is modern psychology which has given the term "anxiety" a categorical density it never previously carried. Perhaps there is an apprehensive quality, characterizing our age, which requires the term to be isolated and then weighted—or even exalted—in our vocabulary. Or it may be we turn in a special way to such a theme as anxiety because our psychological theories, despite the many novel notions they have provided about man's character, deny us other approaches which might be more illuminating. A young movement often must be parochial and even shun traditional knowledge if it is to maintain the enthusiasm necessary for pursuing its inspirations. This is why we counsel the young writer to have his own full say before he resorts to bibliography. But youthful parochialism willfully extended beyond its natural time—that is, shunning every possibility of eventual reconciliation with previous thought—brings a premature senility to the movement which now enshrines rather than extends its early achievements.

If some detachment is possible, now that our youth draws to a close, I think it can be said the psychological theories which support and derive from psychotherapy have proliferated without explicit recourse to the subject of will, with its vast philosophical and theological literature. Will has been the category through which we examine that portion of our life which is the mover of our life. Though man is ceaselessly subjected to a variety of forces, human and nonhuman, the traditional concept of will asserts that alone among these many movers, man's power of volition—however frustrated, however often vanquished—is nonetheless accountable, both in achievement and intention. To speak plainly, it is a serious deficiency in our theories that they contain no responsible mover as it has been described, at its best, since the beginnings of Western history. But at this point it may be of historical interest to recall the manner in which Freud turned aside from the category of will in one of his first essays. When Dora—to Freud's great chagrin—unexpectedly terminated treatment after only a few weeks, at a point when his therapeutic ambitions were at their highest, he wrote, after his outrage had subsided, that he recognized one of the limits to psychotherapeutic influence to be the patient's own "will and understanding."[1] But in the course of this essay he had second thoughts about his therapeutic failure—thoughts about the nature of transference, which now seemed a more revealing way to understand Dora's interruption of treatment. With this step Freud may be said to have abandoned the traditional will as a psychological consideration and instead now found, not unlike Schopenhauer, his mover in the libido. Like many important theoretical principles, transference had both advantages and limitations. But at this date it should be possible, without demeaning the knowledge gained through transference theory, to consider the price we pay for excluding will from our psychologies.

One reason for that exclusion was that the pioneers in psychotherapy at the turn of the century came largely from the medical sciences, so it is understandable that they would be more captivated by the scientific spirit of the time than by the subject of will, with its roots in philosophy and theology: occupations which Freud—and he was not untypical—regarded as, if not curable, at least arrestable once their pathology was identified. Far more exciting were the discoveries in chemistry, biology, physics, anthropology. Still, this is only part of the story and fails really to explain not only why we have no psychology of will, but also why the subject of will fell into general disrepute—even in philosophy which had proudly fostered it for so many centuries. As could be expected, science and scientific philosophy were antagonistic to the tangled metaphysical speculations on will. And, it must be admitted, to some extent the antagonism was earned: much that had been called will badly needed the psychological surgery psychoanalysis was more than ready to offer. If this readiness seems brash or presumptuous today, we should recall the intoxicating conviction shared by the early leaders of the young movement that there was nothing in all of human history—and especially prehistory—which would not yield to the new psychoanalytic weapons. In this regard the argument has been made, with considerable generosity, that will was not excluded: that is, by omission or in absentia, will *is* the principal, though invisible, actor in the psychoanalytic drama. In other words, will is the residue, like Leonardo da Vinci's genius, remaining after psychoanalytic reduction. Thus, so the argument goes, psychoanalysis serves the purpose of clearing away the brush overgrowing the subject of will these many years.

At least some of the responsibility for the will's disfavor, as suggested above, must be credited to the accumulated scholarship on the subject—scholarship which, with certain glaring exceptions, is often so tedious as to be virtually unreadable. But tedium alone, I am afraid, would be an insufficient obstacle, to judge from the fashionable careers of other large issues. Elsewhere I have written:

> And even a cursory inspection of this scholarship will reveal that on the one hand the topic of will has been endlessly exploited for all manner of self-serving moralizing, and on the other hand came increasingly to be the speculative plaything of the academicians who tinkered with it so whimsically; it would be difficult for the reader to know that will had any relevance to human considerations. Thus, either as an ingredient of moral coercion or as a fruitless venture in philosophical or theological academicism, the subject of will gradually lost its connection with existence itself. On this basis alone it is understandable why the psychotherapists at the beginning of the century preferred to abandon—or rather

> bury—this bloodless category. They would have needed both patience and erudition to root out the exceptions to this dreariness—the extraordinary thinkers who grasped the anthropological necessity for the term "will." Whichever emphasis they gave the will—choice, decision, resolution, passion, intentionality, determination, spirit—these exceptional men tried at best to preserve will's identity as responsible mover, whether that mover be individual, communal, or divine. And they had assistance here, for literature was spared the attrition born of academicism. Literature—in whose view the human condition is inevitably a drama of conflict—has always been interested in man as a creature with some capacity, even if only potential, for independent personal volition: the one human capacity above all others that gives both interest and meaning to the literary records of conflicts between man and man, man and the world, or within man himself. It can hardly surprise us to find that the subject of will—*explicitly and literally*—has engaged the interest of authors as diverse as Flaubert, Butler, Goncharov, Tolstoy, Dostoyevsky, Ibsen, and even such moderns as Allen Tate and Lionel Trilling.[2]

Having acknowledged my sympathy for those who preferred to abandon the matter of will, given its tedious, moralistic, and sterile expressions in the scholarship of the past, I should now like to consider the price—or more precisely, the theoretical and practical consequences of this abandonment. The problem may be briefly put in this manner: *without a clear and explicit conception of will as responsible mover, we tend in our psychological systems to smuggle will into our systems under other names—this contraband will being usually an irresponsible mover of our lives.* A corollary to this proposition would be: *when particular aspects of our will-less systems are asked to become or include will, the existential or phenomenological relevance of these aspects is diminished.* Thus, when Freud shifted from will to libido, in the example mentioned earlier, he was forced to slight the phenomenological investigation of sexuality in favor of argument or polemics, insisting on the libido's distinction as prime mover. In his postscript to the case of Dora, he wrote, "I was further anxious to show that sexuality provides the motive power for every single symptom, and for every manifestation of a symptom." It could be said, I think, that every system—including my own—contains a polemic for its particular prime mover, such polemic being antithetical to the phenomenological illumination of the system's prime mover. In other words, when Freud insisted that sexuality be the will of his system, it was his and ultimately our understanding of the place of sexuality in existence which suffered from this double burden.

I shall do no more than list some of the categories which have been made to do the work of the will in various psychologies: unconscious, aggression, dependence, power, inferiority, sado-masochism, guilt, and of course anxiety. But before I move to the matter of anxiety I should like to say a word about the issue of psychological determinism itself, as it pertains to the will. Here I would deal not with prime movers, but myriad small movers which appear to the imagination of the psychotherapist as chains of explanation, the scrutiny of which may reveal to him the order he is intent on discovering in neurotic and psychotic disorder. A critical question here, or so it seems to me, is how may motive be distinguished from will. It would seem that in psychology, at least, when will was abandoned in our theories, motivation became an increasing object of our concern. Motive and will have some superficial resemblance in that they both provoke movement or action. If I disparage my friend's achievements out of envy, envy is the motive for my disparagement. However, envy is not the same as my will, even though my will to disparage may be incited by my motive of envy. In other words, a motive cannot be responsible for an action of my will even though it may provoke or prompt such action. This has been the usual distinction between will and motive. Obviously a psychology of will would not preclude psychic determinism, even though it might deprive determinism of some of the ill begotten prerogatives it has acquired in this century. It is when motive is used as cause that it begins to usurp the will's domain and at the same time defeat the phenomenological venture. If out of envy I will to disparage, I still have the option of willing not to disparage. So far as I know, no such option occurs in disparagement whose cause is envy. The determinism relevant to these considerations seems more a professional tic, peculiar to psychotherapists, and might more accurately be called the compulsion or will toward causality which, inventing in its own image, constructs other wills called motives. If there is a motive provoking the will toward causality, it would not be causality itself, but rather the need for order or perhaps the intolerance of mystery. Such a will, when asked to explore the *what* of a situation, turns instead to the *why*. It is but another example of Yeats' "will trying to do the work of the imagination." The will toward causality, given its imaginative limitations, spawns prior wills, preceded by prior wills, etc. Ideally one hopes that principles may eventually arise out of the imaginative search of the situation itself, but here the principles arrive first and any phenomena developed are at the mercy of these principles.

With these introductory remarks I have tried to suggest the direction of my dissatisfaction with anxiety theory. To begin with, I am never entirely sure what the nature of the experience is that anxiety is meant to describe. It is unusually difficult to know whether anxiety signifies a particular shudder of being, common to us all, or whether anxiety is a general category—a blanket term meant to cover a range of painful states. Before the advent of modern psychology, it was one of many expressions we use to indicate distress: its meaning, according to Webster, is "painful uneasiness of mind respecting an impending or anticipated ill." This meaning, it seems to me, is quite precise when compared with its present swollen and ambiguous condition whereby, depending on the whim of its user, it may indicate—or conceal—a host of distressing responses, with any number of subjective or objective shadings—emotional, cognitive, and physical. What we call anxiety today might in another time be more exactly rendered as apprehension, fear, fright, tremor, uncertainty, uneasiness, dread, restlessness, worry, shakiness, trepidation, desperation, palpitations, queasiness, agitation, anguish, alienation, cowardice, according to which experience we wished to describe. It might be objected that theoretical speculation—if only for the sake of brevity—cannot afford such novelistic precision as it searches for hypothetical principles which will govern its theory. After all, we have many items of theory which are not to be confused with experience—ego, projection, regression, identification, etc. But it must be answered that the abstract nature of these terms was clear from the beginning, whereas with anxiety it was never clear whether the term indicated a particular experience or a way of theorizing about a variety of experiences. As a result, what was at first an abstraction now passes itself off as experience itself rather than a way of talking about experience. In our scientific age it is always a danger that a psychological term may trespass its original scientific boundaries. And once the trespass becomes convention, experience itself is vulgarized, since theories about experience inevitably subvert experience as much as our experience connects our theories.

Those psychological theories which have developed within the medical tradition have given a physical emphasis to anxiety so that the "painful uneasiness" of the older definition is now one of the body rather than of the mind. Even when no description of the experience is attempted, what is implied is a bodily response comparable to that of fright, whose predominant manifestations—subjectively and objectively—are such physical disturbances as rapid heart beat, tremors, dry mouth, overbreathing, sweating, muscular incoordination, insomnia, etc. In this view it is the bodily commotion which is primary, other aspects of our distress being derivative of this disturbance. The seeming advantage of a physical theory of anxiety is that the similarity of objective manifestations in babies and lower mammals allows a biological or evolutionary continuity to be asserted about all of mammalian life when endangered. Partly because the subjectivity of lower animals cannot be inspected, and partly because human danger need not be of the literal order of the jungle, a distinction is usually made in these theories between fear and anxiety. Whatever theoretical virtue this distinction may have, in actuality it is usually rather difficult—if not impossible—to separate objective from subjective danger. Needless to say, it is this bodily view of anxiety which has found common cause with the drug industry.

To pursue further the ambiguity of the experience of anxiety, let us consider briefly several modern definitions whose emphasis is not so exclusively physical. Kurt Goldstein describes anxiety (in part) as the subjective experience of the organism in a catastrophic condition.[3] In spite of the fact that Goldstein's contributions have been in the general area of the medical sciences, it will be noted that his description makes no mention of objective bodily disturbance, but instead refers to subjective experience. Yet anxiety for Goldstein is clearly a categorical abstraction intended to cover a range of experience accompanying catastrophe. In an effort to be more particular about the human experience,

Rollo May defines anxiety as "the apprehension cued off by a threat to some value which the individual holds essential to his existence as a personality."[4] The word "apprehension" has the virtue of having both psychic and physical implications. In contrast, Sullivan's descriptions are indeed abstract, suggesting some sort of unpleasant state brought on by the apprehension of disapproval in interpersonal relations.[5] Perhaps the most exhaustive description of the experience is contained in Karen Horney's definition of "basic anxiety"—namely, "the feeling of being small, insignificant, helpless, deserted, endangered, in a world that is out to abuse, cheat, attack, humiliate, betray, envy."[6] This picture of helplessness in the face of a threatening world has a more hysterical, even paranoid, quality, in that the anxious person feels put upon and persecuted by the will of others but lacks any corresponding will to defend himself.

In summary, then, it seems clear that anxiety is a painful state invoked by threat to human integrity. But in the theories we have considered the experience of anxiety has been relatively neglected in favor of its causes and, more especially, its consequences.

If I may return to an earlier proposition, the phenomenological thinness or ambiguity of the term anxiety as it appears in the theories I have just mentioned is largely the consequence of the burden laid upon it to do the work of the will: that is, though unequal to the task, anxiety has been required to supply force, shape, meaning, and intentionality to the matter of psychological development and/or disability. Unlike the will, which pushes actively toward its goal, whether appropriate or inappropriate, anxiety is an ache which helplessly cries for relief. We are told by these theories that its painful urgency is so compelling it overpowers our discriminations, forcing us to settle for familiar and childish ways which serve us poorly in our life in the world. In passing, however, it should be remarked that the notion of settling for old ways is an unwitting attempt to smuggle the traditional will into the system. Be that as it may, the pathological inevitability of consequence associated with anxiety assists the cause of psychic determinism almost too well, failing to account for those times when, in spite of present or future pain, we choose a course which seems right rather than soothing. In order to contain this eventuality, some theories devise two anxieties, one normal and the other neurotic—the former liberating, the latter constricting. In terms of experience, "normal" anxiety is no different from neurotic anxiety, and therefore is not to be confused with an ontological meaning the term anxiety has carried for centuries—namely, solicitous or earnest desire. An example of this meaning would be "I am anxious to rejoin my friend." While the addition of "normal anxiety" to a system would seem to allow anxiety more of the prerogatives of will, in effect it undercuts the original notion of anxiety as an insistent anguish compelling relief. Here a proposition could be made that whenever a psychological category is asked to do the work of the will in psychopathology, sooner or later a normative version of that category must be added to the theory.

In order to consider further the issue of will and anxiety, I shall now confine myself to the theories and practice of Harry Stack Sullivan. According to him, the self is born of anxiety, or so he says, the self "comes into being as a dynamism to preserve the feelings of security." Being an unpleasant feeling, anxiety requires relief. And the relief it finds is apt to be limiting to the development of the person. Whenever these limitations are overstepped, anxiety arises again and dissociates from awareness these new threats. Whatever existential content there may be to anxiety in his theories, it is evident that his is a most hypochondriacal view of development of self. Unlike the traditional will, anxiety permits no choice, sees no ends, cannot discriminate between one course or another. In fact, since anxiety is always limiting, it would seem it insists on not only immediate but inferior relief. As such the self is a tangle of makeshift adjustments, all hastily and mistakenly contrived for the sake of allayment of anxiety. The system has no room for accident, risk, surprise, mystery, grace. In Sullivan's melancholy view, there seems no hope except through psychotherapy.

It may be interesting here to say something of how his theory shaped his practice. Since Sullivan was one of my teachers, I can be anecdotal about this issue. Some psychotherapists profess one theory, but in practice seem to pursue another. They may write about mankind as a jungle of destructive strife, in which survival is almost accidental, yet in their office life be the most kindly and considerate of men. But I would say of Sullivan that he was one of the most painfully consistent human beings I have known: he not only wrote of anxiety as the center of his theories, but moreover he practiced it. In this he resembled some of the more active Zen masters I have read about—men with devilish skill in inventing all manner of mental and physical devices for unsettling their pupils. In the interest of accuracy, I should say here that Sullivan was a mild man physically: he did not cudgel with sticks, he never raised his voice and his harshest physical mannerism was a glance which never met my own. Believing psychotherapeutic ineptitude, as well as psychological disability in general, to stem from and to consist of our poor efforts to cope with anxiety, he thought any psychotherapy or teaching worth its name must eventually provoke that anxiety in the hope that within his ambience something more satisfactory might at long last occur.

Our first meeting—which had taken several months to arrange, and required the intervention of a mutual friend—was, to put it mildly, distressing. As I described the three patients I was treating at the time, he looked quite discouraged by the supervisory prospect. Two of my patients, he wearily explained, were wholly unsuitable for supervision—and, by inference, for psychotherapy, too. As I was beginning to wonder what presumption had possessed me to seek supervision with this eminent man, he grudgingly agreed to hear about my third patient, although he made it quite clear he expected no good to come of it. This patient was a young man with severe ulcerative colitis, much of whose energy was spent, when he was not hospitalized, in both inviting and defeating the possessive intrusions of his divorced parents. For two hours Sullivan sat in silence as I nervously tried to depict this young man's struggles, hoping all the while my portrayal, while faithful to my patient, would also be intriguing enough to justify Sullivan's continuing to spend time with me in supervision. But he was too scrupulous—or too unimpressed—to indicate, through gesture or word, the tiniest interest in my account. Once or twice, when my desperation verged on sheer panic, I turned helplessly to him for advice, but he refused these overtures with a tired wave of the hand, as though my solicitations were too flagrant or too gross to deign a verbal refusal. When finally I ground to a limp and chaotic halt in my story and made ready to flee this unhappy occasion, Sullivan roused himself to offer what the Zen masters would call a koan. "I would suggest," he said, "that until our next appointment you try to imagine—mind you, not say, *imagine*—what might be your young man's response if you were to ask him what he imagined his mother's reaction would be to his saying, 'Mother, since you insist you are so deeply attached to me, let us go to bed together and have it over with.'" If I may translate this rather involved imaginative exercise, Sullivan was suggesting that out of my own anxiety I was taking my patient's account of his parents' erotic attachment to him much too literally.

When I managed to drag myself to his study two weeks later for our second appointment, he immediately asked me if I had any thoughts about our first session. I confessed I had not really been up to thought; in fact, my anguish had been so paralyzing I had taken to my bed for most of the period. Deliberately, I skipped the details of my anguish, the consuming self-disparagement which led me to question even my choice of profession. His astonishing reply was, "Well, that's rather promising. I hadn't really expected so much." To this day I can still recall almost physically the relief and gratitude that came over me at having, in this wholly unexpected way, earned this man's approval through my suffering.

In this vignette I trust I have conveyed Sullivan's way of practicing what he preached. Unfortunately, what I have been forced to slight in this anecdote is his remarkable clinical shrewdness, as well as his tactful, often compassionate, manner of dealing with disturbance such as mine. It should be noted that, according to his view, it was my anxiety with my patient which led me into gullibility; however, when Sullivan reinvoked that same anxiety, he now provided me with the opportunity for new knowledge about myself and my work with my patient. In a way, this theory resembles a species of folk wisdom which occurs in several forms: anything really good comes hard, or nothing really good comes easy. At first it would seem Sullivan had reversed this belief, so that whatever comes hard is necessarily good. But such an assumption would be a serious underestimation: he was too knowing a psychotherapist and too convinced of the crippling power of anxiety to subscribe to such a reversal. Anxiety requires psychotherapeutic assistance, if the patient or student is not to return to old ways.

I should now like to re-examine the episode from the standpoint of will. Having already pressed the phenomenological question about anxiety as experience, I shall arbitrarily, and perhaps mistakenly, assume in what is to follow that anxiety in Sullivan's theories is a satisfactory rubric for the range of unhappiness which befell me. Somewhere in Sullivan's writings he has a footnote to the effect that he was one of those fortunate human beings without any anxiety to speak of. If this was so, and I have no reason to doubt it, our relationship—in this respect, at least—was somewhat uneven. True, I stood to gain more than he in this inequality, since he would not have the renewing opportunity of old anxiety reinvoked, but at least he would have the more comforting belief in an acumen that needed no assistance, which would have made him vulnerable in his own particular way. To begin with the matter of my own will, I would have to postulate two forms my will took, even as I made the long journey to my first appointment with him. On the one hand, there was the will to become a psychotherapist, which could be expressed as an enduring and wholehearted wish to become a sufficient member of this profession. This expression is more explicit than the fact that I pursued a goal or was pursued by it, without so baldly formulating this pursuit. Such will came and went, depending on discouragement, my shifting estimation of what psychotherapy might be, my wavering as to the worldly ways in which best to find my professional career, and of course the doubts plaguing me from time to time as to whether psychotherapist in any important way described the man I wished to become. At any rate, it was this will which effected the intricate arrangements which culminated in my time with Sullivan. In referring to this will, I delete my backslidings and hesitations and confusions when this will gave way to a more self-conscious stubborn determination to trudge through this course of psychoanalytic apprenticeship—regardless of how my mind and body lagged in the process, regardless of the fatigue and boredom associated with this tiring and tiresome program. On the one hand, I wished to have supervisory time with this renowned teacher in order to become a psychotherapist—whatever that was; and on the other hand, I wished to impress this man so that I could become a favored pupil on my way to a diploma—and I knew what *that* was.

Sullivan's strategy or technique during our first meeting could be characterized as his will not to respond. Regardless of his intention, his deliberate indifference opposed my own will in two different ways. To the extent to which I gave myself wholeheartedly to my task, with all resources joined to my will to become a psychotherapist under his tutelage, there was a dialogic possibility open to us, whose rebuff no doubt led to the agonizing questioning of my suitability for this profession I had chosen. At a lower, more self-serving and self-seeking level, my determination to win his admiration was easily routed by his will not to respond. I could no more will to admire him than I could will him to admire me. If I try to will my admiration of another, all I can grasp is the visage or posture of admiration: its actuality will elude me. If I try to will another to admire me, I shall self-consciously select only those gestures which are coercive of my end: regardless of my powers, he would have to be gullible indeed to be won by such manipulation. Willing what cannot be willed is by necessity an uneasy, even frantic, misdirection of the will: no cunning is required on the part of an adversary to bring such distress into frank and painful prominence. My guess is that as every overture of mine was repudiated, my distress or anxiety grew and, moreover, I was increasingly deprived of the few intellectual powers which were available to me, so that toward the end of our first appointment, my will to impress Sullivan stood in harsh contrast with the uninspired and labored account to which I had been reduced. Even when he was later encouraged by the anxiety he had aroused in me, my relief was tempered by my awareness that while he could will anxiety in me, I could not will anxiety in myself—only the mannerisms of anxiety would be accessible to me and these not only would fool no one, but would defeat our joint pedagogical and therapeutic goal.

Out of my particular miseries with Sullivan, I wish now to define the relation between will and anxiety. In my understanding, the word anxiety is a broad term for human distress containing a range of psychic and physical manifestations. With the exception of one additional phrase, anxiety in my usage does not differ essentially from Webster's definition—namely, a painful uneasiness of mind and body respecting an impending or anticipated ill. At any given moment, depending on which manifestations are most pressing, the experience of anxiety may be more exactly identified as uneasiness, trepidation, etc. (see page 282), without losing its tie to the parent category, anxiety. But by whatever name it is called, *anxiety is that range of distress which attends willing what cannot be willed*. In other words, anxiety can be located in the ever-widening split between the will and the impossible object of the will. As the split widens, the bondage between the will and its object grows, so that one is compelled to pursue what seems to wither or altogether vanish in the face of such pursuit.

Before considering the implications of this definition, I should like to stress that my formulation is intended to be a phenomenological definition. As such, it would supplement rather than contradict other definitions of anxiety, mentioned earlier, which are concerned for the most part with the causes and/or consequences of anxiety. Thus, in regard to Kurt Goldstein's definition, mine would explore the nature of "the subjective experience," as well as something of the "catastrophic condition" into which the "organism" falls in anxiety. In regard to Rollo May's definition, my definition does not attempt to contend with the "threat" to values which causes anxiety, but rather with the experience itself which follows such a threat. My purpose is to extend phenomenologically what Rollo May calls "apprehension."

If my life in the world is threatened by loss, betrayal, failure, disapproval, injury, I may respond in various ways depending on who and where I am in my world and the exact nature and relevance of the threat endangering me. Melancholy, grief, despair, remorse, enlightenment are but a few of the possibilities open to me, *even* when the threat is to values I deem essential to my existence. *But anxiety,* I would emphasize, *is not my lot until I resort to my will to counter such threat and now will what cannot be willed*. The severity of my impairment will vary according to the degree to which the will, in its bondage to its object, is isolated from faculties such as reason, imagination, etc., and the degree to which the object being willed recedes and diminishes in the rush of will. It is important to stress that the disability is principally one of will, because a serious deficiency of anxiety theory has been the inability of anxiety itself to account for the human mishaps it would explain. We need no special clinical background to remind ourselves of those who are privately and visibly anxious without any particular disorder in their lives as a result of anxiety. This must mean that, in the midst of anxiety, crucial faculties are still available. On the other hand, we should be equally familiar with those who neither have nor have had any great anxiety in their lives, yet their difficulties are enormous. Here it is simply not enough for anxiety theory to invoke the-little-man-who-wasn't-there psychologism, asserting anxiety *could* be there if it weren't so immediately assuaged by defensive and inferior stratagems. Since this inference cannot be argued, demonstrated, nor—more important—confirmed in the experience of the placid ones, belief in it must remain an article of faith in the dogma of anxiety theory. It is but another instance of making anxiety do the work of the will, such work unfortunately being shoddy and unconscious. It is worth remarking on, however, that when either the anxious ones or the placid ones are asked to investigate the circumstances surrounding their anxiety or placidity, the result may be salutary even though it may not prove the theory. Salutary, because in either case the will has been offered a suitable endeavor for its efforts, which hopefully will help return the world which has been lost or acquire a world which never was.

It follows that to characterize my encounter with Sullivan merely as anxiety would do it phenomenological injustice. At the same time, for theoretical purposes to abstract anxiety as the psychological mover toward either constriction or enlightenment would be equally fallacious. Anxiety may be an ache which cries for relief, but whether or what will occur cannot be anxiety's decision. Unlike the will, anxiety must be considered morally (or psychologically) *inert,* which is to say that whether good or evil follows anxiety will depend on forces other than anxiety. Though seriously shaken, my will to become a psychotherapist allowed me to contend with my more meretricious need to impress Sullivan. And I doubt very much that the anxiety which accompanied my willing what could not be willed—given his will not to respond—was itself generative of insight about myself or my patient. My recognition of my own gullibility in my work with my patient was, as far as I can see, a response to Sullivan's clinical shrewdness—not because of but *in spite of anxiety*. Conceivably I might have chosen another way in which, indicting the man as cruel, arrogant, and a poor teacher, I did not return. Such a conclusion could have been willed only by blinding myself to my discriminations of this remarkable man. And had that been my way, no doubt I should have told myself and a few close friends that I was forced to discontinue because of the anxiety he provoked in me.

As has already been suggested, the more stubborn the will's pursuit of its intractable goal, the sooner the will becomes separated from those faculties which might allow its bondage to be objectified, diverted, dispelled. In isolation from such powers as intellect and imagination, the will can only will, reflection about its own adversities being beyond its capacity. The failure of meaning, which is said to be characteristic of anxiety, stems from the deprivation of resources and the withering of the will's goal in the face of the will's demands. Because of this failure, eventually the anxious person may no longer be able to say what he is anxious about. However, his failure should not be attributed, as is the habit, to the repression of the cause of his anxiety, but rather to the falling away of those rational powers which might assist the will but which cannot return until—for one reason or another—there is an end to willing what cannot be willed. This same failure in self-reflection has often been used to distinguish anxiety from fear whose reason—or so it is assumed—is actual and exterior. According to this view, the danger in anxiety is "inner" and unknown, while the danger provoking fear is "outer" and known. Even if we try to preserve a legitimate distinction between anxiety and fear, although I believe psychology has misused this distinction, it can readily be seen that both experiences have their inner and outer dimensions. So far as the present definition is concerned, fear does not merge into anxiety until willing what cannot be willed takes over. If I am summoned to an interview with a superior who, I am warned, will be sharply critical of my performance, my troubled anticipation of this event will contain, in addition to my willing, a mingling of subjective and objective considerations, but I doubt that it is either useful or possible to disentangle which portion of my apprehension is inner anxiety and which portion outer fear.

A burst of thunder in a darkening sky can frighten me with the possibility that the plane in which my family is flying home will be caught in the same impending storm. Again, the inner and outer features of my unhappy state seem less critical than the degree to which I now fall into willing what cannot be willed: clear skies, gifted pilot, indestructible plane. Untempered by imagination and reason, not to mention information from the weather bureau and airport, my isolated will *wills*—that is, it demands its object absolutely, however futile that demand may be. And with each new crack of thunder, I shall no doubt swing from the willed certainty of safety to the certainty of disaster, so that now the storm battering that fragile plane is violent and the pilot hopelessly inept. Both obsessive extremes, with their attendant anxiety, are products of my isolated will. Should I, still in the mood of disaster, muse about how to bury my family and now take up my life alone, my musings are born of that same isolated will rather than a hostile, if unacceptable, instinct for their destruction. Were I to assume such a motive supported my will in its authorship of these melancholy reveries, my disorder would still lie in willing what cannot be willed—namely, the storm's destruction of plane and family. Moreover, for the sake of completeness, I should have to assume a more considerate motive to account for my insistence on their safety.

If only because of their extreme and uncommon character, the conventional illustrations of fear to be found in the usual anxiety theory tend to reveal the effort to rid the problem of contamination by subjectivity: the armed burglar in the night, the rabid bat in the bedroom, the car careening toward us on the wrong side of the road. Yet even these examples, so weighted on the objective side, would seem to fail their purpose. Presumably the immediate overpowering fright will give way to anxiety at the point we retrospectively resort to willing what cannot be willed. But even that very first fright, so far as we can penetrate the experience, carries no lesson in the epistemology of danger from without. Little reflection is required to realize that it too must mingle both inner and outer aspects. Clearly, it is as hard to construct an anxiety which is only inner as it is to imagine a fear which is only outer.

In the disability of will we have been considering, anxiety is not the only experience. As the will is increasingly stripped of supporting faculties, and as what is being willed recedes further from the will's impositions, the will itself comes to be experienced as impotent thrust. Here it is the very powerlessness of the power pressing toward its refractory goal which accounts for the helplessness and uncertainty most writers believe to be essential characteristics of anxiety. As discernment fails, what can most painfully be discerned are those bodily manifestations of distress which have occupied the medical approach to the subject of anxiety. Thus the split between the will and its object, if extended in time and severity, enforces finally another split between mind and body in which our world—already diminished by the bondage described—shrinks still further to that cramped cell where all we can do is suffer and observe those painful commotions of our flesh. And these bodily discomforts again oppose, even as they invite, the activities of our isolated will. This is the arena, peculiarly modern, which can loosely be described as fear of fear or anxiety about anxiety. More accurately, it is the shrunken state in which, as actor and audience of our body's disabilities, we will not to have anxiety, such willing bringing more anxiety in its wake. This impasse may well be the existential source for the biological or medical views of the problem of anxiety.

This has been called the Age of Anxiety. Considering the attention given the subject by psychology, theology, literature, and the pharmaceutical industry, not to mention the testimony from our own lives, we could fairly conclude that there is more anxiety today and, moreover, that there is definitely more anxiety about anxiety now than in previous epochs of history. Nevertheless, I would hesitate to characterize this as an Age of Anxiety, just as I would be loath to call this an Age of Affluence, Coronary Disease, Mental Health, Dieting, Conformity, or Sexual Freedom, my reason being that none of these labels—whatever fact or truth they may involve—goes to the heart of the matter. Much as I dislike this game of labels, my preference—which could be anticipated—would be to call this the Age of the Disordered Will. It takes only a glance to see a few of the myriad varieties of willing what cannot be willed that enslave us: we will to sleep, will to read fast, will to have simultaneous orgasm, will to be creative and spontaneous, will to enjoy our old age, and—most urgently—*will to will*. If anxiety is more prominent in our time, that anxiety is the product of our particular modern disability of will. To this disability, rather than anxiety, I would attribute the ever increasing dependence on drugs affecting all levels of this society. While drugs do offer relief from anxiety, their more important task is to offer the illusion of healing the split between the will and its refractory object. The resulting feeling of wholeness may not be a responsible one, but at least within that wholeness—no matter how willful the drugged state may appear to an outsider—there seems to be, briefly and subjectively, a responsible and vigorous will. This is the reason, I believe, that the addictive possibilities of our age are so enormous.

With or without drugs, at the same time that our lives are occupied by deliberate efforts of will—toward both appropriate and inappropriate ends—we suffer a mounting hunger for a sovereign and irreducible will, so wedded to our reason, our emotions, our imagination, our intentions, our bodies, that only after a given enterprise has come to an end can we retrospectively infer that will was present at all. In other words, within such totality will, being unconscious, would not be a matter of experience, even though we might later try to portray the essence of the enterprise as one in which we wished with our whole heart or willed with all our being. The predominant experience within this realm of will would be one of freedom, as opposed to the bondage of the isolated will. And the goal of will within this realm would be one of direction rather than a specific object or achievement, though naturally the course of this will would be dotted inconspicuously by such concrete items. Never a permanent state, and always limited in duration, it would give way over and over again to the more self-conscious will with which we are necessarily more familiar. Needless to say, the utilitarian opportunities for this more self-conscious will are vast in this technological age—in fact, it could be said our technology could not have been accomplished without it. To move my hand, add a column of figures, even earn a psychoanalytic diploma—these are all discrete and feasible objects for this will. However, there is no activity I could mention—however trivial—which in the service of the joined realm of will, would not lose its utilitarian countenance and become part of the flow in a particular direction. I may say I went to the library to look at a book I thought might be interesting. By all standards this is an ordinary statement about an ordinary errand, requiring no comment except that the errand and the statement about it are singularly unmuscular in nature and point merely in the direction of possible interest. If I am asked, on my return from the library, for the physical details of my trip, I shall probably—and fortunately—not remember them. However, when my utilitarian will engineers this errand, something ordinary is now splintered into many things arduous. *Book* now becomes the principal object of this expedition, but of course there are subsidiary objects too: I must pick the proper time, choose the right route, park on a crowded street, deal with a difficult librarian, etc. Once the book is found, *reading the book* can splinter into similar tedious efforts of will—all open to memory, should someone be foolish enough to inquire. Though tedious and arduous, these actions are still feasible, and in their difficulty will not compare with the anxiety which arises when this same utilitarian will is asked to will what it cannot will.

Consideration of the historical origins of our present situation lies outside my purpose and competence. I would, however, ask this question: Could it be that the disordered will, with its paradoxical privilege for technology and all manner of scientific fact, and the hunger for another will from which we suffer, are the consequence of the death of God proclaimed by Nietzsche in the last century? If so, few of us, I suspect—believers and non-believers alike—have been spared. Depending on which side of Nietzsche's divide we stand historically, the other side is almost unimaginable. For this reason, the contemporary issue is not of the order proposed by Kirilov in Dostoyevsky's *The Possessed:* "To recognize that there is no God and not to recognize at the same instant that one is God oneself is an absurdity, else one would certainly kill oneself." Kirilov's choice, springing from its apparent logical necessity, has the terrified—yet abstract—quality of one who, while still on the other side of the divide, has glimpsed the loss, but that loss has not yet penetrated and shaped his life in all those subtle and pedestrian ways that make Nietzsche's proclamation for most of us merely another old-fashioned theological generalization. With the disappearance of the divine Will from our lives, we have come to hunger not for *His Will*—neither in the sense of living *in* His Will nor *usurping* His Will for ourselves—but rather for our *own* sovereign will, which is our modern way, this side the omnipotence of suicide or madness. And all exhortations not withstanding, this will we cannot will.

NOTES

1 Sigmund Freud, "Analysis of a Case of Hysteria," in *Collected Papers* 3; London: Hogarth Press, 1933; p. 131.

2 Leslie H. Farber, "Introduction to the Problem of Will," *Review of Existential Psychology and Psychiatry*, Vol. V, No. 1, Winter, 1965.

3 Rollo May, *The Meaning of Anxiety,* New York: The Ronald Press Co., 1950; p. 49.

4 *Ibid.*, p. 191.

5 *Ibid.*, p. 148

6 Karen Horney, *The Neurotic Personality of Our Time,* New York: W. W. Norton & Co., 1937; p. 92.

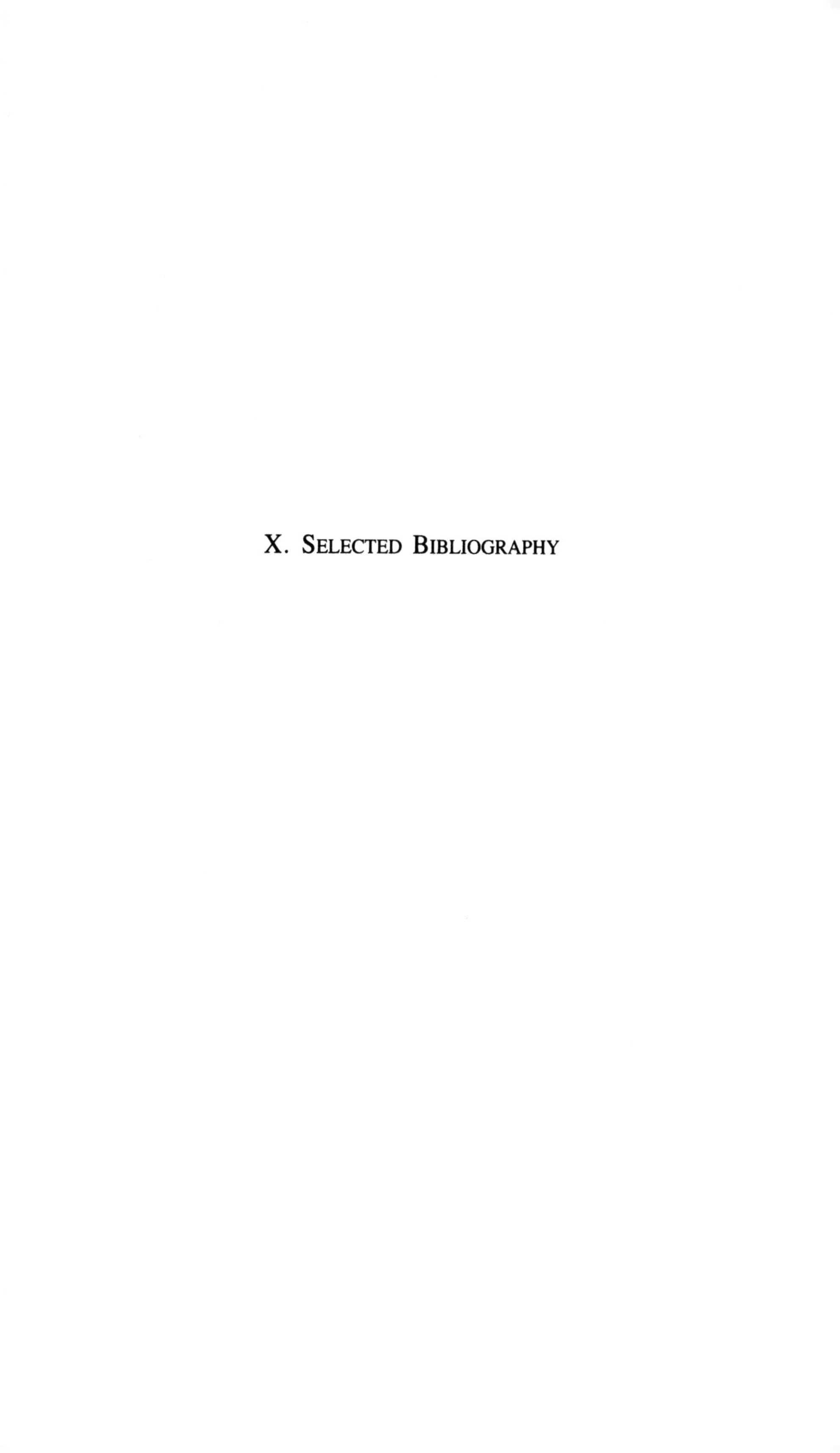

X. Selected Bibliography

Selected Bibliography of Existential Psychology & Psychiatry

COMPILED BY KEITH HOELLER

Allers, Rudolf. *Existentialism and Psychiatry.* Springfield: C. C. Thomas, 1961.

Allport, Gordon W. *Becoming: Basic Considerations for a Psychology of Personality.* New Haven: Yale University Press, 1955.

Bannan, John F. *The Philosophy of Merleau-Ponty.* New York: Harcourt Brace & Jovanovich, 1967.

Barnes, Hazel E. *An Existentialist Ethics.* Chicago: University of Chicago Press, 1985.

Barrett, William. *Irrational Man: A Study in Existential Philosophy.* New York: Doubleday, 1958.

Barton, Anthony. *Three Worlds of Therapy: An Existential-Phenomenological Study of the Therapies of Freud, Jung, and Rogers.* Palo Alto: National Press Books, 1974.

Bateson, Gregory. *Steps to an Ecology of Mind.* New York: Ballantine Books, 1972.

Beauvoir, Simone de. *The Second Sex,* trans. H. M. Parshley. New York: Random House, 1952.

Bergantino, Len. *Psychotherapy, Insight, and Style: The Existential Moment.* Boston: Allyn and Bacon, 1981.

Bernauer, James. *Michel Foucault's Force of Flight: Toward an Ethics for Thought.* New York: Humanities Press, 1990.

Binswanger, Ludwig. *Being-in-the-World: Selected Papers of Ludwig Binswanger,* ed. & trans. Jacob Needleman. London: Souvenir Press, 1975.

Boss, Medard. *Existential Foundations of Medicine and Psychology,* trans. Stephen Conway and Anne Cleaves. New York: Jason Aronson, 1979.

Boss, Medard. *I Dreamt Last Night,* trans. Stephen Conway. New York: Gardner Press, 1977.

Boss, Medard. *Psychoanalysis and Daseinsanalysis,* trans. Ludwig B. Lefebre. New York: Da Capo Press, 1982.

Boyers, Robert, and Orrill, Robert (eds.). *R. D. Laing & Anti-Psychiatry.* New York: Harper & Row, 1971.

Breggin, Peter. *The Psychology of Freedom*. Buffalo: Prometheus Books, 1980.

Buber, Martin. *I and Thou*. New York: Scribners, 1970.

Bugental, James F. T. *The Art of the Psychotherapist*. New York: Norton, 1987.

Bugental, James F. T. *The Search for Authenticity: An Existential-Analytic Approach to Psychotherapy*. New York: Holt, Rinehart and Winston, 1965.

Bugental, James F. T. *The Search for Existential Identity: Patient-Therapist Dialogues in Humanistic Psychotherapy*. San Francisco: Jossey-Bass, 1976.

Camus, Albert. *The Myth of Sisyphus,* trans. Justin O'Brien. New York: Random House, 1956.

Castel, Robert. *The Regulation of Madness: The Origins of Incarceration in France,* trans. by W. D. Halls. Berkeley: University of California Press, 1988.

Charlesworth, Max. *The Existentialists and Jean-Paul Sartre*. New York: St. Martin's Press, 1976.

Charme, Stuart. *Meaning and Myth in the Study of Lives: A Sartrean Perspective*. Philadelphia: University of Pennsylvania Press, 1984.

Collier, Andrew. *R. D. Laing: The Philosophy and Politics of Psychotherapy*. New York: Pantheon, 1977.

Colm, Hanna. *The Existentialist Approach to Psychotherapy with Adults and Children*. New York: Grune & Stratton, 1966.

Cooper, David. *The Death of the Family*. New York: Random House, 1970.

Craig, Erik (ed.). *Psychotherapy for Freedom: The Daseinsanalytic Way in Psychology and Psychoanalysis*. Special Issue of *The Humanistic Psychologist,* Vol. 16 (1988).

De Armey, Michael H. and Skousgaard, Stephen (eds.). *The Philosophical Psychology of William James*. Washington, D.C.: University Press of America, 1986.

De Koning, A. J., and Jenner, F. A. (eds.). *Phenomenology and Psychiatry*. New York: Grune & Stratton, 1982.

Detrick, Douglas W. and Detrick, Susan P. *Self Psychology: Comparisons and Contrasts*. Hillsdale: The Analytic Press, 1989.

Deurzen-Smith, Emmy Van. *Existential Counseling in Practice*. Los Angeles: Sage, 1988.

SELECTED BIBLIOGRAPHY

De Waehlens, Alphonse. *Schizophrenia: A Philosophical Reflection on Lacan's Structuralist Interpretation,* trans. Wilfred Ver Eecke. Pittsburgh: Duquesne University Press, 1978.

Dreyfus, Hubert L. and Rabinow, Paul. *Michel Foucault: Beyond Structuralism and Hermeneutics.* Chicago: University of Chicago Press, 1983.

Edie, James M. *William James and Phenomenology.* Bloomington: Indiana University Press, 1987.

Edwards, David. *Existential Psychotherapy: The Process of Caring.* New York: Gardner Press, 1982.

Elizur, Joel and Minuchin, Salvador. *Institutionalizing Madness: Families, Therapy, and Society.* New York: Basic Books, 1989.

Ellenberger, Henri F. *The Discovery of the Unconscious: The History and Evolution of Dynamic Psychiatry.* New York: Basic Books, 1970.

Esterson, Aaron. *The Leaves of Spring: Schizophrenia, Family and Sacrifice.* London: Tavistock, 1970.

Evans, C. Stephen. *Søren Kierkegaard's Christian Psychology: Insight for Counseling & Pastoral Care.* Grand Rapids: Zondervan, 1990.

Evans, Richard I. *Carl Rogers: The Man and His Ideas.* New York: E. P. Dutton, 1975.

Farber, Leslie. *The Ways of the Will: Essays Toward a Psychology and Psychopathology of the Will.* New York: Basic Books, 1966.

Fell, Joseph P. *Emotion in the Thought of Sartre.* New York: Columbia University Press, 1965.

Feyerabend, Paul K. *Against Method.* New York: Routledge, Chapman, & Hall, 1988.

Fischer, Constance T. and William F. "Phenomenological-Existential Psychotherapy." In: *The Clinical Psychology Handbook,* ed. Michel Hersen, Alan E. Kazdin, and Alan S. Bellack. New York: Pergamon Press, 1983.

Foucault, Michel. *The Foucault Reader,* ed. Paul Rabinow. New York: Pantheon, 1984.

Foucault, Michel. *The History of Sexuality: An Introduction.* New York: Pantheon, 1978.

Foucault, Michel. *Madness and Civilization,* trans. Richard Howard. New York: Random House, 1965.

Foucault, Michel. *Mental Illness & Psychology,* trans. Alan Sheridan. Berkeley: University of California Press, 1987.

Foucault, Michel. "Nietzsche, Freud, Marx." In: *Transforming the Hermeneutic Context: From Nietzsche to Nancy.* Albany: State University of New York Press, 1990, pp. 59-67.

Foucault, Michel and Binswanger, Ludwig. *Dream & Existence,* trans. Forrest Williams. Seattle: Review of Existential Psychology & Psychiatry, 1986.

Frankl, Viktor. *The Doctor and the Soul: From Psychotherapy to Logotherapy,* trans. Richard and Clara Winston. New York: Alfred Knopf, 1966.

Frankl, Viktor E. *Man's Search for Meaning: An Introduction to Logotherapy.* New York: Simon & Schuster, 1959.

Frankl, Viktor. E. *Psychotherapy and Existentialism.* New York: Washington Square Press, 1967.

Frey, David H. *Existential Theory for Counselors.* Boston: Houghton-Mifflin, 1975.

Friedenberg, Edgar Z. *R. D. Laing.* New York: Viking Press, 1973.

Fromm, Erich. *Escape from Freedom.* New York: Rinehart, 1941.

Gendlin, Eugene T. *Experiencing and the Creation of Meaning.* Glencoe: The Free Press, 1962.

Gendlin, Eugene T. *Focusing.* New York: Bantam Books, 1981.

Gendlin, Eugene T. *Let Your Body Interpret Your Dreams.* Wilmette: Chiron Publications, 1986.

Giorgi, Amedeo. *Psychology as a Human Science: A Phenomenologically Based Approach.* New York: Harper & Row, 1970.

Goffman, Irving. *Asylums: Essays on the Social Situation of Mental Patients and Other Inmates.* Garden City: Doubleday, 1961.

Greening, Thomas C. (ed.). *Existential Humanistic Psychology.* Belmont: Brooks/Cole, 1971.

Gurwitsch, Aron. *Studies in Phenomenology and Psychology.* Evanston: Northwestern University Press, 1966.

Gutting, Gary. *Michel Foucault's Archaeology of Scientific Reasoning.* Cambridge: Cambridge University Press, 1989.

Hall, Calvin and Lindzey, Gardner. "Existential Psychology." In their book: *Theories of Personality.* New York: Wiley, 1978 (3rd Ed.), pp. 311-45.

Heidegger, Martin. *Basic Writings,* ed. David Farrell Krell. New York: Harper & Row, 1977.

Heidegger, Martin. *Being and Time,* trans. John Macquarrie and Edward Robinson. New York: Harper & Row, 1962.

Heidegger, Martin. *Existence and Being,* ed. Werner Brock. Chicago: Henry Regnery, 1949.

Heidegger, Martin. *The Question Concerning Technology and Other Essays,* trans. William Lovitt. New York: Harper & Row, 1978.

Heller, Erich. *The Importance of Nietzsche.* Chicago: University of Chicago Press, 1988.

Henry, Jules. *Culture Against Man.* New York: Random House, 1963.

Henry, Jules. *Pathways to Madness.* New York: Random House, 1971.

Hoeller, Keith (ed.). *Heidegger and Psychology.* Seattle: Review of Existential Psychology & Psychiatry, 1988.

Hoeller, Keith (ed.). *Merleau-Ponty and Psychology.* Seattle: Review of Existential Psychology & Psychiatry, 1985.

Hoeller, Keith. "Phenomenological Foundations for the Study of Suicide." *Omega: The Journal of Death & Dying,* Vol. 3 (1973), pp. 195-208.

Hoeller, Keith (ed.). *Readings in Existential Psychology & Psychiatry.* Seattle: Review of Existential Psychology & Psychiatry, 1990.

Hoeller, Keith (ed.). *Sartre and Psychology.* Seattle: Review of Existential Psychology & Psychiatry, 1983.

Husserl, Edmund. *The Crisis of European Sciences and Transcendental Phenomenology,* trans. David Carr. Evanston: Northwestern University Press, 1970.

Husserl, Edmund. *Ideas Pertaining to a Pure Phenomenology and to a Phenomenological Philosophy, Book I,* trans. Fred Kersten. Boston: Kluwer, 1983.

Husserl, Edmund. *Phenomenological Psychology: Lectures, Summer Semester, 1925,* trans. John D. Scanlon. The Hague: Martinus Nijhoff, 1977.

Ingleby, David (ed.). *Critical Psychiatry: The Politics of Mental Health.* New York: Pantheon, 1980.

Izenberg, Gerald. *The Existentialist Critique of Freud: The Crisis of Autonomy.* Princeton: Princeton University Press, 1976.

James, William. *The Principles of Psychology,* 2 Vols. New York: Dover Publications, 1950.

Jaspers, Karl. *General Psychopathology,* trans. J. Hoenig and M. W. Hamilton. Chicago: University of Chicago Press, 1963.

Johnson, Richard E. *Existential Man: The Challenge of Psychotherapy.* New York: Pergamon, 1971.

Jourard, Sidney M. (ed.). *To Be or Not to Be: Existential-Psychological Perspectives on the Self.* Gainesville: University of Florida Press, 1967.

Jourard, Sidney M. *The Transparent Self.* New York: D.Van Nostrand, 1971.

Kaufman, Walter (ed.). *Existentialism from Dostoyevsky to Sartre.* New York: Meridian Books, 1956.

Kaufmann, Walter. *Nietzsche: Philosopher, Psychologist, Antichrist.* Princeton: Princeton University Press, 1969 (rev. ed.).

Keen, Ernest. *Three Faces of Being: Toward an Existential Clinical Psychology.* New York: Appleton-Century-Crofts, 1970.

Kestenbaum, Victor (ed.). *The Humanity of the Ill: Phenomenological Perspectives.* Knoxville: University of Tennessee Press, 1982.

Kierkegaard, Søren. *The Concept of Anxiety,* trans. Reidar Thomte and Albert B. Anderson. Princeton: Princeton University Press, 1980.

Kierkegaard, Søren. *Either/Or,* Vols. I & II, ed. & trans. Howard V. and Edna H. Hong. Princeton: Princeton University Press, 1987.

Kierkegaard, Søren. *Fear and Trembling/Repetition,* trans. Howard V. and Edna H. Hong. Princeton: Princeton University Press, 1983.

Kierkegaard, Søren. *The Sickness Unto Death,* trans. Howard and Edna Hong. Princeton: Princeton University Press, 1980.

Knowles, Richard T. *Human Development and Human Possibility: Erikson in the Light of Heidegger.* Washington, D.C.: University Press of America, 1986.

Kockelmans, Joseph J. *Edmund Husserl's Phenomenological Psychology: A Historico-Critical Study.* Pittsburgh: Duquesne University Press, 1967.

Kockelmans, Joseph J. *Heidegger and Science.* Washington, D.C.: University Press of America, 1985.

Kockelmans, Joseph J. *Phenomenological Psychology: The Dutch School.* Boston: Martinus Nijhoff, 1987.

Kockelmans, Joseph J. (ed.). *Phenomenology: The Philosophy of Edmund Husserl and Its Interpretation.* New York: Doubleday/Anchor, 1967.

Koestenbaum, Peter. *The Vitality of Death: Essays in Existential Psychology and Philosophy*. Westport: Greenwood, 1971.

Kotarba, Joseph A. and Fontana, Andrea (eds.). *Existential Self in Society*. Chicago: University of Chicago Press, 1987.

Kruger, Dreyer. *An Introduction to Phenomenological Psychology*. Pittsburgh: Duquesne University Press, 1981.

Kuhn, Thomas S. *The Structure of Scientific Revolutions*. New York: New American Library, 1970 (2nd ed.).

Lacan, Jacques. *Écrits,* trans. Alan Sheridan. New York: Norton, 1977.

Laing, R. D. *The Divided Self: An Existential Study in Sanity and Madness*. New York: Pelican, 1960.

Laing, R. D. *The Politics of Experience*. New York: Random House, 1961.

Laing, R. D. *Self and Others*. New York: Random House, 1961.

Laing, R. D. and Esterson, Aaron. *Sanity, Madness and the Family*. New York: Pelican, 1963.

Lana, Robert E. *The Foundations of Psychological Theory*. Hillsdale: Lawrence Erlbaum Associates, 1976.

Lawrence, Nathaniel and O'Connor, Daniel (eds.). *Readings in Existential Phenomenology*. Englewood-Cliffs: Prentice-Hall, 1967.

Levin, David Michael. *The Body's Recollection of Being: Phenomenological Psychology and the Deconstruction of Nihilism*. London: Routledge, Kegan & Paul, 1985.

Lyons, Joseph. *Psychology and the Measure of Man: A Phenomenological Approach*. New York: Free Press, 1963.

Mackey, Louis. *Kierkegaard: A Kind of Poet*. Philadelphia: University of Pennsylvania Press, 1971.

Mahrer, Alvin P. *Experiential Psychotherapy: Basic Practices*. New York: Brunner/Mazel, 1983.

Mallin, Samuel B. *Merleau-Ponty's Philosophy*. New Haven: Yale University Press, 1979.

Maranhão, Tullio. *Therapeutic Discourse and Socratic Dialogue: A Cultural Critique*. Madison: University of Wisconsin Press, 1986.

Marcel, Gabriel. *Being and Having: An Existentialist Diary*. New York: Harper & Row, 1965.

Margulies, Alfred. *The Empathic Imagination.* New York: W. W. Norton, 1989.

Maslow, Abraham. *Toward a Psychology of Being.* Princeton: Van Nostrand, 1969 (rev. ed.).

Maslow, Abraham. *The Psychology of Science: A Reconnaissance.* New York: Harper & Row, 1966.

Masson, Jeffrey M. *Against Therapy: Emotional Tyranny and the Myth of Psychological Healing.* New York: Atheneum, 1988.

Masson, Jeffrey M. *The Assault on Truth: Freud's Suppression of the Seduction Theory.* New York: Penguin Books, 1985.

May, Rollo. *The Art of Counseling.* New York: Gardner Press, 1989 (Revised ed.).

May, Rollo. *The Discovery of Being: Writings in Existential Psychology.* New York: W. W. Norton, 1983.

May, Rollo. *Existential Psychology.* New York: Random House, 1969 (2nd ed.).

May, Rollo. *Love and Will.* New York: W. W. Norton, 1969.

May, Rollo. *The Meaning of Anxiety.* New York: W. W. Norton, 1977 (rev. ed.).

May, Rollo. *Psychology and the Human Dilemma.* New York: D. Van Nostrand, 1967.

May, Rollo, Angel, Ernest, and Ellenberger, Henri F. *Existence: A New Dimension in Psychology & Psychiatry.* New York: Simon & Schuster, 1958.

May, Rollo and Yalom, Irvin D. "Existential Psychotherapy." In: *Current Psychotherapies,* ed. Raymond Corsini and Danny Wedding. Itasca: Peacock Publishers, 1989 (4th ed.), pp. 363-402.

McCall, Raymond. *Phenomenological Psychology: An Introduction.* Madison: University of Wisconsin Press, 1983.

McCarthy, Vincent A. *Phenomenology of Moods in Kierkegaard.* Boston: Kluwer, 1978.

McCleary, Richard C. *The Writings of Sartre* (2 Vols.). Evanston: Northwestern University Press, 1974.

Meek, Clinton R. *Existence, Culture and Psychotherapy.* New York: Philosophical Library, 1985.

Merleau-Ponty, Maurice. *Consciousness and the Acquisition of Language,* trans. Hugh J. Silverman. Evanston: Northwestern University Press, 1973.

Merleau-Ponty, Maurice. *The Essential Writings of Merleau-Ponty,* ed. Alden L. Fisher. New York: Harcourt, Brace & Jovanovich, 1969.

Merleau-Ponty, Maurice. *Phenomenology of Perception,* trans. Colin Smith. New York: Humanities Press, 1962.

Merleau-Ponty, Maurice. *The Primacy of Perception,* ed. James M. Edie. Evanston: Northwestern University Press, 1964.

Merleau-Ponty, Maurice. *The Structure of Behavior,* trans. Alden L. Fisher. Pittsburgh: Duquesne University Press, 1984.

Mijuskovic, Benjamin. *Loneliness.* Milwood: Associated Faculty Press, 1985 (2nd ed.).

Minkowski, Eugene. *Lived Time: Phenomenological and Psychopathological Studies,* trans. Nancy Metzel. Evanston: Northwestern University Press, 1970.

Misiak, Henryk, and Sexton, Virginia Staudt. *Phenomenological, Existential, and Humanistic Psychologies: A Historical Survey.* New York: Grune & Stratton, 1973.

Morano, Donald V. *Existential Guilt: A Phenomenological Study.* Assen: Van Gorcum, 1973.

Moustakas, Clark (ed.). *The Child's Discovery of Himself* (formerly Existential Child Therapy). New York: Basic Books, 1966.

Moustakas, Clark. *Loneliness.* Englewood-Cliffs: Prentice-Hall, 1961.

Mowrer, O. Hobart. *Morality and Mental Health.* Chicago: Rand McNally, 1967.

Natanson, Maurice (ed.). *Phenomenology and the Social Sciences,* 2 Vols. Evanston: Northwestern University Press, 1973.

Nietzsche, Friedrich. *The Basic Writings of Nietzsche,* trans. and ed. Walter Kaufmann. New York: Modern Library, 1968.

Nietzsche, Friedrich. *The Gay Science,* trans. Walter Kaufmann. New York: Random House, 1974.

Nietzsche, Friedrich. *The Portable Nietzsche,* trans. and ed. Walter Kaufmann, 1954.

Nietzsche, Friedrich. *Thus Spoke Zarathustra,* trans. Walter Kaufmann. New York: Viking, 1954.

Nietzsche, Friedrich. *The Will to Power,* trans. Walter Kaufman and R. J. Hollingdale. New York: Random House, 1967.

Pfänder, Alexander. *The Phenomenology of Willing and Motivation.* Evanston: Northwestern University Press, 1967.

Polkinghorne, Donald. *Methodology for the Human Sciences: Systems of Inquiry.* Albany: State University of New York Press, 1983.

Pontalis, J.-B. *Frontiers in Psychoanalysis: Between the Dream and Psychic Pain,* trans. by Catherine and Philip Cullen. New York: International Universities Press, 1981.

Price, Linda Whitson. *The Implications of Existential Psychology for the Black Experience (with Application to Education).* Palo Alto: R & E Research Associates, 1982.

Ramsland, Katherine M. *Engaging the Immediate: Applying Kierkegaard's Theory of Indirect Communication to the Practice of Psychotherapy.* Lewisburg: Bucknell University Press, 1989.

Reeves, Clement. *The Psychology of Rollo May.* San Francisco: Jossey-Bass, 1977.

Review of Existential Psychology & Psychiatry (1961-Present). Ed. Keith Hoeller. Seattle, WA.

Richardson, William J. *Heidegger: Through Phenomenology to Thought.* The Hague: Martinus Nijhoff, 1967.

Ricoeur, Paul. *Freud and Philosophy: An Essay on Interpretation,* trans. Denis Savage. New Haven: Yale University Press, 1970.

Rieff, Philip. *The Triumph of the Therapeutic: Uses of Faith After Freud.* Chicago: University of Chicago Press, 1987.

Rogers, Carl R. *Carl Rogers: Dialogues,* ed. Howard Kirschenbaum and Valerie Land Henderson. Boston: Houghton-Mifflin, 1989.

Rogers, Carl R. *The Carl Rogers Reader,* ed. Howard Kirschenbaum and Valerie Land Henderson. Boston: Houghton-Mifflin, 1989.

Ruitenbeek, Hendrik M. (ed.). *Going Crazy: The Radical Therapy of R. D. Laing and Others.* New York: E. P. Dutton, 1972.

Ruitenbeek, Hendrik M. (ed.). *Psychoanalysis and Existential Philosophy.* New York: E. P. Dutton, 1962.

Sartre, Jean-Paul. *Anti-Semite and Jew,* trans. George Becker. New York: Schocken Books, 1948.

Sartre, Jean-Paul. *Being and Nothingness,* trans. Hazel Barnes, New York: Philosophical Library, 1956.

Sartre, Jean-Paul. *The Emotions: Outline of a Theory,* trans. Bernard Frechtman. New York: Philosophical Library, 1948.

Sartre, Jean-Paul. *Existential Psychoanalysis,* trans. Hazel Barnes. Chicago: Regnery, 1962.

Sartre, Jean-Paul. *The Freud Scenario,* ed. J.-B. Pontalis, trans. Quentin Hoare. Chicago: University of Chicago Press, 1988.

Sartre, Jean-Paul. *Nausea,* trans. Lloyd Alexander. New York: New Directions, 1949.

Scheff, Thomas J. *Being Mentally Ill.* New York: Aldine, 1984 (2nd ed.).

Scheper-Hughes, Nancy and Lovell, Anne M. (eds.). *Psychiatry Inside Out: Selected Writings of Franco Basaglia,* trans. Anne M. Lovell and Teresa Shtob. New York: Columbia University Press, 1987.

Schrader, George Alfred (ed.). *Existential Philosophers: Kierkegaard to Merleau-Ponty.* New York: McGraw-Hill, 1967.

Scott, Charles E. *Boundaries in Mind: A Study of Immediate Awareness Based on Psychotherapy.* New York & Chico: Crossroads Publishing and Scholars Press, 1982.

Scott, Charles E. *On Dreaming: An Encounter with Medard Boss.* Soundings, Vol. LX (1977).

Scull, Andrew. *Social Order/Mental Disorder: Anglo-American Psychiatry in Historical Perspective.* Berkeley: University of California Press, 1989.

Seidman, Bradley. *Absent at the Creation: The Existential Psychiatry of Ludwig Binswanger.* Roslyn Heights: Libra Publishers, 1983.

Sharma, Sohan Lal. *The Therapeutic Dialogue: A Theoretical and Practical Guide to Psychotherapy.* Albuquerque: University of New Mexico Press, 1986.

Sheridan, Alan. *Michel Foucault: The Will to Truth.* London: Tavistock, 1980.

Silverman, Hugh J. (ed.). *Philosophy and Non-Philosophy Since Merleau-Ponty.* New York: Routledge, 1988.

Smith, Joseph H. (ed.). *Psychiatry and the Humanities,* Vol. 1. New Haven: Yale University Press, 1976.

Spiegelberg, Herbert. *The Phenomenological Movement.* Boston: Kluwer, 1982 (3rd rev. ed.).

Spiegelberg, Herbert. *Phenomenology in Psychology and Psychiatry: A Historical Introduction.* Evanston: Northwestern University Press, 1972.

Strasser, Stephan. *Phenomenology of Feeling: An Essay in the Phenomena of the Heart,* trans. R. E. Wood. Pittsburgh: Duquesne University Press, 1977.

Straus, Erwin W. *Man, Time, and World.* Pittsburgh: Duquesne University Press, 1982.

Straus, Erwin W. *Phenomenological Psychology: The Selected Papers of Erwin W. Straus,* trans. Erling Eng. New York: Basic Books, 1966.

Straus, Erwin W. *The Primary World of Senses: A Vindication of Sensory Experience.* Glencoe: The Free Press, 1963.

Straus, Erwin W., Natanson, Maurice, and Ey, Henri. *Psychiatry and Philosophy,* trans. Erling Eng and Stephen C. Kennedy. New York: Springer, 1969.

Sturdivant, Susan. *Therapy with Women: A Feminist Philosophy of Treatment.* New York: Springer, 1980.

Szasz, Thomas S. *The Ethics of Psychoanalysis.* Syracuse: Syracuse University Press, 1988.

Szasz, Thomas S. *The Myth of Mental Illness.* New York: Harper & Row, 1974 (2nd ed.).

Szasz, Thomas S. *The Myth of Psychotherapy: Mental Healing as Religion, Rhetoric, and Repression.* Syracuse: Syracuse University Press, 1988.

Szasz, Thomas S. *Schizophrenia: The Sacred Symbol of Psychiatry.* New York: Basic Books, 1976.

Szasz, Thomas S. *The Theology of Medicine.* Syracuse: Syracuse University Press, 1988.

Tillich, Paul. *The Courage to Be.* New Haven, Yale University Press, 1952.

Valle, Ronald S. and Halling, Steen (eds.). *Existential-Phenomenological Perspectives in Psychology: Exploring the Breadth of Human Experience.* New York: Plenum, 1989.

Valle, Ronald S. and King, Mark (eds.). *Existential-Phenomenological Alternatives for Psychology.* New York: Oxford University Press, 1978.

Van den Berg, J. H. *A Different Existence: Principles of Phenomenological Psychopathology.* Pittsburgh: Duquesne University Press, 1972.

Van den Berg, J. H. *The Phenomenological Approach to Psychiatry: An Introduction to Recent Phenomenological Psychopathology.* Springfield: C. C. Thomas, 1955.

Van Kaam, Adrian. *Existential Foundations of Psychology.* Pittsburgh: Image Books, 1966. Also: Washington, D. C.: University Press of America, 1984.

Vatz, Richard E. and Weinberg, Lee S. (eds). *Thomas Szasz: Primary Values and Major Contentions.* Buffalo: Prometheus Books, 1983.

Wann, T. W. (ed.). *Behaviorism and Phenomenology: Contrasting Bases for Modern Psychology.* Chicago: University of Chicago Press, 1964.

Weisman, Avery D. *The Existential Core of Psychoanalysis: Reality Sense and Responsibility.* Boston: Little, Brown & Co., 1965.

Wheelis, Allen. *How People Change.* New York: Harper & Row, 1973.

Wheelis, Allen. *The Illusionless Man.* New York: Harper & Row, 1966.

Wild, John D. *The Radical Empiricism of William James.* New York: Doubleday, 1969.

Wilshire, Bruce. *William James and Phenomenology: A Study of "The Principles of Psychology."* Bloomington: Indiana University Press, 1968.

Yalom, Irvin D. *Existential Psychotherapy.* New York: Basic Books, 1980.

Yalom, Irvin D. *Love's Executioner & Other Tales of Psychotherapy.* New York: Basic Books, 1989.

ACKNOWLEDGEMENTS*

Allen, Jeffner. "The Role of Imagination in Phenomenological Psychology." Vol. XV, no. 1 (1977), pp. 52-60.

Boss, Medard. "Anxiety, Guilt, and Psychotherapeutic Liberation." Vol. II, no. 3 (1962), pp. 173-95.

———. "The Unconscious—What is It?" This is the first English translation of this article. It was originally read in Portuguese at the "Simposio internacional de Indigação sobre o Inconsciente," April 7, 1981, Rio de Janeiro, and published in *Tempo Psicoanalitico* (Rio de Janeiro: Orgão oficial do Instituto de Medicina Psicologica), Vol. IV (1981), pp. 28-40. The first German edition of this article appeared in Boss' *Von der Spannweite der Seele* (Bern: Bentali Verlag, 1982), pp. 132-50. Reprinted by permission of Dr. Boss.

Conkling, Mark. "Sartre's Refutation of the Freudian Unconscious." Vol. VIII, no. 2 (1968), pp. 86-101.

Farber, Leslie. "Despair and the Life of Suicide." Vol. II, no. 2 (1962), pp. 125-39.

———. "Will and Anxiety." Vol. IV, no. 3 (1964), pp. 195-212.

Frankl, Viktor. "Logotherapy and the Challenge of Suffering." Vol. I, no. 1 (1961), pp. 3-7.

Gendlin, Eugene T. "Schizophrenia: Problems and Methods in Psychotherapy." Vol. IV, no. 2 (1964), pp. 168-79.

Hoeller, Keith. "An Introduction to Existential Psychology & Psychiatry." This article was written especially for this volume.

———. "Selected Bibliography of Existential Psychology & Psychiatry." This bibliography was prepared especially for this volume.

Iturrate, Miguel. "Man's Freedom: Freud's Therapeutic Goal." Vol. XV, no. 1 (1977), pp. 32-45.

Kvale, Steinar and Grenness, Carl Erik. "Skinner and Sartre: Towards a Radical Phenomenology of Behavior." Vol. II, no. 2 (1967), pp. 128-50.

Laing, R. D. "Minkowski and Schizophrenia." Vol. III, no. 3 (1963), pp. 195-207.

* All articles either originally appeared in the *Review of Existential Psychology & Psychiatry* (Seattle, WA) or else are published here for the first time (as noted above).

May, Rollo. "The Meaning of the Oedipus Myth." Vol. I, no. 1 (1961), pp. 44-52.

———. "On the Phenomenological Bases of Psychotherapy." Vol. IV, no. 1 (1964), pp. 22-36.

———. "Will, Decision, and Responsibility." Vol. 1, no. 3 (1961), pp. 249-58.

Rogers, Carl. "Ellen West—And Loneliness." Vol. I, no. 2 (1961), pp. 94-101. This article was later reprinted in a slightly revised form in Rogers' *A Way of Being* (Boston: Houghton-Mifflin, 1980), pp. 164-80, as well as in *The Carl Rogers Reader,* ed. Howard Kirschenbaum and Valerie Land Henderson (Boston: Houghton-Mifflin, 1989), pp. 157-68. We have reprinted the later version by permission of Houghton-Mifflin.

Tillich, Paul. "Existentialism and Psychotherapy." Vol. I, no. 1 (1961), pp. 8-16.

Van Kaam, Adrian. "Existential Psychology as a Comprehensive Theory of Personality." Vol. III, no. 1 (1963), pp. 11-26.

Woocher, Jonathan. "From Guilt Feelings to Reconciliation: Images of Modern Man." Vol. XV, nos. 2 & 3 (1977), pp. 186-209.

CONTRIBUTORS

JEFFNER ALLEN is Associate Professor of Philosophy, State University of New York, Binghamton. She is the co-editor (with Iris Young) of *The Thinking Muse: Feminism and Modern French Philosophy* (Indiana University Press) and author of numerous articles in phenomenological philosophy and psychology.

MEDARD BOSS (1903–1990) was Director of the Daseinsanalysis Institute for Psychotherapy and Psychosomatics in Zurich and Professor of Psychotherapy at the University of Zurich. He is the author of *Psychoanalysis and Daseinsanalysis* (Da Capo Press), *I Dreamt Last Night* (Halsted Press), and *Existential Foundations of Medicine and Psychology* (Jason Aronson).

MARK CONKLING resides in Sante Fe, New Mexico. He is the author of several articles in existential philosophy and psychology, including "Consciousness and the Unconscious in William James's *Principles of Psychology*," (*Human Inquiries*) and "Ryle's Mistake About Consciousness" (*Philosophy Today*).

LESLIE FARBER (1912-1981) was for many years in private practice in New York City. A frequent contributor to the *Review of Existential Psychology & Psychiatry,* he also authored *The Ways of the Will: Essays Toward a Psychology and Psychopathology of Will* (Harper & Row) and *Lying, Despair, Jealousy, Envy, Sex, Suicide, Drugs, and the Good Life* (Basic Books).

VIKTOR FRANKL is Professor of Neurology and Psychiatry at the University of Vienna Medical School and Distinguished Professor of Logotherapy at the United States International University, San Diego, Calif. He is the originator of the school of logotherapy, and the author of numerous books, including *Man's Search for Meaning* (Simon & Schuster), and *Psychotherapy and Existentialism* (Washington Square Press).

EUGENE GENDLIN is Professor of Psychology, University of Chicago. He is the former Editor of *Psychotherapy: Theory, Research and Practice.* In 1970 he was chosen the Distinguished Professional Psychologist of the Year by the Psychotherapy Division of the American Psychological Association. He is the author of *Experiencing and the Creation of Meaning* (Free Press), *Focusing* (Bantam), and *Let Your Body Interpret Your Dreams* (Chiron Publications).

CARL ERIK GRENNESS is Professor of Psychology at the University of Oslo, Norway.

KEITH HOELLER is the Editor of the *Review of Existential Psychology & Psychiatry,* and its companion book series, *Studies in Existential Psychology and Psychiatry,* Seattle, Wash. He is also author of numerous articles in existential psychology and philosophy, including "Phenomenological Foundations for the Study of Suicide" (*Omega: The Journal of Death & Dying*) and "Phenomenology, Psychology, and Science, Parts I & II" (*Review of Existential Psychology & Psychiatry*).

MIGUEL ITURRATE (1920-1987) was for many years a practicing psychoanalyst in New York. He was the author of *Psicoanalisis y Personalidad (Psychoanalysis and Personality)* and numerous articles on existential psychoanalysis including "Man as the Meaning-Giver: An Existential-Psychoanalytic Approach" (*Review of Existential Psychology & Psychiatry*).

STEINAR KVALE is Professor of Educational Psychology and Director of Qualitative Research, Aarhus University, Denmark. He is the author of *Prufung und Herrschaft* (Berlin: Weinheim), and editor of *Issues of Validity in Qualitative Research* (Lund: Studentliteratur).

R. D. LAING (1927-89) was President of The Philadelphia Association (London, England), which pioneered the setting up of households as sanctuaries for people to work through their personal problems. He authored *The Divided Self* (Pantheon), *The Politics of Experience* (Pantheon), *The Voice of Experience* (Pantheon), and co-authored (with Aaron Esterson) the ground-breaking study of schizophrenia, *Sanity, Madness, and the Family* (Pantheon).

ROLLO MAY practices therapy in Tiburon, California, and is Director of the Rollo May Institute of Humanistic Studies, San Francisco, Calif. He is the co-editor (with Ernest Angel and Henri Ellenberger) of *Existence: A New Dimension in Psychology & Psychiatry* (Basic Books) and the author of over a dozen books, including *The Discovery of Being* (W. W. Norton), and *The Art of Counseling* (Garden Press).

CARL ROGERS (1902-1987) founded "client-centered" therapy at the University of Chicago, and was for many years a resident fellow at the Center for Studies of the Person at La Jolla, California. He authored numerous books, including *Counseling and Psychotherapy, Client-Centered Therapy,* and *On Becoming a Person* (all published by Houghton-Mifflin).

PAUL TILLICH (1886-1965) taught philosophy and theology at several universities in Europe and America. At the time of his death he was Professor of Theology at the University of Chicago Divinity School. Perhaps most well-known for his book *The Courage to Be* (Yale), he authored several other books, including *The New Being* (Scribners) and the three volume work, *Systematic Theology* (Chicago).

ADRIAN VAN KAAM is Director of the Institute of Formative Spirituality, Duquesne University. He is the author of *Existential Foundations of Psychology* (Image Books), *The Art of Existential Counseling* (Dimension Books), and *Religion and Personality* (Image Books). During the 1960s, he served as the first Editor of the *Review of Existential Psychology & Psychiatry.*

JONATHAN WOOCHER is Executive Vice-President of the Jewish Educational Service of North America. He is the author of *Sacred Survival: The Civil Religion of American Jews* (Indiana University Press) and co-editor of *Perspectives in Jewish Population Research* (Westview Press).